$49⁹⁵

BS
1140.3
P48
2004

YO-EMG-686

ESSAYS ON BIBLICAL LAW

ESSAYS ON BIBLICAL LAW

ANTHONY PHILLIPS

T & T CLARK INTERNATIONAL
A Continuum imprint
LONDON • NEW YORK

Colorado Christian University
Library
180 S. Garrison
Lakewood, Colorado 80226

Published by T&T Clark International
A Continuum imprint
The Tower Building, 11 York Road, London SE1 7NX
15 East 26th Street, Suite 1703, New York, NY 10010

www.tandtclark.com

Copyright © 2002 Sheffield Academic Press
First published as JSOTS 344 by Sheffield Academic Press
This edition published 2004

All rights reserved. No part of this publication may be reproduced or transmitted
in any form or by any means, electronic or mechanical, including photocopying,
recording or any information storage or retrieval system, without permission in
writing from the publishers.

British Library Cataloguing-in-Publication Data
A catalogue record for this book is available from the British Library

ISBN 0567043800 (paperback)

Typeset by Sheffield Academic Press
Printed on acid-free paper in Great Britain by The Bath Press, Bath

For Vicky,
in gratitude for her love
and support throughout the
years in which these essays
were written.

CONTENTS

Part II
SHORTER ESSAYS

PREFACE

The essays collected together in this book were published over a considerable period of time and in the main sought to build on my doctoral thesis published as *Ancient Israel's Criminal Law: A New Approach to the Decalogue* (Oxford: Basil Blackwell, 1970). Having briefly practised as a solicitor, I endeavoured to apply my legal training to the study of biblical law arguing that ancient Israel consciously distinguished between crimes and torts. These essays modify, augment and expand into other areas of that original study. Inevitably there is some overlap between different essays, but I hope that by publishing them together in one volume to stand alongside other scholars' similar collections, the further study of the legal issues raised here will be made easier. References are to the Masoretic text throughout.

I am much indebted to Professor David J.A. Clines of Sheffield Academic Press for agreeing to publish this collection in the JSOT Supplement Series. My special thanks are due to the editorial staff at the Press with whom it has been a pleasure to work.

Anthony Phillips
6 August 2002

ABBREVIATIONS

AICL	Anthony Phillips, *Ancient Israel's Criminal Law: A New Approach to the Decalogue* (Oxford: Basil Blackwell, 1970).
AJSL	*American Journal of Semitic Languages and Literatures*
AnBib	Analecta biblica
ANET	James B. Pritchard (ed.), *Ancient Near Eastern Texts Relating to the Old Testament* (Princeton, NJ: Princeton University Press, 1950)
AOAT	Alter Orient und Altes Testament
ArOr	*Archiv orientálni*
BA	*Biblical Archaeologist*
BDB	Francis Brown, S.R. Driver and Charles A. Briggs, *A Hebrew and English Lexicon of the Old Testament* (Oxford: Clarendon Press, 1907)
BEvT	Beiträge zur evangelischen Theologie
BHT	Beiträge zur historischen Theologie
Bib	*Biblica*
BibOr	Biblica et orientalia
BJRL	*Bulletin of the John Rylands University Library of Manchester*
BWANT	Beiträge zur Wissenschaft vom Alten und Neuen Testament
BZ	*Biblische Zeitschrift*
BZAW	Beihefte zur *ZAW*
CBC	Cambridge Bible Commentary
CBQ	*Catholic Biblical Quarterly*
EI	*Eretz Israel*
ExpTim	*Expository Times*
GThT	*Gereformeerd Theologisch Tijdschrift*
HTR	*Harvard Theological Review*
HUCA	*Hebrew Union College Annual*
IB	*Interpreter's Bible*
ICC	International Critical Commentary
IDB	George Arthur Buttrick (ed.), *The Interpreter's Dictionary of the Bible* (4 vols.; Nashville: Abingdon Press, 1962)
JANESCU	*Journal of the Ancient Near Eastern Society of Columbia University*
JAOS	*Journal of the American Oriental Society*

JBL	*Journal of Biblical Literature*
JBLMS	*Journal of Biblical Literature*, Monograph Series
JJS	*Journal of Jewish Studies*
JNES	*Journal of Near Eastern Studies*
JPOS	*Journal of the Palestine Oriental Society*
JQR	*Jewish Quarterly Review*
JRAS	*Journal of the Royal Asiatic Society*
JSOT	*Journal for the Study of the Old Testament*
JSOTSup	*Journal for the Study of the Old Testament*, Supplement Series
JSS	*Journal of Semitic Studies*
JTS	*Journal of Theological Studies*
KAT	Kommentar zum Alten Testament
KB	Ludwig Köhler and Walter Baumgartner (eds.), *Lexicon in Veteris Testamenti libros* (Leiden: E.J. Brill, 1953)
NCBC	New Century Bible Commentary
NEB	*New English Bible*
OTL	Old Testament Library
OTS	*Oudtestamentische Studiën*
PEQ	*Palestine Exploration Quarterly*
RB	*Revue biblique*
RE	*Realencyklopädie für protestantische Theologie und Kirche*
RIDA	*Revue Internationale des Droits de l'Antiquité*
RSV	Revised Standard Version
RTP	*Revue de théologie et de philosophie*
SBL	Society of Biblical Literature
SBLDS	Society of Biblical Literature, Dissertation Series
SBT	Studies in Biblical Theology
SJLA	Studies in Judaism and Late Antiquity
SOTS	Society for Old Testament Study
SOTSMS	Society for Old Testament Study, Monograph Series
VT	*Vetus Testamentum*
VTSup	*Vetus Testamentum*, Supplements
WMANT	Wissenschaftliche Monographien zum Alten und Neuen Testament
ZAW	*Zeitschrift für die alttestamentliche Wissenschaft*

ACKNOWLEDGMENTS

The author wishes to thank the editors and publishers concerned for their kind permission to republish his essays in this volume. With the exception of a uniform housestyle and very minor alterations, they have been reprinted as originally published though the opportunity has been taken to run together two essays on the Sinai Pericope and two essays on Family Law. The essays and notes were originally published as follows:

Essays

Chapter 1, 'The Decalogue—Ancient Israel's Criminal Law', *JJS* 34 (1983), pp. 1-20.

Chapter 2, 'A Fresh Look at the Sinai Pericope—Part 1', *VT* 34.1 (1984), pp. 39-52, and 'A Fresh Look at the Sinai Pericope—Part 2', *VT* 34.3 (1984), pp. 282-94.

Chapter 3, 'Another Look at Murder', *JJS* 28 (1977), pp. 105-26.

Chapter 4, 'Another Look at Adultery', *JSOT* 20 (1981), pp. 3-25, and 'A Response to Dr. McKeating', *JSOT* 22 (1982), pp. 142-43.

Chapter 5, 'The Laws of Slavery: Exodus 21.2-11', *JSOT* 30 (1984), pp. 51-66.

Chapter 6, 'Some Aspects of Family Law in Pre-Exilic Israel', *VT* 23 (1973), pp. 349-61, and 'Another Example of Family Law', *VT* 30 (1980), pp. 240-45.

Chapter 7, 'Animals and the Torah', *ExpTim* 106 (1995), pp. 260-65.

Chapter 8, 'Respect for Life in the Old Testament', *King's Theological Review* 6 (1983), pp. 32-35.

Chapter 9, 'The Attitude of Torah to Wealth', in Andrew Linzey and Peter J. Wexler (eds.), *Heaven and Earth: Essex Essays on Theology and Ethics* (Worthing: Churchman Publishing, 1986), pp. 69-86.

Chapter 10, 'Prophecy and Law', in Richard Coggins, Anthony Phillips and Michael Knibb (eds.), *Israel's Prophetic Tradition: Essays in Honour of Peter Ackroyd* (Cambridge: Cambridge University Press, 1982), pp. 217-32.

Chapter 11, Torah and Mishpat—a Light to the Peoples', in Wilfrid Harrington (ed.), *Witness to the Spirit: Essays on Revelation, Spirit, Redemption* (*Proceedings of the Irish Biblical Association*, 3; Manchester: Koinonia Press, 1979), pp. 112-32.

Chapter 12, 'The Book of Ruth—Deception and Shame', *JJS* 37 (1986), pp. 1-17.

Chapter 13, 'The Place of Law in Contemporary Society', *Christian Jewish Relations* 14 (1981), pp. 43-51; (*South African Outlook* 111 [1981], pp. 3-6; and *ExpTim* 93 [1982], pp. 108-112).

Shorter Essays

Chapter 14, 'The Interpretation of 2 Samuel xii 5-6', *VT* 16 (1966), pp. 242-44.

Chapter 15, 'The Case of the Woodgatherer Reconsidered', *VT* 19 (1969), pp. 125-28.

Chapter 16, '*Nebalah*—A Term for Serious Disorderly and Unruly Conduct', *VT* 25 (1975), pp. 237-42.

Chapter 17, 'Uncovering the Father's Skirt', *VT* 30 (1980), pp. 38-43.

Chapter 18, 'Double for All her Sins', *ZAW* 94 (1982), pp. 130-32.

Chapter 19, 'The Undetectable Offender and the Priestly Legislators', *JTS* 36 (1985), pp. 146-50.

Chapter 20 (with Lucy Phillips), 'The Origin of "I AM" in Exodus 3.14', *JSOT* 78 (1998), pp. 81-84.

Chapter 21, 'Old Testament and Moral Tradition', *ExpTim* 108 (1997), pp. 231-32.

The publishers of *Expository Times* are T. & T. Clark, Edinburgh, and the publishers of *Journal of Theological Studies* are Oxford University Press, Oxford.

Part I

Essays

Chapter 1

THE DECALOGUE: ANCIENT ISRAEL'S CRIMINAL LAW

In 1970 I published my *Ancient Israel's Criminal Law: A New Approach to the Decalogue*.[1] The main thesis of my book was the contention that the Decalogue in an original short form given at Sinai constituted pre-exilic Israel's criminal law. From both the legal and narrative material, I argued that ancient Israel distinguished between crimes and torts, the former always demanding the exaction of the death penalty by the community, the latter payment of damages to the injured party. In contrast to torts where the action lay between the individuals themselves as plaintiff and defendant, criminal offences were not the personal concern of any individual who may have suffered injury, but of the community at large upon whom the responsibility for conviction rested.[2] Failure to comply with the requirements of the Decalogue brought direct divine punishment on the community which could only ward off such action by the execution of the criminal. It was not the apodictic form of the Decalogue that indicated its Israelite origins, but its content which on entry into Canaan had to be superimposed on and integrated with the indigenous law resulting in the *mišpāṭîm* of the Book of the Covenant, which clearly differentiate between crimes and torts, a distinction which again underlies Deuteronomy.

In my book I connected this thesis with Mendenhall's assertion that the description of the inauguration of the covenant at Sinai in the Exodus narrative and its theological interpretation was modelled on the form of the

---

1.   A. Phillips, *Ancient Israel's Criminal Law: A New Approach to the Decalogue* (Oxford: Basil Blackwell, 1970 [hereafter cited as *AICL*]).

2.   M.J. Buss, 'The Distinction between Civil and Criminal Law in Ancient Israel', in *Proceedings of the Sixth World Congress of Jewish Studies 1973* (Jerusalem: World Union of Jewish Studies, 1977), pp. 51-62, also recognizes the importance of distinguishing between crime and tort in ancient Israel's law, though on many particular issues we hold different opinions.

Hittite suzerainty treaties.[3] Indeed I believed that I was in fact strengthening Mendenhall's argument by establishing the inner unity of the Ten Commandments. While Rogerson in his review of my book thought that this connection with the Hittite treaties was vital to my thesis,[4] Nicholson rightly surmised that my understanding of the Decalogue as Israel's criminal law code could be maintained independently of Mendenhall's views.[5] It is now clear to me following the work of both McCarthy[6] and Nicholson[7] that although the suzerainty treaty form does influence the later compilation of the Sinai narrative in Exodus, as well as Deuteronomy, it only entered Israel's theology following the fall of the northern kingdom to Assyria. Consequently if the Decalogue derives from earliest times, the treaty form plays no part in its original composition and interpretation. Similarly my use of the Nothian view of the amphictyony,[8] also considered by Rogerson as vital to my thesis,[9] is in fact peripheral to my main argument, though I would with McCarthy[10] seek to caution against a too sweeping rejection of any tribal unity in pre-monarchic Israel. While Mayes[11] has shown that the amphictyonic hypothesis as elaborated by Noth can no longer be maintained, nonetheless ancient Israel was not a total disunity as the emergence of the monarchy confirms. There were common religious traditions which did single out the Hebrews from the indigenous population of Canaan and which in my view were secured by the Decalogue. It thus remains my contention that it was the Decalogue which both created Israel as a distinct community, and, though from time to time reinterpreted and remoulded, secured her survival from the earliest days of the settlement until exile in Babylon.

3.   G.E. Mendenhall, 'Ancient Oriental and Biblical Law', *BA* 17 (1954), pp. 26-46, and 'Covenant Forms in Israelite Traditon', *BA*, 17 (1954), pp. 50-76.

4.   J. Rogerson, review of *AICL*, by Anthony Phillips, in *PEQ* 104 (1972), p. 157.

5.   E.W. Nicholson, review of *AICL*, by Anthony Phillips, in *Theology* 75 (1972), pp. 154-55.

6.   D.J. McCarthy, *Treaty and Covenant: A Study in Form in the Ancient Oriental Documents and in the Old Testament* (AnBib, 21A; Rome: Biblical Institute Press, new edn, 1978).

7.   E.W. Nicholson, *Exodus and Sinai in History and Tradition* (Oxford: Basil Blackwell, 1973).

8.   M. Noth, *Das System der zwölf Stämme Israels* (BWANT, 4.1; Stuttgart: W. Kohlhammer, 1930).

9.   Rogerson, review of *AICL*, p. 157.

10.   McCarthy, *Treaty and Government*, p. 282.

11.   A.D.H. Mayes, *Israel in the Period of the Judges* (SBT, 29; London: SCM Press, 2nd edn, 1974).

Two main objections have been advanced against my thesis: (1) that the Decalogue itself is a late composition,[12] perhaps Deuteronomic;[13] and (2) that the biblical evidence itself does not warrant my assertion that the Decalogue constituted pre-exilic Israel's criminal law, and thereby established legal principles which distinguished her law from that of all other ancient Near Eastern legal collections.[14] I have already sought to defend myself against these charges, both reasserting the early date of the Decalogue[15] and, in studies of murder[16] and adultery,[17] the distinctive nature of Israel's criminal law as derived from it. Here I summarize, modify and augment my arguments.

I

If the Decalogue carried such significance as I have suggested, it is perhaps strange that reference to it is so rare in the Old Testament. While it is set out in both Exod. 20 and Deut. 5 in the accounts of the inauguration of the covenant at Sinai/Horeb, the only other allusions to it occur in Hos. 4.2 and Jer. 7.9 where apparent reference is made to some specific commandments concerned with offences against the person. While such partial citing of particular commandments cannot be taken as conclusive evidence of the existence of the whole collection of Ten Commandments, it does, however, seem to me that in both cases deliberate appeal is being made to the Decalogue.[18] Yet, as I argued in my essay 'Prophecy and

12. A.D.H. Mayes, *Deuteronomy* (NCBC; London: Oliphants, 1979), pp. 161-65.

13. E.W. Nicholson, 'The Decalogue as the Direct Address of God', *VT* 27 (1977), pp. 422-33.

14. See in particular, M. Greenberg, review of AICL, *JBL* 91 (1972), pp. 535-38; B.S. Jackson, 'Reflections on Biblical Criminal Law', *JJS* 24 (1973), pp. 8-38 (repr. in *idem*, *Essays in Jewish and Comparative Legal History* [SJLA, 10; Leiden: E.J. Brill, 1975], pp. 25-63).

15. A. Phillips, 'A Fresh Look at the Sinai Pericope—Part 1', *VT* 34.1 (1984), pp. 39-52, and 'A Fresh Look at the Sinai Pericope—Part 2', *VT* 34.3 (1984), pp. 282-94 (reprinted below as Chapter 2).

16. A. Phillips, 'Another Look at Murder', *JJS* 28 (1977), pp. 105-126 (reprinted below as Chapter 3).

17. A. Phillips, 'Another Look at Adultery', *JSOT* 20 (1981), pp. 3-25 and *idem*, 'A Response to Dr. McKeating', *JSOT* 22 (1982), pp. 142-43 (both reprinted below as Chapter 4).

18. H.W. Wolff, *Hosea* (*Hermeneia*; Philadelphia: Fortress Press, 1974), pp. 67-68.

Law',[19] in neither case does the citing of the specific commands of the Decalogue form an integral part of the prophetic material, nor indeed of the prophets' message as a whole. Thus while Hos. 4.1 indicates the general charge against Israel and Hos. 4.3 the direct consequences of its breach, v. 2 seems to be a later interpretation of what conduct actually constituted lack of *ʾemet ḥesed* and *daʿat ʾelōhîm*. For neither the rest of Hosea's prophecy, nor that of his fellow prophet to the north, Amos, points to that state of general chaos which would of necessity have followed the conduct described in Hos. 4.2. Similarly while Jer. 7.5b-6 indicates the course of action which Israel is to follow to avoid Yahweh's judgment, the specific reference to provisions in the Decalogue in v. 9 seems intrusive for nowhere else in Jeremiah is any reliance placed on breach of the Decalogue as the reason for Judah's rejection. In my view, both in Hos. 4.2 and Jer. 7.9 the Decalogue is being used theologically as a blanket expression to indicate total rejection of Yahweh which in the case of Hosea justifies the fall of Samaria, and of Jeremiah the fall of Jerusalem. Like the insertion of *bᵉrît* in Hos. 8.1,[20] and the use of the covenant theology in Jeremiah, this is the work of the Deuteronomistic redactors concerned to show the utter rejection of the Decalogue, in their eyes the sole covenant law of Horeb (Deut. 4.13; 5.22).

Indeed what is striking in the eighth-century prophetic material (apart from Hos. 4.2) is the total lack of condemnation of those acts for which sanctions were prescribed and enforced by the courts. This does not necessarily mean that such acts were never perpetrated, but we must assume that when they occurred they were dealt with under the law, the criminal suffering execution in the prescribed manner. Had the prophets been able to condemn a more obvious breakdown in law and order, they would certainly have done so. Instead, detailed examination of the prophetic traditions indicates that Amos, Micah and Isaiah rested their indictment solely on the general charge of lack of humaneness and maladministration of justice, the kind of actions already condemned in the Book of the Covenant (Exod. 22.20–23.9).[21] While such conduct could never be

19. A. Phillips, 'Prophecy and Law', in R. Coggins, A. Phillips and M. Knibb (eds.), *Israel's Prophetic Tradition* (Festschrift P.R. Ackroyd; Cambridge: Cambridge University Press, 1982), pp. 217-32 (reprinted below as Chapter 10).

20. L. Perlitt, *Die Bundestheologie im Alten Testament* (WMANT, 36; Neukirchen–Vluyn: Neukirchener Verlag, 1969), pp. 190ff.

21. The references to idolatry in Micah (1.7; 5.10-15) and Isaiah (2.8, 18, 26) are redactional as also is the comment on murderers at the end of Isa. 1.21 (O. Kaiser, *Isaiah 1–12* [OTL; London: SCM Press, 2nd edn, 1983], p. 39).

precisely defined, nor enforced by the courts through legal sanctions, it was the prophets' contention that its very unnaturalness should have been obvious to Israel (Amos 1–2.8; Isa. 1.3).[22] Their innovation was then to hold that Israel's election depended not merely on appropriate cultic practice or observance of enforceable law, but also on those general principles of natural law which of necessity could never be precisely defined but which rational men ought to be able to discern for themselves. The other prophetic tradition is that of Hosea, who condemns Israel for her lack of loyalty to Yahweh due to her syncretistic cult. This he interprets as apostasy. Because in Deuteronomic eyes such apostasy accounted for both the fall of Samaria and Jerusalem, this tradition now dominates the biblical material, though both eighth-century prophetic traditions are found in the Deuteronomic laws and are brought together in Jeremiah, itself the result of Deuteronomistic redaction.[23]

But the fact that the Decalogue is only set out in full in Exod. 20 and Deut. 5, and then in a form which betrays a late compilation, need not of itself cause surprise. For it must be remembered that not all ancient Israel's theological traditions had to be recalled in subsequent literature, which still depended on those traditions for its interpretation. So, as has often been pointed out, no further mention is made in the Old Testament of the Eden narrative of Gen. 3. The author (J) having established the predicament of man in the world in which God had set him, the rest of the Old Testament could be understood against that basic theological assessment of man's condition. There is then no *prima facie* reason why this should not also be true of the Decalogue if it too established the conditions for Israel's position in the world in which God had set her. Indeed it is apparent that those to whom the prophets proclaimed judgment did not see themselves as under threat, even as late as the time of Jeremiah (6.14; 8.11). Rather, both in their excessive religious zeal and, we must assume from the prophetic silence, in their outward maintenance of enforceable law and order, the people believed that Yahweh was ensuring their protection as his elect (Jer. 7.4). Hence the business community in the time of Amos make no attempt to breach the sabbath requirements, thereby confirming that, in spite of every intention of continuing their dishonest

---

22. J. Barton, 'Natural Law and Poetic Justice in the Old Testament', *JTS* 30 (1979), pp. 1-14, 'Ethics in Isaiah of Jerusalem', and *idem, JTS* 32 (1981), pp. 1-18.

23. E.W. Nicholson, *Preaching to the Exiles* (Oxford: Basil Blackwell, 1970); R.P. Carroll, *From Chaos to Covenant* (London: SCM Press, 1981).

business practices, outward conformity with the requirements of the Decalogue determined their actions (Amos 8.4-6).

In fact those who hold that the Decalogue is a Deuteronomic composition can give no satisfactory theological explanation for its collection at that time based on its contents. Indeed these bear very little relation to the main thrust of the Deuteronomic laws to which the Decalogue now acts as the preface. Certainly no one could have composed the Decalogue as a summary of Deuteronomic legal concern. Rather the reverse is the case, for as now presented the Deuteronomic laws are to be understood as deduced from the Decalogue. By inserting the Decalogue into the original book of Deuteronomy, the Deuteronomistic redactors give the new law collection a proper pedigree, thereby validating its legitimacy.[24] Further the redactors' deliberate alteration of the Sinai narrative (Exod. 19–24; 32–34) enabled the Deuteronomic laws associated with Josiah's reform to supersede all previous law as the sole canonical statement of Yahweh's covenant requirement.[25] This involved the omission of (1) the Book of the Covenant by immediately introducing the tablets of the law following the giving of the Decalogue (Deut. 5.22) and (2) the laws of Exod. 34.11-26 by asserting that only the Decalogue was written on the second set of tablets (Deut. 10.4). The fact that in contrast to the Book of the Covenant, the Deuteronomic law collection almost totally omits all civil law, further indicates that its concern is with that law that can cause divine rejection, namely the criminal law derived from the Decalogue and, following the prophetic protest, the laws of humaneness and maladministration of justice (Amos, Micah and Isaiah) and apostasy (Hosea).

While there is no direct evidence that the Decalogue originally consisted of short apodictic commands, nor if it did can we be certain of their precise form, the fact that the Deuteronomic version shows a deliberate theological development from the Exodus version, which in turn in the case of the sabbath commandment has also been subjected to later reinterpretation by the Priestly theologians, indicates that in the text of Exod. 20 and Deut. 5 we have the product of a period of reflection and

---

24. Deut. 5.1–6.3; 9.1–10.11 form the major insertions of the first Deuteronomistic redactors into the original book of Deuteronomy which resulted in the formation of the Deuteronomistic History Work (Deuteronomy–2 Kings) for which the Deuteronomistic redactors composed Deut. 1–3 as the introduction. Later a second redaction took place which included the insertion of Deut. 4.1-40 (A.D.H. Mayes, 'Deuteronomy 4 and the Literary Criticism of Deuteronomy', *JBL* 100/101 [1981], pp. 23-51).

25. Phillips, 'A Fresh Look'.

reassessment necessitated by successive changes in Israel's theological outlook.

Clear indication of the adaptation of the Sinai Decalogue of Exod. 20 to Deuteronomic legal concern is found both in the commandments concerning parents and coveting. So in Deut. 5.16 the Deuteronomistic redactors add to the promise of longevity the additional promise of prosperity in the land which God gives them. This conforms with the Deuteronomic extension of the motive clauses designed to secure obedience to the unenforceable laws of humaneness and righteousness already found in the Book of the Covenant (Exod. 22.20b, 22-23, 26; 23.9) to include the idea of prosperity for the performance of certain apparently uneconomic injunctions.[26] Though obedience to such commands did not on the face of it look as if it could possibly bring the performer any material blessing, Yahweh would in fact secure him personal gain (Deut. 14.29; 15.4-6, 10, 18; 23.21). Similarly, the reversal of house and wife in the commandment on coveting is a deliberate move by the Deuteronomistic redactors to conform with the Deuteronomic law under which for the first time women were treated as equal with men under the law (Deut. 7.3; 13.7; 15.12-17; 17.2-5; 22.22). No longer could a wife be listed alongside her husband's other chattels. She herself had acquired rights under the law and was herself a member of the elect community with all the privileges and duties which that entailed (Deut. 12.12, 18; 16.11, 14; 29.11, 18).

Further, by a subtle modification of the Sinai Decalogue of Exod. 20, the Deuteronomistic redactors were able to emphasize one new concern of the exilic situation which formed no part of the original Deuteronomic law collection (Deut. 12–26). This they achieved by (1) introducing the exodus as an explanation for keeping the sabbath (Deut. 5.15) and inserting the ox and the ass in the list of those who should do no work on it (Deut. 5.14), thereby securing verbal links with both the beginning and end of the Decalogue; and (2) running together the short apodictic injunctions of the last four commandments. As a result, the sabbath commandment was now thrust into a dominant position at the centre of the Decalogue, so underlining its new overall importance in the different circumstances facing exilic Israel.[27] In exactly the same way the Priestly theologians built on to the sabbath commandment in Exod. 20 the connection with their creation theology in Gen. 1, in which they interpreted the sabbath as the sign that

---

26. B. Gemser, *The Importance of the Motive Clause in Old Testament Law* (VTSup, 1; Leiden: E.J. Brill, 1953), pp. 50-66.

27. N. Lohfink, 'Zur Dekalogfassung von Dt 5', *BZ* 9 (1965), pp. 17-32.

God could never repudiate his election of Israel. Since the sabbath was fixed in creation, and the only people in the world who kept the sabbath were the Jews, they too were fixed in creation. Only failure to appropriate their election could invalidate it.[28]

These examples of Deuteronomistic and Priestly reinterpretation of the Decalogue clearly show that the text was in no way sacrosanct, but as with other Hebrew law could be reinterpreted and remoulded to take cognizance of the changed legal and theological situations facing Israel, usually the result of political upheaval. What was important was that in whatever new circumstances Israel found herself the fundamental demands of the Decalogue should continue to reflect Yahweh's will for his elect people.

Indeed it has been my contention that the commandments on images, the name of Yahweh, sabbath, parents and coveting all reflect earlier pre-Deuteronomistic remoulding of the original short apodictic commandments consequent upon a new theological position, itself the result of political change, namely the fall of the northern kingdom leading to Hezekiah's reform (2 Kgs 18).

Since the first commandment prohibits relationships with all other gods, it is clear that originally the commandment on images would have been concerned solely with representations of Yahweh. These would have been in human form since that is how Israel thought of her God (Deut. 4.16; Isa. 44.13; Hab. 2.18-19; Ps. 115.4-8) But the change of person in Exod. 20.5 indicates that whoever expanded the commandment took the first two commandments as one and interpreted the images as those of other gods. Further, these images are now envisaged as representations from the animal world. The same picture is reflected in the laws of Exod. 34.11-26, where Exod. 34.17 again takes the first two commandments together and, as the context indicates, obviously refers back to the golden calf of Exod. 32, itself associated with the bull images of Jeroboam I (1 Kgs 12.28). Further, both in the expanded second commandment (Exod. 20.5) and in Exod. 34.17, Yahweh is described as jealous, a term only used of him when his claims over Israel are threatened by other gods.[29]

Both in *AICL*[30] and in a subsequent article,[31] I have examined the laws of Exod. 34.11-26 and concluded that they reflect Hezekiah's reform, the

---

28. A. Phillips, *God B.C.* (Oxford: Oxford University Press, 1977), p. 48.

29. H.T. Obbink, 'Jahwebilder', *ZAW* 47 (1929), pp. 264-74; R. Knierim, 'Das Erste Gebot', *ZAW* 77 (1965), pp. 20-39 (33).

30. Phillips, *AICL*, pp. 167-79.

31. Phillips, 'A Fresh Look'.

whole Sinai narrative Exod. 19–24, 32–34 being the work of the Proto-Deuteronomists in Jerusalem writing in the light of that reform and the threat to Judah.[32] They are responsible for the Covenant Code framework in its present form (Exod. 19.3-8; 20.22-23; 24.3-8), and the introduction into the Sinai narrative of both the Book of Covenant and the tablets of the law on which they understood both the Decalogue and the Book of the Covenant to have been written (Exod. 24.12), a summary of the more important provisions of which they set out on the second set of tablets (Exod. 34.11-26)[33] Further, they now introduce the Book of the Covenant with a new preface prohibiting molten images and stressing the necessary simplicity of Israelite sanctuaries (Exod. 20.22-26). This radical theological revision of the Sinai narrative resulted from reflection on the changed political situation following the vindication of Hosea's prophecy in the Assyrian conquest. These southern theologians saw that disaster as due to Israel's apostasy symbolized in her bull images.[34] This led Hezekiah in his reform to eject from the temple even the serpent Nehushtan, although attributed to Moses (2 Kgs 18.4). It also explains the central role which the incident of the golden calf now plays in the Sinai narrative (Exod. 32),[35] commandments on molten images both prefacing the Book of the Covenant (Exod. 20.23), and being repeated in the laws on the second set of tablets (Exod. 34.17). These same ideas underlie the Proto-Deuteronomists' expansion of the second commandment now interpreted

---

32. In *AICL*, I used the term 'JE redactor' to describe these authors. But because (1) the whole issue of what is meant by E is now in dispute (B.S. Childs, *Introduction to the Old Testament as Scripture* [London: SCM Press, 1979], p. 122), and (2) the thought and language of these theologians foreshadows what comes to be known as Deuteronomistic theology, it is better to link them with their successors rather than their uncertain predecessors.

33. Only when Deuteronomy was attached to the Tetrateuch to form the Pentateuch was there an attempt to reconcile the Sinai narrative with the Deuteronomic account that only the Decalogue (the Ten Words) was written on the second set of tablets (Deut. 10.2, 4). So the Pentateuchal editors inserted the Deuteronomistic phrase, the Ten Words, in Exod. 34.28. This explains why scholars have found it so difficult to isolate ten commandments in Exod. 34.11-26. There never were nor was it ever intended that there should be Ten Words in Exod. 34.11-26 (Phillips, 'A Fresh Look').

34. On Jeroboam I's purpose in establishing bull images at Dan and Bethel (1 Kgs 12.28) see W.F. Albright, *From the Stone Age to Christianity* (Baltimore: The Johns Hopkins University Press, 2nd edn., 1946), pp. 203, 229.

35. 'For a discussion of the origin of the story of the golden calf, see *AICL*, pp. 170-73.

as prohibiting images of other gods in animal form of which Nehushtan and the bulls form examples. Later, the commandment was to be expanded further in the final Deuteronomistic redaction of Deuteronomy when astral worship associated with the last years of the Davidic monarchy (2 Kgs 21.3-6) becomes associated with it (Deut. 4.19).

Following their introduction of the Book of the Covenant into the Sinai narrative, the Proto-Deuteronomists added to the sabbath commandment the list of those who should do no work on the sabbath, their purpose being to make the commandment conform to Exod. 23.12. By the use of the term holy, Israel is reminded that the sabbath is the creation of Yahweh on whose election alone her existence depends. Later, the Deuteronomistic redactors were to justify the sabbath commandment by reference to Israel's slavery in Egypt and Yahweh's deliverance of her (Deut. 5.15). Similarly, the hortatory expansions of the commandments on the name and on parents are also the work of the Proto-Deuteronomists who as in Exod. 20.10 refer to God by the third person form. The reason that they did not do so in their expansion of the commandment on images was that by taking the first and second commandments together, they were conditioned by the 'before me' of Exod. 20.3. In fact, the third person form was much more suited to their parenetic style. Further, just as the Proto-Deuteronomists introduced motive clauses into the laws of humaneness and righteousness in the Book of the Covenant (Exod. 22.20b, 22-23; 23.9),[36] so they introduce such a clause into the commandment on parents. The question of longevity in the land was of course uppermost in the people's minds as they faced the Assyrian threat. Later, as we have seen, both in the Deuteronomistic version of this commandment and in the Deuteronomic laws, the new motive of the promise of prosperity for obedience to apparently uneconomic laws was inserted, support for parents being considered a financial burden. The tenth commandment was also expanded by the Proto-Deuteronomists as part of their emphasis on the laws of humaneness and righteousness. By an additional *ḥāmad* clause they extended it to include all other property which an Israelite might have acquired by agreement, purchase or gain, which explains the absence of children and confirms that 'house' cannot be interpreted as 'household'. Later under the influence of Isa. 5.8 and Mic. 2.2 the Deuteronomistic redactors added 'field' to the list.

Let me sum up my argument so far. While the apparent reference to

36. While the laws of humaneness and righteousness are in the 'thou' form, the additions are in the plural, like the Covenant Code framework (Exod. 19.3-8; 20.22-23; 24.3-8), also the work of the Proto-Deuteronomists.

the Decalogue in Hos. 4.2 and Jer. 7.9 appears to be the work of the Deuteronomistic redactors, the prophetic silence on the Decalogue can be explained in other ways than ignorance of its existence, for their indictment does not indicate that total chaos in society which would result from its breach. Indeed the people appear fully confident of Yahweh's continued election. Further, the Deuteronomistic redactors use the Decalogue theologically to give support to their law seen as superseding all previous laws in the Sinai narrative, being the complete expression of the will of Yahweh. The Deuteronomistic development of the Sinai Decalogue to reflect Deuteronomic legal concern, seen again in the Priestly theologians introduction of their creation theology into the sabbath commandment, indicates that the Decalogue was subject to continuous revision in the light of new theological ideas, themselves often the consequence of political events. This explains the expansion of the short apodictic commandments by the Proto-Deuteronomists following the fall of Samaria interpreted as due to northern apostasy, and leading to Hezekiah's reform. It is then my contention that before the Proto-Deuteronomists re-wrote the Sinai narrative Exod. 19–24; 32–34, the Decalogue existed as a series of short apodictic commandments. Can we be more precise about its origins?

II

In criticising my book, *Ancient Israel's Criminal Law*, Greenberg[37] curiously failed to recognize the debt I owed to his seminal essay, 'Some Postulates of Biblical Criminal Law'.[38] In this he concluded that a basic difference in the evaluation of life and property separated biblical law from other ancient Near Eastern law. While in non-biblical law an economic and political evaluation pre-dominated, biblical law was governed solely by a religious evaluation. This resulted in three main postulates: (1) biblical law being a statement of God's will made pardon or mitigation impossible: consequently both the murderer and the adulterer had to be executed; (2) no property offence was punishable by death; (3) vicarious punishment was ruled out.

In my book I sought to confirm these postulates by arguing that (1) all

---

37. See n. 14.
38. M. Greenberg, 'Some Postulates of Biblical Criminal Law' in M. Haran (ed.), *Yehezkel Kaufmann Jubilee Volume* (Jerusalem: Magnes Press, 1960), pp. 5-28 (repr. in Greenberg, *Studies in the Bible and Jewish Thought* [Philadelphia: Jewish Publication Society of America, 1995], pp. 25-41).

ten commandments concerned either an injury to God or to the person of a fellow Israelite, but never his property; (2) the penalty for breach of every commandment was death, the exaction of which was mandatory, but which was never required for a property offence; (3) while apostasy would result in the extermination of all males within a family so that the family would be entirely blotted out (2 Kgs 9.26), the substitution of someone for execution for another's crime was never permitted (Exod. 21.31).

Before I seek to defend my thesis, I must rebut the suggestion of McKeating that I take 'it for granted that we know how Israelite law "worked"; how it functioned in society'.[39] On the contrary, I fully recognize that the material is extremely fragmentary; much remains uncertain; some is idealistic; part could never have been enforced; all has been subjected to theological considerations. Indeed the law collections, with the exception of the *mišpāṭîm* of the Book of the Covenant (Exod. 21.12–22.16), are not so much instructions to the judiciary as sermons to the nation. Rather than legal codes establishing a judicial system, these collections constitute theological literary works concerned with the maintenance of Israel's election. But since it was Israel's theology which made her a distinct people in the ancient Near East, it seems reasonable to assume that the various collections might provide sufficient evidence to indicate that at certain points Israel's law was different in principle from other ancient Near Eastern law. Of course we are dealing with probabilities, even possibilities, not certainties. But it remains my assertion that the Old Testament contains enough evidence to show that Greenberg's postulates as elaborated and extended by myself can be established, even if much of my case must of necessity rest on the argument from silence.

In his criticism of Greenberg, Paul[40] and myself, Jackson argues that there were three instances when property offences resulted in the exaction of the death penalty: (1) brigandage (2) kidnapping and (3) sacrilege.[41] But (1) Jackson's distinction between theft and brigandage[42] is irrelevant to the

39. H. McKeating, 'A Response to Dr. Phillips by Henry McKeating', *JSOT* 20 (1981), pp. 25-26 (26).

40. S.M. Paul, *Studies in the Book of the Covenant in the Light of Cuneiform and Biblical Law* (VTSup, 18; Leiden: E.J. Brill, 1970).

41. Jackson, 'Reflections', p. 17.

42. B.S. Jackson, 'Some Comparative Legal History: Robbery and Brigandage', *Georgia Journal of International and Comparative Law* 1 (1970), pp. 45-103; *idem*, *Theft in Early Jewish Law* (Oxford: Clarendon Press, 1972), pp. 1-40, 180-81, 251-53. On Jackson's interpretation of the distinction between *gnb* and *gzl* see J. Milgrom,

administration of early Israelite law; (2) man-theft is not a property offence for which damages are paid (Exod. 21.37), but a crime which requires the exaction of the death penalty (Exod. 21.16), for the offender is no ordinary thief but is specifically described as 'the stealer of the life of one of his brethren' (Deut. 24.7), the equivalent of a murderer; and (3) there is no indication of a particular offence of theft of sacred objects in the Old Testament comparable to Laws of Hammurabi (LH) 6 and 8. Of the cases cited by Jackson, Achan and his family were not executed for theft, but because his action had brought them within the ban to which Jericho was already subject (Josh. 7); Jacob's order that the person with whom Laban's household gods are found should be executed merely indicates the power of the *paterfamilias* at that time (Gen. 31.32); and there is no indication that Joseph or his steward thought that death was the appropriate penalty for theft of his cup (Gen. 44.1-17). The possibility of such a punishment only enters the conversation because the brothers were so certain of their innocence that they were able to make such an extravagant offer. All we have in these last two accounts is stories of the pursuit of thieves on the discovery of loss of property, not a reference to a special offence of sacrilege. It remains then my assertion that no property offence was punishable by death.

Both Jackson and McKeating have criticized Greenberg and myself for our opinion that execution for murder and adultery was mandatory, Jackson arguing that in the *mišpāṭîm* 'there is no explicit statement of general principle, whether allowing or prohibiting composition'.[43] He believes that there was a period in which composition for homicide was permitted and, following Loewenstamm,[44] points to Prov. 6.32-35 'as evidence that adultery could be settled by payment of an agreed amount of compensation'.[45] McKeating adopts the same view,[46] noting that there is little direct evidence of the death penalty being applied for adultery. Indeed in

---

'The Missing Thief in Leviticus 5:20ff.', *RIDA* 22 (1975), pp. 71-80 (repr. in *Cult and Conscience* [SJLA, 23; Leiden: E.J. Brill, 1976], pp. 89-102).

43. Jackson, 'Reflections', pp. 21-26.

44. S.E. Loewenstamm, 'The Laws of Adultery and Murder in Biblical and Mesopotamian Law', *Beth Miqra* 13 (1962), pp. 55-59 (Hebrew) (repr. in *idem, Comparative Studies in Biblical and Ancient Oriental Literatures* [AOAT, 204; Neukirchen–Vluyn: Neukirchener Verlag, 1980], pp. 146-53).

45. Jackson, 'Reflections', p. 34.

46. H. McKeating, 'Sanctions against Adultery in Ancient Israelite Society with Some Reflections on Methodology in the Study of Old Testament Ethics', *JSOT* 11 (1979), pp. 57-72.

his view, while Deut. 22.22 and Lev. 20.10 command execution as a matter of course, in fact its infliction in the end rested on the attitude of the husband.

Kōphēr is only mentioned once in the *mišpāṭîm* when an ox known by its owner to have a propensity to gore kills a man or woman (Exod. 21.30). Uniquely the owner is permitted to save his life by paying *kōphēr* to the injured family. But this is no exception to the rule that in every case the murderer must be executed, because the ox is still stoned to death as the murderer, which explains why its flesh cannot be eaten. The biblical law of the goring ox is then in sharp contrast to Laws of Eshnunna (LE) 54–55 and LH 250–52, which are only concerned with compensating the injured party but provide no penalty for the ox. So while Babylonian law treats injury caused by a goring ox both to men and animals as a civil offence, making provision for pecuniary compensation, biblical law sharply contrasts the death of a man by an ox as a criminal offence with the death of an ox by an ox which, as in Babylonian law, leads to a civil action for damages (Exod. 21.35-36). The fact that under biblical law, even death caused by an animal requires exaction of the death penalty, confirms its mandatory nature. Where there is no difference in principle, biblical and Babylonian law remain identical (LE 53; Exod. 21.35).[47]

Jackson points out though that the way in which *kōphēr* is introduced into the law of the goring ox indicates that it was a well-known practice. But that does not mean that Israelite law countenanced it. Rather its absence from the *mišpāṭîm* in the face of the absolute demands of Exod. 21.12, 15-17 indicates that in contrast to the hitherto common Canaanite practice of *kōphēr* (2 Sam. 21.4), Israelite law was making execution for murder mandatory. Exceptionally, Exod. 21.30 amends earlier law (Exod. 21.29) to allow the owner as accessory to the goring ox to pay *kōphēr*. But in demanding the death of the ox as a murderer, indigenous Canaanite law is being modified due to the principles of Hebrew law.[48]

Further evidence that as a crime, murder was the responsibility of the local community to expiate, rather than of direct concern to the family of

---

47. For further discussion see Phillips, 'Murder', pp. 109-11.

48. Jackson also cites Exod. 21.22 and Exod. 21.32 as envisaging 'monetary payment as the consequence of homicide' ('Reflections', p. 23). But the whole point of Exod. 21.22 (in contrast to Exod. 21.23-25) is that there is no taking of life, the assault on the pregnant woman being treated as a tort for which damages are paid. While Exod. 21.32 demands the death of the murderer—the ox—the owner is treated as a tortfeasor and pays damages to the slave's master (Phillips, 'Murder', pp. 116-17).

the deceased, comes from the ancient provision on the unknown murderer (Deut. 21.1-9).[49] As the reference to elders indicates, this comes from a time before professional judges were appointed.[50] The nearest town to the corpse is made responsible for propitiating Yahweh in order that no punishment should fall on the community. Forbidden by the principles of Hebrew law to execute a substitute for the murderer, the killing of a heifer is prescribed. No blood is shed and the animal's carcass is simply abandoned. As McKeating indicates by connecting this provision with the killing of the seven sons of Saul (2 Sam. 21),[51] Canaanite ideas on fertility underlie the heifer ritual, the rite being designed to prevent drought and consequent famine, interpreted as the most frequent form of direct divine punishment. But despite this reliance on Canaanite practice, Deut. 21.1-9 retains the distinctive principles of Israel's criminal law. In contrast to LH 24 and Hittite Laws (HL) 6, no interest is shown in the deceased or his family; no attempt is made to identify him or contact his family; the community and not a specific individual are responsible for the heifer ritual; no mention is made of any compensation.

As I have already noted, Loewenstamm, Jackson and McKeating have cited Prov. 6.35 as evidence for the payment of *kōphēr* for adultery. However, they fail to recognize that *kōphēr* is also used of an illegal payment designed to avoid prosecution for an offence already committed. It is to this illegal sense of a cover-up operation by the payment of a bribe or hush-money to judges to pervert the course of justice that *kōphēr* in 1 Sam. 12.3 and Amos 5.12 refers, as it does in Prov. 13.8, where a rich man always subject to the threat of blackmail is contrasted with a poor man who has nothing with which to buy off the blackmailer. Similarly *kōphēr* in Prov. 6.35 describes hush-money as the parallel use of *šōḥad*, the normal Old Testament word for the payment of money to pervert the course of justice ('bribe'), confirms. What is being contemplated is the

---

49. For full discussion, see Phillips, 'Murder', pp. 124-26.

50. See below, pp. 21-23. Those provisions in Deuteronomy which mention elders administering justice (19.12; 21.1-9, 18-21; 22.13-21; 25.7-10), while still current law at the time Deuteronomy was promulgated, must antedate Jehoshaphat's reform (2 Chron. 19.5; cf. Deut. 16.18-20). Hence the introduction of 'judges' in Deut. 21.2. The compiler of the Deuteronomic legal corpus probably interpreted this ancient law as referring to the death of someone killed in battle, which explains its present position in the middle of the war laws (Mayes, *Deuteronomy*, pp. 53, 284).

51. H. McKeating 'The Development of the Law on Homicide in Ancient Israel', *VT* 25 (1975), pp. 46-68 (62-64).

possibility of a cover-up operation whereby the adulterer would escape criminal prosecution by bribing the husband to keep quiet. Since the husband could in any event divorce his wife at will under family law and need give no reason, the criminal law was always liable to be treated with contempt if the bribe offered to the husband was sufficiently attractive, especially because the prosecution normally rested on him. But the sage points out that an adulterer would be very foolish to rely on such a possibility of escaping his criminal responsibility, for usually the husband's jealousy would seek vengeance in the adulterer's total ruin.[52]

Nor can I accept McKeating's view that it was only with Deuteronomy and the Holiness Code that an attempt was made to make death for adultery mandatory.[53] While it is true that no such provision appears in the Book of Covenant, neither Deut. 22.22 nor Lev. 20.10 are entirely new enactments. Rather, both have been expanded to bring the offending woman within the scope of criminal liability to which the adulterer had long been subject, and which results in the case of Deuteronomy in the carefully framed legislation of Deut. 22.13-29. This is clear both from the singular *môt yumāt* in Lev. 20.10, and the emphasis placed on 'both of them' in Deut. 22.22, who are then again specifically identified,[54] and is another example of the way in which women were brought within the scope of the law by the Deuteronomists.[55] Before this extension of the criminal law it would have been left to the husband to deal with his adulterous wife as he saw fit under family law (Hos. 2.4, Jer. 3.8), though as in all family law he had no power of life or death over her.[56] Normally

52. See further Phillips, 'Murder', pp. 117-18, *idem*, 'Adultery', pp. 17-18. Prov. 6.27-35 reflects postexilic law. As v. 33 indicates, the adulterer is now no longer executed. Nonetheless he is to be totally disgraced in a way from which he will never recover. This refers to the postexilic penalty of excommunication from the community (Lev. 18.29), which except in cases of murder replaced the death penalty for crimes (*AICL*, pp. 28-32, 124-29), Loewenstamm ('The Laws of Adultery and Murder in the Bible', *Beth Miqra* 18–19 [1964] pp. 77-78 [Hebrew] [repr. in *idem*, *Comparative Studies in Biblical and Ancient Oriental Literatures* (AOAT, 204; Neukirchen–Vluyn: Neukirchener Verlag, 1980), pp. 171-72]) rightly rejects M. Weinfeld's assertion that nothing can be learnt about actual legal practice from Prov. 6.32-35 ('The Concept of Law in Israel and among her Neighbours', *Beth Miqra* 17 [1964], pp. 58-63 [Hebrew]).

53. McKeating, 'Sanctions', pp. 63-65.

54. Phillips, 'Adultery', p. 6.

55. See above, p. 8.

56. A. Phillips, 'Some Aspects of Family Law in Pre-exilic Israel', *VT* 23 (1973), pp. 349-61, and *idem*, 'Another Example of Family Law', *VT* 30 (1980), pp. 240-45 (reprinted as Chapter 6 below).

he would have divorced her, which as elsewhere in the ancient Near East would have included stripping the wife and driving her from the matrimonial home (Hos. 2.5). This stripping cannot then be understood as an alternative punishment to death.

It remains then my view that the criminal law governing murder and adultery in Israel was unique in the ancient Near East. Both demanded community, not private, action leading to the execution of the murderer and the adulterer, and after the Deuteronomic reform of the adulteress as well. The injured party could not pardon the criminal, take any private act of revenge,[57] or settle for damages. The only thing which concerned him, as it did the community at large, was that the criminal should be tried, convicted and executed, and he was under a duty to do all that he could to effect this. Indeed he would often have been the chief witness in the prosecution. In my view, this situation could only have arisen because ancient Israel came into being through accepting a distinctive set of demands which made her a peculiar people among other ancient Near Eastern peoples. Could this have been other than the Decalogue?

Jackson rightly cautions against a synthetic view of non-biblical ancient Near Eastern law, holding that each collection must be considered on its own.[58] But it is clear that no non-biblical collection made the rigid distinction between criminal and civil offences based on whether the offence was against person or property. Yet it is the necessity to make this distinction which underlies the compilation of the *mišpāṭîm*, the earliest section of the Book of the Covenant (Exod. 21.12–22.16) normally dated to the period of the settlement, and clearly directed at the judiciary.

The *mišpāṭîm* begin with a series of crimes all of which require the exaction of the death penalty by the community: murder (Exod. 21.12); assault on parents (Exod. 21.15); man-theft (Exod. 21.16); and repudiation of parents (Exod. 21.17).[59] Then follows a collection of precedents differentiating murder from assault (Exod. 21.18-27). These lead on to a number of rulings on animals which include injury caused by an ox, injury caused to an ox or ass, and theft of an ox, sheep or ass (Exod. 21.28–22.3). This

---

57. For my understanding of the office of *gō'ēl hadām* as an official of the local community, see *AICL*, pp. 102-106, and Phillips, 'Murder', pp. 111-14. There is no evidence of the exercise of blood vengeance in Israel.

58. Jackson, 'Reflections', p. 14.

59. For this interpretation see H.C. Brichto, *The Problem of 'Curse' in the Hebrew Bible* (JBLMS, 13; Philadelphia: Society of Biblical Literature and Exegesis, 1963), pp. 132ff.

section also deals with the killing of a thief caught breaking in. Further precedents concerning damage or illegal appropriation of personal property including seduction of a virgin conclude the laws (Exod. 22.4-16).

For all civil offences including assault, theft, damage to, or illegal appropriation of property, damages are payable by the offender to the injured party, which may be punitive (Exod. 21.37; 22.6-9), the aim being to compensate the injured and deter further similar actions. Clearly, the four absolute demands of the criminal law are being differentiated from the provisions of the civil law: murder from assault, the body being treated as part of a man's personal property; man-theft from theft of property. Exceptionally, assault on parents as well as their repudiation carries the death penalty, while seduction of a virgin—in contrast to adultery (Lev. 20.10; Deut. 22.22)—results in damages. What situation has necessitated the compilation of the *mišpāṭîm* and why do these four particular crimes head the list of precedents?

Canaan, of course, already possessed an established legal system long administered by the elders in the gate. Like other Canaanite practices, whether cultic or secular, this would have been taken over by the Hebrews on entry into the land, but made subject to any overriding principles of Hebrew law. Clearly, the Hebrew compiler of the *mišpāṭîm* aims to place an absolute duty on the community to execute certain criminals for particular offences against persons, while at the same time to affirm that offences against property should be settled by payment of compensation to the injured party. Where it is unclear whether certain action results in a crime or tort, as in the case of injury leading to death (e.g. Exod. 21.18-19.), the compiler provides a ruling. In this way he imposes the mandatory demands of the four criminal laws (Exod. 21.12, 15-17) on the administration of justice of his day.

Apart from the fact that the four criminal laws all concern offences against persons and not property, their inner connection would not be obvious were it not that the Decalogue also contains commandments on parents, murder and theft. Although *gānab* in Exod. 20.5 carries no object, this must refer to the person of a fellow Israelite,[60] for as the context makes clear, the objectless commandments on murder and adultery, like that on theft, are all to be understood as committed against one's neighbour as specified in the commandment on false witness. This is even more obvious in the Deuteronomic version of the Decalogue where the four

---

60. A. Alt, 'Das Verbot des Diebstahls im Dekalog', in *idem*, *Kleine Schriften zur Geschichte des Volkes Israel*, I (Munich: C.H. Beck, 1953), pp. 333-40.

commandments are run together (Deut. 5.17-20). Just as Exod. 21.12 makes explicit what is meant by 'kill' in Exod. 20.13, so Exod. 21.16 does the same for 'steal' in Exod. 20.15. Further, interpreting *gānab* as man-theft explains the strange order of the commandments cited in Hos. 4.2: third, ninth, sixth, eighth and seventh—two kinds of spoken crimes, two kinds of murder (Deut. 24.7 calls the man-thief 'the stealer of life') and adultery (cf. Jer. 7.9).

The *mišpāṭîm* thus provide evidence that from earliest times the Hebrews imposed certain fundamental principles on the indigenous law which appear to derive from the Decalogue, namely that while certain offences against the person required the exaction of the death penalty by the community, injuries to property are a matter for the parties themselves to be settled by the payment of damages. This explains the otherwise curious phenomenon that unlike other cases of assault (Exod. 21.18-19), exceptionally assault on parents carries the death penalty (Exod. 21.15), a far stiffer penalty than LH 195. It is then a mistake to describe the casuistic laws of the *mišpāṭîm* as Canaanite in origin. Like the apodictic commands, they derive from the new situation in Canaan caused by the entry of the Hebrews into the land and reflect the distinctive principles of their law.

Once again it needs to be stressed that even if Exod. 21.12, 15-17 do refer to three of the commandments of the Decalogue, the citing of some of the commandments does not prove the existence of the full collection of ten. Nonetheless, the sharp distinction which the *mišpāṭîm* introduce between offences against persons and offences against property points to a particular theological concern which we have also seen reflected throughout the pre-exilic period in the laws on murder and adultery. Such a distinction also underlies Nathan's parable (2 Sam. 12.1-14).[61]

The prophet describes how a rich man appropriates a poor man's one ewe lamb to feed a visitor. David is so incensed that he declares that the offender should be put to death like any common criminal. The rich man has, however, not committed a crime but the civil offence of theft of a sheep, for which damages are prescribed which even if punitive constitute an entirely inadequate remedy in view of both the callous nature of the rich man's action and his immense wealth. But when Nathan declares that David is the man, it is not to convict him of the civil offence of theft of property, but of the crime of adultery and murder which carry the death

---

61. Phillips, 'The Interpretation of 2 Samuel xii 5-6', *VT* 16 (1966), pp. 242-44 (reprinted below as Chapter 14). Cf. Jackson, *Theft*, pp. 144-48.

penalty. David is only spared through the direct intervention of God.

Finally, I return to the tenth commandment, perhaps the least accepted part of my original thesis. While breach of the other commandments could have resulted in legal action, the injunction not to covet could not, for mental attitudes, however reprehensible, can only become the object of legal concern once a move is made to implement them.[62] Many scholars have, of course, sought to establish that the verb *ḥāmad* carries with it not merely the idea of mental desire, but also the physical steps necessary to gratify it. This seems very unlikely and lacks etymological support both from Hebrew and cognate languages. Further there is clear evidence that to indicate change of possession, *ḥāmad* must be followed by an additional verb of taking (Deut. 7.25; Josh. 7.21; Mic. 2.2).[63] In any event the Deuteronomistic redactors by their use of the alternative *'awâ* in Deut. 5.21b confirm that they understood *ḥāmad* in terms of desire alone.

There is general agreement that the commandment originally covered the house only. Therefore any explanation of its original purpose must take account of why the house should be so picked out. In my book, I argued that the concern of the commandment was not with the house as such, but with the status of elder which was automatically conferred on the owner of a house with the responsibility of taking part in the local community's affairs.[64] Principal among these was the administration of justice intended to be exercised by the heads of all houses.[65] Consequently, judicial matters could only have been properly administered so long as citizens remained free householders. In my view, it was the purpose of the original commandment to achieve this.

In my book I argued that the original short apodictic commandment had contained a verb of taking. But with the change in the administration of justice from the elders to professional judges under Jehoshaphat's reform (2 Chron. 19.5),[66] confirmed by the Deuteronomic law (Deut. 16.18-20),

62. B.S. Jackson, 'Liability for Mere Intention in Early Jewish Law', *HUCA* 42 (1971), pp. 197-207.

63. Exod. 34.24 should not be considered an exception. The verse indicates that when the Israelites go up to worship at the central sanctuary, there will be no one left to desire their land because everyone else will have been expelled (*AICL*, pp. 149-50).

64. Phillips, *AICL* pp. 151-52.

65. E.W. Davies, *Prophecy and Ethics: Isaiah and the Ethical Traditions of Israel* (JSOTSup, 16; Sheffield: JSOT Press, 1981), pp. 92, 100-102.

66. W.F. Albright, 'The Judicial Reform of Jehoshaphat', in S. Leiberman (ed.), *Alexander Marx Jubilee Volume* (New York: Jewish Theological Seminary of America, 1950), pp. 61-82; R. Knierim, 'Exodus 18 und die Neuordnung der Mosaischen

the commandment lost its purpose and was spiritualized by the insertion of the verb *ḥāmad*. While I still maintain that the singling out of the house must be connected with the status of elder which house ownership conferred, it now seems to me more probable that when the Decalogue was originally set in its Sinai narrative context in Exodus, the tenth commandment was already spiritualized, the verb *ḥāmad* being used. Clearly, soon after the settlement the commandment would have lost its original purpose, for in the changed economic situation in Canaan dispossession of property could take place legally. While sale of property followed by purchase would not lead to any loss of status as an elder,[67] economic pressures could result in an Israelite having to sell himself into slavery for insolvency, so losing his legal status within the community (Exod. 22.2b). Although Exod. 21.2-4 specifically ensured that a Hebrew slave could recover that status after six years' slavery, the ceremony of making slavery permanent (Exod. 21.5-6) confirms that few felt able to take advantage of it. There was little point in exchanging security without freedom for freedom without security. Nonetheless, the ideal of a slaveless property-owning society in which each family had a stake in the community's decisions remained valid and was preserved by the tenth commandment, which in effect became an early example of the laws on humaneness and righteousness. This explains why Isaiah and Micah, who presupposed that the administration of justice was in the hands of professional judges (Isa. 3.2; Mic. 3.1-2, 9-11), continued to condemn seizure of realty by the rich (Isa. 5.8; Mic. 2.2), though there is no need to assume that illegal means were used.[68] It was part of that conduct which was against God's will and could bring judgment on his people, for in effect it operated against the principles of natural justice. The spiritualization of the commandment also accounts for its absence from the Deuteronomistic insertions in Hos. 4.2

Gerichtsbarkeit', *ZAW* 73 (1961), pp. 146-71 (162-71); *AICL*, pp. 17-20; Mayes, *Deuteronomy*, pp. 263-64; Davies, *Prophecy and Ethics*, pp. 96-97, who, however, on the strength of Ezra 10.8, 14 argues that professional judges acted alongside the local elders.

67. I cannot accept that realty could not be sold out of the family for ever. Lev. 25.23 is part of the idealized Jubilee law. Neither Isaiah nor Micah appeal to it, nor make any mention of the Jubilee. There is no reason to assume that Ahab's request to purchase Naboth's vineyard was in any sense improper (1 Kgs 21). Naboth merely resorts to an appeal to filial piety to get out of an awkward situation (H. Seebass, 'Der Fall Naboth in 1 Reg. XXI', *VT* 24 [1974], pp. 474-88).

68. Davies, *Prophecy and Ethics*, p. 69.

and Jer. 7.9 which refer to specific crimes which could be prosecuted.[69] It remains then my view that the original tenth commandment concerned the person of the individual Israelite and not his property. It was with the Proto-Deuteronomists that the emphasis of the commandment changed as they added a further clause to include all other property which an Israelite might have acquired by agreement, purchase or gain, later expanded further by the Deuteronomistic insertion of field.[70]

As Greenberg sensed, I believe that there is then within the oldest legal traditions of the Old Testament clear indication of the rigid division of crime and tort based on whether the person or his property was the subject of the offence. It is this distinction which the compiler of the *mišpāṭîm* integrates into local Canaanite legal practice, thus from the first differentiating Israel's legal collections from those of all other ancient Near Eastern law. Can the origin of this distinction lie elsewhere than in the Decalogue? In earliest times, the criminal law derived from the Decalogue would have been administered by the clan elders like any other ancient customary law (Lev. 18.6-18). During the settlement period it appears that there were officials appointed to maintain general oversight over and obedience to Hebrew law (Judg. 10.1-5; 12.7-15; 1 Sam. 7.16), though they may have exercised their authority over a much more limited area than previously thought.[71] This would have been a difficult period as the distinctive traditions of Hebrew law were imposed on the indigenous population. The *mišpāṭîm* contain a collection of their authorized rulings. But with the advent of the monarchy, the ultimate responsibility for the administration of law passed to the king. It was his duty to uphold justice (Ps. 72; Isa. chs 9 and 11). Indeed I have argued that the original Book of the Covenant built around the *mišpāṭîm*, but before the Proto-Deuteronomistic revision, dates from the early days of the Davidic monarchy.[72] Throughout the pre-exilic period, legal power increasingly became centred in the monarchy as Jehoshaphat brought the administration of justice much more firmly under his authority and Hezekiah both reformed the law and attempted some centralization of worship, which under Josiah was finally

69. I would not now connect the final phrase of Hos. 4.2 with Exod. 22.1-2a (see Phillips, *AICL*, p. 152), but rather translate it 'and crime follows crime'.

70. See above, p. 11.

71. Mayes, *Israel*, pp. 65-67.

72. Phillips, *AICL*, pp. 158-61 and in a review of *The If-You Form in Israelite Law* (SBLDS, 15; Missoula, MT: Scholars Press, 1975), by H.W. Gilmer, in *JTS* 27 (1976), pp. 424-26 (425-26).

secured, together with a further reform of the law. But during this period, there is no indication of any attempt by the king to abolish the distinction between crime and tort based in my view on the Decalogue.

It therefore still seems most natural to accept Mendenhall's contention, though not his attempt to prove this from the Hittite suzerainty treaties, that the Decalogue created Israel as a peculiar people both in its religious and legal practice.[73] But these were not distinct parts of Israelite life, for, as well as the distinction between crime and tort based on injury to person or property, monolatry,[74] the absence of images[75] and black magic,[76] and the institution of the sabbath[77] all derived from the Decalogue. Law through which her religion found its expression thus characterized Israel from Sinai to Babylon. It has characterized Judaism ever since.

73. See above, n. 3.
74. Phillips, *AICL*, pp. 37-47.
75. Phillips, *AICL*, pp. 48-52.
76. Phillips, *AICL*, pp. 53-63.
77. Phillips, *AICL*, pp. 64-79.

Chapter 2

A Fresh Look at the Sinai Pericope[*]

Professor E.W. Nicholson's considerable contribution to the study of the Sinai narrative in Exodus is well known both from his monograph *Exodus and Sinai in History and Tradition*, and his numerous articles.[1] In Part 1 of this article I shall consider his treatment of Exod. 20.22-23 contained in one such article, 'The Decalogue as the Direct Address of God'. In Part 2 I shall offer an interpretation of the development of the Sinai narrative Exod. 19–24; 32–34 as a whole, in which Exod. 20.22-23 plays the key role.

Part 1

The main purpose of Nicholson's article 'The Decalogue as the Direct Address of God' was to consider 'why in Exodus the Decalogue is proclaimed directly to the people by God whilst the remaining laws (the Book of the Covenant), though also written in the first person singular as a speech of God, are transmitted at second hand, so to speak, by Moses'. He rejected the then generally held view that the Decalogue originally followed Exod. 20.18-21, the continuation of the theophany account in Exod. 19, which was thought to have been transposed to accommodate the Book of the Covenant in the Sinai narrative. Instead, he found the answer to his question in Exod. 20.22-23, arguing that these verses were not to be connected with the theophany traditions of Exod. 19, but referred to the

---

*   This essay is based on a paper given to the Evangelisch-Theologische Fakultät in the University of Munich, January 1982.

1.   'The Interpretation of Exodus xxiv.9-11', *VT* 24 (1974), pp. 77-97; 'The Antiquity of the Tradition in Exodus xxiv.9-11', *VT* 25 (1975), pp. 69-79; 'The Origin of the Tradition in Exodus xxiv.9-11', *VT* 26 (1976), pp. 148-60; 'The Decalogue as the Direct Address of God', *VT* 27 (1977), pp. 422-33; 'The Covenant Ritual in Exodus xxiv.3-8', *VT* 32 (1982), pp. 74-86.

Decalogue as Yahweh's direct address to Israel. Like the insertion of the Decalogue itself, they derived from a Deuteronomic redactor and reflected the Deuteronomic 'apologetical emphasis upon the Decalogue as God's direct address to Israel' as repeatedly expressed in Deut. 4–5. So Exod. 20.22 had Yahweh speaking 'from heaven' as in Deut. 4.36, which was immediately followed by the prohibition of the making of images in Exod. 20.23 corresponding to the same prohibition in Deut. 4.16-18, also based on Yahweh's transcendence, for at Horeb his 'form' was not seen (Deut. 4.15). While, for Nicholson, before the insertion of the Decalogue in Exod. 20, the theophany of Exod. 19 was the basis upon which obedience to Yahweh was evoked (Exod. 20.18-21), Exod. 20.22 now 'invokes God's speaking "from heaven" as the immediate basis'. So the direct address of Yahweh from heaven marked the climax of the narrative. Theophany and law were thereby brought together: the gift of the commandments 'came to Israel as part and parcel of her election'.

Finally, Nicholson made three suggestions consequent upon his treatment of Exod. 20.22-23. First, both the Decalogue and Exod. 20.22-23 are held to derive from the same Deuteronomic redactor. Second, it is thought probable that the insertion of the Decalogue and the related verses Exod. 20.22-23 into the Exodus narrative is subsequent to the inclusion of the Decalogue in Deuteronomy, the author of Exod. 20.22 presupposing Deut. 4.1-40. Third, the Book of the Covenant is seen as belonging to an earlier stage in the development of the Sinai narrative than the Decalogue. Nicholson therefore concludes that the position of the Decalogue in the Sinai narrative in Exodus is not due to editorial but primarily theological reasons. His argument depends entirely on his interpretation of Exod. 20.22-23. For, unlike Deut. 4–5, there is no explicit statement in Exod. 19–24 that the Decalogue was given directly to the people.

One of Nicholson's concerns in his treatment of the Sinai narrative has been to counteract what B.S. Childs described as 'the failure of most critical commentaries to deal with the final shape of the text', but instead to concentrate on form-critical and source analysis which 'has tended to fragment the text and leave the reader with only bits and pieces'.[2] But in his treatment of Exod. 20.22-23 Nicholson only considered these verses in terms of the Decalogue and not their present position as forming part only of the preface to the Book of the Covenant. For Exod. 20.22-23 is followed by the law of the altar in Exod. 20.24-26 set out, in contrast to Exod. 20.22-23, in the 'thou' form and widely believed to have been an

---

2.   Childs, *Exodus* (OTL; London: SCM Press, 1974), pp. xiv-xv.

ancient enactment, probably originally part of the cultic laws at the end of the Book of the Covenant (Exod. 23.10-19). Exod. 20.22-23 cannot then be considered independently from Exod. 20.24-26. Both these provisions have been deliberately placed in their present emphatic position.

While it is possible that Exod. 20.24-26 already acted as a preface to the Book of the Covenant before Exod. 20.22-23 was inserted, this is unlikely. It would have been moved to its present prominent position only for specific theological reasons. Since Exod. 20.24-26 assumes a plurality of sanctuaries at which sacrifice could be offered, this new emphasis on the ancient altar law could not have been the work of the Deuteronomistic redactors for whom all worship had been centralized at Jerusalem (Deut. 12.5). Nor can they have been responsible for combining Exod. 20.22-23 with Exod. 20.24-26, an enactment which contradicted their own policy of a single sanctuary.

In fact, it is no accident that has led to the ancient enactment of Exod. 20.24-26 being singled out to act with Exod. 20.22-23 as the introduction to the Book of the Covenant. For the prohibition of metal images and the command to build an earthen altar are part and parcel of one idea—a purification of Israel's sanctuaries to a much simpler and primitive form. This deliberate theological construction which, as we shall see, reflects the subsequent Sinai narrative in Exodus (32–34), must then derive from a pre-Deuteronomic attempt to reform Israel's worship. This raises the possibility that rather than Exod. 20.22-23 being dependent on Deut. 4.1-40, those late Deuteronomistic redactors drew on the Exodus narrative. For Mayes has shown both the unity of Deut. 4.1-40, and its late insertion into Deuteronomy after the original book had already been redacted.[3] Let us examine Nicholson's arguments.

Nicholson contends, as other commentators have done, that the words 'from heaven' in Exod. 20.22 point to Yahweh's transcendence and therefore lead on to the prohibition of images in Exod. 20.23. While Deut. 4.36 makes no mention of images, Deut. 4.15-19 prohibits them on the grounds that no form of Yahweh was seen at Horeb where God's voice was heard out of the fire (Deut. 4.12), described as burning 'to the heart of heaven' (Deut. 4.11).

---

3. Mayes, *Deuteronomy*, pp. 43-46, 148-58, and *idem*, 'Deuteronomy 4', argues both for the unity of Deut. 4.1-40 and that it formed part of a later Deuteronomistic redaction into the Deuteronomistic History Work. On the other hand, Deut. 5.1–6.3, which includes the Decalogue, was part of the earlier Deuteronomistic redaction which resulted in the formation of that History Work.

Comparison of Exod. 20.23 with Deut. 4.15-19 indicates, however, that the two provisions on images have very different concerns. The emphasis of Exod. 20.23 falls on the substance out of which the images might be made, silver and gold, whereas Deut. 4.15-19 is a far-reaching reinterpretation of the second commandment which is later than the present form of that commandment in both versions of the Decalogue. Not only does it take account of the extension of the commandment from images in human form to include images from nature (Exod. 20.4b; Deut. 5.8b), but it also deals with astral cults associated with the last years of the Davidic monarchy (2 Kgs 21.3-6). Deut. 4.15-19 is therefore a highly sophisticated late Deuteronomistic interpretation of the second commandment, and its concern is much wider than the very specific and limited interest of Exod. 20.23.

Further, the association of the fire on the mountain with heaven in Deut. 4.11 is found neither in the Sinai narrative in Exodus, nor in the earlier work of the Deuteronomistic redactors who understand Yahweh to speak from the fire (Deut. 5.22, 24-26; 10.4). It has all the marks of an attempt to reconcile two contradictory ideas as to the location of Yahweh's voice. If this is so, and we accept the unity of Deut. 4.1-40, then the authors of Deut. 4.11 must be drawing on the Sinai narrative in Exodus where the sudden introduction of the voice from heaven in Exod. 20.22 seems at variance with the earlier description of Yahweh descending on the mountain 'in fire' (Exod. 19.18). The difficulty of effecting such a reconciliation is confirmed by the clumsy and overloaded Deut. 4.36 with its reference both to the voice from heaven and to the words from the fire.

It is not, however, the introduction of this voice from heaven which most arrests the reader of Deut. 4.36, but the Deuteronomistic explanation that it was given for disciplinary purposes, an interpretation which is confirmed from the frequent use of *yāsar* in the training of a child (Deut. 8.5; Prov. 19.18; 29.17) or in general correction (1 Kgs 12.11, 14; Jer. 10.24; 30.11).[4] It is the connection of the voice from heaven with the idea of discipline which requires an explanation, which, as I shall show later, is to be directly connected with Exod. 20.23 for which Exod. 20.22 formed the basis. The fact that the Deuteronomistic redactors felt it necessary to stress repeatedly that the Decalogue was the direct address of God to the people, when nothing is made of this in Exod. 19–24, indicates a new theological emphasis.

---

4. S.R. Driver, *Deuteronomy* (ICC; Edinburgh: T. & T. Clark, 3rd edn, 1902), p. 76; Mayes, *Deuteronomy*, p. 158.

Nicholson's suggestion that the Decalogue was first inserted in Deuteronomy and then later in Exodus cannot be accepted, though it is, of course, clear that the Exodus version of the fourth commandment on observing the sabbath has subsequently been brought into line with Priestly theology (Exod. 20.11). It was the Deuteronomistic insertion of Deut. 5.1–6.3 which incorporated the Decalogue into the original book of Deuteronomy where it was hitherto neither referred to nor presupposed. But the Deuteronomistic redactors were only following the Sinai narrative in Exod. 19–24, 32–34 in which the Decalogue was already present, as is confirmed by their other major insertion describing the incident of the golden calf and the issue of the second set of tablets (Deut. 9.1–10.11), though, as we shall see, they make important theological alterations to it. Nor can it be argued that, because the Decalogue did not form part of the original book of Deuteronomy, it did not yet exist when this book was compiled, for the original book of Deuteronomy was not concerned with the covenant at Horeb—part of the Deuteronomistic redaction which led to the Deuteronomistic History Work—but with the proclamation of the law to Israel in Moab just before her entry into Canaan.[5] I shall consider the origin of the Decalogue in Part 2 of this article: here it is sufficient to note that its position in the Sinai narrative in Exodus preceded its Deuteronomistic use.

This conclusion is confirmed from detailed examination of the Deuteronomic version of the Decalogue which shows clear signs of having been altered from the Exodus version in order to comply with Deuteronomic legal concerns. So in the fifth commandment concerning parents, the Deuteronomists add to the promise of longevity the additional promise of prosperity in the land which God gives them. This is in accord with their extension of the motive clauses in the laws of humaneness and righteousness already found in the Book of the Covenant (Exod. 22.20b, 22-23, 26; 23.9) to include the idea of prosperity for the performance of certain apparently uneconomic injuctions.[6] Though obedience to these laws did not look as if it could possibly bring personal advantage, it would in fact secure material gain for those who complied with them through the direct intervention of Yahweh (Deut. 14.29; 15.4-6, 10, 18; 23.21). This is, of course, in line with the Deuteronomic theology of blessing and cursing following obedience or disobedience of the law (Deut. 28). Similarly, the

---

5. Mayes, *Deuteronomy*, pp. 161-65. He argues that 'both the Exodus and Deuteronomic versions of the Decalogue point to the Deuteronomic milieu as the context of their collection and presentation'.

6. Gemser, 'The Importance of the Motive Clause', pp. 50-66.

reversal of house and wife in the tenth commandment on coveting is a deliberate move to conform with Deuteronomic law which treated women as equal with men under the law (Deut. 7.3; 13.7; 15.12-17; 17.2-5; 22.22). No longer could the wife be included with a list of chattels. She herself had rights under the law and was a member of the covenant community (Deut. 12.12, 18; 16.11, 14; 29.11, 18).

Exod. 20.22 clearly exhibits linguistic similarities with Exod. 19.3–4. So we find in Exod. 19.3-4: 'Thus shalt thou say to the house of Jacob and tell the people of Israel: You yourselves have seen...', while Exod. 20.22 reads: 'Thus shalt thou say to the people of Israel: You yourselves have seen...' This can hardly be coincidence.

In his monograph, *Exodus and Sinai in History and Tradition*[7], Nicholson, in the wake of L. Perlitt,[8] argued that Exod. 19.3b-8 together with Exod. 24.3-8 in its present form was the work of a 'later, probably Deuteronomic, redactor' who introduced the covenant terminology into the Sinai narrative in Exodus. Dale Patrick has similarly pointed to the linguistic and stylistic evidence for the common authorship of Exod. 19.3b-8, 20.22-23, 24.3-8 which, he argued, constituted a narrative framework to the Covenant Code 'composed for the purpose of setting the Code in the context of the revelation at Sinai'.[9] In addition to having parallel words and phrases, these passages were all in the plural form of address including the commandment Exod. 20.23 attached to Exod. 20.22. Patrick noted that, while there was clear evidence of 'points of contact' with Deuteronomy and Deuteronomistic literature, nothing demonstrated dependence or common authorship. Indeed, since the Deuteronomic collection Deut. 12–26 was clearly dependent on the Book of the Covenant for both its legal and parenetic traditions, Patrick argued that there was no *prima facie* reason why the Deuteronomists should not also draw on terminology already connected with the framework of the Sinai narrative in Exodus for its leading theological expressions. If Patrick were right, the present Deuteronomistic narrative with its stress on a covenant theology inserted into the original book of Deuteronomy might not then be an innovation of the Deuteronomistic redactors which was later read back by them into the Sinai narrative in Exodus, but rather owe its origin to that narrative itself.

In 'The Decalogue as the Direct Address of God', Nicholson points to

7. Nicholson, *Exodus and Sinai*, pp. 70-74.
8. Perlitt, *Die Bundestheologie*, pp. 190ff.
9. Patrick, 'The Covenant Code Source', *VT* 27 (1977), pp. 145-57 (156).

the importance which the Deuteronomic author places on the Decalogue as the sole content of the covenant law given at Horeb (Deut. 4.13; 5.22). Since he 'appears to have known of no other commandments given at Horeb', Nicholson suggests that this may indicate that 'he did not know the Sinai pericope in its present form' (p. 425). But Nicholson fails to recognize that the Deuteronomistic redactors may have deliberately rejected the Exodus tradition by affirming that nothing else was added to the Decalogue. This they achieved in two ways. First, they introduced the two tablets immediately after the giving of the Decalogue (Deut. 5.22), whereas in the Exodus account they do not appear until after the Book of the Covenant has been mediated to Israel by Moses (Exod. 24.12). Second, they reconstructed the account of their replacement. So in Deut. 9.1–10.11, after the incident of the golden calf, the Deuteronomistic redactors described Moses breaking the two tablets of the law inscribed with the Decalogue and going back up the mountain taking the fresh-hewn replacement tablets on which it is specifically asserted that the Decalogue was rewritten by God himself (Deut. 10.4). But in Exod. 32–34, it is recorded that, on going back up the mountain, Moses received a new set of laws from Yahweh (Exod. 34.11-28), which are inscribed on the two new tablets apparently by Moses rather than God. Here the reference to the Ten Words, found elsewhere only in Deuteronomy (4.13; 10.4), is clearly a late attempt, to bring the Sinai narrative in Exodus into line with the Deuteronomistic account.

Nicholson is then right to emphasize that for the Deuteronomistic redactors the Decalogue alone was given at Horeb but he misses the point of their assertion. Their purpose was to suppress both the Book of the Covenant and the laws on the second set of tablets in Exod. 34.11-26. This also explains why in Deut. 4–5 they constantly insist that the Decalogue was the direct address of Yahweh to his people in contrast to Exod. 19–24 which makes nothing of it. It was the Book of the Covenant and the laws in Exod. 34.11-26 which according to the Sinai narrative in Exod. 19–24 were specifically mediated by Moses to Israel, which laws the Deuteronomistic redactors were intent on suppressing.

The Sinai narrative in Exodus is, then, entirely superseded by the new Deuteronomistic revision of the original book of Deuteronomy. For the Deuteronomistic redactors the Decalogue, from which the laws in Deut. 12–26 are pictured as deduced, is the sole covenant law, obedience to which determines Israel's relationship with her God. The Deuteronomic laws thus have the same force as the Decalogue: if ever Israel was again to cross the Jordan and inherit Canaan, here was the law, obedience to which alone could secure her future in the land Yahweh wills to give her. This Deuteronomistic revision thus became the Torah, the complete expression of the will of Yahweh.[10]

Accordingly it can no longer be maintained that the Deuteronomistic redactors were concerned to edit the Exodus account of the Sinai narrative. What they were intent on doing was to produce an alternative version to replace that earlier account—a version which would in effect carry sole canonical authority.[11] While Nicholson correctly recognized that the Deuteronomistic redactors would hardly have introduced the Book of the Covenant and the Decalogue into the Exodus narrative at the same time in view of their assertion that the Decalogue was the only law given at Horeb, this basic assertion of the Deuteronomistic redactors makes it equally impossible that they would have inserted the Decalogue into an account which already held that other laws (the Book of the Covenant and the laws of Exod. 34.11-26) were given at Sinai. This means not only that the Decalogue's position in the Sinai narrative owes nothing to the Deuteronomistic redactors, but also that we should not in any event expect to find their hand in the Sinai narrative in Exodus. Only after the detachment of Deuteronomy from the Deuteronomistic History Work and attachment to the Tetrateuch did later Pentateuchal editing lead to some fusion of the material, of which the note about the Ten Words in Exod. 34.28 appears to be an example. Rather, what we have in the Deuteronomistic revision is a radical reappraisal of the Sinai narrative in Exodus by the Deuteronomistic redactors who draw on that narrative, but adapt it for their own theological purposes. Their aim is to provide the only authoritative statement of the nature of Israel's relationship with her God based on their covenant theology. In a similar manner the prophet of the exile was to exhort his hearers to obliterate from their memory the exodus from Egypt in the face of an even more spectacular deliverance which Yahweh was even then inaugurating (Isa. 43.16-21). When the Priestly theologians rejected the Deuteronomistic theological assessment, they were able to use the discredited Sinai narrative as part of the framework of their Work.[12]

---

10. Barnabas Lindars, 'Torah in Deuteronomy', in P.R. Ackroyd and B. Lindars (eds.), *Words and Meanings* (Cambridge: Cambridge University Press, 1968), pp. 117-36.

11. Cf. R.E. Clements, *God's Chosen People* (London: SCM Press, 1968), pp. 89-105.

12. On the question whether 'P should be considered an independent literary source or a redaction of earlier literary material', see Childs, *Introduction*, pp. 122-23.

If the Deuteronomistic revision of the original book of Deuteronomy makes it impossible to hold that the Deuteronomistic redactors edited the Sinai narrative in Exodus, how are the clear points of contact between that narrative and Deuteronomy to be explained? The solution lies not in reading back into the Sinai narrative in Exodus Deuteronomistic theology, but rather in examining that narrative itself to determine its own theological position. Critical studies of the Old Testament have placed far too much reliance on linguistic similarities without applying the necessary check on the proper consideration of the theological implications of the material as it stands. When that is done with that part of the Sinai narrative in Exod. 19–24, 32–34 in which scholars have seen signs of Deuteronomic influence, it becomes clear that what we have in the Exodus material is theological ideas which become fully worked out only in Deuteronomy, though because the Deuteronomistic redactors went beyond these theological roots they found it necessary to deny their source. In other words, in the rest of this essay I shall argue that Deuteronomistic theology developed from the work of those southern theologians in Jerusalem who compiled the Sinai narrative in Exod. 19–24, 32–34, and who may therefore appropriately be called Proto-Deuteronomists. But since new theological ideas appear only as a result of reflection on particular circumstances, it will be necessary to identify those events which led the Proto-Deuteronomists to redact the then existing Sinai narrative in Exodus. The solution to this problem lies in the laws alleged to have been written on the second set of tablets, Exod. 34.11-26.

For many years these laws were understood as part of J and termed the Ritual Decalogue in contrast to Exod. 20 attributed to E, and called the Ethical Decalogue. However, this distinction can no longer be maintained. In the first place, Exod. 34.11-26 is not a Decalogue, but contains more than ten provisions. And second, Exod. 34.11-26 is not an alternative version of the requirements found in the Decalogue and the Book of the Covenant, but a subtle reapplication of this material to meet the requirements of a particular political situation. I have previously argued that Exod. 34.11-26 reflected Hezekiah's reform recorded in 2 Kgs 18.4 in which following the fall of the northern kingdom, Hezekiah launched a full-scale attack on Canaanite syncretism.[13] Examination of the material shows that it entirely fits such a milieu. Thus Exod. 34.11-16 warns against fraternizing with the Canaanites: forbidding the making of a

---

13. Phillips, *AICL*, pp. 167-79.

covenant with them (v. 12); ordering the destruction of their altars and cult apparatus (v. 13); commanding worship of Yahweh alone (vv. 14-15); and counselling against the intermarriage of Israelite men with the daughters of the indigenous population (v. 16).

Nicholson, following others, has argued that 'it seems clear that the material in Exod. 34.11-16 has a marked Deuteronomic stamp'.[14] But examination of the related material in Deut. 7.1-3, 6, probably part of the original book of Deuteronomy, indicates that the Deuteronomic author was introducing new ideas not found in the earlier material in the Sinai narrative in Exodus, whether in Exod. 23.20-33 or in Exod. 34.11-16, but present in the Deuteronomic laws, Deut. 12–26. So in Deut. 7.2 the emphasis falls not on the command not to make a covenant with the inhabitants of the land, but on putting them to the ban, considered elsewhere in Deuteronomy as the appropriate fate for the Canaanites as opposed to other peoples (Deut. 20.10-18), but nowhere applied to the Canaanite population in the Sinai narrative in Exodus (cf. Exod. 23.32, 34.12, 15).[15] Further, whereas Exod. 34.16 merely warns against foreign marriages between Israelite men and Canaanite women, Deut. 7.3 absolutely prohibits them, and extends the provision to cover Israelite daughters as well. This is, of course, in accord with the Deuteronomic innovation already referred to whereby women were made subject to the law equally with men (cf. Deut. 5.21; 13.7; 15.12-17; 17.2-5; 22.22). Here again we have a clear instance of that lack of precision among Old Testament scholars in their use of the term 'Deuteronomic'. Deuteronomy 7 shows a distinct theological development from the Sinai narrative in Exodus which indicates that that narrative must reflect an earlier situation which prompted its composition—in my view Hezekiah's reform.

This is confirmed from the rest of the law on the second set of tablets in Exod. 34.11-26. So Exod. 34.17 prohibits the making of a molten god, in the context obviously referring back to the golden calf of Exod. 32, and that explains why Hezekiah was not afraid to destroy the bronze serpent Nehushtan even though its creation was attributed to no less a person than Moses (2 Kgs 18.4). Finally, there follows in Exod. 34.18-26 the re-emphasis on the festal calendar of Exod. 23.14-17 which both introduces the law of the first born (cf. Exod. 22.28b-29) as a supplementary Passover

---

14. Nicholson, *Exodus and Sinai,* p. 76.

15. In Exod. 22.19 those who sacrifice to other gods are to be put to the ban. But the injunction is clearly addressed to the Hebrews who might apostasize (*AICL*, pp. 40-47).

law,[16] and explicitly requires the centralization of the celebration of the three main festivals at Jerusalem (Exod. 34.23-24). That some kind of centralization took place is confirmed by the Rabshakeh's speech (2 Kgs 18.22) and perhaps by the record of Hezekiah's Passover celebrations (2 Kgs 23.21-23), though it is extremely improbable that Hezekiah intended the destruction of all sanctuaries. While certain high places would have been destroyed, the ancient shrines such as Hebron and Beersheba would merely have been purified. Indeed, Nicholson himself has argued that the origin of the dogma of the central shrine is to be associated with Hezekiah.[17]

Who then is responsible for the creation of Exod. 34.11-28. In my view it is those theologians who have been termed the Proto-Deuteronomists and who, following the fall of the northern kingdom in the wake of the announcement of judgment by the canonical prophets and in the light of Hezekiah's reform, have sought to reflect on the theological basis of Israel's relationship with her God in order that southern Judah might not suffer Samaria's fate. To do this they took over the traditions of both the north and the south and overlaid them with their own theological assessment of why Yahweh had allowed the destruction of the north. Here lies the present significance of the account of the making of the golden calf in Exod. 32.

Undoubtedly, this account is intended to refer to the bull images associated with the northern kingdom, criticized in Hosea (8.5-6; 10.5; 13.2), and originating from Jeroboam I's action in installing them in his principal sanctuaries at Bethel and Dan (1 Kgs 12.28-29.). Although only one calf was involved in Exod. 32, this connection has now been made explicit by Exod. 32.4 being made to conform with 1 Kgs 12.28—perhaps another instance of late Pentateuchal editing. Probably underlying Exod. 32 was an aetiological account supporting Jeroboam's action in demy-thologizing the Canaanite bull images, rather as the story of Num. 21.8-9 justified the retention of the Canaanite Nehushtan in the Davidic sanctuary at Jerusalem. This explains the inability of the present author to condemn Aaron who sees the calf as appropriate to a Yahweh festival (Exod. 32.5). Probably, Jeroboam's bulls, like the ark, were to act as pedestals for the invisible Yahweh, and so in contrast to their Canaanite versions were

16. This connection is further developed in Exod. 13 (Phillips, *AICL*, p. 176).

17. E.W. Nicholson, 'The Centralisation of the Cult in Deuteronomy', *VT* 13 (1963), pp. 380-89.

deliberately left riderless.[18] But in Exod. 32 these images are now seen as apostate representations of other gods, the cause of the breaking of the covenant inaugurated in Exod. 19–24. It is therefore my contention that the Proto-Deuteronomists in reinterpreting the old tradition concerning Jeroboam's bulls to explain Yahweh's rejection of the northern kingdom were in fact faithfully reflecting the reaction in Jerusalem which led to Hezekiah's reform, itself recorded by them in the second set of tablets in Exod. 34.11-28. It was this reinterpretation which the Deuteronomists took over and applied to their interpretation of Israel's history.

At this point I return to Exod. 20.22-23 which must be considered with Exod. 20.24-26, the two provisions making up the preface to the Book of the Covenant. The prominent position of these verses with their stress on molten images and a simple altar must be due to the same distinct theological concern which we have found in both the narrative of the making of the golden calf and the laws written on the second set of tablets (Exod. 32–34). Thus Exod. 32.5-8 records that not only was the golden calf made, but an apostate altar built before it on which sacrifices were offered to the molten image. In its present position Exod. 20.22-26 is intended to act as the basic summary of the covenant law which follows, just as Exod. 19.3-8 acts as a summary of the whole account of the inauguration of the covenant in Exod. 19–24. It is these specific laws on images and a primitive altar which have been broken in the making of the golden calf and sacrifice to it, and which must be reiterated in the laws set out on the second set of tablets marking the reinauguration of the covenant (Exod. 34.17). While Hezekiah's reform apparently allowed that there might be more than one sanctuary, as the use of Exod. 20.24-26 in the new preface to the Book of the Covenant confirms, those that survived that reform were to be purged of all Canaanite accretions (Exod. 34.13), and return to their primitive state. While the *'ašērâ* was probably always regarded as improper and condemned, it appears that even Hosea had felt no need to condemn the *maṣṣēbâ* (Hos. 3.4), its destruction being an innovation of Hezekiah's reform.

It is the connection of Exod. 20.23 with the incident of the golden calf which explains the curious introduction of 'discipline' in Deut. 4.36 as an explanation for the voice from heaven and indicates that those late Deuteronomistic redactors, like their predecessors, continued to draw on the Sinai narrative in Exodus (see n. 3 above). In Exod. 20.22 the

---

18. Obbink, 'Jahwebilder', pp. 264-74; Albright, *From the Stone Age*, pp. 203, 229.

introduction of the voice from heaven of the transcendent Yahweh is immediately followed by the commandment on molten images and acts as its *raison d'être*. This commandment is broken in the making of the golden calf and the sacrifice to it on the newly built altar (Exod. 32.1-6), and so leads to Yahweh's direct punishment of his people (Exod. 32.35).[19] It is to these events that Deut. 4.36 alludes. Only someone already familiar with the Sinai narrative in Exodus, in which failure to heed the precise words of the voice from heaven prohibiting molten images led to direct divine punishment, could have composed Deut. 4.36.

Part 2

I shall now consider how the Sinai narrative in Exodus reached its present shape. I am, of course, aware of the almost unlimited hazards which confront any attempt to answer this question. My purpose is simply to offer some comments which arise from the recognition of the key position of Exod. 20.22-26.

We have already seen that Exod. 20.22-23 comes from the same hand as Exod. 19.3-8, which is itself related to Exod. 24.3-8 in its present form. This means that, if my earlier identification of Exod. 20.22-23 as connected with Hezekiah's reform is accepted, the narrative framework to the Sinai account in Exod. 19–24, which describes the establishment of a covenant at Sinai on the basis of obedience to law, must also be attributed to the Proto-Deuteronomists. While the use of the plural form of address both in this framework and in the Deuteronomistic insertions Deut. 5.1– 6.3 and 9.1–10.11 might be thought to indicate a common redactional hand in both Exodus and Deuteronomy, the fact that the Deuteronomistic redactors were intent on deliberately suppressing the Sinai narrative in Exodus rules this out. Rather, the use of the plural form of address in the narrative framework appears to have been a deliberate stylistic device intended to highlight the Proto-Deuteronomists' redactional activity in Exod. 19–24, and so to emphasize their covenant theology, though, as we shall see, in their continuation of that narrative itself (Exod. 23.20-33; 24.12-15; 32.1–34.28) they return to the singular form of address because

19. The introduction of the Levites who execute the ban on the apostate people in accordance with Exod. 22.19 is an independent tradition concerning the origin of the Levitical priesthood and originally had nothing to do with the incident of the golden calf. But it has been incorporated here to reflect the contention that Jeroboam I appointed non-Levitical priests for his royal sanctuaries (1 Kgs 12.31; 13.33).

they have no need to distinguish their work from an earlier account.

Patrick held that the narrative framework was composed to set the Book of the Covenant in the Sinai narrative—in his opinion before E was combined with J.[20] Childs has also argued[21] that the Book of the Covenant was inserted into Exod. 19–24 by the JE redactor, who saw the covenant sealed on the basis of both the Decalogue and the Book of the Covenant. This is certainly made explicit in Exod. 24.3 where Moses tells the people both the 'words' (the Decalogue, Exod. 20.1) and the 'ordinances' (the Book of the Covenant, Exod. 21.1) on which the covenant is made. Although in *AICL* I also used the term 'JE redactor', I would not now want to do so. Not only is the whole issue of what is meant by E in dispute,[22] but I also see no need as Childs does for holding that an original J version underlay the provisions of Exod. 34.11-26;[23] rather these represent a deliberate combination and elaboration of laws drawn from the Decalogue and the Book of the Covenant reflecting the interests of Hezekiah's reform. Thus I believe that it was those theologians in Jerusalem whom we have called the Proto-Deuteronomists, because they foreshadow what comes to be known as Deuteronomistic theology, who in the light of the fall of the northern kingdom compiled the narrative framework Exod. 19.3-8, 20.22-23, 24.3-8 in its present form, and inserted the Book of the Covenant into Exod. 19–24, following this with the creation of Exod. 32–34.

However, it must not be thought that all I am doing is to modify Nicholson's views expressed in his *Exodus and Sinai in History and Tradition* by placing the emergence of the covenant terminology in the work of the Proto-Deuteronomists, a possibility which, in effect, he himself considered in his monograph.[24] Of course, Judah's uncertain future after Assyrian expansionism would provide an appropriate setting for the development of a theology which sought to guarantee possession of the land through obedience to covenant law. Indeed, this was the assurance which the Proto-Deuteronomists sought to give to Judah badly shaken by the destruction of Samaria. Hence the creation of the narrative framework Exod. 19.3-8; 20.22-23; 24.3-8 in its present form, and the account of the golden calf and reinauguration of the covenant in Exod. 32–34. Further,

20. Patrick, 'The Covenant', pp. 156-57.
21. Childs, *Exodus*, pp. 344-51.
22. Childs, *Introduction*, p. 122.
23. Childs, *Exodus*, p. 607.
24. Nicholson, *Exodus and Sinai*, pp. 74-76.

such a late emergence of the covenant concept would explain the often remarked almost total absence of the term *bᵉrît* in the work of the eighth-century prophets, Hos. 6.7 and 8.1 being the exceptions. While the interpretation of Hos. 6.7 remains uncertain,[25] Hos. 8.1 does seem to owe its origin to Deuteronomistic redaction. For here 'my *tōrâ*' is used in its Deuteronomic sense of the complete expression of the will of Yahweh and paralleled with 'my *bᵉrît*'.

Again, care needs to be exercised over drawing hasty conclusions from the presence or absence of particular words without making an adequate check on the theological ideas in the material in question. In the first place, an idea may already be part of Israel's faith before any specific word has been coined to define it. So, as Mayes points out[26] while election was part of Israel's theology from earliest times (Amos 3.2), it was the Deuteronomists who introduced *bāḥar* to express it. Second, the absence of a particular term may be due to other reasons than ignorance of it.

In any event, D.J. McCarthy has pointed to what he describes as the 'very un-Deuteronomic' phrase 'the blood of the covenant' in Exod. 24.8,[27] which indicates that, contrary to Perlitt, the idea of *bᵉrît* already formed part of the sacrificial ritual in Exod. 24.4-6 before the Proto-Deuteronomists built on this to make the conclusion of their narrative framework. Indeed, since the reference to 'young men' offering the sacrifice in Exod. 24.5 seems to indicate a time before the establishment of the Levitical priesthood, it appears that what we have in Exod. 24.4-6, 8 is an early covenant ritual which must pre-date the monarchy. Further indication of the antiquity of the covenant terminology is to be found in its association with Shechem which, as Mayes notes, would never have been retained in the Deuteronomistic literature with its emphasis on a single sanctuary at Jerusalem had there not been a strong pre-Deuteronomic covenant tradition located there.[28]

25. The *bᵉrît* of Hos. 6.7 may be connected with the violation of the law concerning the cities of refuge, two of which are referred to in Hos. 6.8-9. So (Ramoth-) Gilead, restored to Israel by Jeroboam II, is pictured as full of those who ought to have been executed, while those who should have been given asylum at Shechem are murdered *en route* by the priests (B. Dinur, 'The Religious Character of the Cities of Refuge and the Ceremony of Admission into Them', *EI* 3 [1954], pp. 135-46 [142]. See further M.J. Dahood, 'Zacharia 9,1 *'ên 'Ādām'*, *CBQ* 25 [1963], pp. 123-24).

26. Mayes, *Deuteronomy*, pp. 64-65.

27. D.J. McCarthy, '*bᵉrît* in Old Testament History and Theology', *Bib.* 53 (1972), pp. 110-21 (117).

28. Mayes, *Deuteronomy*, p. 68.

Nicholson has now accepted McCarthy's reasoning, and so modified his earlier views set out in *Exodus and Sinai in History and Tradition* and has conceded that the ritual described in Exod. 24.8 is a covenant ceremony, though he reserves judgement as to both authorship and date.[29] For him the blood ritual is not to be understood in terms of forming relationships of friendship or 'brotherhood' created between naturally unrelated groups or individuals, but rather consecrates the Hebrews as Yahweh's holy people. It is this idea which is taken up in the preface Exod. 19.3-8, which summarizes the whole narrative Exod. 19–24, in designating Israel as 'a kingdom of priests and a holy nation' (Exod. 19.6a). As a result of this covenant ritual, the pre-Yahwistic theophany tradition of Exod. 24.1-2, 9-11[30] is used to illustrate that, in contrast to Exod. 19 where the people cannot go near the holy mountain, now as a consecrated nation they can eat in God's presence in safety.

If the covenant terminology so emphasized by the Proto-Deuteronomists and the Deuteronomistic redactors did not originate with them, is this also the case with the Decalogue, for which the latter coined the phrase 'the Ten Words' (Deut. 4.13, 10.4)? Could it be that covenant and Decalogue were after all associated together in the Sinai narrative from the first, obedience to the Decalogue's provisions both establishing and maintaining the identity of the elect people of Yahweh? The Decalogue itself is set out only in Exod. 20 and Deut. 5, though apparent reference is made to it in the collection of specific commands concerning offences against the person found in Hos. 4.2 and Jer. 7.9. But in my essay 'Prophecy and Law',[31] I have argued that these verses were the work of Deuteronomistic redactors concerned to indicate that the Decalogue, in their eyes the sole law given at Horeb (Deut. 4.13; 5.22), had been broken in both Samaria and Jerusalem. The consequent catastrophes to these cities could then be understood.

Detailed examination of the eighth-century prophetic material discloses two traditions of prophetic condemnation. Amos, Micah and Isaiah rest their indictment solely on the general condemnation of lack of humaneness and righteousness, the kind of actions commanded in Exod. 22.20–23.9, which of necessity could not be specifically defined nor

---

29. Nicholson, 'The Covenant Ritual', p. 81. Nicholson interprets Exod. 24.5 as referring not to young men but to subordinate cultic officials, 'priests' servants' as in 1 Sam. 2.13-17.

30. Nicholson, 'The Interpretation', pp. 77-97.

31. See Chapter 10 below.

enforced by the courts: and that explains why these provisions carry no sanctions. The other tradition is that of Hosea, who condemns Israel for her syncretism which he interprets as apostasy.

What is striking in both prophetic traditions is the total lack of reference (apart from Hos. 4.2) to those wrongdoings for which Israelite law provided sanctions to be enforced by the courts.[32] This is not to say that such capital crimes as murder or adultery were never committed. Rather, we must assume that, when they occurred, they were dealt with under the law. Had these eighth-century prophets been able to condemn a more obvious breakdown in law and order, they would certainly have done so. Instead, they spoke to a people confident in their election by Yahweh not only in their excessive religious zeal, but also, we must assume, from the prophetic silence, in their outward maintenance of law and order. The innovation of the eighth-century prophets thus lay in the content of their message: to an apparently orderly and confident society engaged in devout religious practice and, at any rate in Amos' time, enjoying considerable prosperity which was interpreted as God's blessing, they proclaimed divine judgment, on the one hand for inhuman and unjust practices and on the other for syncretism.

While the humanitarian concern of Amos, Micah and Isaiah was to be re-emphasized in the motive clauses added to the laws of humaneness and righteousness in the Book of the Covenant (Exod. 22.20b, 22-23; 23.9), and later by further humanitarian provisions in Deuteronomy, it was the influence of Hosea's prophecy uttered just before the fall of Samaria which dominated both the Proto-Deuteronomists' creation of the present Sinai narrative in Exod. 19–24, 32–34, and the Deuteronomic redaction to the original book of Deuteronomy. For this reason the Deuteronomists redacted Hosea so that uniquely among the eighth-century prophets we have in Hosea appeal to both the Decalogue (4.2) and 'my $b^e r\hat{i}t$' (8.1). The Deuteronomistic redactors intended Hosea's preaching to be understood against the background of an utterly rejected Decalogue, *the covenant law* of Horeb. So while in 4.1 Hosea indicts Israel for having 'no knowledge of God', the Deuteronomistic redactors define this in terms of general breach of the Decalogue, even though the eighth-century prophets indicate by their silence that no such total breakdown of law and order as would result from such conduct had occurred. In other words, breach of the Decalogue is used by the Deuteronomistic redactors as a blanket expression

---

32. The references to idolatry in Micah (1.7; 5.12-13) and Isaiah (2.8, 18, 20) must be regarded as redactional, as also the comment on murderers at the end of Isa. 1.21.

indicating Israel's absolute renunciation of Yahweh. This is also true of the temple sermon in Jer. 7 where the two traditions I have isolated in the prophetic condemnation come together in vv. 5b-6: the proper exercise of humaneness and justice and the avoidance of apostasy. But into this sermon, itself a Deuteronomistic construction based on an incident in Jeremiah's lifetime (Jer. 26), the Deuteronomistic redactors have again introduced breach of the Decalogue as a blanket statement to indicate total renunciation of Yahweh. Outside Jer. 7.9 no reliance is placed on the Decalogue for Judah's condemnation.

In view of all this, the views of Nicholson, Mayes and others that the Decalogue is a Deuteronomic compilation would appear to gain support. But the earlier discussion of *bᵉrît* should caution against too hasty a judgment. For the absence of any mention of general lawlessness such as would result from a general abrogation of the Decalogue can be interpreted as due to the fact that the people knew that their very election depended on keeping its injunctions. Evidence for this is found in the reference to unwilling sabbath observance by the business community in the time of Amos (8.4-6). Certainly, the manifest confidence of the people in the face of the prophetic protest, even in the time of Jeremiah (Jer. 7.4), indicates that they considered themselves loyal to Yahweh and that he would protect them.

Is there any evidence from the history of ancient Israel's law which would support an early date for the Decalogue? Of course, our information is only partial for we by no means have a complete legal system in the Old Testament law collections. Indeed, these owe their composition primarily to theological rather than legal considerations. They are both fragmentary and on occasion idealistic, more concerned with what should be than what was in fact capable of being secured by the law. Nonetheless, I believe that we have in the collections sufficient information to enable us to make some positive statements.

Mayes has argued that the history of any single commandment must be distinguished from the history of the collection of ten: while some of the commandments may be old and may have formed small collections of two or three, there is in his view no evidence of the collection of ten before the seventh century, for not even Hos. 4.2 refers to all ten.[33] But if we are to give the Decalogue a late date, can we explain why these particular commandments should at that time be placed together? While the command-

---

33. Mayes, *Deuteronomy*, pp. 162-65.

ments now act as a preface to the laws in Deuteronomy which are seen as deduced from them, they in fact bare very little relation to them. Certainly, no one would have collected the Decalogue as a summary of Deuteronomic legal concern. It is the most serious defect in the argument for a Deuteronomic origin of the Decalogue that those who hold such a view can give no satisfactory reason based on its contents for its collection at that time. On the other hand, there are a number of factors which, although not conclusive, yet point to an early date for the Decalogue and make sense both of the history of Israel's law and of Israel herself.

First, it seems that offences which require the exaction of the death penalty are all to be traced back to the Decalogue.[34] This explains the severity of the law on repudiating parents (Exod. 21.15, 17) compared with LH 195.[35] Second, examination of the *mišpāṭîm* in the Book of the Covenant (Exod. 21.12–22.19)—the nearest we have to an Israelite law code for the use of judges—appears to indicate that the compiler is consciously trying to distinguish crimes requiring the death penalty from civil offences for which damages are paid to compensate the injured party. So murder (Exod. 21.12) is contrasted with assault (Exod. 21.18-19), and man-theft (Exod. 21.16) with theft of property (Exod. 21.37; 22.2b-3). Repudiation of parents (Exod. 21.15, 17) carries the death penalty; seduction of a virgin (in contrast to adultery) results in damages (Exod. 22.15-16). If with A. Alt we understand the commandment on theft to refer to man-theft,[36] then these crimes all relate to injunctions of the Decalogue. As I have argued,[37] the compiler aims to assimilate local indigenous legal practice which had long been administered by the elders in the gate to the overriding principles of Yahwism as set out in the Decalogue, for breach of which the community required the death penalty, because the offender had put himself outside the elect people of God. This explains why, in contrast to other ancient Near Eastern practice, in Israel there was an absolute duty to execute both the murderer[38] and the adulterer,[39] and

---

34. This is the thesis of *AICL*, which is not dependent on the fact that I linked this to Mendenhall's views on the Hittite suzerainty treaties (Mendenhall, 'Ancient Oriental and Biblical Law', pp. 26-46; *idem*, 'Covenant Forms', pp. 50-76) (see Chapter 1 above).

35. *ANET*, p. 175.

36. Alt, 'Das Verbot', pp. 333-40.

37. Phillips, *AICL*, pp. 158-61.

38. Phillips, 'Murder', pp. 105-26 (reprinted below as Chapter 3).

39. Phillips, 'Adultery', pp. 3-25 (reprinted below as Chapter 4).

composition was absolutely forbidden. Third, the same need to distinguish a crime requiring the death penalty (adultery and murder) from a civil offence for which damages are paid (theft of an animal) underlies Nathan's parable in 2 Sam. 12.[40] In my view, there is enough here to indicate that Israel had a distinctive legal system which apparently sprang from a recognition of the unique place of the Decalogue whose provisions delineated the elect people of God, and separated them from all other ancient Near Eastern peoples.

As we have seen, the aim of the Deuteronomistic redactors in inserting the Decalogue before the Deuteronomic law and describing how it alone formed the contents of the second set of tablets was to suppress the Sinai narrative in Exodus with its record of the mediated laws of the Book of the Covenant and the laws of the second set of tablets (Exod. 34.11-26). At the same time this insertion of the Decalogue gave the Deuteronomic law a proper pedigree. In my view, then, rather than holding that the Decalogue was a new Deuteronomic creation, we should recognize that the Deuteronomistic redactors were directly appealing to that ancient collection—in their eyes the sole law given at Horeb. Although the Decalogue had little immediate relevance to the Deuteronomic laws themselves, nonetheless the redactors by their skilful suppression of the Sinai narrative validated their legitimacy as the Torah, the sole test of Israel's obedience to her God. Chief among them was the centralization of all worship at Jerusalem.

The Deuteronomistic redactors were, however, able to use the Decalogue to emphasize one new concern which formed no part of the original Deuteronomic law collection (12–26). By modifying the original Decalogue, both by introducing the exodus and the ox and the ass into the sabbath commandment to provide verbal links with the beginning and the end of the Decalogue, and also by running together the short apodictic injunctions of the sixth to the tenth commandments, they thrust the sabbath commandment into a prominent position at the centre of the Decalogue, which clearly reflected the new importance of the sabbath in the exilic situation.[41]

Returning then to the Sinai narrative in Exod. 19–24, can we now offer an explanation of how it reached its present form? Clearly, as originally constructed the people's fear resulted from the theophany, Exod. 20.18-21

---

40. Phillips, 'The Interpretation', pp. 242-44 (reprinted below as Chapter 14).
41. Lohfink, 'Zur Dekalogfassung von Dt 5', pp. 17-32.

following on from Exod. 19.19.[42] But Yahweh's terrifying appearance, while securing his acceptance by the people, must also have provided the means whereby they could both prove their allegiance, and in doing so define their identity as a distinctive people. This is secured by the announcement of the Decalogue, which, since Yahweh's authority had already been accepted, could be presented as a *fait accompli*. This explains why the Decalogue constitutes a series of commands without legal sanctions, though in my view these commands were to determine the whole nature of Israel's legal system because they defined who made up the elect community. But the Proto-Deuteronomists, following the eighth-century prophetic protest, sought to reinterpret the covenant law in terms of both the Decalogue and the Book of the Covenant, and so inserted the latter in the Sinai narrative. To do this they re-arranged Exod. 20.18-21 after the Decalogue, with the result that it is only when the people hear the absolute demands of Yahweh that fear breaks out. This leads to the request that Moses act as mediator to ensure that the people are able to keep the absolute demands of the Decalogue, which they are enabled to do because Moses reveals to them the provisions of the Book of the Covenant.

I would argue with McCarthy[43] and Childs[44] against Nicholson[45] and Mayes,[46] that the Decalogue was originally part of the Sinai narrative, and that it is only as a result of the re-arrangement of Exod. 20.18-21 that it can be interpreted as addressed to the people directly, though nothing was made of this by the Proto-Deuteronomists unlike their successors the Deuteronomistic redactors. It was because the Deuteronomistic redactors wanted to suppress the earlier mediated laws of the Book of the Covenant and the second set of tablets in Exod. 34.11-26 that they came to stress the direct address of the Decalogue to the people, a fact which they could deduce from the Sinai narrative but which had hitherto had no theological significance.

The Proto-Deuteronomists, who were making a theological judgment on current historical events, above all else saw the prohibition of molten images as a test of the people's loyalty. It is this loyalty which is found wanting in Exod. 32. For this reason they prefaced the Book of the

42. Cf. M. Greenberg, '*'nsh* in Exodus 20 20 and the Purpose of the Sinaitic Theophany', *JBL* 79 (1960), pp. 273-76.

43. McCarthy, *Treaty and Covenant*, pp. 243-52.

44. Childs, *Exodus*, pp. 347-51; *Deuteronomy*, pp. 388-401.

45. Nicholson, 'The Decalogue'.

46. Mayes, *Deuteronomy*, pp. 161-65.

Covenant with a new introduction, the provisions on molten images
(Exod. 20.23) and the simple altar (Exod. 20.24-26). This explains the
prominent position of Exod. 20.23-26 in the Sinai narrative. It now
supersedes the Decalogue as the basic covenant law and provides the key
to the understanding of the whole Sinai narrative Exod. 19-24, 32-34. We
can thus agree with Nicholson that the position of the Decalogue is due
primarily to theological not editorial reasons, though our argument for
doing so differs markedly from his.

For the sake of completeness we should note that other material
attributable to the Proto-Deuteronomists is also to be found in Exod. 19–
24. Thus while the parenetic anti-Canaanite epilogue in Exod. 23.20-33
displays similarities to Deuteronomic theology, it anticipates rather than
presupposes it, and provides a fitting introduction to the episode of the
golden calf. In my view, it is also probable that it was the Proto-
Deuteronomists who built on to the original short apodictic injunctions of
the Decalogue. Certainly, in the extended second commandment (Exod.
20.4-6) and in the laws on the second set of tablets (Exod. 34.11-16), the
concern is with the worship of images of other gods rather than the making
of an image of Yahweh as envisaged by the original commandment.
Further, in both Exod. 20.5 and 34.14 Yahweh is described as jealous, an
expression used only when his claims over Israel are threatened by other
gods. Nor can the fact that the expansion of the commandment is concerned with the making of images from nature be coincidence. It is probable too that the motive clauses, which are also in the plural as in the
framework to the Sinai narrative and have been inserted into the 'thou'
laws of humaneness and righteousness, are the work of the Proto-
Deuteronomists and reflect the eighth-century prophetic protest (Exod.
22.20b, 22-23; 23.9).[47] Later, as we have seen, the Deuteronomists
extended these clauses to include promising prosperity for obedience to
apparently uneconomic laws.

Lastly, it would seem that the introduction of the tablets of the law into
the Sinai narrative is also due to the Proto-Deuteronomists who used them
as the means of describing the breaking and the renewal of the covenant in
Exod. 32–34. The tablets suddenly appear in Exod. 24.12 without any
explanation of their nature or number. But, as the equally sudden mention
of Joshua in Exod. 24.13 (cf. Exod. 32.17) indicates, Exod. 24.12-15

---

47. Since existing material is being redacted, the Proto-Deuteronomists again use
the plural form (see above pp. 37-38).

anticipates Exod. 32-34 to which it acts as the link with the account of the inauguration of the covenant in Exod. 19–24.

As the phrase *tōrâ* and *miṣwâ* in Exod. 24.12 indicates, it is assumed that what was written on the first set of tablets was the Decalogue and the Book of the Covenant, a summary of the more important provisions of which now appears on the second set of tablets, and is designated 'the words of the covenant' (Exod. 34.28). Only later, in the light of the Deuteronomic insistence that the Decalogue was the sole law of Horeb, was the assertion that the contents of the second set of tablets were the Ten Words (Exod. 34.28) introduced into the Sinai narrative. This explains why scholars have found it so difficult to isolate only ten commandments in the laws in Exod. 34.11-26. The Proto-Deuteronomists were not intent on writing a new Decalogue. The original tablets had in their scheme of things contained both the Decalogue and the Book of the Covenant, and the second constituted a summary of their more important provisions. It is only through the late insertion of the phrase 'the Ten Words' that the number of the provisions in Exod. 34.11-26 has become an issue to puzzle later commentators. There never were, nor was it ever intended that there should be, Ten Words in Exod. 34.11-26.

So the Proto-Deuteronomists, recognizing that the provisions of the original tablets (the Decalogue and the Book of the Covenant) had been broken in the northern apostate kingdom, in the light of Hezekiah's reform strengthened those provisions. They achieved their aim by introducing the specific prohibition of molten images (Exod. 34.17) and by their attempt at some centralization of worship (Exod. 34.23-24). The fact that Moses rather than Yahweh appears to have written the laws on the second set of tablets (Exod. 34.27-28) may indicate that the reader is to identify king Hezekiah as a 'second Moses' who interceded for his people (cf. Exod. 32.32) and introduced the reform which saved Judah from Samaria's fate.[48]

If the tablets were introduced into the Sinai narrative only at a late date, then the connection between the Decalogue and the ark must be an even

---

48. It is this idea of vicarious suffering found in Exod. 32.32 which the Deuteronomistic redactors took up (Deut. 1.37; 3.26; 4.21-22) and Deutero-Isaiah used as the model for his suffering servant (A. Phillips, '*Torah* and *Mishpat*—a Light to the Peoples', in W. Harrington [ed.], *Witness to the Spirit* [*Proceedings of the Irish Biblical Association*, 3; Manchester: Koinonia Press, 1979], pp. 112-32; reprinted as Chapter 11 below); *idem*, 'The Servant—Symbol of Divine Powerlessness', *ExpTim* 90 [1978–79], pp. 370-74).

later development. That this is the case is confirmed from the Deuteronomistic phrase 'ark of the covenant' (Deut. 10.8; 31.9, 25, etc.) and the
emphasis that the ark contained nothing but the two tablets of stone (1 Kgs
8.9).[49] In the Sinai narrative in Exodus no mention is made of the placing
of the tablets in the ark. Though the basic meaning of *'rôn* as 'box' or
'chest' indicates that from the first the ark acted as a container, its
historical origins are uncertain. It certainly played a prominent role in the
war with the Philistines (1 Sam. 4), and it has been suggested that it may
have contained the covenant document or symbol which bound the tribes
together in that war.[50]

By introducing the tablets, the Proto-Deuteronomists were clearly drawing on the language associated with the making and breaking of political
treaties which was found throughout the ancient Near East. This is not
surprising in view of the fact that Hezekiah was himself engaged as a
vassal in renouncing his suzerainty to Assyria. Such treaties were inaugurated by being recorded in duplicate, one copy being retained by each
party and placed in his sanctuary. This explains the necessity for two
tablets in the Sinai narrative in Exodus,[51] though it would seem that it was
the Deuteronomists who, confirming the political treaty analogy, dealt
with the location of their deposit (Deut. 10.5). Further to indicate that the
treaty was broken, the tablet on which it had been recorded was smashed.[52]
For it to be restored fresh tablets were required. It therefore seems that the
understanding of Yahweh's covenant with Israel in terms of a political
treaty, which is reflected in Deuteronomy and was once widely held by
scholars (including myself) to be found in the original Sinai narrative, in
fact derives from the Proto-Deuteronomists' reassessment of the relationship of Israel with her God consequent upon the fall of Samaria, and that it
led to Hezekiah's reform. It is their theology which results in the present
Sinai narrative Exod. 19–24, 32–34, and in spite of the Deuteronomistic
redactors' attempt at suppressing that narrative, it now underlies Deuteronomic theology itself.

49. Mayes, *Deuteronomy*, pp. 203-204.

50. J. Maier, *Das altisraelitische Ladeheiligtum* (BZAW, 93; Berlin: W. de Gruyter, 1965), pp. 58ff.

51. M.G. Kline, *Treaty of the Great King: The Covenant Structure of Deuteronomy*
(Grand Rapids: Eerdmans, 1963), pp. 17-19.

52. K. Baltzer, *Das Bundesformular* (Neukirchen–Vluyn: Neukirchener Verlag,
1960), p. 27.

Chapter 3

Another Look at Murder[*]

Recent studies of ancient Israel's law by Moshe Greenberg,[1] Shalom Paul[2] and myself[3] have concentrated on establishing definitive principles from the biblical law collections. But this approach has now been subjected to searching criticism by Bernard Jackson.[4] It will be my purpose to consider his criticism with particular reference to murder.

Clearly the first issue that arises is to establish the nature of the collections of laws in the Old Testament. Can these in fact be termed 'codes' with all that that implies for the administration of justice? Now it is clear that every codification of Israel's law was undertaken in a theologized form. As they stand, none of these collections is a simple set of commands and precedents drawn up to enable Israel's judges to administer her law. There is much parenetic material; some of the laws appear to be idealized pictures of what ought to happen; many could never have been the subject of enforcement through the courts. Further, that part of the collections which might be directly related to the actual practice of Israelite courts is obviously insufficient to comprise a fully constituted legal system. But Israel's law was not addressed to the judiciary but to the nation. It represented Yahweh's instruction or teaching—the proper meaning of tōrâ— on how Israel should conduct her affairs, whether or not that conduct could be the subject of legal enforcement through the courts. The material that appears in the collections is there solely because of its theological importance. Other laws which regulated Israel's day-to-day affairs have been omitted. Thus although, as Jackson concedes, much of the content of

---

[*]   This essay is based on a paper given to Bristol Theological Society, October 1976.
    1.   Greenberg, 'Postulates', pp. 25-41.
    2.   Paul, *Studies* (*AICL*).
    3.   Phillips, *AICL*.
    4.   Jackson, 'Reflections'.

these biblical legal collections 'may still have been taken from the real legal world'[5] the collections themselves are in effect theological literary works. But it was, of course, Israel's theology which made her a 'peculiar people'. It would therefore seem reasonable to suppose that since these literary collections of Israel's law were theologically based, they would reflect certain fundamental principles on which Israelite society was itself founded. For instance, if it could be shown that for theological reasons laws governing certain specific issues were included in the collections while other particular concerns were omitted, then this could itself establish important principles of Israelite law. The fact that Israel's legal collections cannot be defined as law codes for her judges to administer does not *prima facie* rule out the possibility that principles can still be established in spite of the very limited material available, and the recognition that much of Israel's legislation nowhere appears in these collections.

Jackson defines a principle as 'any formulation of more general application than the text from which it is inferred'.[6] While he does not deny that principles existed in biblical law he argues that it is:

> only when they assume an explicit form that we can be confident (a) that they exist; (b) that they were consciously articulated; (c) that a certain minimum value, sufficient for their inclusion, was placed upon them; (d) that their range can be determined within reasonable limits… Maxims such as 'a life for a life' deserve primary, if not exclusive, consideration when postulates are sought.[7]

Jackson's criticism is aimed at the use of laws and/or narratives to establish principles alleged to be implicit in this material. Of course there are dangers in such an approach: the same material in the hands of different scholars may lead to the construction of very varied principles. But this is true of almost every aspect of biblical criticism. The answers are not spelt out but have to be inferred, and then subjected to general scholarly criticism. To limit one's enquiry to that which is explicit and therefore assured would reduce research in biblical law to a process of cataloguing and comparison with catalogues of other legal systems. Of course principles enunciated on the basis of what is held to be implicit are recognized as only hypotheses, but it is on such a basis, and only on such a basis, that the study of ancient Israel's law can proceed. But such study is not merely

5. Jackson, 'Reflections', p. 29.
6. Jackson, 'Reflections', p. 34.
7. Jackson, 'Reflections', p. 32.

an enquiry into an ancient legal system. As with the prophetic and wisdom material, it is, whether the commentator likes it or not, part of the study of Israel's theology, which, whatever view we take of her law, was undoubtedly unique among the people of the ancient Near East.

Inevitably in seeking to establish principles in ancient Israel's law comparison is made with other laws of the ancient Near East. But here considerable caution must be exercised. In the first place the same reservations already made about biblical law apply to the description of these other collections of law as codes in the sense that this implies a definitive series of statutes and precedents for the judges to administer. As Jackson has pointed out of the Laws of Hammurabi, whose importance over a very long period can hardly be exaggerated, 'in no law-case so far known are the laws quoted or cited'.[8] Rather it appears that the Babylonian law collections were primarily apologia to the gods to vindicate the king in the exercise of the mandate which they had given him.[9] What actual influence the provisions of a collection such as Hammurabi's had on the day-to-day administration of justice remains very uncertain. But what is clear is that in any event the sparse material of the various collections of ancient Near Eastern law give a very incomplete picture of the legal practice of the ancient Near East. Further Jackson rightly criticizes the tendency to classify all ancient Near Eastern law under the all embracing term of 'cuneiform law' and then to contrast it with the biblical law: 'It is misleading to classify together such diverse cultures as those appearing from the Middle Assyrian and the Hittite laws'.[10]

It might seem then in view of these necessary reservations that rather than compare systems of ancient Near Eastern law, the commentator is left with the possibility of a specific law in one ancient Near Eastern collection illuminating the interpretation of a provision in the biblical corpus. This aspect will, of course, form an important part of his work. But because of the theological basis of biblical law, it would still seem that the possibility of establishing a distinctive principle of Israelite law over against other ancient Near Eastern law cannot be entirely ruled out.

Despite what has been said about the nature of the so-called biblical law codes, it does seem that the collection of *mišpāṭîm* contained in Exod. 21.12–22.16 are intended as a statement of actual statutes and precedents

8. Jackson, 'Reflections', p. 27.

9. Paul, *Studies*, pp. 24-26; B.S. Jackson, 'From Dharma to Law', *American Journal of Comparative Law* 23 (1975), pp. 490-512 (492-93).

10. Jackson, 'Reflections', p. 33.

to be put into effect by Israel's judges.[11] All the laws specify sanctions which can be enforced, whether it is execution or damages. Further there is no parenetic material. These *mišpāṭîm* begin with four offences— murder, assault on parents, man-theft, and repudiation of parental authority—[12] all of which carry the death penalty (Exod. 21.12, 15-17). There then follows a series of specific precedents differentiating murder from assault for which damages are payable (Exod. 21.18-27). The *mišpāṭîm* continue with a number of precedents on animals which includes injury caused by an ox, injury caused to an ox or ass, and theft of an ox, sheep or ass (Exod. 21.28–22.3). This section also deals with the killing of a thief caught breaking in. Further precedents concerning personal property follow concluding with a provision on the seduction of a virgin (Exod. 22.4-16).

As is well known, Alt divided the *mišpāṭîm* on the basis of form and concluded that while those laws which were in the casuistic form were inherited from Canaan, those in the apodictic form were the distinctive Israelite material.[13] But quite apart from Gerstenberger's redefinition of Alt's concept of apodictic and casuistic law,[14] it has been shown that both types of law existed together over a wide area of the ancient Near East.[15] The definition can in fact tell us nothing about the foreign or indigenous nature of the *mišpāṭîm*. Rather what we have are a number of laws which absolutely prohibit certain actions, and then a series of precedents based on particular concrete cases. And it seems entirely probable that these

11. I would agree with Paul that the formal legal corpus of the Book of the Covenant is contained in Exod. 21.1–22.16, to which I have argued a small criminal law coda has been added, Exod. 22.17–19, 27 (*AICL*, pp. 158-61). But the law on slaves, Exod. 21.2-11, is part of family law which is outside the jurisdiction of the courts being administered privately by the head of each household (Phillips, 'Family Law' [reprinted below as Chapter 6]).

12. Brichto, *The Problem of 'Curse'*, pp. 132-33, shows that *qillel* is not simply to be rendered 'curse' but has the wider meaning of 'repudiate'. Thus the commandment to honour one's parents requires total submission to their authority (*AICL*, pp. 80-82).

13. A. Alt, 'The Origins of Israelite Law', in his *Essays on Old Testament History and Religion* (Oxford: Basil Blackwell, 1966), pp. 81-132 (repr. Bib Sem, 9; Sheffield: JSOT Press, 1989).

14. E. Gerstenberger, *Wesen und Herkunft des 'apodiktischen Rechts'* (WMANT, 20; Neukirchen–Vluyn: Neukirchener Verlag, 1965); *idem*, 'Covenant and Command-ment', *JBL* 84 (1965), pp. 38-51.

15. For a summary of form-critical study of Israelite law, see H.W. Gilmer, *The If-You Form in Israelite Law* (SBLDS, 15; Missoula, MT: Scholars Press, 1975), pp. 1-26.

precedents do in fact reflect the indigenous Canaanite law administered by the elders in the gate. But it is my contention that Canaanite law was not taken over simply as it stood, but was in fact made subject to certain fundamental laws which the Hebrews brought with them on entry into Canaan, and which had already defined them as a peculiar people. This is the significance of the four absolute prohibitions at the beginning of the *mišpāṭîm* addressed to the judges for breach of which the death penalty was to be exacted (Exod. 21.12, 15-17). My concern is principally with the first, the prohibition of murder.

Taken at face value, Exod. 21.12 would seem simple enough. A murderer is to be put to death. As with the son who assaults his parents, the man-thief, the son who repudiates his parents (Exod. 21.15-17) and incidentally with the man who commits bestiality (Exod. 22.18),[16] the community has no choice. For Greenberg, Paul and myself, the absolute way in which Exod. 21.12 is formed leads us to infer the principle that Israelite law ruled out the possibility of composition for homicide. Only

---

16. This provision forms part of an additional criminal law coda (Exod. 27.17-19, 27) (see above n. 11). For a discussion of the crime, See Phillips, *AICL*, p. 121. It is interesting to note that in contrast to the law on the goring ox (Exod. 21.28-32) there is no penalty prescribed for the animal. This is because the goring ox was regarded as the criminal being the actual murderer, whereas the animal with whom bestiality was committed was the passive victim of the criminal. Later the Holiness Code prescribed that the animal must also be executed (Lev. 20.15-16). This reflects the extension of punishment in crimes involving sexual intercourse to include both parties. Thus the crime of adultery originally only required the execution of the adulterer, the woman being treated as the passive victim whom the husband was free to divorce at will (Phillips, 'Family Law', pp 351-56). But the crime was extended by Deut. 22.24 and Lev. 20.10 to include the woman too (Phillips, *AICL*, pp. 110-11). This extension was prompted by the Deuteronomic reform whereby women were made equal members of the covenant community with men and so subject to the covenant law (cf. Deut. 7.3; 13.7; 15.12-17; 17.2-5; 22.22). So Lev. 20.16 extends the crime of bestiality to include women. But Exod. 21.28-32 had already recognized that an animal could be treated as a criminal: it was therefore only logical that the Holiness Code which demanded execution for the adulterer's partner (Lev. 20.10), should do the same for the animal victim of the man or woman who committed bestiality (Lev. 20.15-16). Similarly the partners in incest and sodomy are also to be executed (Lev. 20.11-14). Only in the case of adultery with a betrothed woman in open country is the partner still regarded as a passive victim (Deut. 22.25-27). See B.S. Jackson, 'The Goring Ox', *Journal of Juristic Papyrology* 18 (1974), pp. 55-93, (repr. in *idem*, *Essays in Jewish and Comparative Legal History* [SJLA, 10; Leiden: E.J. Brill, 1975], pp. 108-152 [here ref. is to pp. 119-20]).

once do the *mišpāṭîm* mention composition—in the case of the owner of an ox who knew that his beast had a propensity to gore (Exod. 21.30). But this is not in effect an exception to the rule that in every case the murderer must be put to death, for the ox is still to be executed as the murderer. Exodus. 21.30 merely permits the owner as an accessory to murder the opportunity of saving his life. However, at more or less every point, Jackson has challenged our inferred principle:

> The import of the *mišpāṭîm* may be put thus. There is no explicit statement of general principle, whether allowing or prohibiting composition. There are certain cases, all of them special in some way, in which it is contemplated. No certain principle can be inferred, such as will tell us whether composition was or was not allowed in other cases. But the formulation of Ex. 21:30 suggests that *kōphēr* was not an unusual expedient, and this is confirmed by non-legal sources.[17]

Let us begin with the law on the goring ox. For Jackson, the ox cannot be considered a murderer.[18] In the first place none of the biblical texts specifies that communal stoning was the penalty for murder. Rather the murderer's execution was a private affair, the duty falling on the *gō'ēl hadām* as representative of the family, who most probably would have used a sword. Second, Jackson notes that Exod. 21.28-32 makes no mention of the ox actually being stoned to *death*. For him, the original purpose of the stoning, which he connects with Israel's semi-nomadic past, was to drive away into the desert a dangerous animal. It was thus 'an utilitarian measure designed to protect the community'.[19] But while it is true that the word 'death' does not appear in connection with the stoning of the ox, since the very next phrase consists of a prohibition against eating the ox, we must assume that the intention behind the stoning was to kill the beast. Otherwise such a prohibition, which is an integral part of the command to stone, would have been unnecessary, or at least would have been framed to indicate that it governed the exceptional case of the death of the ox. In fact Exod. 21.28 assumes that death will directly result from the stoning. Further there is no reason at all to connect the provision with semi-nomadic conditions. The *mišpāṭîm* are directed at a settled agricultural community (cf. Exod. 22.4-5) which needs to know what action to take should a normally harmless domestic animal, the ox, become wild. Jackson's theory is, of course, an attempt to account for the remarkable

17. Jackson, 'Reflections', p. 45.
18. Jackson, 'The Goring Ox', pp. 108-12.
19. Jackson, 'The Goring Ox', p. 120.

difference between Israel's law which insists on the execution of the ox, and LE 54–55 and LH 250–52 which are only concerned with compensating the injured and provide no penalty for the ox. For him this is explained by the fact that in contrast to the *mišpāṭîm*, Babylonian law was addressed to a settled community: 'The population of a permanently settled community is more dispersed than that of a semi-nomadic group. The threat to human life posed by a vicious animal is thus proportionately less. The wild ox becomes a menace to agriculture (Num. 22.4) rather than to life.'[20] But like the biblical law, the Babylonian law is not concerned with damage to agriculture, nor does it regard the loss of human life through a goring ox as a remote possibility. The same situation is envisaged by both the Laws of Eshnunna, the Laws of Hammurabi and the Book of the Covenant, but while the Babylonian law deals with it entirely in terms of civil injury and lays down pecuniary compensation, the biblical law concentrates on the criminal nature of the case, and the penalty which the community must exact. Where no difference in principle applied, as in the case of an ox not previously known to be dangerous goring to death another ox, then the biblical and Babylonian law remained near identical (LE 53: Exod. 21.35). Thus Exod. 21.28-32 is to be understood as consciously asserting the distinctive principle of Israelite law that in all cases of murder, the murderer must be executed. Inferred as it must be, it is difficult not to draw the conclusion that earlier Canaanite law is here being modified by special Israelite practices.

It might be thought that the conscious ruling out of vicarious punishment in Exod. 21.31 provided further evidence of this assertion of basic Israelite principles in contrast to other ancient Near Eastern law (LH 116; 209–210; 230; Middle Assyrian Laws [MAL] A 50, 55). But as Jackson has shown the use of the opening *'ôw* (cf. Exod. 21.36) and the reference to *kamišpāt*, also found in Lev. 5.10 and Num. 15.24, indicates that Exod. 21.31 is a late insertion.[21] In my view it is the work of the Priestly legislator who, as we shall see, had again to assert the basic principles of Israelite law following the exile in Babylon. But even though Exod. 21.31 may be a late insertion into the law on the goring ox, it is almost certainly restating a general principle of Israelite law, rather than introducing a new directive. Certainly there is no indication of vicarious punishment

20. Jackson, 'The Goring Ox', p. 115.

21. Jackson, 'The Goring Ox', pp. 151-52. Jackson explains this insertion not as a reaction to vicarious punishment found outside Israel, but as a 'scholastic addition' designed not to alter the law but to fill it out. 'It was, in one sense, an "empty phrase"'.

elsewhere in the Old Testament. Though sons might be executed *with* their guilty father (2 Kgs 9.26), a practice prohibited under the Deuteronomic reform (Deut. 24.16), they would not have been punished *instead* of him.

But even if the ox is executed by communal stoning, how can this be equated with Jackson's contention that the execution of the murderer was a private affair for the nearest kinsman of the deceased. Paul does not consider this problem: Greenberg does not recognize it.[22] It is, of course, true that nowhere is stoning specified as the penalty for murder—indeed, no mention is made of any method of execution in the *mišpāṭîm*, other than for the goring ox. But neither do the *mišpāṭîm* make mention of the *gō'ēl hadām*, not even in the insertion concerning sanctuary at the local altar (Exod. 21.13-14). Indeed, with the apparent exception of 2 Sam. 14.11, the *gō'ēl hadām* is only referred to as executing the murderer in the context of his escape from the local community to seek asylum at one of the cities of refuge which because of local prejudice early replaced the right to sanctuary at the local shrine.[23] Further the fact that, again with one exception (Num. 35.12), this supposed nearest kinsman cannot be referred to by his normal title of *gō'ēl*, but only by the precise expression *gō'ēl hadām*, seems to indicate two different offices. In my view, as I argued in *AICL*[24] following an original suggestion by Sulzberger,[25] the *gō'ēl hadām* was the official designated by the murderer's city to inflict execution on their behalf once the murderer had left their jurisdiction in an attempt to obtain sanctuary at his city of refuge. Clearly the community would have chosen the man whose physical strength and fitness (cf. Deut. 19.6) was most likely to achieve this. Were this duty left to the next of kin, there would have been many occasions on which he simply could not have been able to undertake the task or would himself run the risk of injury. It is true that once, in Num. 35.12, *gō'ēl* alone is used of the avenger of blood. But the fact that all the major versions read the full phrase, *gō'ēl hadām*, which also appears in all six subsequent uses of the term in Num. 35, indicates that either, and more probably *hadām* has dropped out of the Masoretic Text, or that it was inserted in the versions because of the necessity to indicate that this was not the person ordinarily understood by the designation *gō'ēl*.

22. Cf. his review of Phillips, *AICL* in *JBL* 91 (1972), pp. 535-36.
23. Phillips, *AICL*, pp. 99-101.
24. Phillips, *AICL*, pp. 102-106.
25. M. Sulzberger, *The Ancient Hebrew Law of Homicide* (Philadelphia: J.H. Greenstone, 1915), pp. 55ff.

But let us return to Exod. 21.12 itself. Since this is framed in exactly the same way as Exod. 21.15-17, it would seem reasonable to suppose that the legal processes were identical in each case. Deuteronomy 21.18-21 describes precisely what action parents are to take in the face of repudiation by their son. They are themselves to initiate a prosecution before the elders of the son's city. On the son's conviction, he is to be executed by communal stoning. Although this precedent contains the characteristic Deuteronomic purging formula,[26] it is much older than the promulgation of Deuteronomy itself, for it envisages trial before the elders and so antedates the appointment of professional judges to replace the elders, perhaps as a result of Jehoshaphat's reform (2 Chron. 19.5).[27] Certainly Deuteronomy envisages trial before such professional judges (Deut. 16.18). Confirmation that Deut. 21.18-21 reflects the normal legal process in the case of a crime is provided by the trial of Naboth (1 Kgs 21). And the fact that the *mišpāṭîm* themselves also order the stoning of the goring ox raises the strong presumption that there too this procedure was understood as the recognized method of execution. Is there any reason why this should not have been the fate of the human murderer? 2 Samuel 14 provides, I believe, the answer.

This has long proved an embarrassment to those who still believe that blood vengeance operated in ancient Israel, that is that the clan which had suffered the death exacted retribution from the clan which had caused it through the agency of the next of kin. But a blood feud can only arise between members of different clans. If the murder occurs within a clan, then the murderer is dealt with by clan law. But if this is what is happening in 2 Sam. 14, then as de Vaux saw, the mention of the *gō'ēl hadām* in v. 11 has to be explained away.[28] In a recent article on homicide, McKeating admits that in Israel, as elsewhere, there is little evidence that blood vengeance was exacted within the clan, and so resorts to a novel interpretation of the incident in 2 Sam. 14:

> It is therefore possible that the woman is appealing to the king to restrain the kin group from prosecuting the slayer with a vengeance that was seen as

26. Deut. 13.7; 17.7, 12; 21.21; 22.21, 22, 24; 24.7; cf. 19.13; 21.19. This purging formula is only used in connection with capital crimes.

27. Albright, 'Judicial Reform', pp. 61-82; *AICL*, pp. 17-20.

28. R. de Vaux, *Ancient Israel: Its life and Institutions* (London: Darton, Longman & Todd, 1961), p. 12. D.A. Leggett, *The Levirate and Goel Institutions in the Old Testament with Special Attention to the Book of Ruth* (Cherryhill, NJ: Mack Publishing, 1974), pp. 134-37, fails to appreciate the problem.

over-rigorous... This would mean that the king is not being asked to prevent the law taking its normal course, but to ensure that it should take its normal course.[29]

But this would seem to make very little sense of David's obvious reluctance to intervene until the question of guilt had been determined (2 Sam. 14.9). For guilt can hardly fall on David for ensuring that the 'law should take its normal course'. In fact McKeating can find no unambiguous example of the normal exercise of blood vengeance in Israel. Thus he recognizes that in contrast to Abner's legitimate slaughter of Asahel in battle (2 Sam. 2.18-23), Joab's act of revenge (2 Sam. 3.27) 'was far from normal'. 'Joab's killing is not a regular judicial act, but the important fact for our purposes is that he can manage plausibly to pass it off as one'. But as the text makes plain, Joab's action was immediately recognized as murder (2 Sam. 3.29) for he had sought to avenge in peace blood shed in war (1 Kgs 2.5). Only his personal power put him temporarily above the law (1 Kgs 2.32).

It is my contention that since the Book of the Covenant regards Israel as one kin group, blood vengeance is automatically ruled out. Instead the group deals with the murderer according to its own law, namely Exod. 21.12, a provision not even mentioned by McKeating in his article. In other words, like assault on parents, manstealing, and repudiation of parental authority, murder was regarded as a crime being an offence committed against the community who must take the appropriate steps to inflict the prescribed penalty of execution. Only when there was a total breakdown within the Israelite community resulting in the re-emergence of different group identities could blood vengeance arise, for then there would no longer be one kin group. This is what occurred following Saul's action against the Gibeonites, and resulted in retribution being exacted through the death of members of Saul's own family (2 Sam. 21). Only by this means would the Gibeonites once again (Josh. 9) be brought within the community of Israel.[30]

What then is the situation envisaged in 2 Sam. 14? In the first place *mišpāḥâ* should be understood as referring not to the deceased's immediate family, but rather to the local clan, that is the several families

---

29. McKeating, 'The Development', pp. 50-51.

30. F.C. Fensham, 'The Treaty between Israel and the Gibeonites', *BA* 27 (1964), pp. 96-100; J. Blenkinsopp, *Gibeon and Israel* (SOTSMS, 2; Cambridge: Cambridge University Press, 1972), pp. 28-40, 91-94.

living at Tekoa who together made up the local community.[31] It is clear
that they have found the surviving brother guilty of murder. They believe
that he is hiding at his mother's house and demand that she gives him up
for communal execution in accordance with the clan law (Exod. 21.12).
There is certainly no thought of any private action by the *gō'ēl hadām*. It
seems probable that we have here a reflection of the customary law which
forbade entry into another's house (cf. Deut. 24.10-11), evidence of which
is found elsewhere in the ancient Near East (LH 16; Shurpu Tablet 2.
47).[32] The king seeks to postpone making a decision and orders the woman
back to her house. At her further petitioning he directs that she shall in no
way be molested. The king is still playing for time. But in fact the son is
not in his mother's house. As in the case of Absalom, on which the story is
modelled, he had fled from his home. But the woman knows that once his
absence is discovered, the local community will dispatch the *gō'ēl hadām*
to execute him. He cannot acquire the protection of his city of refuge for
death following a blow in a quarrel was undoubtedly regarded as murder
(Exod. 21.18-19).[33] Hence the mother specifically asks the king to prevent

31. J. Pedersen, *Israel: Its Life and Culture*, 1-2 (Oxford: Oxford University Press;
Copenhagen: Branner og Korch, 1926), pp. 46-55; de Vaux, *Ancient Israel*, pp. 8, 21.

32. D. Daube, *Studies in Biblical Law* (Cambridge: Cambridge University Press.
1947), pp. 202, 205-220, notes this element in the account of Laban's pursuit of Jacob
(Gen. 31.25-35).

33. This is confirmed by the use of *wᵉniqqâ* in v. 19. Nor has any attempt been
made to alter this phrase following the insertion of the right to asylum for an
unpremeditated killing (Exod. 21.13-14). However, Jackson regards the assault as
unpremeditated and therefore falling within Exod. 21.13-14. For him premeditation
rather than intention is the necessary factor in determining a case of murder ('The
Problem of Exodus 21:22-5 [*IUS TALIONIS*]', *VT* 23 [1973], pp. 273-304 (288-89)
[repr. in *idem*, *Essays*, pp. 75-107 (here 91-92)]). But such a definition is too narrow
for it fails to take into account that under ancient Israelite law irrespective of premeditation, engaging in any dangerous action likely to cause death would also warrant
sufficient evidence to sustain a charge of murder (cf. Exod. 21.29). Thus premeditation
is irrelevant if one strikes another person with a stone (Exod. 21.18; Num. 35.17), beats
a slave so that he dies that day (Exod. 21.20), or through fighting with another causes
death to a third party (Exod. 21.22-25). In such cases, the death could not be said to be
an act of God (Exod. 21.13) for its likelihood could have been foreseen. Only when
death was entirely accidental would a charge of murder be reduced to manslaughter
(Deut. 19.5). So deliberately to strike a man with a dangerous weapon regardless of
premeditation or intention to kill will amount to murder if the victim dies (Num. 35.16-
18) as well as any premeditated action to cause death (Num. 35.20-21). But if the death
was entirely accidental and could not reasonably have been expected to have followed

the *gō'ēl hadām* from slaying 'any more'. S.R. Driver rejects this translation on the grounds that the *gō'ēl hadām* has not yet destroyed at all.[34] But this most likely rendering immediately becomes acceptable once it is recognized that it does not refer to a kinsman wanting to exercise blood vengeance, itself ruled out by v. 7 which clearly envisages communal execution. Rather the *gō'ēl hadām* indicates the officer appointed by the local community who would earlier have acted in other cases of murder and may well have shed blood. Once the king grants an absolute pardon, the runaway son can return home in safety. The woman is, of course, out to achieve a similar safe homecoming for Absalom.

But my argument so far would be quite irrelevant if Jackson's contention that '*kofer* was not an unusual expedient' could be upheld. What is the basis of his contention? First he argues that the way in which *kōphēr* is introduced into the law on the goring ox hardly looks as if this is a remedy 'to meet a highly exceptional situation. It does not say "if the circumstances are such and such, a ransom may be accepted". Rather, the ransom is first mentioned in a subordinate protasis: "If a ransom is laid upon him".'[35] It must therefore reflect a well-known practice. This is, of course, not denied for 2 Sam. 21.4 clearly shows that the Gibeonites envisaged such a possibility in their request for vengeance on the house of Saul. But we have already seen that 2 Sam. 21 is not describing the options open under Israelite law, but rather concerns the taking of blood vengeance following the total breakdown of the covenant through which the Gibeonites had become part of Israel (Josh. 9).[36] That the practice of *kōphēr* was known at the time the Book of the Covenant was evolving is not in question: what is at issue is whether such a practice was permitted in spite of the apparent absolute statement in Exod. 21.12.

Examination of the precedents on the goring ox would seem to indicate that Exod. 21.30 is a later insertion. Having established the basic principle

---

from the action which caused it then it only constituted manslaughter (Num. 35.22-23). Naturally lack of premeditation would be an important element in the evidence establishing the accidental nature of one's action. But Jackson is mistaken in regarding Num. 35.22 as referring to 'intentional but unpremeditated homicide' and v. 23 as governing 'accidental homicide', for v. 23 merely illustrates by a particular precedent what is envisaged by v. 22b.

34. *Notes on the Hebrew Text and the Topography of the Books of Samuel* (Oxford: Clarendon Press, 2nd edn, 1913), p. 307.

35. 'Reflections', p. 44.

36. See above p. 58.

that an ox which gores a man or woman to death is to be treated as a murderer, though its owner is not liable either as a criminal or tortfeasor (Exod. 21.28), the *mišpāṭîm* go on to consider the position of an owner who knew that his ox had a propensity to gore. Like LE 54–55 and LH 251–52, first the case of the goring to death of a free man or woman is considered (Exod. 21.29), and then that of a slave (Exod. 21.32). We have already agreed with Jackson that the clause on the free man's son or daughter (Exod. 21.31) is a later addition.[37] Both in the case of the free man or woman and of the slave, the ox is to be executed as a murderer under the general rule established in Exod. 21.28. But where the death of a free man or woman occurs, the owner is also treated as an accessory to the murder and likewise to be executed: while in the case of the death of a slave, the owner is merely regarded as a tortfeasor and pays fixed damages to the slave's master to compensate for the loss of his personal property. The owner may have done all he could to keep the animal from causing injury: but as Greenberg and Paul failed to see, this is immaterial.[38] The owner is subject to strict liability.

Clearly Exod. 21.30 interrupts the flow of this legislation. Further it is quite unnecessary if *kōphēr* was a regular practice of Israelite law known to be possible whenever a murder occurred. Why has it been felt necessary to spell it out in this one case? The answer can only be that something exceptional is being introduced into the legislation. What the addition of Exod. 21.30 does is to amend the law of Exod. 21.29 by in effect, though not in practice, putting the owner of the ox known to be dangerous in the position of a tortfeasor in all cases. Because a free man or woman cannot have an average market price like a slave, the amount of *kōphēr* must be assessed for each individual case probably in the same way as that laid down in Exod. 21.22.[39] But because technically the owner remained a criminal, to effect his purpose the interpolator used the hitherto well-known custom of *kōphēr* (2 Sam. 21.4), now relegated to cases of blood feud with people outside the community of Israel when Exod. 21.12 no longer operated. The owner is thus seen as ransoming his life, and there still remains the possibility that he could be executed rather than simply enslaved for failure to pay damages (cf. Exod. 22.2). But it would

37. See above p. 55.
38. Thus Greenberg introduces the concept of criminal negligence ('Postulates', p. 13), and Paul speaks of failure to take 'the necessary precautions to safeguard his ox' (*Studies*, p. 80).
39. Phillips, *AICL*, pp. 89-90.

obviously be in the interests of all parties for *kōphēr* to be paid for only then would the deceased's family receive any compensation. Seen as an amendment to earlier legislation the wording and position of Exod. 21.30 is then entirely explicable.[40]

But for Jackson Exod. 21.30 is not the only example in the *mišpāṭîm* which envisages 'monetary payment as the consequence of homicide'. For in reply to Greenberg's contention that in biblical law the 'taking of life cannot be made up for by any amount of property',[41] Jackson cites Exod. 21.22 and Exod. 21.32.[42] But the whole point of Exod. 21.22 in contrast to Exod. 21.23-25 is that there is no 'taking of life'. So the man who commits the assault on the pregnant woman is treated as a tortfeasor and pays damages. This is one of a number of precedents differentiating the tort of assault from the crime of murder—very important under Israelite law when the murderer had no opportunity of avoiding the death penalty through the payment of *kōphēr*. There is therefore no question here of the assailant having to save his life by the payment of a monetary sum, for his life was never in danger. If *kōphēr* were payable at all, it would be payable under Exod. 21.23-25 where, however the precedent is interpreted, life was considered to have been taken.[43] But as elsewhere in the earlier

---

40. Care should betaken in comparing Exod. 21.30 with the law establishing a right of asylum (Exod. 21.13-14), also an amendment to earlier legislation of an absolute nature (Exod. 21.12). The owner of the ox could not take advantage of the right to asylum for if death followed from engaging in a dangerous act then premeditation was irrelevant (Exod. 21.18-25) (see above n. 33 and below n. 43). Hence the legislator continues to regard the owner as a criminal liable for murder but exceptionally allows him to pay *kōphēr*.

41. Greenberg, 'Postulates', p. 18.

42. Jackson, 'Reflections', pp. 44-45.

43. Jackson, 'The Problem', pp. 75-107, argues that Exod. 21.23 is not concerned with the death of the woman. Rather v. 22 governs the premature birth of the child whereas v. 23 concerns a miscarriage for which substitution has to be provided (cf. MAL A 50). This interpretation has been followed by J. Weingreen, 'The Concepts of Retaliation and Compensation in Biblical Law', *Proceedings of the Royal Irish Academy* 76 (1976), pp. 1-11. Both Jackson and Weingreen argue that as the assault was unpremeditated then in view of Exod. 21.13-14 there can be no charge of murder. But premeditation is irrelevant, for engaging in dangerous action always results in strict liability for murder if death follows (cf. Exod. 21.29) (see n. 33). The biblical law may then be closely paralleled with LH 209–214 which also does not differentiate between a deliberate and an unintentional assault on the woman. But in any event the *lex talionis* has been inserted into the Book of the Covenant (J. Morgenstern, 'The Book of the Covenant—Part II', *HUCA* 7 [1930], pp.19-258 [68ff.]), as it has been into

cases contrasting assault with murder (Exod. 21.18-21), no mention is made of it.

And we have already seen that while Exod. 21.32 still demands the death of the murderer—the ox, there is again no question of considering the owner a criminal.[44] The money he pays to the slave's master is a straight-forward case of damages for loss of personal property which here are fixed. Although the *mišpāṭîm* do recognise that a free Israelite could be guilty of the crime of murder for the killing of a slave (Exod. 21.20), they were clearly reluctant to do so, restricting murder to the most extreme case. It is therefore not surprising that where death was caused by an ox, it alone was treated as the criminal and the owner as a mere tortfeasor.

Jackson concludes his argument by asserting that the practice of *kōphēr* is found in five non-legal texts: 1 Sam. 12.3; 1 Kgs 20.39; Amos 5.12; Prov. 6.35; and Prov. 13.8. While the original meaning of the root *kpr* appears uncertain, the verb *kipper* is generally rendered by 'to cover over', and is, of course, frequently used of atoning for sin. The noun *kōphēr* thus refers to a payment which in some way covers over an offence and so brings about reconciliation between the parties, whether man and his neighbour or man and God. But *kōphēr* can also be used of an illegal payment designed to avoid facing the consequences of previous improper actions and so covering over one's liability. Quite clearly it is this illegal sense of a cover up operation that is referred to in 1 Sam. 12.3 and Amos 5.12. Both passages refer to the payment of bribes or hush money to judges with the intention of perverting the course of justice. Is *kōphēr* also used in this sense of hush money elsewhere in the Old Testament?

Proverbs 13.8 compares the rich man with the poor. But here wealth is not seen as an asset but a liability. This means that the *māšāl* cannot be about the possibility of having enough money to ransom one's life. In fact it concerns the likelihood of blackmail. While the poor man is immune from such a threat, having nothing with which to buy the blackmailer off, the rich man can constantly be preyed upon to make cover up payments. Hence here too *kōphēr* is used of hush money.

---

the Holiness Code (Lev. 24.19-20) and Deuteronomy (19.21) (*AICL*, pp. 96-99). Originally as in the two precedents in Exod. 21.18-21, Exod. 21.22-23 contrasted a case of assault requiring the payment of damages with a case of murder requiring the exaction of the death penalty. If Exod. 21.22-23 is concerned with possible injury to the foetus, rather than with the prospective mother, then it indicates that under Hebrew law murder included the 'death' of a child still unborn (cf. HL 17–18).

44. See above p. 61.

Proverbs 6.20-35 is not concerned with murder, but with adultery. It warns the young man against the folly of such a course by describing the inevitable fate which would befall him. Rather surprisingly in view of the precedent on the seduction of a virgin (Exod. 22.15-16), the *mišpāṭîm* do not include any law on adultery. But it is clear from Deut. 22.22 and Lev. 20.10 that this was a crime, the adulterer being executed. Further, as Greenberg has pointed out, 'there is no question of permitting the husband to mitigate or cancel the punishment'.[45]

But Jackson contends that Prov. 6.35 clearly shows that the payment of *kōphēr* was possible: 'Prov. 6:32–5 condemns the adulterer as a fool. The husband will be jealous and will not accept *kōphēr*. His non-acceptance is the result of the human attribute of jealousy, not of any legal prohibition.'[46] Though the payment of *kōphēr* for adultery is nowhere else alluded to in the Old Testament Jackson's assessment may seem reasonable enough until one looks at the *māšāl* as a whole. When this is done, it is seen that *kōphēr* is used in parallel with *šōḥad*, the normal word in the Old Testament for the payment of money to pervert the course of justice and generally rendered as 'bribe'. Its only other use relates to payments made to foreign monarchs to take sides on Israel's behalf (1 Kgs 15.9; 2 Kgs 16.8). But such bribes, financed in part from temple treasures, are also to be understood as improper payments for they lead to Judah's dependence on other nations and their gods and not on Yahweh. Significantly Cyrus needs no such payment for he is Yahweh's anointed (Isa. 45.13). In fact what is being contemplated in Prov. 6.35 is an illegal cover-up operation which flouts the absolute injunction that the adulterer must be brought to court as a criminal by bribing the husband to keep quiet. Since a husband could in any event divorce his wife at will, there was always the possibility that for an illegal payment he might be prepared to protect the adulterer. The only effective deterrent to such action was the husband's natural jealousy which would seek vengeance in the adulterer's total ruin. Thus as the parallel use of *šōḥad* confirms, *kōphēr* is again being used of hush money.

If I may digress a moment, Prov. 6.27-35 is itself of considerable interest as it clearly reflects postexilic law. As v. 33 indicates, there is now no question of the adulterer being executed. But nonetheless he is to be totally disgraced in a way from which he can never recover. This refers to

45. Greenberg, 'Postulates', p. 12.
46. Jackson, 'Reflections', p. 60.

the postexilic penalty of excommunication from the community (Lev. 18.29), which except in the case of murder replaced execution.[47] Further v. 31 alludes to a thief paying 'seven times over'. This may simply be a proverbial expression for full restitution,[48] but it has been argued that this sevenfold payment represents a later increase in the amount of punitive damages payable for theft.[49] Support for this contention is found in the LXX rendering of 2 Sam. 12.6 where 'sevenfold' replaces the Masoretic Text's 'fourfold'.

We are now left with 1 Kgs 20.39. The prophet's story describes the capture of a prisoner who is placed in the custody of a guard during the remainder of the battle. Clearly there is no intention that the prisoner is to be executed when his captor returns. He could quite well have done this in the battle itself. Rather the prisoner represents the man's personal booty and will either become his slave or be sold. But should the guard allow the prisoner to escape, then he would have to take his place as a slave or compensate the master for what in effect, as Gray recognized, amounts to a breach of pledge.[50] Such an exorbitant sum is fixed—100 times the price of a slave in Exod. 21.32—that in practice the guard would in any event have ended up in slavery. There is then no reference here to *kōphēr*, nor is the word used. Indeed 'only with the specific mention of the *herem* in v. 42 does the death of the prisoner become an issue. Benhadad was not Ahab's personal booty to do with as he liked: rather he had been devoted to Yahweh and should have been destroyed. Ahab would now take his place (1 Kgs 22). It is interesting to note that the prophet uses exactly the same technique as Nathan in 2 Sam. 12. In both instances the subject of the story commits an offence which is not punishable by death, and is sharply rebuked by the king, who is then immediately convicted of an actual capital offence. In contrast to damages for theft of an animal, David should die for his capital crime of adultery with Bathsheba: in contrast to enslavement for letting a prisoner escape, Ahab should die for his failure to inflict the ban. The similarity would be even more striking if the suggested interpolation of the NEB into v. 40 was accepted so that the verse read: 'The king of Israel said to him, "You deserve to die". And he said to

47. Phillips, *AICL*, pp. 28-32.
48. De Vaux, *Ancient Israel*, p. 160.
49. S.A. Cook, *The Laws of Moses and the Code of Hammurabi* (London: A. & C. Black, 1903), pp. 215-16. Morgenstern, 'The Book', p. 98.
50. J. Gray, *I and II Kings* (OTL; London: SCM Press, 2nd edn, 1970), pp. 432-33.

the king of Israel, "You have passed sentence on yourself".'[51]

In my view then no part of Jackson's argument alters Greenberg's, Paul's and my assertion that Exod. 21.12 absolutely rules out the possibility of composition for homicide, which is reiterated in Num. 35.31-32 even for the unintentional murderer who has fled to his city of refuge. The reason for this extension is that under the priestly legislation, the unintentional murderer was now detained at the city of refuge until the death of the high priest (Num. 35.28).[52] Jackson has, however, argued that this *kōphēr* provision in postexilic legislation would have been unnecessary if its payment had not recently been practised.[53] McKeating agrees: 'On the assumption that law givers do not legislate against things that no one is inclined to do, it seems likely that even up to the exile and perhaps beyond there were those who supported the system of monetary payments in recompense for homicide'.[54]

Now it is, of course, perfectly true that communities do not legislate against something which is not contemplated, which is, however, not quite the same thing as not practised. Clearly *kōphēr* for murder was a possibility for the priestly legislator. He was laying down the basic legislation on murder for postexilic Israel against a background of Babylonian law and practice. Against such foreign influence the necessity to reiterate the fundamental principles of Israelite law is entirely explicable. Indeed I have already argued that the provision in the law of the goring ox ruling out vicarious punishment (Exod. 21.31) is also a later priestly addition reminding Israel of the basic principles of her law (cp. LH 116; 209–10; 230; MAL A 50, 55).[55] I also believe that the late insertion of the *lex talionis* into the Book of the Covenant (Exod. 21.23-25), the Holiness Code (Lev. 24.19-20) and Deuteronomy (Deut. 19.11) was a further result of foreign influence.[56] By forbidding *kōphēr* the priestly legislator ensured that the distinctive nature of Israel's ancient law of murder would not be modified through contact with foreign legal practices.

---

51. See further Phillips, 'The Interpretation' (reprinted below as Chapter 14).

52. The purpose of this detention was to secure the purity of the worshipping community from a man who had shed blood until atonement could be made for his inadvertent act. This could not be done by the sacrifice of animals, but only through the death of the high priest (*AICL*, pp. 107-108).

53. Jackson, 'Reflections', pp. 45-46.

54. McKeating, 'The Development', pp. 55-56.

55. See above p. 55.

56. Cf. Phillips, *AICL*, pp. 96-99; Jackson, 'The Problem', pp. 106-107.

We must now consider other ancient Near Eastern law. Greenberg maintains that 'outside of the Bible, there is no parallel to the absolute ban on composition between the murderer and the next of kin. All Near Eastern law recognises the right of the slain person's family to agree to accept a settlement in lieu of the death of the slayer.'[57] Paul is more cautious: Israel's 'absolute ban on composition for homicide is without parallel in all Near Eastern law'.[58] Jackson rightly points to the paucity of the material available. And Gurney, arguing that there is no general statement on the law of murder in either the Laws of Hammurabi, the Middle Assyrian Laws or the Hittite Laws, concludes that 'the silence of the other oriental codes on this matter is due to the fact that murder was still extrajudicial, a thing to be settled by private vengeance'.[59] But for him the difference between this law and Israelite law, where he admits 'the crime is treated at length', is not substantial for he believes that under the latter all the judicial authorities had to do was to hand the murderer 'over to the vengeance of the gō'ēl, the "redeemer", i.e., the next of kin'. But we have already noted that blood vengeance did not operate in Israel which instead as one kin group dealt with the murderer according to its general statement on the law of murder (Exod. 21.12).[60] Further, this explains why, in contrast to other ancient Near Eastern law collections, all Israel's law collections deal with murder in some detail (Exod. 21; Num. 35; Deut. 19).

But in spite of the lack of material there are still some indications in the other ancient Near Eastern legal material of a very different attitude to murder. So MAL A 10 and B 2 give the next of kin of the murdered man the option of demanding the murderer's death or taking his property. The fate of the murderer is thus an entirely personal affair for the victim's next of kin rather than the community at large. The Hittite Proclamation of Telipinus also allows the next of kin to decide whether he will kill the murderer or make restitution. But Neufeld argues that as no reference to such a choice appears in the Hittite Laws, private vengeance must by then have been entirely suppressed.[61] For him, HL 1–2 deal with murder, and HL 3–4 with manslaughter. Death as a result of a blow during a quarrel is regarded as intentional murder in the Book of the Covenant (Exod. 21.18-

57. Greenberg, 'Postulates', p 14.

58. Paul, *Studies*, p. 61.

59. O.R. Gurney, *The Hittites* (Harmondsworth: Penguin Books, rev. edn, 1961), pp. 97-98.

60. See above p. 58.

61. E. Neufeld, *The Hittite Laws* (London: Luzac, 1951), pp. 129-30.

19),[62] but not in LH 206. Both HL 1–2 and HL 3–4 require substitution rather than death in order that the fighting and working strength of the deceased's community can be maintained. For Greenberg this 'view of life as a replaceable economic value' reaches its ultimate expression in HL 43 where 'the culprit is not punished but incorporated':[63] 'If a man customarily fords a river with his ox, another [man] pushes him aside, seizes the tail of the ox and crosses the river, but the river carries the owner of the ox away, they shall receive that very man'.

But Gurney[64] and Jackson[65] maintain that HL 1–4 do not contain a general statement on the law of murder, but only concern unpremeditated and accidental killings. Murder, that is a premeditated killing, is only found in HL 5 which provides a scale of payments for the killing of a merchant. So Jackson argues that the Proclamation of Telipinus and the Hittite Laws are complementary not contradictory. But even if Jackson is right, in my view, Hittite law clearly envisaged a very different situation from the biblical one with its insistence in all cases on the death of the murderer. I have already mentioned that in contrast to Exod. 21.28-32, LE 54–55 and LH 250–52 make no provision for the fate of the goring ox.[66] Their sole concern is the owner's liability for damages whereas the biblical law emphasizes the necessity for the execution of the murderer— the ox.

Additional confirmation that biblical law was based on very different principles to other ancient Near Eastern law is provided by comparing the punishment of the adulterer. For Israel, adultery as a crime was again a community not a family concern, and required the exaction of the death penalty (Lev. 20.10; Deut. 22.22). To seek to keep the husband quiet by the payment of hush money was strictly illegal (Prov. 6.35).[67] But in spite of signs of state intervention, LH 129, MAL A 14–16, 23, and HL 197–98 show that the concern of these laws was to redress the husband for his injury. So with the exception of HL 198, it is he alone who determines the fate of the adulterer, his punishment or his pardon.

In my view then, while other ancient Near Eastern legal material may

---

62. See above p. 59.
63. Greenberg, 'Postulates', p. 17.
64. Gurney, *The Hittites*, p. 97.
65. Jackson, 'Reflections', pp. 47-48; 'Two or Three Witnesses', in *idem*, *Essays*, pp. 154-71; 'From Dharma to Law', p. 504.
66. See above p. 55.
67. See above p. 64.

show the gradual growth of state intervention in matters of murder and adultery, it contains nothing to compare with Israel's insistence from earliest times that the murderer must be executed for his crime, and the consequent prohibition of any composition between him and his victim's family. It remains to determine what was the reason behind this principle.

For Greenberg the explanation is a religious one. It lies in man's supreme worth as made in the image of God. This is clearly set out in Gen. 9.5-6 and regardless of the lateness of this material is confirmed for Greenberg by the early law of the goring ox.[68] McKeating, however, sees Gen. 9.5-6 as a Priestly development whereby murder is placed 'in the orbit of sacral law'.[69] But he stresses that in spite of this it is man who must inflict punishment on the murderer: '"Whoever sheds man's blood *by man* shall his blood be shed" (Gen. IX.5f.) Any suggestion that sanctions could safely be left to the deity is explicitly discouraged by this statement.' Jackson adopts a very different position. Rendering *bā'ādām* (with the NEB) so as to read 'for that man his blood shall be shed', he understands Gen. 9.5-6. as 'part of the law to be administered by God, not by man'.[70] For him it forms a guarantee that God will not allow the un-detected murderer permanent conquest of his victim's blood.

In Gen. 9.1-7 the Priestly theologian seeks to confirm that in spite of the catastrophe of the flood, God's promise and blessing to man at creation stands. He is still to have total dominion over the created order save that he must recognize the ancient principle that all blood belonged to God, the creator of life. In other words the Priestly theologian is intent on stressing the new covenant of sheer grace which is characteristic of Ezekiel's, Deutero-Isaiah's and his theology. Despite her failure, God will not let Israel go, but continues to bless her. Into this context he introduces his remarks on homicide. But he is not concerned with guaranteeing divine punishment for the undetected murderer whether animal or human. Rather he is reiterating the ancient principle of Israelite law that a murderer must die, again emphasized in P at Num. 35.33. The Priestly theologian needed to do this because, as I have shown in *AICL*, excommunication appears to have replaced execution as the penalty for crime in postexilic Israel.[71] But murder was to be the exception. The anomaly has nothing to do with murder polluting the land (Num. 35.33-34) for sexual offences also defiled

68. Greenberg, 'Postulates', p. 15.
69. McKeating, 'The Development', p. 65.
70. Jackson, 'Reflections', pp. 46-47.
71. Phillips, *AICL*, pp. 28-32.

the land and yet under priestly legislation were punished by excommunication (Lev. 18.24-30). Rather the explanation lies in the ancient belief
that the murderer gained possession of his victim's blood. But all blood
belonged to God, to whom it had to be returned, and whom the Old
Testament pictures as actively seeking its recovery (Gen. 9.5; 42.22; Ps.
9.13; Ezek. 3.18, 20; 33.6, 8; cf. 2 Chron. 24.22). Only execution could
achieve this.

It is then my contention that the origin of Israel's distinctive law of
murder is not to be found in Gen. 9.5-6. In the changed circumstances of
postexilic Israel, this reiterates the principle, but it does not explain it. We
must return to the *mišpāṭîm*.

As we have seen, Exod. 21.12, 15-17 impose an absolute prohibition on
murder, assault on parents, man-theft, and repudiation of parents, and
provide for the death penalty to be exacted on the offender. Clearly this
body of laws framed so similarly and yet comprising such an apparently
strange collection of topics has a common origin. This can only be the
Decalogue, where as Alt argued the commandment on theft must be interpreted as originally referring to man theft.[72] The nature of the *mišpāṭîm*
then becomes explicable. The compiler aims to assimilate the local
indigenous legal practice as administered by the elders in the gate to the
overriding principles of Yahwism as contained in the Decalogue. In the
new situation of the settlement in Canaan, Israel's law was to retain its
own peculiar nature for its observance guaranteed her election as God's
chosen people. Hence death was demanded for breach of any of the commandments. Thus the *mišpāṭîm* carefully distinguish between murder and
assault, and man-theft and loss of other personal property. For assault and
loss of personal property, damages are to be paid. But in the case of
murder, man-theft, and repudiation of parents compensation was categorically ruled out because Israel's criminal law derived from the Decalogue
had made her a distinct people. This explains why exceptionally assault on
parents is treated as a crime being deemed action amounting to parental
repudiation and so demands exaction of the death penalty. In contrast LH
195 provides that the son should have his hand cut off.

Thus Greenberg is right that a religious explanation underlies the
Israelite principle that there shall be no composition for homicide. He is
also right in going on to recognize the very different way in which Israelite
law deals with persons as opposed to property which is in sharp contrast to

----

72. Alt, 'Das Verbot', pp. 333-40.

other ancient Near Eastern law.[73] While property could always be replaced and its loss compensated, people could not. Consequently it is they who have to be protected by the ultimate sanction of the death penalty. And this emphasis on persons rather than property is taken even further in the laws on charity designed to protect those without legal status, the widow, orphan and the resident alien, and in the provisions for the poor. Such provisions may not have been enforceable through the courts, but they represented God's law, his instruction, for breach of which Israel was to be condemned as the prophets proclaimed. It is therefore no surprise to find in Deuteronomy an almost total lack of interest in laws safeguarding personal property. Their absence confirms, albeit negatively, the distinctive theological principles of Israel's law.[74]

Finally let me return to the basic issue with which I have been concerned, the law of murder, and consider a text to which I have so far made no reference. Deuteronomy 21.1-9 deals with the case of the unknown murderer. Although included in Deuteronomy, the law is an ancient one and, as the reference to elders indicates, dates from the time before professional judges were appointed.[75] It thus points to the sacral nature of the law of murder from early times. A breach of criminal law has occurred which if not atoned for will cause direct divine punishment to fall upon the community. The nearest town to the corpse is made responsible for propitiating God and so seeing that this did not happen.

73. Greenberg, 'Postulates', pp. 16-20, cf. Jackson, 'Reflections', pp. 36-54. But Jackson's distinction between theft and brigandage is irrelevant to early Israelite law; man-theft is not a property offence for which damages are paid (e.g. Exod. 21.37), but a crime which demands the exaction of the death penalty (Exod. 21.16) for the offender is no ordinary thief, but is specifically described as 'the stealer of the life of one of his bretheren' (Deut. 24.7), i.e. the equivalent of a murderer; there is no indication of a particular offence of theft of sacred objects in the Old Testament (cf. *AICL*, p. 141).

74. E. Good, 'Capital Punishment and its Alternatives in Ancient Near Eastern Law', *Stanford Law Review* 19 (1967), pp. 947-77 (977): 'One finds in Israel a religious ethic that is sometimes explicitly adduced in explanation of legislation, whereas Babylonian ethics would seem to be based entirely upon social or utilitarian considerations. The religious rationale for Israelite ethics may, to be sure, have been overlaid upon a previously existent social structure. But the penetration of religion puts a face on the details of Israelite law different from the one presented by the religiously neutral Babylonian legal formulations.'

75. See above p. 57.

However, Deut. 21.1-9 makes no attempt to provide a substitute for the offender because only the actual murderer would have gained possession of his victim's blood. Consequently there is no question here of any execution by communal stoning. Instead the elders are to take an unmated[76] and unworked heifer to a valley where there is permanent running water and in which the soil has not been disturbed by ploughing or sowing[77] and there break its neck. The elders then wash their hands over the animal and disclaim all responsibility for the murder. No blood is shed and the animal's corpse is simply abandoned. Nor is any attempt made to transfer any guilt on to the heifer as in the case of the ritual scapegoat (Lev. 16.21). Rather the washing and confession by the elders alone effects expiation for the murder and secures God's pardon on the community at large. What is the purpose of the heifer in the ritual?

McKeating provides the answer by connecting Deut. 21.1-9 with the killing of the seven sons of Saul by the Gibeonites (2 Sam. 21).[78] There again the victims were not stoned to death,[79] and instead of being buried their bodies were abandoned in open country, though in this case a relative took it on herself to guard them. Clearly 2 Sam. 21 reflects Canaanite ideas of fertility.[80] The killing took place after three years of famine and the bodies were exposed until the rains came. Famine was, of course, understood as the most common form of direct divine punishment.[81] It is to prevent such a possibility that ancient Canaanite ideas are taken over and incorporated in the Israelite procedure for dealing with a case of murder by a person or persons unknown. Deuteronomy 21.1-9 thus confirms that under Israelite law murder was a matter for the community who were directly responsible to God.

But it is not until comparison is made with other ancient Near Eastern law that the distinctiveness of Deut. 21.1-9 becomes fully apparent. Thus LH 24 provides that where in the course of a robbery murder took place

76. G.R. Driver, 'Three Notes', *VT* 2 (1952), pp. 356-57 (356).

77. Rather than a remote and wild place, this may indicate land lying fallow (Exod. 23.11) (Phillips, *AICL*, pp. 75-76). This would fit in well with the provision's connection with fertility. Land near a perennial stream would certainly have been used for agricultural purposes.

78. McKeating, 'The Development', pp. 62-64.

79. Phillips, *AICL*, pp. 25-28.

80. H. Cazelles, 'David's Monarchy and the Gibeonites Claim', *PEQ* 87 (1955), pp. 165-75.

81. Such a famine may have formed the background to the trial of Naboth (1 Kgs 21) (Gray, *I and II Kings*, p. 440).

and the murderer was not caught, then the city and governor of the place where the robbery occurred must compensate the victim's family. Similarly HL 6 again provides for compensation to be paid where a man dies in another town. Liability falls on the owner of the land on which the corpse is found. If the land is not in private ownership, the neighbouring village assumes responsibility. But Deut. 21.1-9 shows no interest in the deceased or his family. No attempt is made to identify him or to contact his family; no role is assigned to his next of kin in the atoning ritual; no mention is made of any compensation.[82] Is this pure chance?

Of course the argument for the distinctive nature of Deut. 21.1-9 is ultimately based on silence. But in arguing for the payment of *kōphēr* Jackson resorts to a similar basis when he asserts that:

> it may be that the concern of the author of Deut. 21:1-9 was solely with the aspect of ritual expiation. In the light of the striking expiatory ceremony prescribed in this case, there would be no risk that a public payment to the kin might be confused with expiation. It is, then, quite possible that such a payment was made, but we have no way of knowing for sure.[83]

Alas nothing is, of course, certain but the striking failure of Deut. 21.1-9 to substantiate the view that punishment for murder was a matter for the family acting through the next of kin to whom compensation could be paid is none the less remarkable, especially when other ancient Near Eastern law is taken into account. While clearly the onus of proof lies on those who would establish a principle, it remains my contention that the Old Testament contains sufficient evidence to show that Israel's attitude to murder was distinct from that of other ancient Near Eastern law. It can only be understood as reflecting her theological position as the chosen people of God to whom she was absolutely liable for failure to keep the provisions of the criminal law derived from the Decalogue.

Perhaps I may end by quoting some words of S.A. Cook which I found written by him in pencil on one of his own articles. He was referring to Budde: I refer to my friend Bernard Jackson: 'He criticises my views pretty adversely, but either through pigheadedness or ignorance I am not convinced'.

---

82. J. Finkelstein, 'The Goring Ox: Some Historical Perspectives on Deodands, Forfeitures, Wrongful Death and the Western Notion of Sovereignty', *Temple Law Quarterly* 46 (1973), pp. 69-290 (192-93, 273ff.).

83. Jackson, 'Reflections', p. 49.

Chapter 4

ANOTHER LOOK AT ADULTERY[*]

Recent study of Old Testament law has shown a marked polarization between those who hold that, from the first, such law exhibited distinctive principles marking it off from the general body of ancient Near Eastern law, and those who have seen biblical law as part and parcel of general ancient Near Eastern law evolving in much the same way as private concerns gave way to public ones. Exponents of the former view have been Moshe Greenberg,[1] Shalom Paul[2] and myself,[3] and of the latter Bernard Jackson[4] and Henry McKeating.[5] I have already examined Jackson's criticism of the assertion that distinctive principles governed ancient Israel's law of murder;[6] in this essay I turn to adultery.

In his essay, 'Some Postulates of Biblical Criminal Law', Greenberg,[7] following Neufeld[8] and Kornfeld,[9] argued that while Babylonian, Assyrian and Hittite law all saw adultery as an offence committed against the husband whose decision whether to punish his wife determined not only her fate but also the fate of her lover, in Israel adultery was regarded as a sin against God which in all cases demanded exaction of the death penalty. This was a principle of biblical law. Punishment was not designed to redress the injury done to the husband but was exacted at the express

*   This essay was given as a paper to the Augustine Society, University of Exeter, November 1980.

1.   Greenberg, 'Postulates'.

2.   Paul, *Studies*.

3.   Phillips, *AICL*.

4.   Jackson, 'Reflections'.

5.   McKeating, 'The Development.

6.   Phillips, 'Murder' (above Chapter 3).

7.   Greenberg, 'Postulates', pp. 12-13.

8.   E. Neufeld, *Ancient Hebrew Marriage Laws* (London: Longmans, Green, 1944), pp. 163ff.

9.   W. Kornfeld, 'L'adultère dans l'oriente antique', *RB* 57 (1950), pp. 92-109.

command of God. That such a principle existed has now been radically challenged by McKeating,[10] though he makes no reference to the work of Greenberg, Paul or myself, or indeed to that of Jackson.

Before outlining McKeating's argument, a preliminary point needs to be made. I do not intend in this essay to examine in detail the ancient Near Eastern law of adultery outside Israel. Rather my concern is to establish that Israel's law of adultery rested on a distinctive principle found nowhere else in the ancient Near East. Indeed, as Talmon has indicated, comparison with external parallels should only be undertaken after the phenomenon under consideration is examined in its biblical context.[11] While Jackson has questioned Greenberg's assumption of the uniformity of the Babylonian, Assyrian and Hittite law in respect of the husband's discretion to pardon,[12] nowhere does this non-Israelite law make the exaction of the death penalty for adultery *mandatory*. Yet it will be my contention that in pre-exilic times this was the distinctive principle of Israel's law of adultery: it is this assertion that McKeating seeks to disprove.

McKeating approaches the subject by isolating what he understands as the different sanctions prescribed for adultery. He begins by noting that while sanctions are missing from the Decalogue (Exod. 20.4; Deut. 5.18), Lev. 18.29 provides that the adulterer (Lev. 18.20) should be cut off from his people, that is, excluded from the cultic community. Here, argues McKeating, we are with the Decalogue 'still in the realm of religious law'. On the other hand Deut. 22.22 and Lev. 20.10 both lay down the death penalty to be inflicted on both parties, though McKeating notes that there is no instance of the exaction of such a penalty recorded in the Old Testament. Further, as Jackson had already contended,[13] Prov. 6.32-35 indicates that this death penalty was not, as Greenberg asserted, mandatory, for the husband could be bought off through the payment of *kōphēr*. Indeed, examination of certain other wisdom texts (Prov. 7.5-27, 9.13-18; Qoh. 7.26; Sir. 9.1-9) shows that though often referring to death for the adulterer, they are to be interpreted as metaphorical. Their chief concern is with loss of reputation and the anger of the husband. Though death may sometimes have been inflicted, nowhere is it demanded. Indeed these wisdom writers 'appeal to other sanctions often enough and clearly enough to

10. McKeating, 'Sanctions'.

11. S. Talmon, 'The "Comparative Method" in Biblical Interpretation—Principles and Problems' (VTSup, 29; Leiden: E.J Brill, 1978), pp. 320-56.

12. Jackson, 'Reflections', pp. 60-61.

13. Jackson, 'Reflections', p. 60.

make it certain that adultery was not infrequently dealt with outside the framework of the law'. McKeating then argues that Hos. 2.5; Jer. 13.22, 26-27; Ezek. 16.37-39; 23.19 and possibly Nah. 3.5 refer to an alternative rather than an additional penalty for adultery, namely 'that of disgracing the woman by stripping her naked in public', a practice widely found throughout the ancient Near East. This leads McKeating to assert 'categorically' that the death penalty for adultery 'was not always resorted to': and indeed 'the probability is on the balance of evidence, that it was not resorted to very often'. McKeating concludes this section of his article by noting various references to the possibility of direct divine action for adultery (Gen. 12.10–13.1; 20.1-8; 26.10; 39.9; 2 Sam. 12.13; Wis. 3.16-19; cf. 4.6). Alongside fear of human retribution, fear of God acted as an important deterrent.

Having isolated the alleged alternative sanctions for adultery, McKeating then reconstructs the history of the treatment of this offence. First he argues that it is D and H who remove adultery from family law and see it as an offence against God which requires punishment by the whole community through the mandatory exercise of the death penalty. Their concern is that divine displeasure may fall on the community at large if adultery is not punished but 'left to the private discretion of offended husbands'. But McKeating holds that this attempt to make adultery a sacral crime could only have been a partial success, for in the first place the alternative penalty of humiliation remained in force, and second the Proverbs references indicate that the 'inflexible laws of D and H' were not always applied.

Finally McKeating makes a number of methodological observations which caution against using the laws 'as a starting point for any discussion of Israelite ethics'. The appearance of a law does not guarantee that it was applied. Rather for McKeating it is the narrative accounts which provide the best beginning for they offer 'examples of actual behaviour'.[14] And even more important are the wisdom writings for they 'may well bear witness to the existence of constraints which we might not have guessed at simply from perusal of the laws'. McKeating concludes by arguing that the different penalties show that while the law indicated what was

---

14. The narrative accounts are, of course, of considerable importance as I shall show in this essay, but they may only be intelligible when reference is made to the laws. Thus I have argued that both Nathan's parable in 2 Sam. 12.1-6 ('The Interpretation: repr. below as Chapter 14) and that of the unnamed prophet in 1 Kgs 20.39-43 ('Murder', pp. 118-19) can only be properly understood once it is recognized that in ancient Israel crimes were sharply distinguished from civil offences.

desirable, the fact that it was rarely applied showed that adultery was not so far beyond the bounds of the tolerable. Consequently, he asserts, we must distinguish between the ethics of the Old Testament, an ideal theological construction, and the ethics of ancient Israel, 'the principles by which real Israelites actually lived'. While 'the Old Testament defines adultery as a sacral crime, an offence against God, and therefore to be punished by the whole community, the same Old Testament preserves evidence that the Israelites frequently did not treat it in this way, but that many of them persisted in dealing with it as a largely private issue'. McKeating's thesis thus argues for a tension between private (family) law and public (sacral/criminal) law. While, following D and H, the community motivated by religious theory was commanded to exact the death penalty for adultery as a matter of course, in fact its infliction in the end rested on the attitude of the husband.

But McKeating's essay is itself subject to a serious methodological error. He assumes that because the law of adultery first appears in D and H, then the attempt to make the death penalty for adultery mandatory must date from the issue of those law collections. But because we have no record of an earlier injunction, it does not *necessarily* mean that the community was not already under such a mandatory duty. Israel's legal collections by no means contain the full expression of her law. Further, McKeating does not consider the possibility that the laws in D and H may themselves exhibit signs which indicate that they are not in fact entirely new enactments, but the product of legal development, which certainly one narrative (Gen. 20) appears to confirm. Let us examine these laws.

Leviticus 20.10 prescribes the death penalty for both the adulterous man and the wife. But it is clear from the use of singular *mot yumat*[15] that originally this enactment only concerned the man, the woman being added later.[16] Leviticus 20.10 thus indicates that earlier law is being built upon, and that therefore the law of adultery prescribing the exaction of the death penalty for the adulterous man is older than the issue of the Holiness Code.

---

15. Buss, 'The Distinction', p. 56, has argued that this phrase does not command the exaction of the death penalty but that it may be carried out at the discretion of the husband. But Exod. 21.12-13 confirms by the provision of sanctuary that this phrase amounts to a legal pronouncement giving sentence for breach of the criminal law which results in the mandatory exaction of the death penalty (cf. Gen. 26.11; Exod. 19.12; Judg. 21.5) inflicted by communal stoning (Lev. 20.2, 27; 24.16; Num. 15.35).

16. M. Noth, *Leviticus* (OTL; London: SCM Press, rev. edn, 1977), p. 150.

Further, although Deut. 22.22 lays down that both the adulterous man and the woman in question shall die, it is clear from the emphasis placed on 'both of them', who are then again specifically identified, that something new is being set out. Were this recognized procedure, there would have been no need to have said the same thing twice. This can only mean that the woman is now also being made subject to the criminal law of adultery. Elsewhere there is substantial evidence that it was one of the chief innovations of the Deuteronomists to bring women within the scope of the law. Examples can be found in Deut. 7.3; 13.7; 15.12-17; 17.2-5, and in the other laws concerning adultery.

Let us first consider Deut. 22.13-19. This deals with the case of a man who brings a false charge against his wife. His purpose is not just to obtain a divorce,[17] for he could get this at any time at will, divorce being a matter of family law and therefore quite outside the jurisdiction of the courts.[18] Rather his aim is to recover the bride price (*mōhar*) paid to the father of the girl at betrothal,[19] and not recoverable on divorce.

The charge in Deut. 22.13-19 has usually been interpreted as an accusation of lack of virginity on marriage. In defence the parents of the girl are pictured as producing the blood-stained bed-covering of the wedding night as proof of their daughter's virginity on marriage. But a moment's thought indicates that no husband would leave his marriage bed to bring an accusation of lack of virginity if all the parents had to do was go to that bed and produce the stained bed-covering. Wenham has rightly argued that the concern here is not with the loss of virginity, but with the possible pregnancy of the bride.[20] Basing his argument on his contention that *bᵉtūlâ* does not mean 'virgin' but 'a girl of marriageable age', Wenham asserts that *bᵉtūlîm* in v. 13 refers 'to the age and marks of adolescence and not to virginity'. In his view the parents produce certain blood-stained material as proof of the girl's menstruation immediately before her marriage, thus indicating that she was not pregnant at that time.

In *AICL*, I argued that the concern of the law of adultery was not with

---

17. Contra Driver, *Deuteronomy*, p. 254; G. von Rad, *Deuteronomy* (OTL; London: SCM Press, 1966), p. 142.

18. Phillips, 'Family Law'; 'Another Example of Family Law' (repr. below as Chapter 6).

19. De Vaux, *Ancient Israel*, p. 33.

20. G.J. Wenham, 'BᴱTULAH "A Girl of Marriageable Age"', *VT* 22 (1972), pp. 326-48.

protecting a husband's property, as is often argued,[21] for a wife's position is not to be confused with that of a daughter.[22] By her marriage the wife became an 'extension' of the husband himself (Gen. 2.24), and it was through their children that his name was perpetuated. This was of vital importance in a society which did not believe in life after death but rather that a man's personality went on in his children. It also explains why the law of adultery is restricted to sexual intercourse with a married or betrothed woman (Deut. 22.23-27), and is unconcerned with a husband's sexual fidelity. It is not sexual ethics but paternity which is uppermost in the legislator's mind.[23] This is further confirmed by Num. 5.11-31 which lays down the procedure to be adopted by a husband who suspects that his wife has committed adultery and might therefore bear him a child which was not his own, but who has no concrete evidence, and so cannot institute normal legal proceedings through the courts. Indeed it is probable that prosecution for adultery could only be undertaken if the couple were caught *in flagrante delicto* (Num. 5.13), which explains why cases which rested on unsubstantiated accusations of adultery are missing from Deuteronomy (cf. LH 131–32).[24] Instead the husband may bring his wife to the priest who forces her to utter a self-curse, the outcome of which is decided by drinking certain waters.[25] Though this primitive ordeal, originally to be undertaken at the local sanctuary, has now been brought within Yahwism, the precise details of what was expected to happen to a guilty wife are uncertain. It is, however, clear that they relate in some way to pregnancy, probably resulting in a miscarriage or sterility.[26] But an

21. E.g. Neufeld, *Ancient Hebrew*, pp. 163ff.

22. Phillips, *AICL*, pp. 117-21.

23. Further support for my view is provided by Susan Niditch, 'The Wrong Woman Righted: An Analysis of Genesis 38', *HTR* 72 (1979), pp. 143-49.

24. M. Fishbane, 'Accusations of Adultery: A Study of Law and Scribal Practice in Numbers 5:11–31', *HUCA* 45 (1974), pp. 25-46 (35), argues that Num. 5.12-14 envisages two different situations: '(1) an allegation (vv. 12-13) of conjugal infidelity apparently substantiated by probable cause, common knowledge, or prima facie evidence—but wherein the wife has neither been seen nor caught *in flagrante delicto* by her husband or witnesses; (2) an allegation v. 14 of conjugal infidelity based on suspicion, pure and simple. There is no reasonable justification for the allegation.' But Fishbane is too dependent on LH 131–32.

25. Whether this water is to be understood as 'the water of bitterness' (RSV) or 'the water of contention' (NEB) remains uncertain.

26. G.R. Driver, 'Two Problems in the Old Testament Examined in the Light of Assyriology', *Syria* 33 (1956), pp. 70-78 (74-78). But Brichto, *The Problem of*

innocent wife had nothing to fear. Any children born to her could safely be regarded as the husband's. Thus Num. 5.11-31 is an ancient paternity rite designed to determine the legitimacy of the husband's children. Numbers 5.31 should not then be interpreted as referring to the possible punishment of the wife by the community under the criminal law. Rather this summary verse, probably to be attributed to the Priestly legislator himself, simply indicates that while the jealous husband shall be free from any punishment regardless of the result of the ordeal (cf. Deut. 22.13-21), the guilty wife would not escape the consequences of her secret action.

There is then every reason to associate Deut. 22.13-19 with the possibility of the wife's pregnancy. The husband suspects that during betrothal his wife has become pregnant because during the first month he does not find $b^e t\hat{u}l\hat{i}m$ in her—that is, the signs of menstruation. To counteract this charge, the parents produce blood-stained clothing, so alleging that on marriage the girl was not pregnant. Of course, as Wenham points out, they could forge the evidence, but even if there was no corroboration such as visible signs of pregnancy, and the court gave the girl the benefit of the doubt, the matter could always be put right if subsequently it turned out that an obvious error had been made.[27]

But this provision, unlike the rest of the material on sexual ethics, is not a Deuteronomic innovation, which explains why it has been taken up first in this section of the legislation.[28] The reference to elders in v. 15 indicates that it dates from a time when justice was still administered in the gate. In

---

'Curse', p. 49, and *idem*, 'The Case of the *SOTA* and a Reconsideration of Biblical "Law"', *HUCA* 46 (1975), pp. 55-70 (66), argues that it is the state of pseudocyesis (false pregnancy) that is envisaged.

27. The necessity for a woman to wait before contracting a second marriage for fear of pregnancy through her first husband is extensively dealt with under Talmudic law (R. Yaron, 'Ad secundas nuptias convolare', in *Symbolae Iuridicae et Historicae Martino David Dedicatae*, I (Leiden: E.J. Brill, 1968), pp. 263-79. Note in particular b.Yeb 35a, where even though there has been no prior marriage, an unmarried woman who has taken part in sexual intercourse whether willingly or not must wait three months before marriage.

28. G.J. Wenham and J.G. McConville, 'Drafting Techniques in Some Deuteronomic Laws', *VT* 30 (1980), pp. 248-52, argue for the essential unity of Deut. 22.13-29 on the grounds of the formal structure of each law, the logical order of the cases, the chiastic order of the punishments, and the triadic division of the whole section. But while this may be true of the Deuteronomic presentation of the laws, it does not mean that all these laws must originate at the same time. Their present arrangement is due to the Deuteronomist building on an already existing piece of legislation, Deut. 22.13-19.

contrast Deuteronomy envisages the administration of justice as in the hands of professional judges (Deut. 16.18). Probably this change took place under Jehoshaphat's reform (2 Chron. 19.5).[29] Since the book of Kings makes no mention of this reform, the historicity of the Chronicler's account has been questioned, but it would seem that it should be upheld,[30] for as far as the southern kingdom of Judah is concerned both Isa. 3.2 and Mic. 3.1, 2, 9-11 assume that in their time the handling of the administration of justice was by professional judges.[31] There are a number of references to the elders in the Deuteronomic legislation, in all cases indicating that that legislation is older than the Deuteronomic collection (Deut. 19.12; 21.1-9, 19-20; 25.7-8).

This pre-Deuteronomic provision then sets out the consequence of the failure of the husband's suit. Although v. 18 has usually been interpreted as referring to the infliction of corporal punishment, this is in fact uncertain, for elsewhere the verb *yāśār* is only used generally of 'admonish', 'discipline'. Where Deuteronomy does refer to corporal punishment the different verb *nākâ* occurs (Deut. 25.1-3).[32] Verse 18 may therefore merely indicate that the husband must be admonished, v. 19 specifying what that admonishment is to be, namely the payment of 100 shekels of silver to the girl's father. This is not to be interpreted as a fine, that is a penalty fixed by the criminal law, for Hebrew criminal law did not exact such payments. Rather the case is a civil one: the husband is seeking damages from the father of the girl, whose property she has been up until her marriage, namely the return of the bride price. Recovery of this would put him in the same position he was in before the marriage took place: he would be no worse and no better off. This was the normal result of a successful civil action for damages under Hebrew law (Exod. 21.36; 22.4-5, 13) though exceptionally punitive damages could be inflicted (Exod. 21.37; 22.2b-3, 6, 8). But if the husband failed in his action, then he must compensate the father for wrongfully accusing him of passing off his daughter as already pregnant, whether knowingly or not. Deuteronomy 22.29 indicates that the bride price had become standardized at 50 shekels. In Deut. 22.19, then, we have a further example of the infliction of

---

29. Phillips, *AICL*, pp. 18-19.
30. Albright, 'Judicial Reform'.
31. Knierim, 'Exodus 18', pp. 162ff.; Mayes, *Deuteronomy*, pp. 263-64.
32. Mayes, *Deuteronomy*, p. 310, but cf. von Rad, *Deuteronomy*, p. 142. We have no indication for what circumstances whipping would have been prescribed under Deut. 25.1-3. Probably it was for conduct likely to result in a breach of the peace.

punitive damages, these being double what the husband would have recovered had he been successful. In addition the unsuccessful husband
loses his right to divorce his wife at will. This deterrent measure is to be
interpreted as a new Deuteronomic enactment, for, in contrast to Exod.
22.15-16, Deut. 22.29 also deprives the husband of this basic right. This
restriction is part of the Deuteronomists' general reliance on a deterrent
theory of punishment found elsewhere in their criminal law provisions
(Deut. 17.13; 19.20; 21.21), but here brought into the family law of
divorce which normally was of no concern to the courts (cf. Deut.
22.29).[33] Thus though the Deuteronomic law continues to recognize the
property rights of the father and to compensate him with damages for the
slander, it also, as in Deut. 22.29, recognizes that an injury has been
inflicted on the girl.[34] This is entirely in accord with Deuteronomy's
humanitarian ideals, particularly towards those who had no means of
protecting themselves through the courts (Deut. 10.18; 24.17-22).

Deuteronomy 22.20-21 is to be understood as a Deuteronomic addition
to the pre-Deuteronomic provision, Deut. 22.13-19, originally dealt with
by the elders in the gate. This is seen in the introduction of a criminal
dimension to what was purely a matter of civil law, as the Deuteronomic
purging formula makes plain (cf. Deut. 13.6; 17.7, 12; 19.19; 21.21; 22.22,
24; 24.7). This is not found outside Deuteronomy, and in all cases refers to
crimes which require the exaction of the death penalty.[35] The fact that
Deuteronomy now brings women within the scope of the criminal law of
adultery (Deut. 22.22) has led to the addition of Deut. 22.20-21 to Deut.
22.13-19. The original provision had simply been concerned with the case
of a husband who failed in his suit for the return of the bride price, and the
consequent damages to be paid to the girl's father: now what was once
purely a matter of civil law has to be brought into line with the extension
of the criminal law. If the husband does succeed, it is no longer simply a
matter of recovering the bride price under civil law and the possibility of
divorcing his wife under family law: the girl has commited adultery during

---

33. Phillips, 'Family Law', pp. 351-56.

34. M. Weinfeld, *Deuteronomy and the Deuteronomic School* (Oxford: Clarendon
Press, 1972), p. 285.

35. Mayes, *Deuteronomy*, p. 233, notes that Deut. 19.19 is an exception, but on pp.
289-90 accepts my suggestion that the proceedings envisaged by Deut. 19.16-21 are
limited to criminal cases which required the exaction of the death penalty. The
malicious witness is seeking the death of another through a miscarriage of justice
(*AICL*, p. 143).

betrothal and must be executed as a criminal. But since a husband who failed in his suit would have to compensate the father, so in this new criminal law provision, where the husband succeeds, the father too must suffer the community's disapproval because, knowingly or not, he has been guilty of fraud in accepting the bride price for a girl he has allowed to become pregnant while still in his care. So instead of the girl being taken out to the gate of the city for stoning in the usual manner (Deut. 17.5; 22.24), she is executed at the door of her father's house. The girl is described as having committed $n^e b\bar{a}l\hat{a}$ in Israel, an expression often found in conjunction with sexual offences (Gen. 34.7; Judg. 19.23-24; 20.6, 10; 2 Sam. 13.12), though not confined to them (Josh. 7.15; 1 Sam. 25.25; Job 42.8; Isa. 9.16; 32.6; Jer. 29.23). As I have argued elsewhere, $n^e b\bar{a}l\hat{a}$ is to be understood as a general expression for serious disorderly and unruly action resulting in the break up of an existing relationship whether between tribes, within the family, in a business arrangement, in marriage or with God.[36]

So far then the Deuteronomic legislation repeats a pre-Deuteronomic prescription of the civil law (Deut. 22.13-19) which is of concern to the Deuteronomists not merely because they can add to it their humanitarian and deterrent provisions but because, since women are now brought within the scope of the criminal law of adultery (Deut. 22.22), they must amend it. Hence the addition of Deut. 22.20-21. But having made the adulterous woman also liable to the exaction of the death penalty, the Deuteronomists then have to consider whether such a woman was a willing partner in the act or whether she was forced, and so could defend herself from the criminal charge on the grounds that she acted involuntarily. This explains the following enactment, Deut. 22.23-27.

These provisions specifically refer to a betrothed girl, who, as v. 24 confirms, was for the purposes of the law of adultery in the same position as a wife. The bride price had been paid, and she was therefore contracted to another whose children she was to bear. The reason for such precision here may be due to the previous legislation in Deut. 22.13-21 which acts as the basis for the subsequent new Deuteronomic provisions: the legislator is still considering the possibility of a man marrying a girl who could already be pregnant at marriage. But it may also indicate that the betrothed girl had a greater freedom than a wife, and that therefore the situation envisaged in Deut. 22.23-27 was more likely to happen to her. We must

---

36. A. Phillips, 'NEBALAH—A Term for Serious Disorderly and Unruly Conduct', *VT* 25 (1975), pp. 237-42 (reprinted below as Chapter 16).

certainly assume that this ruling would also apply to a wife.

As the purging formula indicates, this is new legislation necessitated by the Deuteronomists bringing women within the scope of the law of adultery. Deuteronomy 22.23-24 provides that if sexual intercourse took place in the city, then there is a presumption of guilt on the woman's part since she could have cried out for help with reasonable expectation that someone would have come to her aid.[37] Consequently both the man and the woman must be executed as criminals in the normal way, that is by stoning by the community at the city gate, the place of judgment. But Deut. 22.25-27 enacts that if the offence took place in the open country, then there is a presumption of innocence on the woman's part since, even if she had cried out, it was unlikely that anyone would have heard her. No doubt her evidence could be adduced to override either presumption. But in lieu of such evidence, the courts recognized possibility that the woman could have been forced, and therefore ought not to be convicted as a partner in the crime. As in the case of murder (Deut. 19.4-6), the Deuteronomic legislation thus explicitly held that intention must determine criminal responsibility, even though in the case of adultery intention had to be presumed in a somewhat rough and ready manner.

Having dealt with the crime of adultery, Deuteronomy then re-enacts the provisions of the civil law concerning seduction of a girl who has never been betrothed (Deut. 22.28-29), already set out in the list of casuistic civil law precedents on property offences in the Book of the Covenant (Exod. 22.15-16).[38] Such a girl is the property of her father to whom damages must be paid to recompense him for the loss of the bride price which following her seduction he would not now normally get. This explains why both in Exod. 22.15 and Deut. 22.28 the Hebrew makes it plain by the use of a passive perfect instead of a passive participle (cf. Deut. 22.23, 25, 27) of *'āras* that this enactment only concerns a girl who has never been betrothed, rather than (as in the RSV rendering) one who is not (at present) betrothed, so excluding a girl whose betrothal has for some reason been broken off before marriage. Since her father would have received the

---

37. Howard Jacobson, 'A Legal Note on Potiphar's Wife', *HTR* 69 (1976), p. 177, argues that this is the reason why Potiphar's wife repeatedly asserts that she screamed when Joseph approached her (Gen. 39.10-18).

38. The view that Exod. 22.15-16 is supplementary to Deut. 22.23-29 (Morgenstern, 'The Book', pp. 119ff.) cannot be accepted; F.C. Fensham, 'Aspects of Family Law in the Covenant Code in the Light of Ancient Near Eastern Parallels', *Dine Israel* 1 [1969], pp. 5-19 [12]).

mōhar for her on her betrothal, he would suffer no damages even if, though unmarried and still living with him following the break up of her betrothal, she was subsequently seduced.[39] There is then no punitive element in this provision, the father being no better off than if he had arranged his daughter's marriage in the normal way. Indeed in many cases we must assume that all that had happened was that the young man who intended to marry a particular girl had acted precipitately. While Exod. 22.15-16 left the amount of damages payable to be assessed by the court according to the girl's circumstances, Deut. 22.29 standardizes these at 50 shekels of silver (cf. Deut. 22.19), probably to be understood as an average bride price, thus simplifying the legal procedure.[40] But as a further deterrent, the seducer must now marry the girl whom he is subsequently prevented from divorcing. Under the Book of the Covenant the father could withhold his daughter from her lover who, if he did marry the girl, was still free to divorce her at any time at will in accordance with the normal practice of family law. Again the Deuteronomic legislators may have in mind Deut. 22.13-21. As a result of her seduction, the girl may have become pregnant which could lead to further legal proceedings should the father hasten to marry her off to someone else. But as in Deut. 22.19, this restriction on divorce is also intended both as a humanitarian measure in respect of the girl and as a deterrent measure to a would-be lover.

Attempts have been made to explain this Deuteronomic deprivation of the husband's right to divorce his wife by arguing that while Exod. 22.15-16 implies that the girl was persuaded by her lover to consent to the act, Deut. 22.28-29 envisages rape.[41] This cannot, however, be maintained.[42] For the verb *ṭāpas* used in Deut. 22.28 does not indicate force but means quite generally 'hold', 'handle'. As Deut. 22.25 indicates, where the Deuteronomists need to specify that force was used, then the hiphil of *ḥāzaq* occurs (cf. Deut. 25.11). Nor should the verb *'ānâ* found in both Deut. 22.24 and Deut. 22.29 be interpreted as indicating that the woman was humiliated through rape. Rather, as its use in Deut. 21.14 confirms, it simply reports that sexual intercourse has taken place.[43] Accordingly in Deut. 22.28-29 the Deuteronomic legislators should be understood as

39. D.H. Weiss, 'A Note on אשר לא ארשה', *JBL* 81 (1962), pp. 67-69.

40. Driver, *Deuteronomy*, p. 258; C.M. Carmichael, *The Laws of Deuteronomy* (Ithaca, NY: Cornell University Press, 1974), p. 169.

41. Morgenstern, 'The Book', pp. 118ff.

42. Weinfeld, *Deuteronomy*, pp. 286-87.

43. Mayes, *Deuteronomy*, pp. 304, 312-13.

directly amending Exod. 22.15-16 in the light of both their standardization of damages, and their humanitarian and deterrent aims.

The Deuteronomic legislation does not deal with sexual intercourse with a slave-girl, but Lev. 19.20-22 confirms that since she was not a free woman, even if betrothed to another, this would not amount to a criminal action for adultery but a civil one for damages. This seems the best explanation for the unique Hebrew word *biqqoret*.[44] While normally damages for injury to a slave girl would have been paid to her owner, in the case of a betrothed slave girl, damages would have been paid to her fiancé, since the owner would already have received the *mōhar*.[45]

But one further Deuteronomic provision confirms my argument, the law concerning remarriage with a former wife (Deut. 24.1-4). This is an old law, another reference to it being found in Jer. 3.1.[46] It now has attached to it the Deuteronomic abomination formula (cf. Deut. 7.25; 16.21-22; 18.9-14, 22.5; 23.18-19; 25.13-16),[47] and as a result of Jer. 3.1, an even later addition in v. 4 referring to pollution of the land. But the Deuteronomists have made a further amendment to the law in the introduction in v. 1 of the clause giving the reason for the husband's action. As Mayes indicates, this has a new beginning seen in the word *wᵉhāyâ* (cf. Deut. 18.19).[48]

Deuteronomy 24.1 now envisages the initial divorce occuring when the husband finds in his wife *'erwāt dābār*, literally 'the nakedness of a thing'. This cannot refer to adultery since by extending the crime of adultery to women, the Deuteronomists removed the adulterous wife from the sphere of private family law. Indeed it is this change in the law which has resulted in the insertion of this new clause. The Deuteronomists, who were not legislating for divorce in general but for a particular situation, have inserted the phrase *'erwāt dābār* to make sure that there should be no ambiguity in their legislation. It has been deliberately constructed not as a technical term, but as a general expression denoting anything, however

44. E.A. Speiser, 'Leviticus and the Critics', in M. Haran (ed.), *Yehezkel Kaufmann Jubilee Volume* (Jerusalem: Magnes Press, 1960), pp. 29-45 (33ff.); Noth, *Leviticus*, pp. 142-43. But cf. J. Milgrom, 'The Betrothed Slave-Girl, Lev. 19:20-22', *ZAW* 89 (1977), pp. 43-50.

45. G.J. Wenham, *The Book of Leviticus* (Grand Rapids: Eerdmans, 1979), pp. 270-71.

46. T.R. Hobbs, 'Jeremiah 3:1-5 and Deuteronomy 24:1-4', *ZAW* 86 (1974), pp. 23-29 (24).

47. On the abomination formula, see Weinfeld, *Deuteronomy*, pp. 267-74.

48. Mayes, *Deuteronomy*, p. 322.

slight (Deut. 24.3), which the husband found unbecoming in his wife *other than her adultery*.[49] Had women not been made subject to the criminal law of adultery, this additional clause in Deut. 24.1 would never have been needed. That the expression *'erwāt dābār* should be understood as describing quite generally what is unbecoming rather than what is immoral is confirmed from Deut. 23.15, where it is used in connection with ensuring the purity of the Israelite camp from anything which could be considered offensive to Yahweh. Yaron finds the motive for this law in the need to protect the second husband,[50] but the fact that remarriage is even prohibited following his death rules this out.[51] Instead Wenham suggests, following the principles of affinity laid down in Lev. 18 and 20, that Deut. 24.1-4 regards the restoration of the marriage as a type of incest. By the marriage the woman became part of the husband's family—a sister to him and his brothers—and therefore following the logic of the affinity rules, should that marriage be dissolved neither the brother nor the husband could subsequently marry her.[52] But this law in no way sought to limit the husband's absolute right to divorce his wife at will and for whatever reason.[53]

The Deuteronomic legislation on adultery and seduction is therefore not to be understood as the repetition of ancient laws somehow of no concern to the Book of the Covenant.[54] Rather it clearly reflects the contemporary interests of the Deuteronomists and directly results from their innovatory legislation in bringing women within the scope of the criminal law of adultery. As both Lev. 20.10 and these Deuteronomic laws indicate, although not mentioned in the Book of the Covenant, adultery must already have been a crime before the issue of D and H. Further confirmation for this assertion seems to be provided by the narrative of Sarah and Abimelech in Gen. 20. As Daube argues, the linguistic parallels between this narrative and Deut. 22.22 particularly in the use of the phrase *bᵉûlat*

---

49. Phillips, *AICL*, pp. 111-12; Phillips, 'Family Law', pp. 355-56.

50. R. Yaron, 'The Restoration of Marriage', *JJS* 17 (1966), pp. 1-11.

51. Carmichael, *The Laws*, pp. 203-207. In his *Women, Law and the Genesis Traditions* (Edinburgh: Edinburgh University Press, 1979), pp. 8-21, Carmichael argues that this law arose from reflection on the specific case of the patriachal wife in Gen. 20. But cf. my review in *JJS* 31 (1980), pp. 237-38.

52. G.J. Wenham, 'The Restoration of Marriage Reconsidered', *JJS* 30 (1979), pp. 36-40.

53. As has been argued by Driver, *Deuteronomy*, p. 272; Neufeld, *Ancient Hebrew*, pp. 176ff.; Kline, *Treaty of the Great King*, p. 115.

54. See Weinfeld, *Deuteronomy*, p. 284 n. 1.

ba'al, unique to these two passages, presupposes that at the time when the narrative was written there was a specific law like but not necessarily identical to Deut. 22.22 demanding the exaction of the death penalty for adultery.[55] But this would in fact only have been for the adulterer (Gen. 20.3, 7) since, as in Gen. 12 and 26, punishment of the patriarchal wife is nowhere envisaged. Certainly Deut. 22.22 cannot be modelled on the narrative in Gen. 20, for in the first place the problem of liability for adultery committed in error cannot have been dealt with before the punishment of adultery in general had been established, and second Deut. 22.22 envisages the woman's joint liability which is not even considered in the narrative.[56]

McKeating has, however, argued that there is strong evidence that both before and after D and H death was not the only penalty exacted for adultery. But McKeating failed to consider the possibility that women were not liable under the criminal law of adultery before D and H. Once this is accepted, then the earlier material immediately falls into place. While the adulterer would have been executed in the normal way under the criminal law, it would have been left to the husband to deal with his wife as he saw fit under family law. Normally he would have divorced her (Hos. 2.4; Jer. 3.8). Certainly there is no indication that before the Deuteronomic legislation the husband could himself execute his wife, for despite the absolute authority of the head of the household in cases of family law, he nonetheless had no power of life or death over those under his protection whether wife, child or slave.[57] As I have noted, this explains why there is

---

55. D. Daube, 'Concerning Methods of Bible-Criticism', *ArOr* 17 (1949), pp. 89-99. Daube points out that the money given to Abraham as compensation is paid to him as Sarah's *brother* and guardian, not as her husband (Gen. 20.16), so avoiding any suggestion that damages were being paid to the husband for adultery.

56. For the discussion of the dating of Gen. 20 cf. J. van Seters, *Abraham in History and Tradition* (New Haven: Yale University Press, 1975), pp. 167-91, and the review of this book by E.W. Nicholson, *JTS* 30 (1979), pp. 220-34.

57. Phillips, 'Family Law', pp. 349-61; *idem*, 'Another Example of Family Law', pp. 240-45 (reprinted below as Chapter 6). The case of Tamar may look like an exception (Gen. 38.24). But she is not being charged with adultery, for she is a widow (Jackson, 'Reflections', p. 60), but treated as a prostitute. Though the reference to burning may indicate the power of the *paterfamilias* in patriarchal times, it is more probable that this is a Priestly gloss following the insertion of the hitherto unknown punishment into the Holiness Code (Lev. 20.14; 21.9) probably due to Babylonian influence (G.R. Driver and J.C. Miles, *The Babylonian Laws*, I [Oxford: Clarendon Press, 1952], pp. 495-96 n. 12).

no suggestion that either Sarah[58] or Rebekah, and for that matter Bathsheba,[59] would have been or was liable for the crime of adultery (Gen. 12.10-20; 20.1-18; 26.6-11; 2 Sam. 11–12). And although, as McKeating indicates, direct divine punishment is envisaged for this offence (cf. also Gen. 39.9; Wis. 3.16-19; 4.6), as indeed for any direct affront to God, he fails to notice that in the pre-exilic texts this punishment falls not on the woman, but the guilty man alone (Gen. 12.17-19; 20.3, 17-18; 26.10; 2 Sam. 12.14). Only in the late Wisdom of Solomon is there any suggestion that the woman also is liable for her action (4.6).

As evidence that there were alternative punishments for adultery, McKeating notes the procedure for stripping the wife found in Hos. 2.5 and, citing Gordis for support,[60] argues that while elsewhere in the ancient Near East this ritual was part of a divorce procedure, in Israel it survived as a substitute for the death penalty for adultery. But only failure to recognize that in Hosea's time there was no question of the woman being executed for adultery could have led to this conclusion. As Jer. 3.8 confirms, the man alone was liable until the Deuteronomic reform. The husband's remedy lay in his absolute right under family law to divorce his wife. Like all such law, this was exercised not in a court[61] but in the matrimonial home, the husband securing the divorce by pronouncing the appropriate formula (Hos. 2.4) whereby the wife became known as $g^e r\hat{u}\check{s}\hat{a}$, the expelled. But as elsewhere in the ancient Near East, where divorce was for adultery,[62] before the husband pronounced the divorce formula, the wife was stripped naked (Hos. 2.5). This was not simply to indicate that her husband was no longer under any obligation to clothe his wife,[63] but to proclaim publicly the shameful reason for the divorce. The wife was no ordinary divorcee but had acted like a common prostitute and was to be treated as such.[64] While a Nuzi tablet indicates that the children

58. Daube, 'Concerning Methods', pp. 89-99.

59. H.W. Hertzberg, *I and II Samuel* (OTL; London: SCM Press, 1964), p. 309.

60. R. Gordis, 'Hosea's Marriage and Message: A New Approach', *HUCA* 25 (1954), pp. 9-35 (20-21 n. 30a).

61. As argued by J.L. Mays, *Hosea* (OTL; London: SCM Press, 1969), pp. 35-38; H. McKeating, *Amos, Hosea, Micah* (CBC; Cambridge: Cambridge University Press, 1971), pp. 83-84.

62. The most usual reason for divorce was childlessness (Pedersen, *Israel*, 1-2, p. 71).

63. Wolff, *Hosea*, p. 34.

64. D.R. Hillers, *Treaty Curses and the Old Testament Prophets* (*Bib.Or*, 16; Rome: Pontifical Biblical Institute, 1964), pp. 58-60.

were responsible for the stripping,[65] there is no suggestion of this in Hos. 2, though apparently the children born of their mother's adultery would have been expelled with her (Hos. 2.6). This again indicates that the concern of the law of adultery was with paternity rather than sexual ethics. Hosea 2.4-5 thus reflects normal pre-exilic legal procedure under family law and is not to be confused with the criminal law which until the Deuteronomic reform regarded only the adulterer as liable to execution. The death penalty for the wife is not an issue.

McKeating also finds evidence of this stripping procedure in Jer. 13.22, 26-27; Ezek. 16.37-39; 23.29 and probably Nah. 3.5, and notes how both Eichrodt[66] and Neufeld[67] see this as a prelude to trial and stoning. But since Jer. 13 and Nah. 3 are both pre-Deuteronomic, the question of the execution of the wife does not arise. Further, as McKeating's own analysis of Ezek. 16.35-43 indicates, the situation envisaged there, and for that matter in Ezek. 23 too, is not that of a real trial resulting in a sentence for adultery, for in both instances it is the lovers who perform the sentence, whereas they ought also to be suffering the penalty for adultery. Both passages are highly metaphorical, Israel being seen as having prostituted herself among the nations. It is these nations, her erstwhile lovers, whom Yahweh now uses to punish her for her faithlessness to him. The dominant concern is then with idolatry, though, since Israel is pictured as a prostitute, she suffers the customary humiliation reserved for such a woman. But since both Ezek. 16 and 23 clearly envisage the exaction of the death penalty on the adulteress Israel, these admittedly complex chapters cannot be regarded as support for the view that stripping was an alternative penalty to that of death for adultery. It could only be an additional one inherited from family law, and perhaps still carried out by the husband (Ezek. 16.37).

Nor should the possible reference in Ezek. 23.25 to mutilation before execution for adultery be understood as an Israelite criminal law penalty.[68] Apart from the fact that only in Deut. 25.11-12 is there any reference to mutilation under Israelite law,[69] if reference is being made to actual legal practice, then it is under foreign law (Ezek. 23.24)[70] for which there are

---

65. C.H. Gordon, 'Hos. 2:4–5 in the Light of New Semitic Inscriptions', *ZAW* 13 (1936), pp. 277-80.

66. W. Eichrodt, *Ezekiel* (OTL; London: SCM Press, 1970), p. 209.

67. Neufeld, *Ancient Hebrew*, pp. 161ff.

68. Neufeld, *Ancient Hebrew*, p. 167.

69. Phillips, *AICL*, pp. 94-95.

70. Eichrodt, *Ezekiel*, p. 329.

both Assyrian and Egyptian precedents.[71] But the allusion in this highly metaphorical passage may rather be to the normal fate of defeated people under Babylonian military victory, including mutilation and plunder (Ezek. 23.26).[72]

As further evidence that the death penalty for adultery was not mandatory, McKeating cites the reference to *kōphēr* in Prov. 6.35. Here I can do no more than repeat my argument already set out in reply to Jackson.[73] There I pointed out that while *kōphēr* could be used of a legal payment of money which brought about reconciliation between the parties—though there is no evidence of this ever being practised in Israel—it could also be used of an illegal payment designed to avoid prosecution for offences already committed. It is to this illegal sense of a cover-up operation by the payment of a bribe or hush money to judges to pervert the course of justice that 1 Sam. 12.3 and Amos 5.12 refer. It is also in this sense that *kōphēr* is to be understood in Prov. 13.8 where a rich man always subject to the threat of blackmail is contrasted with a poor man who has nothing with which to buy off a blackmailer. Ironically the rich man's wealth becomes a liability rather than an asset for he can constantly be preyed upon to pay hush money.

But Jackson contends that Prov. 6.35 clearly shows that the payment of *kōphēr* was possible: 'Prov. 6:32-35 condemns the adulterer as a fool. The husband will be jealous and will not accept *Kofer*. His non-acceptance is the result of the human attribute of jealousy, not of any legal prohibition.'[74] His argument looks plausible enough until one realizes that *kōphēr* is used in parallel with *šōḥad*, the normal Old Testament word for the payment of money to pervert the course of justice, and generally translated 'bribe'. Its only other use relates to payments made to foreign monarchs to support Israel (1 Kgs 15.9; 2 Kgs 16.8). But such bribes, financed in part from temple treasures, are also to be understood as improper payments for they lead to Judah's dependence on foreign nations and their gods and not on Yahweh. Significantly Cyrus needs no such payment for he is Yahweh's anointed (Isa. 45.13). In fact, as the parallel use of *šōḥad* confirms, *kōphēr* in Prov. 6.35 is again being used of hush money. What is being

71. K.W. Carley, *The Book of the Prophet Ezekiel* (Cambridge: Cambridge University Press, 1974), p. 157.

72. W. Zimmerli, *Ezekiel*, I (*Hermeneia*; Philadelphia: Fortress Press, 1979), pp. 488-89.

73. Phillips, 'Murder', pp. 117-18.

74. Jackson, Reflections', p. 60.

contemplated is the possibility of a cover-up operation whereby the adulterer would escape criminal prosecution by bribing the husband to keep quiet.[75] Since the husband could in any event divorce his wife at will and need not give a reason, the law was always liable to be treated with contempt if the bribe offered to the husband was sufficiently attractive. But the sage points out that an adulterer would be very foolish to rely on such a possibility of avoiding his criminal responsibility, for normally the husband's natural jealousy would seek vengeance in the adulterer's total ruin.

Finally, we should note, as Prov. 6.33 confirms, that in the postexilic period the practice of execution of the adulterer lapsed. This made the possibility of an illegal cover-up all the more likely. But this change in the penalty for adultery was not because this offence became a civil wrong of no interest to the criminal law, but because, apart from murder,[76] the death penalty was no longer exacted.[77] Instead, the criminal was excommunicated from the sacral community of Israel. This reflects the post-exilic constitution of Israel as a religious community protected by a high priest rather than as a nation under a king. It was the purity of the cult that now mattered, for this ensured the God–man relationship.

Though McKeating refers to the excommunication formula in Lev. 18.29 in connection with adultery, he fails to recognize either the lateness of this provision or its significance. Leviticus 18, like Lev. 20, is now arranged as a comprehensive list of sexual crimes for the postexilic period. To the ancient customary law prohibitions of sexual relations with certain women whom one would expect to find in one's tent[78] has been added an assortment of sexual crimes. Leviticus 20.10-16 indicates that such relations originally required the exaction of the death penalty. But in the changed situation of the postexilic period this requirement is replaced by excommunication from the cult community. This is expressed by the *niphal* of *kārat* ('cut off'), with the individual to be punished as the subject and usually the community as the indirect object, and it is only found in the Priestly legislation.[79] So while, like the Holiness Code (Lev. 20.10),

---

75. This interpretation was accepted by Neufeld, *Ancient Hebrew*, p. 167.

76. Phillips, *AICL*, pp. 95-96.

77. Phillips, *AICL*, pp. 28-32.

78. Cf. K. Elliger, 'Das Gesetz Leviticus 18', *ZAW* 26 (1955), pp. 1-25; J.R. Porter, *The Extended Family in the Old Testament* (Occasional Papers; Social and Economic Administration, 6; London: Edutext Publications, 1967).

79. Cf. Gen. 17.14; Exod. 12.15, 19; 30.33, 38; 31.14; Lev. 7.20, 21, 25, 27; 17.4, 9, 14; 18.29; 19.8; 20.17, 18; 22.3; 23.29; Num. 9.13; 15.30, 31; 19.13, 20.

Proverbs still alludes to death for adultery (2.18-19; 7.25-27), the addition to the instruction in Prov. 5.9-14 prescribes exclusion from the community.[80] But the idea that vv. 9-10 picture the husband recovering damages in a civil action must be rejected, for v. 9 is to be understood as referring to loss of dignity rather than of wealth,[81] and v. 10 to hard-earned wealth falling into foreign hands.[82] Even though the adulterer was no longer executed, he remained a criminal and was punished by the community, the husband deriving no personal gain from the prosecution. This change in criminal procedure explains why the other wisdom references cited by McKeating (Prov. 9.13-18; Qoh. 7.26; Sir. 9.1-9) do not demand the death penalty for adultery. But contrary to McKeating's assertion, nowhere is it indicated that adultery was 'dealt with outside the framework of the law'.

In conclusion, then, this 'another look at adultery' in the Old Testament confirms the assertion of Greenberg, Paul and myself that the law covering adultery in Israel was unique in the ancient Near East, adultery being treated as a crime and not as a civil offence. Consequently it demanded community—not private—action leading to the execution of the adulterer, and, after the Deuteronomic reform, of the adulteress too. The husband could neither pardon the criminal(s), take any private act of revenge, nor settle for damages, since adultery was a crime and not a civil offence for which damages would properly be paid. The only thing which concerned him, as it did the community at large, was that the criminal(s) should be publicly tried, convicted and executed, though in the postexilic period excommunication from the cult community replaced exaction of the death penalty. In my view this situation could only have arisen because ancient Israel came into being through accepting a distinctive law which made her a peculiar people among the other ancient Near Eastern peoples.[83] This could only have been the Decalogue.

80. Cf. W. McKane, *Proverbs* (OTL; London: SCM Press, 1970), p. 317.

81. D.W. Thomas, 'The Root שנה = *Saniya* in Hebrew II', *ZAW* 55 (1937), pp. 174-75.

82. McKane, *Proverbs*, pp. 315-17.

83. Buss's suggestion, *The Distinction*, p. 56, that adultery in the Old Testament was an offence in which civil and criminal law overlapped must therefore be rejected. While this situation may be reflected in other ancient Near Eastern law as the state itself took notice of what had previously been a private matter, there is no evidence that at any time punishment of adultery in Israel rested with the husband (cf. LH 129; MAL A 12–16; 23; HL 197–98; LE 28 and see the discussion of R. Yaron, 'Matrimonial Mishaps at Eshnunna', *JSS* 8 [1963], pp. 1-16 [8-9]).

A Response to Dr M. Keating

In his response to my essay,[84] Dr McKeating suggests that I misrepresented him at two points. This was certainly not my intention. Perhaps I might take these in turn.

First, Dr McKeating criticizes me for stating that he challenged 'the *existence* of the principle that adultery was a "sacral crime" and ought to be punished by death'. But I hoped that the first paragraph of my article made clear that what I was challenging in the second was McKeating's rejection of the view that 'from the first' such an inflexible principle existed which marked Israel's law off as unique over against the general body of ancient Near Eastern law. My article as a whole could leave the reader in no doubt as to the difference between us which McKeating neatly summarizes in his reply.

Secondly, Dr McKeating implies that I held him to 'assume that because the law making the death penalty for adultery mandatory first appears in D and H that it could not have existed earlier'. Here he seems to misunderstand me. My point was not that McKeating denied that the death penalty for adultery might have pre-existed D and H, but that he assumes that the attempt to make the penalty mandatory must date from the issue of those law collections. This is what he appears to be saying on pp. 63-65 of his article.[85] For instance he writes on p. 64:

> We may guess, tentatively, that the legislators of D and H were not simply inventing the death penalty for adultery. It was certainly provided for in non-Israelite codes from well before their time, though there it is always a *possible* penalty, a maximum sentence which a husband might press for, if he wished. What the D and H lawmakers seem to be doing is making this penalty mandatory. They do not countenance any other possibility.

As I stated in my essay, in my view part of the flaw in McKeating's methodology arises from his failure to 'consider the possibility that the laws in D and H may themselves exhibit signs which indicate that they are not in fact entirely new enactments, but the product of legal development, which certainly one narrative (Gen. 20) appears to confirm'.

For the record, I do not take it for granted as McKeating asserts that 'we know how Israelite law "worked"'. Much remains uncertain, though I

---

84. McKeating, 'A Response'.
85. McKeating, *Sanctions*.

think it very unlikely that the complicated and inter-related provisions of Deut. 22.13-29 were merely theoretical or idealistic enactments. Rather, as their careful drafting indicates, they appear to mark an important stage in the development of the law of adultery as long practised in Israel.

Chapter 5

THE LAWS OF SLAVERY: EXODUS 21.2-11[*]

In a previous article, I have examined the law of making slavery permanent (Exod. 21.5-6).[1] Like marriage, betrothal,[2] divorce and adoption this
was part of family law, itself a category of customary law, mostly unwritten. Its chief characteristics were that it operated not in the courts but
in the home and was effected by the head of the household acting unilaterally, either by making a prescribed declaration and/or by performing a
prescribed ritual. So the master took the slave to the entrance of his house
and there before the household gods[3] pierced his ear with an awl, probably
with the intention of inserting a ring or cord to which a tag would be
attached indicating ownership.[4] Thus the slave became a permanent part of
his master's property and like the household gods would pass with the rest
of the master's estate on the latter's death.

The provision for making slavery permanent is an amendment to the law
of slavery in Exod. 21.2-4 which gave the *'ebed 'ibrî* an absolute right to
freedom after six years' service without any recourse to the courts. This
explains why, although part of family law, it appears in a biblical law
collection. It has arisen due to economic circumstances for the master was
under no obligation to furnish the released slave with any means of
establishing himself again in society. Consequently he would more often

---

[*]   This article owes its origin to a paper given to the Society for Old Testament
Study at its summer meeting at Exeter in July 1983.

1.   Phillips, 'Family Law', pp. 349-61 (reprinted together with n. 2 below as
Chapter 6).

2.   Phillips, 'Another Example of Family Law', pp. 240-45.

3.   C.H. Gordon, 'אלהים in its Reputed Meaning of Rulers, Judges', *JBL* 54
(1935), pp. 139-44; A.E. Draffkorn, 'Ilāni/Elohim', *JBL* 76 (1957), pp. 216-24; Paul
Studies, pp. 49-51.

4.   I. Mendelsohn, *Slavery in the Ancient Near East* (Oxford: Oxford University
Press, 1949), p. 49, considers also the possibility of tattooing.

have enjoyed a greater measure of security by remaining in his master's house than in risking his freedom without any financial support. Further, should the slave have married after enslavement both his wife and any children born to him would have remained the property of the master (v. 4). As the formal declaration by the slave at the ceremony making his slavery permanent indicates (v. 5), this could exercise an overriding influence on the slave's decision to renounce his right to freedom. In this essay I want to examine the reason for the original provision requiring the release of the *'ebed 'ibrî* after six years and ask why the laws of slavery in Exod. 21.2-11, in contrast to other ancient Near Eastern law collections,[5] should head the Book of the Covenant.

The Book of the Covenant begins at Exod. 21.1 to which 20.22-26 now serves as a prologue. While the law on the altar (20.24-26) may originally have been part of the cultic provisions at the end of the Book of the Covenant (22.28-30; 23.12-19), it has now been combined with a later provision on molten gods (20.23) and marks a revision of the Sinai narrative concerned to stress a return to a simpler form of worship and in particular a rejection of Canaanite accretions. I have associated this with Hezekiah's reform.[6] While 23.20-33 is also understood as a later epilogue, there is no general agreement as to how the remainder of the Book of the Covenant reached its present form. After the law on slaves (21.2-11) this falls into two parts: (1) a series of rulings on criminal and civil matters which carry specified penalties to be enforced by the courts (21.12-22.19);[7] and (2) a mixture of humanitarian and cultic injunctions which envisage no legal action for their breach and specify no penalties (22.20-23.19). Instead they appeal to the moral and religious conscience of the people for obedience, sometimes with the support of a motive clause.

It is readily apparent that the laws on slavery have most in common with this latter group. Not only are they in essence humanitarian and prescribe no means of enforcement, but they also begin in the 'if-you' form. While the 'you' of 21.2 has been regarded as intrusive, being an attempt to conform with the introductory v. 1, Gilmer has shown that this 'if-you' form found also in 22.24, 25-26 and 23.4-5 is both an early and independent form and particularly well suited to frame humanitarian laws dependent on

---

5.   Cf. LH 117–19, 278–82.

6.   Phillips, *AICL*, pp. 167-79; *idem*, 'A Fresh Look', pp. 39-52, 282-94 (reprinted above as Chapter 2).

7.   Exod. 22.17-19, 27 is probably a later criminal law coda (*AICL*, pp. 158-59).

persuasion for their performance.[8] It is again found in the slave legislation in Deuteronomy (Deut. 15.12-15) and the Holiness Code (Lev. 25.39-40). *Prima facie* it would then have seemed more appropriate if the laws on slavery in Exod. 21.2-11 had been placed in the second part of the Book of the Covenant (22.20–23.19), along with other humanitarian provisions governing those without legal status, widows, orphans, foreigners and animals, and those whose legal status was threatened, the poor. Instead they have been given pre-eminence.

The dating of the legal collections that make up the Book of the Covenant is notoriously difficult, but most scholars would want to place 21.12–22.16 in the pre-monarchic period. These enactments are the nearest that biblical law has to a code addressed to judges rather than a sermon to the nation. There is, however, no justification for describing these enactments as inherited from Canaanite law. Although, as one would expect, they deal with the same issues as are found in other ancient Near Eastern law collections, yet, as the law on the goring ox indicates,[9] they display distinctive characteristics which in my view indicate that indigenous law was being brought into line with certain legal principles being introduced by the Hebrew settlers. Such principles are to be found in Exod. 21.12-17, widely regarded as different in kind from the precedents which follow (21.18–22.16) and deliberately placed at their head.[10]

In contrast, the laws on humaneness and righteousness (22.20–23.9), together with the slave laws of 21.2-11, betray a more advanced state of social development in which clan society has broken down and dependents such as widows and orphans lack anyone to protect them. Further, there is now a greater disparity of wealth which results in a definable class of poor. This sharp change in the social and economic structure of Hebrew society from the early days of the settlement in Canaan most naturally reflects the period of the united monarchy. Indeed Gilmer has shown that the 'if-you' form is particularly to be associated with wisdom circles connected with the royal court where it was employed in the instruction of officials and in

8.   Gilmer, *The If-You Form*, pp. 45-56.

9.   Phillips, 'Murder', pp. 109-10 (reprinted above as Chapter 3); and cf. Jackson, 'The Goring Ox'.

10.   J. van der Ploeg, 'Studies in Hebrew Law II. The Style of the Laws', *CBQ* 12 (1950), pp. 248-59, 416-27 (423ff.); *idem*, 'Studies in Hebrew Law. III. Systematic Analysis of the Contents of the Collections of Laws in the Pentateuch', *CBQ* 13 (1951), pp. 28-43, 164-71, 296-307 (28ff.).

the broader context of law.[11] On grounds of content, I have myself argued for a Davidic date for the promulgation of the Book of the Covenant (Exod. 21.1–23.19), for it was the particular function of the Davidic king to uphold law and order especially in those fields in which the courts were powerless to act (Ps. 72; Isa. 11).[12] The Book of the Covenant represents the desire that under the united monarchy law should be standardized in accordance with the state's belief in Yahweh.

The chief source of slaves in the ancient Near East was foreign prisoners of war who were enslaved for life (cf. Deut. 20.10-15; 21.10-14). But economic conditions also ensured a regular supply of native-born slaves. These would include minors sold by poor or indebted parents, or adults either selling themselves into slavery or being declared insolvent. While indebtedness which led to slavery could not at this stage of social development have been very considerable, the prohibition on keeping pledged garments over night (Exod. 22.25) or taking in pledge millstones (Deut. 24.6) indicated the very great poverty of those involved. Loans would have involved no more than enough to live on. In an attempt to minimize slavery among Israelites, in contrast to foreigners, the exaction of interest on loans to them was forbidden (Exod. 22.24; Deut. 23.20; Lev. 25.35-37). While there was no means of enforcing such a prohibition, the fact that of the prophets only Ezekiel alludes to the possibility of its breach (Ezek. 18.13) probably indicates that in the main it was obeyed. Elsewhere in the ancient Near East exorbitant interest rates were the chief cause of slavery.[13] Nonetheless, even in Israel where a man was unable any longer to support himself, he or his children would find themselves forced into slavery (2 Kgs 4.1; Neh. 5.1-5; Amos 2.6; Exod. 22.2b).[14] It is these debt slaves who are the subject of Exod. 21.2-11.

Many scholars, mesmerized by the alleged semantic link between *'ibrî* and *ḥabiru* or *'apiru*, and in particular the occurrence of *ḥabiru* in the slave legislation from Nuzi, have argued that *'ibrî* in Exod. 21.2 is not to

11. Gilmer, *The If-You Form*, p. 110. R. Sonsino, *Motive Clauses in Hebrew Law: Biblical Forms and Near Eastern Parallels* (SBLDS, 45; Chico, CA: Scholars Press, 1980), p. 225, argues that the motive clauses used to encourage obedience to the laws of humaneness and righteousness ultimately derive from the teaching function of the wise rather than cultic preaching.

12. *AICL*, pp. 158-61; and see my review of Gilmer, *The If-You Form*, *JTS* 27 (1976), pp. 424-26.

13. I. Mendelsohn, 'Slavery in the Ancient Near East', *BA* 9 (1946), pp. 74-88.

14. There is no evidence that a man would ever sell his wife into slavery, though she would accompany him into it.

be understood as a gentilic but as an appellative. Consequently they hold
that the law does not concern a fellow Israelite forced into slavery, but a
slave of a particular legal or social class.[15] These scholars have been
further influenced by the appearance of *ḥopšî* in Exod. 21.2 which they
identify with the *ḥupšu* of Nuzi and interpret as someone who while freed
from slavery was still dependent on a city state or individual, and therefore
did not enjoy the full status of a free man. So Paul, noting that the *ḥabiru*
of Nuzi were self-enslaved individuals, identifies the *'ebed 'ibrî* with such
a slave, but then, observing that at Nuzi no limit was placed on the length
of service of these slaves, interprets 21.2 as 'a major reform of this
institution', though he offers no explanation as to why the compilers of the
Book of the Covenant should undertake this.[16] But an interpretation which

---

15. Cf. e.g., Alt, 'The Origins', pp. 93-96; M. Noth, *Exodus* (OTL; London: SCM
Press, 1962), pp. 177-78; U. Cassuto, *A Commentary on the Book of Exodus* (Jerusalem: Magnes Press, 1967), p. 265; N.P. Lemche, 'The "Hebrew Slave": Comments
on the Slave Law Exodus XXI 2-11', *VT* 25 (1975), pp. 129-44 (136ff.); H.J. Boecker,
Law and the Administration of Justice in the Old Testament and Ancient East (Minneapolis: Augsburg, 1980), p. 158. Four different uses of *'ibrî* or *'ibrîm* have been identified in the Old Testament: (1) of the Israelites and their God in their sojourn in Egypt
(Gen. 39.14, 17; 40.15; 41.12; 43.32; Exod. 1.15, 16, 19; 2.6, 7, 11, 13; 3.18; 5.3; 7.16;
9.1,13;10.3); (2) of the Israelites in their wars with the Philistines (1 Sam. 4.6, 9; 13.3,
7, 19;14.11, 21; 29.3); (3) archaically of Abraham (Gen. 14.13) and Jonah (1.9); and
(4) in the laws of emancipation of slaves (Exod. 21.2; Deut. 15.12; Jer. 34.9, 14).
Leaving out of account Exod. 21.2, the subject of this article, I see no reason why in all
other cases *'ibrî* and *'ibrîm* should not be understood in an ethnic sense (cf. R. de
Vaux, *The Early History of Israel: From the Beginnings to the Exodus and Covenant
of Sinai* [London: Darton, Longman & Todd, 1978], pp. 209-216). Only 1 Sam. 14.21,
where *'ibrîm* is apparently contrasted with Israelites, might prove an exception, but it is
probably still best understood as describing certain Israelites/Hebrews in the service of
the Philistines who then deserted and returned to their own people to fight. See further
G.E. Mendenhall, 'The Hebrew Conquest of Palestine', *BA* 25 (1962), pp. 66-87.
While E. Lipiński, 'L' "Esclave Hébreu"', *VT* 26 (1976), pp. 120-24, rejected the
identification of *'ibrî* with *ḥabiru*, arguing that in the Old Testament *'ibrî* is a gentilic,
he noted that it was found in contexts stressing the servile nature of the Israelites. He
therefore concluded that 'the Hebrew slave' was an Israelite of low social standing
who had become a slave—between the unenslavable *'iš*, 'patrician', and the foreigner
who could be enslaved for life. But leaving aside the issue of social classes in Israel,
there is no reason to assume that any Israelite was protected from falling into slavery
should economic circumstances dictate it.

16. Paul, *Studies*, pp. 45-47. See also Mary P. Gray, 'The Habiru-Hebrew Problem
in the Light of the Source Material Available at Present', *HUCA* 29 (1958), pp. 135-
202 (184).

relies first on identifying the slave law of 21.2-4 with foreign practice only to draw a sharp distinction from it must be regarded with some suspicion.

Indeed, as much recent Old Testament criticism of the widespread harmonization of biblical and non-biblical legal material has shown, comparative interpretations ought not to be the starting point for an examination of a particular legal enactment.[17] They place too much reliance on apparent resemblances at the expense of essential differences in the societies from which they emanate and which, if recognized, would have rendered any attempt at comparison suspect.[18] This means, as Ringgren[19] and Talmon[20] have argued, that before engaging in a kind of parallel-hunting involving the abstraction of material out of its context, a proper internal analysis of the biblical material must first be carried out. Only then in the light of the complete picture so obtained may comparison with extra-biblical texts be properly undertaken.

Such an analysis becomes even more necessary when, as Paul admits, the phrase 'Hebrew slave' is found to be without parallel in cuneiform sources.[21] On a comparativist's argument, the addition of *'ebed* to *'ibrî* is tautologous. Further, even a superficial reading of the Old Testament indicates that there is no evidence of the social classes found at Nuzi represented by the terms *ḥabiru* and *ḥupšu*. Nor is it anywhere suggested in the Old Testament slave legislation that, when a slave is freed, he is not restored to full membership of Israelite society. This clearly illustrates that the use of a word in one society does not mean that a related word must necessarily be interpreted in the same way in another community of a quite different social background.[22]

17. T.L. Thompson, *The Historicity of the Patriarchal Narratives: The Quest for the Historical Abraham* (BZAW, 133; Berlin: W. de Gruyter, 1974); van Seters, *Abraham in History*.

18. On such rounds, Jackson, 'Reflections', pp. 32-33, rejects the concept 'cuneiform law'. For a comparison of the different cultural and social background to the Laws of Hammurabi and the provisions of the Book of the Covenant, see M. David, 'The Codex Hammurabi and its Relation to the Provisions of Law in Exodus', *OTS* 7 (1950), pp. 149-78.

19. H. Ringgren, 'Israel's Place among the Religions of the Ancient Near East' (VTSup, 23; Leiden: E.J. Brill, 1972), pp. 1-8.

20. Talmon, 'The "Comparative Method"', pp. 320-56.

21. Paul, *Studies*, p. 45.

22. De Vaux, *Ancient Israel*, p. 88. In view of the fact that no time limit is placed on the length of service of *ḥabiru* at Nuzi, it would seem more likely that if parallels are to be drawn with non-biblical law, LH 117 is more appropriate. See, further, n. 27 below.

In the case of the slave law of Exod. 21.2-11, the Old Testament itself provides an inner parallel in Deut. 15.12-18, a clear reinterpretation of the earlier legislation in the light of Deuteronomic legal considerations. Comparison of the two enactments would on the face of it appear to provide a more reliable methodology than turning directly to non-biblical material. As Talmon asserts, the holistic approach is always to be preferred to the atomistic.[23]

Comparison of Exod. 21.2-11 with Deut. 15.12-18 indicates the following differences, all of which must be interpreted as intentional:

1. While there is no mention of the provisions concerning the *'āmâ* in Exod. 21.7-11, Deut. 15.12 extends the right to release from slavery to the *'ibrîyâ*, who could also elect to become a permanent slave (Deut. 15.17);

2. Deuteronomy 15.13-14 enacts that generous provision is to be given to the freed slave and makes no mention of his family;

3. Deuteronomy 15.15 backs the injunction to free the slave with a motive clause referring to Israel's slavery in Egypt;

4. The family law provision enabling a slave to renounce his right to freedom and enter on permanent slavery is retained, but no mention is made either of the slave's love for his family or of the household gods before whom the ceremony was earlier performed (Exod. 21.6). These were now regarded as illegal objects (2 Kgs 23.24);

5. A further motive clause concludes the Deuteronomic enactment (Deut. 15.18), pointing out that fulfilment of this apparently uneconomic injunction to free the slave would nevertheless result in God's blessing.

The extension of the right of release to female slaves is not to be attributed to a moral development in Israelite law which disapproved of female slaves being used for concubinage as provided by Exod. 21.8-11.[24] Rather, it is part of the Deuteronomic legislators' innovation in extending legal responsibility to adult Israelite women. Though as regards personal injuries, damages continued to be paid to their male protector (Deut.

---

23. Talmon, '"The Comparative Method"', p. 356.

24. See E. Ginzberg, 'Studies in the Economics of the Bible', *JQR* 22 (1932), pp. 343-408 (348 n. 10), where this idea is attributed to Professor Louis Ginzberg. The author then contrasts this enactment with the much later canonization of Mohammedan law.

22.29), in other respects they became equally liable with men under the law (Deut. 5.21; 7.3; 13.7; 17.2-5; 22.22). As a result, the laws of the *'āmāh* of Exod. 21.8-11 became redundant as their absence from Deut. 15.12-18 confirms. They had only arisen as a result of Exod. 21.7 specifically ruling that the female slave should not be released like the male. As a result of the Deuteronomic legislation, male and female slaves now enjoyed the same rights and privileges.

But important as this extension to women is, it does not mark the main emphasis of the Deuteronomic revision of the slave law. This is concerned to do all that it can to ensure that the slave seeks his freedom after six years' service. While he can still accept permanent slavery, this is strongly discouraged both by ensuring that generous provision is made for him on gaining his freedom, and, we must assume from the silence on this matter, letting his family go with him whenever he acquired them (cf. Exod. 21.3-4). The slave's marital status is his private concern which has nothing to do with his service. So when in spite of the hope of the legislators, the slave nonetheless renounces his right to freedom, in contrast to Exod. 21.5, he makes no mention of his wife and children as a reason for doing so: it is love for his master and his household alone which causes him to remain a slave, though in his declaration he makes no reference to his master since he is his brother.[25]

The two motive clauses also lend weight to the Deuteronomic desire that the slave should accept his freedom. While in the Book of the Covenant the motive clause concerning slavery in Egypt had been attached to humanitarian concern for the *gēr* (Exod. 22.20; 23.9), the Deuteronomic legislators use it to remind their fellow citizens that Israelites were not intended to be slaves but formed the nation of those redeemed by God himself. Consequently everything should be done to secure their freedom, including the supply of liberal provisions,[26] even though as the other motive clause indicates, this appears to result in economic loss. While this second motive clause apparently attempts to point out that the master had done well enough financially out of the enslavement,[27] it goes on to add

25. Weinfeld, *Deuteronomy*, p. 282; Carmichael, *The Laws*, pp. 55-57.

26. Cf. Daube, Studies, pp. 49-50, for the influence of this law on the exodus narrative and vice versa.

27. Mayes, *Deuteronomy*, pp. 252-53 (following M. Tsevat, 'Alalakhiana', *HUCA* 29 [1958], pp. 109-34 [125-26]), argues that the context requires the sense of 'equivalent'. In my view there is, however, no reason why *mišneh* should not be interpreted as double of time. See A. Phillips, 'Double for all her Sins', *ZAW* 94

that further divine blessing would in any event fall on him for acting against his immediate interests (Deut. 15.18). This idea marks another Deuteronomic innovation—the extension of earlier motive clauses to include divine blessing for acting against self-interest. While obedience to certain Deuteronomic laws could only bring the performer immediate material loss, Yahweh would in fact secure him personal gain (Deut. 5.16; 14.29; 15.4-6, 10; 23.20). Clearly the slave's right to freedom was being rarely claimed; economic conditions had ensured that. It must remain doubtful whether the new Deuteronomic amendments would have rectified the situation. Lev. 25.39-55 would imply not.

In *AICL*, I found an explanation for the release of the *'ebed 'ibrî* in the seventh year in the covenant renewal festival of Deut. 31.10-11 described as taking place at the end of every seven years, at the set time of the year of release.[28] Identifying the *'ebed 'ibrî* with a Hebrew male slave, I argued that since such a slave would have lost his status as a member of the covenant community, then if he was to be able to take part in the covenant ceremony, there must have been some provision which compulsorily ensured his freedom. This was the measure behind Exod. 21.2. I recognized that the weakness of this argument was that there was no indication in 21.2 of any fixed year of release, but I held that with the advent of the monarchy, the seven-year covenant renewal festival once celebrated at the amphictyonic shrine lapsed and with it the necessity for a fixed year of release for Hebrew male slaves. Accordingly Exod. 21.2 merely enacted that slavery should cease after a period of six years' service no matter when this occurred, but did not specify a fixed date. Sometime in the seventh year of service would satisfy the law which secularized what had once been a compulsory religious innovation.

Though Lemche recognized the originality of my suggestion, he rejected it.[29] In his view the validity of the classical amphictyonic thesis was uncertain, and in any event the laws in Deut. 15.1-11 and 12-18 did not originate in the same tradition, for 15.12-18 required the release of the slaves individually after their period of service, rather than collectively

---

(1982), pp. 130-32 (reprinted below as Chapter 18). If so, then the normal three-year contract of hire (Isa. 16.14) is being contrasted with the six-year period of slavery. The *Code of Lipit Ishtar* 14 provides for the release of a debtor once he has given services equivalent to twice the amount of his debt, while LH 117 grants release after three years.

28. Phillips, *AICL*, pp. 73-74.

29. Lemche, '"The Hebrew Slave"', p. 137.

every seventh year. I have recently reassessed my thesis in *AICL* and as a result would not now wish to associate Exod. 21.2-6 with the covenant renewal festival of Deut. 31.10-11.[30] While I would, with McCarthy, caution against a too sweeping rejection of any tribal unity in pre-monarchic Israel,[31] neither the classical amphictyonic theory as elaborated by Noth nor the existence of a pre-monarchic seven-year covenant festival can be maintained.

I also agree with Lemche that the laws of Deut. 15.1-11 and 12-18 come from different stables. Anxious to minimize slavery of Israelites, the Deuteronomists attack the chief cause of such slavery, debts, and provide that in a fixed seventh year these are to be released. But as the second motive clause indicates (Deut. 15.18), it is clear that the Deuteronomic legislators understood that the release of the Hebrew slave was to take place after a full six years' service whenever that might be.[32] It is the later Deuteronomistic editors who understand 15.1-11 as an extension of the law of the release of slaves (15.12-18) which is now to be interpreted in its light as also requiring the release of slaves in a fixed seventh year, as the apparently inconsistent reference 'at the end of the seventh year' in Jer. 34.14 confirms.[33] While the general release of male and female Israelite slaves by Zedekiah may have been a one-off event aimed at replenishing the ranks of those fighting the Babylonians,[34] the Deuteronomistic editors have clearly interpreted it in the light of the legislation of Deut. 15 which they summarize in Jer. 34.14 by running together a phrase from Deut. 15.1 with another from 15.12.[35] As David has argued from Jer. 34.17, one can only speak of a proclamation of liberty if the manumission is not an individual one coming into effect for each slave separately at the end of six years' work, but is administered generally for all slaves simultaneously.[36]

30. A. Phillips, 'The Decalogue—Ancient Israel's Criminal Law', *JJS* 34 (1983). pp. 1-20 (reprinted above as Chapter 1).

31. McCarthy, *Treaty and Covenant*, p. 282.

32. Mayes, *Deuteronomy*, p. 250, overlooks this point.

33. The LXX translators, failing to understand the significance of this phrase, changed 'seventh' to 'sixth'.

34. For a suggested historical reconstruction in which it is argued that Zedekiah released the slaves in 588–587, a sabbatical year, see N. Sarna, 'Zedekiah's Emancipation of Slaves and the Sabbatical Year', in H.A. Hoffner (ed.), *Orient and Occident* (AOAT, 22; Neukirchen–Vluyn: Neukirchener Verlag, 1973), pp. 143-49.

35. N.P. Lemche, 'The Manumission of Slaves—The Fallow Year—The Sabbatical Year—The Jobel Year', *VT* 26 (1976), pp. 38-59 (51ff.)

36. M. David, 'The Manumission of Slaves under Zedekiah (A Contribution to the

Of such a fixed year of release 'at the end of the seventh year' there is no evidence in the Book of the Covenant, neither in the law of the release of the *'ebed 'ibrî* (Exod. 21.2-6) nor in the law on fallowing which clearly envisages the permanent sustenance of the poor and wild beasts (23.10-11), and therefore of some land lying uncultivated every year. It is this new fixed year of release which the Deuteronomistic editors now prescribe shall conclude with a covenant renewal festival (Deut. 31.10-11).[37]

The position is, then, the opposite of that which I argued in my book. Rather than an amphictyonic covenant festival underlying the law of the release of the *'ebed 'ibrî*, it is the Deuteronomistic editors' identification of the release with a fixed year which has led them to create a festival in which those who had lost their membership of the covenant community through slavery could now once more take their place in it. All Israel, male and female, were to gather before Yahweh as free men and free women whom he had delivered from slavery and in consequence affirm their allegiance to him.

The Deuteronomic legislators' emphasis is then on making the law of the release of the *'ebed 'ibrî* (now extended to the *'ibrîyâ*) work. But there is nothing in the detailed amendment of earlier law to show that the Deuteronomic legislators thought that they were introducing something new in specifically identifying the slaves as Israelites. This they assumed, which is why when women were given legal status, the provision was extended to the *'ibrîyâ*. The phrase 'if your brother' arises naturally from the previous legislation in which Israelites and foreigners had been contrasted (Deut. 15.1-11), and to which the law of the release of the *'ibrî* and *'ibrîyâ* has been deliberately attached. It is because the Deuteronomic legislators are clearly working with the provision of Exod. 21.2-11 before them that the term *'ibrî* is archaically retained and extended to include *'ibrîyâ*. Similarly it is clear that in using *ḥopšî* in Deut. 15.12 the Deuteronomic legislators were not thinking of any intermediate social status between slavery and complete freedom, but only envisaged the latter, as Jer. 34.9, 14 confirms.[38]

Laws about Hebrew Slaves)', *OTS* 5 (1948), pp. 63-78 (75).

37. While in his commentary, Mayes, *Deuteronomy*, p. 374, assigned Deut. 31.9-13 to his second Deuteronomistic editor, in *The Story of Israel between Settlement and Exile* (London: SCM Press, 1983), pp. 37-39, he suggests that this passage comes from the hand of an even later editor. See also his article 'Deuteronomy 4'.

38. The use of *ḥopšî* in the singular in Deut. 15.12 indicates that *'ibrîyâ* is an addition: in Jer. 34.9 the plural *ḥopšîm* appears.

It is time to return to Exod. 21.2-11. At first sight this slave law also appears to provide its own internal evidence to support the Deuteronomic assumption that these laws concerned Israelite slaves. It is clear from the reference back to male slaves in v. 7 that the female slave in 7-11 must come from the same background as the male slave of 2-6. But v. 8 goes on to legislate that a master may not sell his rejected female slave to a foreign people. This would seem to indicate that in 7-11 the law was dealing with Israelite girls, and therefore with Israelite men in 2-6.[39]

It has, however, been argued that *l^e 'ām nokrî* does not refer to a foreign people, but to another family, the phrase reflecting the conditions of the patriarchal period when little solidarity was felt beyond the limits of the great family.[40] Again, on Talmon's methodology, this must be considered doubtful. While *nokrî* does not occur again in the Book of the Covenant, its use in the Deuteronomic legislation always indicates non-Israelites (Deut. 14.2; 15.3; 17.15; 23.21).[41] Nor does Gen. 31.15 necessarily provide contrary evidence; for, however *nokrî* is there interpreted, Rachel and Leah deny the charge. Although Jacob may have come from a distant land to which he now proposes to take them, he is not a foreigner: in marrying their cousin, they have married one of their own people. While, until the Deuteronomic reform, there was no specific prohibition on an Israelite girl marrying a foreigner (Deut. 7.3; cf. Exod. 34.16), it was evidently felt improper that an Israelite who broke his contract to marry should be able to sell the girl to a foreigner, the fear being that she would be used as a prostitute.[42] Although the slave was legally a chattel, the law limited the owner's rights (cf. Exod. 22.25-26).

On the other hand, the rejected slave girl could be redeemed by a fellow Israelite (Exod. 21.8). As the law on adultery with a slave girl indicates (Lev. 19.20), this opportunity to redeem is not to be understood as restricted to the girl's father or near kinsman (cf. Lev. 25.48-54).[43] If not redeemed, she remained with the master, who, if he took another wife, had

---

39. S.R. Driver, *The Book of Exodus* (Cambridge: Cambridge University Press, 1911), p. 213; Childs, *Exodus*, p. 468.

40. Z.W. Falk, 'Hebrew Legal Terms: II', *JSS* 12 (1967), pp. 241-43 (243). Cf. Morgenstern, 'The Book', p. 48.

41. David, 'The Manumission', p. 69 n. 20, argues that *nokrî* can never refer to a strange family.

42. Mendelsohn, *Slavery*, pp. 54-55.

43. David, 'The Manumission, p. 68 n. 19, argues that it is impossible from the text to conclude that only the father had a right to redeem his daughter.

to continue to provide her with proper maintenance (Exod. 21.10).[44] Otherwise he had to let her go free (21.11).

Wolff has argued that the reason why Exod. 21.7 does not permit the female slave to be released, like the male, after six years' service is not that the woman counted more as permanent property, but that the man and wife relationship is thought of primarily as a lasting one even with a slave. Should it cease, the slave woman always gets her freedom.[45] But Wolff's argument does not explain why the Deuteronomists introduced the female Israelite slave into their legislation (Deut. 15.12) and automatically gave her freedom after six years' service like the Israelite male slave. As we have seen, their motive was the extension of legal status to adult Israelite women. It is this previous lack of legal status which is the reason for the difference in treatment of male and female slaves in Exod. 21.2-11, and results in specific legislation to deal with the latter humanely.

As we have recognized on grounds of both form and content, the law of slavery would appear to belong with that mixture of humanitarian and cultic regulations which had no means of enforcement and made up the second part of the Book of the Covenant (Exod. 22.20–23.19). As in the law on fallowing (23.10-11), it is probable that release of the male slave was fixed at the end of six years' service with the sabbath in mind (23.12)[46] But the separation of the law of slavery from the other humanitarian and cultic provisions cannot have been due to accident, but a deliberate choice of the compilers.

One suggestion finds the explanation for this separation in a desire to make the Book of the Covenant correspond with the first verse of the Decalogue.[47] As Yahweh brought the Hebrews out of Egypt, 'the house of bondage', so the Israelites in their turn must let their slaves go free. But, quite apart from the literary problems concerning Exod. 20.2, it is curious that this alleged connection with slavery is not explicitly highlighted by the use of the appropriate motive clause. Instead of attaching this to release from slavery, this clause is applied to the foreigner (22.20; 23.9).[48]

---

44. Paul, *Studies*, pp. 59-61, argues that '°*nātâ* should not be rendered 'conjugal rights' but is 'an otherwise unknown equivalent for "oil, ointments"'.

45. H.W. Wolff, *Anthropology of the Old Testament* (London: SCM Press, 1974), pp. 200-201.

46. Driver, *The Book of Exodus*, p. 210.

47. Cassuto, *A Commentary*, p. 266; Paul, *Studies*, pp. 106-107.

48. While Sonsino, *Motive Clauses*, pp. 193-210, argues for the originality of the motive clauses in the Book of the Covenant, it remains my view that Exod. 22.20b,

It was the Deuteronomists who appropriated it for the release of the Israelite slave (Deut. 15.15).

My examination of the internal biblical legal evidence has, however, suggested that in contrast to other slave provisions of the Book of the Covenant (Exod. 21.20-21, 26-27, 32), which applied generally to all slaves both male and female whatever their origin, 21.2 should be understood as limited to male Israelite slaves. This makes very good sense. These indigenous debt slaves, unlike the foreign slaves drawn from prisoners of war, are not to lose their freedom for all time. While enslavement of a male free-born Israelite had become an unfortunate fact of current economic life by the time the Book of the Covenant was compiled, it was deplored and a limit set on its duration. It is this recognition of the Israelite nationality of the male slaves in Exod. 21.2-6 which provides the only satisfactory explanation for the present position of the law of slavery (21.2-11) at the head of the Book of the Covenant, and explains why this law, unlike the other slave provisions of the Book of the Covenant, remained of interest to the Deuteronomists.[49]

For the compilers of the Book of the Covenant, faced with the establishment of a new social and economic order consequent upon the emergence of the united monarchy, the release of the Israelite male slave was not in the end a humanitarian provision like those concerning widows, orphans, foreigners, animals and the poor. Rather it was restoring to a member of Israel his rightful place under the law. For this reason it should precede the rest of the enactments which, if he were free, would be his both to obey and to enforce. While economic pressures no doubt meant that increasingly few could take advantage of their right to freedom, the ideal of a society in which each adult male Israelite had a stake in his community's affairs remained valid, and—in the face of growing disparity in wealth leading to a massive increase in Israelite slaves—needed to be underlined.

In a recent reassessment of the thesis in *AICL*, I argued that the tenth commandment formed another example of this concern for a slaveless society.[50] Originally dealing with the house alone, it prohibited dispossession with the consequent loss of status as an elder which auto-

---

22b-23 and 23.9 are later additions, being the work of the Proto-Deuteronomists who used the plural form.

49. Cf. J. van der Ploeg, 'Slavery in the Old Testament' (VTSup, 22; Leiden: E.J Brill, 1972), pp. 72-87 (81); Lemche, '"The Hebrew Slave"', pp. 135-36.

50. Phillips, 'The Decalogue', pp. 17-19.

matically conferred on the owner of the house the responsibility of taking part in the local community's affairs.[51] But in the changed economic conditions of Canaan, sale of property by Israelites (1 Kgs 21)[52] and permanent slavery of Israelites (Exod. 21.5-6) became facts of life. Consequently, when the Decalogue was inserted into the Sinai narrative, the tenth commandment was spiritualized and in effect became another example of the laws on humaneness and righteousness reaffirming the ideal of a slaveless property-owning society in which each family had a stake in the community's decisions. This explains why, along with other abuses of Israel's humanitarian and juridical ideals, the seizure of realty by the rich continued to be condemned by Isaiah and Micah (Isa. 3.2; Mic. 3.1-2, 9-11), though there is no need to assume that illegal means were used.[53]

We can then conclude that Exod. 21.2-4 owes nothing to non-biblical law. Rather it is a statement of belief about the true nature of Israelite society: it should be made up of free men. Economic necessities may lead an Israelite to renounce his true heritage, but his destiny is not in the end to be subject to purely financial considerations. Exodus 21.2 is no ordinary humanitarian provision, but expresses Israel's fundamental understanding of its true identity. No matter how far reality failed to match the ideal, that ideal must be reaffirmed in successive legislation. So, in gradually worsening economic conditions both Deuteronomy (15.1-18) and the Holiness Code (Lev. 25.39-43) reiterate it. It is the male Israelite's right to release (Exod. 21.2-4) which explains why the laws of slavery (21.2-11) head that legislation which sought to come to terms with Israel's new-found statehood with all its consequent economic problems under the united monarchy.

---

51. Cf. Davies, *Prophecy and Ethics*, pp. 92, 100.

52. I cannot accept that property could not be sold out of the family for ever. Lev. 25.23 is part of the idealized Jubilee law. Neither Isaiah nor Micah appeal to it, nor make any mention of the Jubilee. There is no reason to assume that Ahab's request to purchase Naboth's vineyard was in any sense improper (1 Kgs 21). Naboth merely resorts to an appeal to filial piety to get out of an awkward situation (Seebass, 'Der Fall Naboth', pp. 474-88).

53. See Phillips, 'Prophecy and Law', pp. 217-32 (reprinted below as Chapter 10).

Chapter 6

SOME ASPECTS OF FAMILY LAW IN PRE-EXILIC ISRAEL[*]

In *AICL* I sought to distinguish crimes, that is actions which the community prohibits and which it punishes in its name, from torts or civil wrongs which result in an action by the injured party against the man who wronged him. For instance I argued that in ancient Israel murder was a crime resulting in the execution of the murderer (Exod. 21.12), whereas assault was a tort which resulted in the payment of damages to the injured party (Exod. 21.18-19). Similarly I pointed out that adultery was a crime carrying the death penalty (Lev. 20.10; Deut. 22.22), whereas seduction of an unmarried or unbetrothed girl was a tort for which the girl's father had to be compensated (Exod. 22.15-16). In the same way theft of persons for sale outside the community resulted in criminal prosecution and execution on conviction (Exod. 21.16), whereas theft of animals or other property led only to an action for damages (Exod. 21.37, 22.2b-3). Indeed I pointed out that much of the original legislation contained in the Book of the Covenant was designed to distinguish crime from tort.

By definition crime is that action which the community prohibits and punishes in its name because it endangers their common welfare. But torts too can seriously jeopardize the smooth running of community life. It is therefore of the utmost importance that the breakdown in local relations following any particular injury should be healed as quickly as possible. This becomes even more urgent in the particular social conditions under which the Israelites lived. Thus in ancient Israel torts as well as crimes were treated as matters of general public concern. Consequently cases of both crime and tort were heard in the local court and not left to individuals or families to settle as they thought fit. Until professional judges were appointed, probably under Jehoshaphat's reform (2 Chron. 19.5), the local elders heard all such cases, and determined what action to take against the

   *   Parts I–III of this essay were first given as a paper to the Society for Old Testament Study at its London meeting, January 1972.

accused.[1] Where execution was ordered, it was carried out by the whole adult male community: when damages were payable, their amount was assessed by the court.

But in the Introduction to my book, I pointed out that there were other heads of law in ancient Israel, and cited customary, family and cultic law. In this essay, I want to examine certain instances of family law, which is itself best seen as a self-contained section within general customary law, and show that under this head a very different procedure was adopted to that in crime and tort. For in contrast to the latter, under family law the courts had no jurisdiction, the matter being left entirely in the hands of the individual head of the house. The reason for this is that only free adult males had legal status in ancient Israel, and so the right to appear before the elders in court. All other persons whether women, children or slaves, were in effect regarded as the personal property of the head of the household, and were dependent on him, not the courts, for their protection.[2] How the head of the household dealt with members of his household who were not free adult males was in general his private affair, and in contrast to wrongs inflicted on members of other households, was unlikely to cause any public disorder in the community. Consequently his domestic actions were of no concern to the courts.[3] The cases I have in mind to illustrate my

---

1.   Phillips, *AICL*, pp. 17-20.

2.   Where such persons no longer enjoyed the protection of the head of the household, as with widows and orphans, they were thought to be under Yahweh's special care (Deut. 10.18), and being economically weak were commended as objects of charity to the community at large (Exod. 22.21; Deut. 24.17-22). But while women not under the protection of a male, e.g. widows and prostitutes, could not rely on the courts to protect them, they could appeal to the king as the supreme upholder of law and order on Yahweh's behalf (2 Sam. 14.1-20; 1 Kgs 3.16-28) (cf. F.C. Fensham, 'Widow, Orphan, and the Poor in Ancient Near Eastern Legal and Wisdom Literature', *JNES* 21 [1962], pp. 129-39). Such an appeal is, however, outside the scope of the recognised legal machinery of the courts (*AICL*, p. 21).

3.   It is probable that general customary law prohibited uninvited entry into another's house (cf. Deut. 24.10-11). Evidence of this has been recognised in the story of Laban's pursuit of Jacob (Gen. 31.25-35) (Daube, *Studies*, p. 202). Further LH 16 indicates that the police had no right of entry into the house of someone known to be harbouring a runaway slave. Uninvited entry is also regarded as a serious offence in Shurpu Tablet II § 47 (I. Mendelsohn, *Religions of the Ancient Near East* [Oxford: Oxford University Press, 1955], p. 213). This may in part explain why Exod. 22.1-2a exceptionally absolves an Israelite from a charge of murder should he kill an intruder at night (*AICL*, pp. 92-93).

argument are divorce, the making of slavery permanent, adoption, and betrothal and marriage.

I

The Book of the Covenant provides ample evidence that a woman had no independent legal status but was treated as the personal property first of her father, and then of her husband. Thus a man who seduced an unmarried or unbetrothed girl would be sued as a tortfeasor, and would have had to compensate her father for damage to his property, namely the loss of his daughter's virginity, and so of her eligibility as a bride. Accordingly Exod. 22.15 provides that the seducer must pay the father by way of damages the price which the father could have expected to have received for his daughter on marriage, and which he would not now get. The seducer was also to take the girl as his wife, though the father had the power to withhold her. The father was thus neither better nor worse off than if he had made a marriage for the girl in the normal manner and harmony was restored within the community.[4]

Similarly when a man injured another's wife, he would have had to compensate her husband. So Exod. 21.22 provides that where a man knocks a pregnant woman who thereby suffers a miscarriage but no further hurt, then damages must be paid. The husband evidently sued for a specific sum, which on the case being proved, was scrutinized by court assessors who determined the actual amount payable.[5]

In view of these precedents, it comes as no surprise to find that a man had an unfettered right to dispose of the women under his protection as he liked, whether as a father making a marriage for his daughter, or as a husband divorcing his wife. Neither the daughter nor the wife had any ultimate say in the matter, nor could they appeal to the courts. Their future was determined by family law, and that was an entirely domestic matter. Thus whereas a wife could never divorce her husband, the latter had an absolute right to divorce his wife at any time and for any reason whatsoever.[6] Probably childlessness was the chief ground for divorce.[7]

---

4. For further discussion of this legislation and the Deuteronomic revision (Deut. 22.28-29), cf. Phillips, *AICL*, pp. 112-13.

5. For further discussion, cf. Phillips, *AICL*, pp. 88-90.

6. Z.W. Falk, *Hebrew Law in Biblical Times* (Jerusalem: Wahrmann Books, 1964), pp. 154-57.

7. Pedersen, *Israel* 1-2, p. 71.

That the ceremony terminating the marriage took place in the matrimonial home is clear from Hos. 2.4-5. This does not describe a court scene
as has sometimes been supposed,[8] presumably on analogy with modern
legal practice, but rather pictures an unwilling husband in the very act of
divorcing his wife.[9] At the eleventh hour he urges the children of the
marriage to make a final plea to their mother to wring from her a promise
that she will reform herself and so make it no longer necessary for him to
execute the divorce by expelling the wife from her home (cf. Deut. 24.3;
Isa. 50.1). Having failed himself to get her to change her ways, as a last
resort he relies on her children. Although normally on divorce they would
almost certainly have remained in the custody of their father,[10] in this case
as illegitimate offspring of the wife, they would also have been expelled
from the home (Hos. 2.6). They could succeed neither to the husband's
name nor property.

Having pronounced the appropriate declaration of divorce 'She is not
my wife and I am not her husband' (Hos. 2.4), all the husband had to do to
put the divorce into effect was to drive the wife from the matrimonial
home. Henceforth she was known as $g^e r\hat{u}\check{s}\hat{a}$, 'the expelled' (Lev. 21.7;
22.13; Num. 30.10; Ezek. 44.22). Indeed, as in the case of the making of
slavery permanent (Exod. 21.6),[11] it is in fact probable that the divorce
ceremony itself took place at the door of the house, that is literally over
the threshold. Whether it was performed publicly, that is in the presence of
members of the community other than the immediate family, is nowhere
indicated and ought not to be assumed. The husband had an absolute right
to act unilaterally independently of the community at large. It was his
affair alone and of no concern to others. The divorced woman would
normally have returned to her father's house (Lev. 22.13; cf. Judg. 19.2).

Where the ground for the divorce was the wife's adultery, then as Hos.
2.5 indicates a further ritual was performed. This consisted of stripping off
the wife's clothes and driving her from the home naked. It was not simply
undertaken to indicate that the husband was no longer responsible for the
wife's maintenance, which was always the case whenever there was

---

8.   Cf. Mays, *Hosea*, pp. 35-40; McKeating, *Amos, Hosea, Micah*, pp. 83-84.

9.   C. Kuhl, 'Neue Dokumente zum Verständnis von Hosea 2 4-15', *ZAW* 11
(1934), pp. 102-109; Gordon, 'New Semitic Inscriptions', pp. 277-80; and cf. the criticism of R. Gordis, 'Hosea's Marriage', pp. 20-21; W. Rudolph, *Hosea* (KAT, 13.1;
Gütersloh: Gerd Mohn, 1966), pp. 64ff.

10.   Neufeld, *Ancient Hebrew*, pp. 181-82.

11.   See below pp. 118-19.

divorce, but rather to brand the wife as a shameless person. She was no ordinary divorcee, but someone who had given herself to another. Indeed she was no better than a common prostitute, and was therefore treated as such.[12] As Hosea puts it, her lewdness is to be exposed for her lovers to see (2.12). Similar ideas are present in both Jeremiah (13.26-27) and Ezekiel (16.37-38; 23.10, 29). As a Nuzi tablet indicates, the children themselves may have carried out the stripping.[13]

Of course both Lev. 20.10 and Deut. 22.22 enact that the wife as well as her lover should be executed for the crime of adultery, but these measures reflect the later Deuteronomic law whereby a number of provisions previously restricted to men were extended to apply to women as well (e.g. Deut. 15.12-18).[14] As Hos. 2.4 and Jer. 3.8 confirm, under earlier law divorce not execution was the consequence of the wife's adultery, her lover alone being put to death. Indeed it is clear that when Lev. 20.10 was originally drawn up, it only provided for the execution of one person, namely the husband, the wife being added later. This explains why there is no suggestion that Sarah would have been in any way liable for her adultery with Abimelech nor Bathsheba condemned for her infidelity with David. Probably a woman was assumed to have been forced. Evidently the Deuteronomic legislator reversed this presumption, though he does contrast a case of presumed consent with one of presumed rape in the case of an unbetrothed woman (Deut. 22.23-27). In view of this, it is perhaps probable that the pre-Deuteronomic ritual of stripping the adulterous wife naked was only undertaken when there was concrete evidence of collusion on her part. In this case, instead of returning to her father's house, she may have been forced to live as a prostitute.

Nonetheless, as compared with other ancient Near Eastern legal systems, Israelite law did place a substantial limitation on the husband's authority over his wife. Adultery was a crime, and therefore a matter of public concern, prosecution being undertaken by the state and not the husband, though he no doubt often acted as the chief witness. If the accused were found guilty, the execution of the lover, and after the Deuteronomic reform, of the wife as well, was carried out by the local community. The husband had no power either to stop the execution by pardoning his wife, nor to settle privately with the adulterer for damages. The whole matter

12. Cf. Hillers, *Treaty Curses*, pp. 58-60.
13. Gordon, 'New Semitic Inscriptions', pp. 277-80.
14. Phillips, *AICL*, pp. 15-16, 110-11. Women, however, still remained under the authority of men (Deut. 22.29).

was taken out of his hands. Further if he acted on his own initiative and himself killed the adulterer or his wife, he would have been charged with the crime of murder and executed. At no time did the Israelite head of the house have the power of life or death over those under his protection. This is in marked contrast to the position in other ancient Near Eastern coun- tries where adultery was treated solely as an injury to the husband who himself could determine the fate of his wife, and, in consequence, that of her lover. If he forgave his wife, then her lover had also to be pardoned.[15] In Israel he had no such choice. The state determined the fate of both parties.[16] And even when the non-Israelite state itself took notice of the adultery by punishing the wife rather than leaving this to the husband, it was still primarily carrying out personal vengeance on his behalf.[17]

Clearly as Israelite society became more complex, the simple divorce procedure already outlined proved extremely unsatisfactory, especially when it is remembered that to have sexual intercourse with a married woman would result in a prosecution on a capital charge of adultery. It was therefore extremely important that a divorced woman should have proof that her marriage had been dissolved in order that she might marry again without fear that her former husband should suddenly claim rights over her.[18] This led to the introduction of the bill of divorce, called literally 'deed of cutting' (*sēper kᵉrîtōt*). This either replaced or sup- plemented the simple divorce formula of family law spoken by the husband before the wife's expulsion from the matrimonial home (Hos. 2.4). Certainly by the time of Jeremiah (3.8) and the Deuteronomic

---

15. LH 129; MAL A 14–16, 23; HL 197-98.

16. Phillips, *AICL*, pp. 117-18.

17. While LH 129 no longer envisages punishment by the husband, traces of it can be recognized in MAL A 14–16, 23, though 12–13 seem to imply state execution. Probably the law was in a state of transition under which the husband's powers of acting extra-judicially were being limited, but nowhere is there any indication that he no longer had the right to determine his wife's fate as he pleased. HL 197–98. appear to reflect a similar situation. It has also been argued that LE 28 in fact legislates for the death of the lover, the fate of the wife being left to the husband or father (Yaron, 'Matrimonial Mishaps at Eshnunna', pp. 7ff.).

18. The case of Samson's first marriage has been cited as an example of uncertainty as to whether the parties were divorced (D. Daube, 'Error and Accident in the Bible', *RIDA* 2 [1949], pp. 189-213 [193-194]), but it is possible that the marriage had never been consummated, and was therefore automatically dissolved when the father gave his daughter to another man (Judg. 15.1-2) (G.R. Driver and J.C. Miles, *The Babylonian Laws*, I (Oxford: Clarendon Press, 1952), p. 291.

legislation (24.1-4) such deeds were regularly given by the husband on divorce.[19] But divorce itself continued to remain an entirely private affair, and no resort was made to the courts.

The interpretation of the phrase *'erwāt dābār*, 'the nakedness of a thing', in Deut. 24.1 has long been a matter of scholarly dispute.[20] Some have argued that it specifically refers to adultery. But since Deut. 22.22 legislated that even the wife was to be executed for this crime, clearly such an interpretation cannot be maintained. Indeed I believe that the very opposite is the case. By making the wife liable to execution as an accessory in the crime of adultery, the Deuteronomic legislator removed this act from the sphere of family law. It was in order to take account of this that he inserted the phrase *'erwāt dābār* in his legislation, which phrase is not to be understood as a technical term, but as a general expression denoting anything which the husband found distasteful in his wife *other than her adultery*. Thus while her adultery now resulted in her execution rather than divorce, in all other respects her husband's rights to divorce her for whatever reason he liked remained unchanged. That the expression *'erwāt dābār* has no moral connotation is confirmed from Deut. 23.15 where it is used of what is unbecoming, but not of what is immoral.

Thus Deut. 24.1-4 cannot be used as evidence that the Deuteronomist sought to limit the husband's absolute right to divorce his wife whenever he wished and for whatever reason.[21] While two other pieces of Deuteronomic legislation do limit the right to divorce, in each case this limit amounts to a penalty placed on the husband due to some previous improper conduct on his part. In one instance he had falsely charged his wife with loss of her virginity at the time of her marriage (Deut. 22.19), and in the other had been compelled to marry a girl whom he had seduced (Deut. 22.29).

---

19. R. Yaron, 'On Divorce in Old Testament Times', *RIDA* 4 (1957), pp. 117-28 (126-27), argues that as the Hebrew word for 'cut', *kārat*, is not elsewhere used in the Old Testament in connection with divorce, the practice of giving a bill of divorce may have been introduced comparatively late and from abroad. He also points out that there is no mention of a bill of divorce in the Aramaic papyri from Elephantine, which although dating from the fifth century BCE, are generally regarded as reflecting pre-Deutcronomic law.

20. Cf. Neufeld, *Ancient Hebrew*, pp. 176ff.; Yaron, 'On Divorce', pp. 127-28.

21. Driver, *Deuteronomy*, p. 272; Neufeld, *Ancient Hebrew*, pp. 176ff.; Kline, *Treaty of the Great King*, p. 115.

Accordingly the husband's absolute right to divorce his wife remained entirely unfettered, and he continued to act solely on his own initiative without recourse to any public body.[22] Divorce remained part of family law, and family law was no concern of the courts.

Deut. 25.5-10 does, however, provide an exceptional instance of the courts taking note of a failure to implement customary family law, though they are powerless to do anything about it. This provision enacts that where a brother[23] refuses to carry out the duties of levirate marriage, his deceased brother's widow can have him brought before the court, who will then seek to persuade him to fulfil his obligation under customary family law. If he still refuses the court permits his public humiliation by the woman, but cannot enforce the marriage. It is probable that by the time of Deuteronomy the practice of levirate marriage was already unpopular and was widely rejected. Leviticus 20.21 apparently abolished it, the curse of childlessness being particularly appropriate.[24] This in turn led to the priestly legislation's innovation of permitting daughters to inherit property, and so continue the name of their deceased and sonless father (Num. 27.1-11).

II

Like a wife or daughter, a slave was treated as part of his master's personal property. Thus Exod. 21.32 enacts that if a slave was gored to death by an ox, the owner of the ox had to compensate the master for his loss.[25] By the payment of damages, fixed at the current purchase price of a slave, harmony was restored within the community.

After six years' service, a Hebrew slave was entitled as of right to freedom. His master had to release him without any payment from the slave, who thereby recovered his status as a free adult male within the community (Exod. 21.2). But a slave could renounce his right to freedom, and indeed it would often have been in his interests to do so. For not only would his wife and children have remained his master's property if he had married after his enslavement, but his master was under no obligation to make any financial provision for him on release (Exod. 21.4). There was

22. Yaron, 'On Divorce', pp. 127-28.

23. Originally the duty of levirate marriage would have extended to other relatives (cf. Gen. 38).

24. However, Porter, *The Extended Family*, p. 19, argues that marriage with one's sister-in-law is only prohibited when she has already borne a son to one's deceased brother.

25. The ox was treated as a murderer and executed. Cf. Phillips, *AICL*, p. 90.

therefore little point in exchanging security without freedom for freedom without security.

Exodus 21.6 describes the ceremony whereby the slave became a permanent member of his master's household. 'Then his master shall bring him to *ᵉlōhîm*: he shall bring him to the door or the door-post, and his master shall pierce his ear with an awl, and he shall serve him for life'. Quite clearly the change in status of the slave takes place without any recourse to the courts. Nor is there any indication that the ceremony had to be performed before other members of the local community. It is essentially private in character, being a personal matter between the master and his slave, and of no direct concern to the public at large. By the formal domestic ceremony before *ᵉlōhîm*, that is the household gods, at the entrance to the house,[26] the slave becomes a permanent member of his master's household. He was now part of the family estate, and like the household gods themselves, would on his master's death pass with the property to his heir. Even in the Deuteronomic revision of this law, which both extended the right of freedom to female slaves and also made it easier to accept (Deut. 15.12-18), the ceremony remained an entirely private affair. The pierced ear would, of course, have indicated to the general public the slave's official position. This would explain why no document was ever needed to certify that position.

This ceremony is another example of family law. The courts are not involved because the slave has no legal status. He was his master's property to do with as he liked. Whether the slave renounced his right to freedom or not did not affect the welfare of the local community at large. It therefore remained a private matter between the master and the slave over which the community as a whole exercised no jurisdiction.

But exceptionally where there was a threat to public order the courts would intervene even in the case of those who had no legal status. This would always have been the case where the head of the house murdered a member of his household. Thus Exod. 21.20-21 provides for the prosecution of a master for the murder of his slave if the latter died as a

---

26. The Book of the Covenant indicates that there were both sanctuary *ᵉlōhîm* (Exod. 22.7-8) and domestic *ᵉlōhîm* (Exod. 21.6). While the former were resorted to in civil property dispute cases involving the community where an oath was required before the priests, the latter were used in family law. Exactly the same distinction is found in the Nuzi material (cf. Gordon, 'אלהים in its Reputed Meaning of Rulers, Judges', *JBL* 54 [1935], pp. 139-44; Draffkorn, 'Ilāni/Elohim', pp. 216-24). Cf. further Phillips, *AICL*, pp. 60-62, 136-37.

result of a disciplinary beating, though to be murder the death had to occur during or immediately after the beating which caused the death. If the slave survived a day or two, then his death was attributed to his own internal weakness. The law presumes that no master would want to deprive himself of his own property. Similarly though a slave could normally not have brought an action for damages for assault against his master, as the only person who would be deemed to have suffered loss by the injury would be the master himself, whose property the slave was, where the master caused permanent injury to the slave, then he had to release him (Exod. 21.26-27). This was in effect a payment of damages for tort, being the purchase price of the slave. The slave's freedom would have been enforced by the courts who would have first determined that the injury was permanent. In both these instances the courts would intervene to curtail the master's absolute authority under family law and make him exceptionally liable for crime and tort in respect of a person who had no legal status simply because it was not in the public's interest to have such a vicious member in its midst. He was a danger to the community, and must therefore be punished, for on another occasion his loss of temper might be vented on a free Israelite. Once more, Israelite law indicates that the head of the house had no power of life or death over dependent members in the household. It may be assumed, though other ancient Near Eastern codes are silent on the matter, that elsewhere the slave would not have been entitled to such protection.

III

Children were, of course, like wives and slaves under their father's protection having no legal status. While a daughter would remain her father's personal property until marriage, a son would with puberty become a free adult.[27] But until then it seems certain that were he to suffer any injury then it would have been his father who would have been compensated by the payment of damages. In view of this one would expect to find that like divorce and making slavery permanent, the adoption of a child was also part of family law taking place in the home.

The Old Testament itself contains no laws governing adoption. But considering its widespread practice throughout the ancient Near East, it is inconceivable that it was not also undertaken in Israel. Its purpose would

---

27. L. Köhler, *Hebrew Man* (London: SCM Press, 1956), pp. 87-88.

have been to provide a childless man with a son who would both bury his father on death, and also inherit his name and property.[28]

The procedure for adoption has then to be gleaned from evidence outside the legal corpus of the Old Testament. In the first place, it seems probable that like divorce adoption was in fact effected through the pronouncement of a simple legal formula. This can be deduced from two passages dealing with Israel's understanding of her king's relationship to Yahweh in which he was undoubtedly seen as God's adopted son. Thus in the original account of the institution of the Davidic covenant, Yahweh says of David, 'I will be his father, and he shall be my son' (2 Sam. 7.14), which is again mirrored in Ps. 2.7 where Yahweh addresses the king: 'You are my son, to-day I have begotten you'. Such an adoption formula must have been in regular use for it to have been taken over in this way.

Secondly it appears that the pronouncement of this legal formula was either preceded or followed by a specific outward sign, namely the placing of the prospective adoptive child either on or between the adopter's knees. This can be inferred from certain examples of adoption within the family in the patriarchal narratives in Genesis whereby a child's status, and therefore his right to inheritance, was altered through adoption by a relative. Thus Rachel adopts Jacob's two sons by her maid Bilhah by having them born upon her knees (Gen. 30.3-8), and Jacob in adopting his grandsons Ephraim and Manasseh has the boys upon his knees (Gen. 48.5, 12). Genesis 50.23 also notes that the children of Manasseh's son Makir were born on Joseph's knees. Of course to be adopted by the mother, as in the case of Rachel, is in no way to be compared with adoption by the father, for the former was merely a means whereby a barren woman could be given the status of motherhood. The child was still that of the father whether the mother adopted him or not.[29]

These two parts to the ceremony would therefore confirm that adoption, as in other cases of family law, took place in the home, and was a unilateral act of the adopter. It would also explain why no mention of adoption occurs in the legal sections of the Old Testament, for as part of family law it did not concern the community at large, and therefore no resort was made to the courts. It has already been shown that the same

28. I. Mendelsohn, 'The Family in the Ancient Near East', *BA* (11), 1948, pp. 24-40 (38-39), argues that originally in the ancient Near East adoption was undertaken for economic reasons, providing a cheap labour force. With the later increase in the number of slaves, adoption became much rarer.

29. Pedersen, *Israel*, p. 258.

situation also applied with regard to divorce, for while the practice itself was alluded to in the Deuteronomic legislation, the actual mechanism whereby it was effected is nowhere set out. The ceremony whereby slavery became permanent is only referred to in the Book of the Covenant (Exod. 21.5-6) because it arose specifically from an amendment to earlier law (Exod. 21.2-4).

The only apparent instance of the adoption of an adult rather than a child is Abraham's adoption of his slave Eliezer (Gen. 15.2-3), concerning which comparison has been made with the Nuzi material.[30] Since a slave had no legal status, his adoption would in any event have fallen within the sphere of family law. It would seem that such an adoption was conditional on his master having no subsequent children of his own (Gen. 15.4). There is, however, no actual evidence that this Mesopotamian custom of adopting a slave as one's heir was ever practised in Israel itself, and comparison with the Nuzi material may not, in fact, be justified.[31] Whether in normal cases of adoption the adoptive tie could be severed, and if so on what conditions, we cannot know.[32]

But before leaving the law of adoption, it ought to be noted that as in the case of husbands and masters, parents' authority was similarly severely limited by law. Thus even though repudiation of parental authority carried the death penalty (Exod. 21.15, 17; Deut. 21.18-21), the parents themselves could not take the law into their own hands, but had to secure a criminal conviction in the courts in the usual manner.[33] On a verdict of guilty, execution would take place by communal stoning. Parents had no power of life or death over their children.

To this assertion, there might at first appear to be an exception in Jephthah's execution of his daughter (Judg. 11.30-40) and Jonathan's threatened execution by Saul (1 Sam. 14.24-46). Both these instances result from a vow that in certain circumstances death would be inflicted. But while the point of both stories is that it is the child of the person making the vow who comes within the scope of the curse, in fact it could have been anyone. Accordingly these examples tell us nothing specific

---

30. C.H. Gordon, 'Biblical Customs and the Nuzu Tablets', *BA* 3 (1940), pp. 1-12 (2-3); W.H. Rossell, 'New Testament Adoption—Graeco-Roman or Semitic?', *JBL* 71 (1952), pp. 233-34.

31. De Vaux, *Ancient Israel*, p. 51; idem, *The Early History of Israel*, pp. 236-37, 249.

32. Cf. LH 185–93.

33. Phillips, *AICL*, pp. 80-82.

about the authority of a parent over his child, but rather point to the power of the oath under general customary law.[34]

IV

Finally both betrothal and marriage are part of family law. An example of the former occurs in 1 Sam. 18.21. There Saul pronounces a formal declaration over David which secures his betrothal to Michal, 'Today you shall be my son-in-law'.[35] The only outstanding issue is the bride price. David knows that he cannot possibly provide a sufficient *mōhar* to wed a king's daughter. But Saul, hoping to secure David's death at the hands of the Philistines, provides a way in which David can marry Michal, a bride price of 100 Philistine foreskins (1 Sam. 18.25). While it was normal for the bride price to be a monetary sum, this was by no means always the case (cf. Gen. 29.18). Nor is there anything in 1 Sam. 18 to indicate that Saul is acting other than as a father disposing of his daughter as was his right, and it must therefore be assumed that Saul, although king, is following the normal practice of family law.[36] Once more then we find the head of the house acting unilaterally without recourse to the courts to bring about a change in legal status which as in divorce and adoption is effected by a specific spoken formula.

Hosea 2.21-22 also appears to contain an echo of a betrothal formula in Yahweh's address to Israel, 'I will betroth you to me for ever'.[37] *lᵉ'ōlām* ('for ever') is here used in a legal sense.[38] It similarly appears in the Aramaic marriage contracts from Elephantine.[39] The bride price is then

34. For a discussion of the possibility of child sacrifice in ancient Israel, cf. W. Eichrodt, *Theology of the Old Testament*, I (OTL; London: SCM Press, 1961), pp. 148-52, and H. Ringgren, *Israelite Religion* (London: SPCK, 1966), pp. 174-75, and on sacrifice to Molech, Phillips, *AICL*, pp. 128-29. It is possible that the story of Saul's curse in 1 Sam. 14.24-46 is another Samuel-Saul conflict story (*ibid.*, p. 55 n. 12).

35. This much is clear whatever *bištayim* means; cf. H.P. Smith, *The Books of Samuel* (ICC; Edinburgh: T. & T. Clark, 1912), p. 174; Hertzberg, *I and II Samuel*, p. 159.

36. While the father could make a unilateral declaration of betrothal in respect of his daughter, marriage would more often have taken place after negotiations between the respective parents of the bridegroom and bride, the bridegroom's parents initiating the discussion (Gen. 34.4; Judg. 14.2). See further Neufeld, *Ancient Hebrew*, pp. 135ff.

37. Falk, *Hebrew*, pp. 147-48.

38. Wolff, *Hosea*, p. 52.

39. R. Yaron, *Law of the Aramaic Papyri* (Oxford: Clarendon Press, 1961), p. 47.

spelt out, *ṣedeq* ('righteousness'), *mišpāṭ* ('justice'), *ḥesed* ('steadfast love'), *raḥ^amîm* ('mercy'), and *'^emūnâ* ('faithfulness'), and the verses end with the consummation of the marriage, 'You shall know the Lord'.[40]

Similarly in Tob. 7.12-14, Sarah's father, Raguel, pronounces Tobias to be Sarah's wife, but in this case seals his declaration with a marriage contract. Oddly the Old Testament makes no specific mention of any written marriage contract,[41] though such contracts have been preserved from the Jewish colony at Elephantine.[42] In contrast LH 128 provides that a marriage was invalid unless concluded by formal written contract, and MAL A 34, 36 similarly indicate that a marriage contract was needed in Assyria.[43] This was also the case at Nuzi.[44] Since formal written declarations of divorce were common practice in the Deuteronomic period (Deut. 24.1-3; Jer. 3.8) it would be surprising if written marriage contracts were not also by then part of normal legal procedure, though whether they were actually required for the marriage to be valid cannot be determined.

These further instances of family law indicate the considerable legal power which the head of the house wielded. His daughter was his property to dispose of as he willed. Thus where she was seduced, the father was entitled to damages in tort for the loss of the *mōhar* which he could not now expect to receive, and he could also refuse to allow the daughter's marriage to her lover (Exod. 22.15-16). Later legislation both fixed the damages payable for seduction[45] and apparently compelled the lover to marry the girl whom he was subsequently prohibited from divorcing (Deut. 22.28-29).[46] Clearly these amending provisions were designed as a deterrent, at any rate in the case of the daughter of a poor man. Why the father's right to withhold the girl from her lover was abandoned is not clear, though it is possible that it was to ensure that he should not subsequently seek to pass her off as a virgin (Deut. 22.13-21). Although he

---

40. Mays, *Hosea*, pp. 50-53; Wolff, *op. cit.*, p. 52.

41. Neufeld, *Ancient Hebrew*, pp. 152ff. There is no certainty that Mal. 2.14 refers to a written marriage contract. Cf. Ezek. 16.8; Prov. 2.17.

42. Yaron, *Aramaic Papyri*, pp. 44-64.

43. *ANET*, pp. 171, 183.

44. Mendelsohn, 'The Family', pp. 24-40.

45. 50 shekels probably represents an average bride price (cf. Exod. 21.32). See further Driver, *Deuteronomy*, p. 258; Driver and Miles, *The Assyrian Laws*, pp. 62-65.

46. For a discussion on the relationship between Exod. 22.15-16 and Deut. 22.28-29, see *AICL*, pp. 112-14; Weinfeld, *Deuteronomy*, pp. 284-88. Weinfeld argues that in contrast to the Book of the Covenant, the Deuteronomic amendment is concerned with the welfare of the girl rather than the father's financial interests.

could dispose of his daughter at will, as in other family law cases, there is never any suggestion that the father had power of life or death over her. She was an asset for whom he was entitled to expect proper compensation for his loss, but his legal action was limited to damages for any injury suffered. This is in stark contrast to MAL A 56 which provides that if the virgin has consented in her seduction then her father shall treat her as he wishes,[47] which may well include the possibility of killing her.[48]

At first sight it might be thought that Gen. 38.24, although dealing with a daughter-in-law rather than a daughter, constituted an exception to the limit on the powers of the *paterfamilias*. But in the first place this is not a case of family law, but of adultery, for Tamar is regarded as betrothed to Shelah rather than as a widow living in her father's house (Gen. 38.11). And second, it is by no means certain that the *paterfamilias* had such personal power even in patriarchal times. Certainly the normal punishment for adultery, as for other crimes, was stoning by the community (Lev. 20.10; Deut. 22.22). And as a crime, the matter was taken out of the hands of the husband, the prosecution, conviction and execution all being a community undertaking. But it has been argued that Gen. 28 reflects an earlier situation when the paterfamilias could act unilaterally without recourse to the courts.[49] However, such an argument should be regarded with extreme caution for nowhere else in the Old Testament is it indicated that an individual had power to execute another for adultery.[50] Further the only two other enactments which specify burning as the prescribed penalty both occur in the Holiness Code, Lev. 20.14 requiring burning for incest with one's mother-in-law, and Lev. 21.9 for prostitution by a priest's daughter. Both these provisions are exilic additions to Israelite law and reflect similar enactments in LH 157 and 110.[51] Further, it has been suggested that Judah's order to have Tamar burnt, issued before he has even heard her defence, may also be a priestly gloss reflecting the Babylonian form of punishment now incorporated into the Holiness Code.[52] Tamar had acted as a common prostitute.

---

47. *ANET*, p. 185.

48. Driver and Miles, *The Assyrian Laws*, p. 60.

49. Kornfeld, 'L'adultère', p. 95.

50. It was the Deuteronomic reform which first required the woman as well as her lover to be executed. Before that she was probably deemed to have been forced and her husband would merely have divorced her.

51. *ANET*, pp. 172, 110.

52. Driver and Miles, *The Babylonian Laws*, I, pp. 495-96.

In conclusion, then, in Israel betrothal and marriage were effected unilaterally by the father of the girl pronouncing the appropriate formula in
the home, and were no concern of the courts, nor do provisions concerning
betrothal or marriage appear in the law collections. The only exception
concerns the practice of levitate marriage (Gen. 38) which was clearly
disliked, and an attempt made to regulate it (Deut. 25.5-10), before it was
finally prohibited (Lev. 18.16; 20.21; 22.13; Num. 27.8-11).[53] But even
though Deut. 25.5-6 provided for the public humiliation of the levir before
the local court,[54] the court itself still had no power to enforce the marriage
against the levir's will nor to punish him for his refusal, for marriage
remained a matter of family law and therefore outside its jurisdiction.[55]

Perhaps I may now sum up this essay by making three points: (1) I hope
I have said enough to show that in addition to crime and tort, there was
another category of law in ancient Israel, which I have termed family law;
(2) unlike crime and tort, under this head there was no recourse to the
courts. Instead family law was administered in the home by the head of the
household acting unilaterally. His action would not disrupt the peace of
the local community; (3) but in spite of the absolute authority of the head
of the household in cases of family law, he nonetheless had no power of
life or death over those under his protection.

---

53. Porter, *The Extended Family*, p. 19, argues that Lev. 20.21 merely prohibits
marriage with one's sister-in-law when she had *already* borne a son to one's deceased
brother.

54. Leggett, *The Levirate*, pp. 55-62, suggests that this procedure was designed to
enable the woman to terminate the possibility of levirate marriage. She thereby became
free from any claims on her by the levir and in full control of her affairs. Leggett also
suggests that by the ceremony of the shoe, she might be barring the brother from any
further right to her dead husband's estate.

55. A. Phillips, *Deuteronomy* (CBC; Cambridge: Cambridge University Press,
1973), pp. 168-69.

Chapter 7

ANIMALS AND THE TORAH

The humanitarian outlook of the legislators who compiled the book of Deuteronomy has often been noted. No one could fail to be moved by their overriding concern for the defenceless in society. Those without legal rights and so without any kind of protection from the state—the widow, orphan and resident alien, together with the landless poor—were held to have an unalienable right to the charity of those who enjoyed prosperity. Examples of such charity include the law of release of debts (Deut. 15.1-11) which provided that all debts of fellow-Israelites were to be cancelled every seventh year. Even if that year were imminent, the rich were still enjoined to lend to those in need though there was virtually no chance of repayment being made. Further no interest was permitted on such loans (Deut. 23.20-21). Another example is the provision that what is forgotten in the harvesting of cereals, olives and vines is to be left for the widow, orphan and alien (Deut. 24.19-22). The laws on pledges again seek to protect the poorest members of Israelite society from loss of the basic necessities of life (Deut. 24.6, 10-13, 17-18). Wages had to be paid daily before sunset lest the labourers went hungry that night (Deut. 24.14-15). Even travellers were allowed to sustain themselves on their journeys from the vineyards and fields through which they passed (Deut. 23.25-26).

The humanitarian outlook of the Deuteronomic legislators was not, though, confined to the poor and defenceless in society—it extended to animals too. For instance, Deut. 25.4 enacts that an ox engaged in threshing is not to be prevented from feeding itself from the grain its hooves had beaten out. Like the daily labourer in the field, or the traveller, the working animal was entitled to its sustenance and would work the better for it.

Deuteronomy 22.1-3 orders an Israelite not to ignore a lost domestic animal, but to look after it until claimed by its owner. Otherwise some harm might befall the animal. Further Deut. 22.4 adds that if a domestic animal has fallen in the road, the owner is to be helped to get it up and so avoid injury. While one purpose of these laws was to ensure the protection of the property of a fellow Israelite, the other was to prevent unnecessary suffering by animals. Indeed the older version of this law contained in Exod. 23.4-5 specifically deals with animals of 'your enemy' which in the context means an opponent in a law suit. Even such a situation does not absolve an Israelite from his duty to alleviate suffering of animals.

Humanitarian concerns and concern for the environment are, of course, closely related. The Deuteronomic legislators enacted that when a city was under siege fruit-bearing trees were not to be felled for use in siege works but left to supply food after the siege was over (Deut. 20.19-20). As the legislators movingly enact: 'The trees of the field are not men that you should besiege them'. Similarly when a bird's nest is found with fledglings or eggs in it and the mother on the nest, the Israelite is not to take both mother and young or eggs. The mother is to be allowed to go free so that she can lay again and provide more food (Deut. 22.6-7).

It has often been argued that those whom we call the Deuteronomic legislators come from that class of Hebrew professionals known as the wise. The Hebrews understood by wisdom the ability to see the order in things, how one thing related to another, how nature, science and society functioned. They looked at relationships, objects and ideas, and tried to discern their pattern, structure, rule and order. Their concern was that people should be able to live the best and fullest lives and not come to any mishap. The wise were then early scientists, psychologists and sociologists. Believing that God had created a natural order, they set out to determine how the world worked. Provided people complied with that order which God had determined in creation, their lives would be prosperous and happy.

Like modern civil servants, the activity of the wise extended to the political sphere as they serviced the royal bureaucracy at Jerusalem. It was here in the pre-exilic period that at distinct times in Israel's history laws were grouped together and issued in the collections we now know as the Book of the Covenant (Exod. 21.1–23.19), the Holiness Code (Lev. 16–26) and Deuteronomy. These collections were not law codes but rather sermons to the nation: they could never have secured the running of the state. Old Testament law is not an all-embracing system concerning every aspect of life: rather it is as the Deuteronomists recognized, an injunction to do what is right and good (Deut. 6.18) of which some examples are given in the specific legislation which follows (Deut. 12–26).

Nor were all laws enforceable through the normal judicial machinery of the courts. Indeed many, such as the laws of charity, simply appealed to the conscience of those addressed. It is their responsibility alone to work out for themselves how best they can obey.

How far such laws were in fact followed we cannot know. Increasingly Hebrew legislation becomes more and more idealistic. But in their collections the wise indicate that law for the Hebrew is not merely what is legally enforceable, but rather reflects what is the nature of God. So while the Hebrew word for law, *tōrâ*, originally meant an instruction or ruling of which examples can be found in Hag. 2.11-13, it came under the Deuteronomists to indicate the very will of God himself, reflecting his character. And that character had shown in the choice of foreign slaves as his elect people God's concern for the poor and dispossessed.

Human nature being what it is, it is clear that the charitable laws were not readily obeyed. They had therefore from earliest times to be supported by motive clauses which themselves reflect God's nature. So Exod. 22.20 supports the injunction not to wrong a stranger or oppress him by appealing to the sympathy of those addressed in reminding them that they were once strangers in the land of Egypt. Further the command not to afflict the widow or orphan in Exod. 22.21-23 is backed by an appeal to fear: God will punish any who disobey this injunction by himself securing their death with the result that their wives will be widows, and their children orphans. God is both sympathetic to the needy but also a righteous God who will ensure that his punishment fits the crime.

But it is the Deuteronomists who set out a far more fundamental reason for obeying the humanitarian injunctions designed to protect the poor and defenceless. Not only would such charity prevent violent action being taken by those who had nothing to lose: it also provided the means for stimulating economic activity from which the wealthy themselves would ultimately benefit. So following the law on release of debts which at face value seems a kind of economic suicide, Deut. 15.4-5 sagely comments: 'But there will be no poor among you (for the Lord will bless you in the land which the Lord God gives you for an inheritance to possess) if only you will obey the voice of the Lord your God, being careful to do all this commandment which I command you this day'.

The Deuteronomists' recognition that obedience to this apparent unprofitable injunction of torah would lead to material blessing is not then pietistic hope but sound economic sense—and this applies both to the muzzled ox, the mother bird with her young, and fruit trees in time of war, as well as the poor and needy. Hebrew law has then something to say to contemporary politicians consumed by national greed both about aid to third world countries including their crippling debts as well as supporting the concerns of the Greens. As the wise knew there was a natural order which God had ordained in creation. People's prosperity depended on the discovery of that order and complying with it. For it was God's will that people should enjoy the creation which he had so richly provided. Had he not brought the liberated slaves to a land flowing with milk and honey where he hoped they would luxuriate? It was failure to obey torah with its injunctions to support the poor that led to exile in Babylon.

But how are people to enjoy that creation, particularly in relation to the animals? What is God's purpose for them in his scheme of things, and how are people to relate to them?

We have already noted the Deuteronomic legislators' humanitarian and environmental concerns. But is there a closer connection between humans and the animal world? There can be no doubt from the *mišpāṭîm*, that series of legal precedents drawn up in Exod. 21.12–22.16, that animals were regarded as the personal property of their owners and were dealt with under the general principles of Hebrew property law. These required that any damage or loss to personal property should be compensated for by payment of damages restoring the injured party to the position he was in before the injury occurred. So Exod. 21.33-34 enacts: 'When a man leaves a pit open, or when a man digs a pit and does not cover it, and an ox or an ass falls into it, the owner of the pit shall make it good; he shall give money to its owner, and the dead beast shall be his'. Clearly were the owner of the dead animal allowed to keep it, he would be better off than before the injury occurred. Where no one is liable, the effects of the injury are shared. So Exod. 21.35-36 provides: 'When one man's ox hurts another's, so that it dies, then they shall sell the live ox and divide the price of it, and the dead beast also they shall divide. However, if one party already knew his ox to be dangerous, then he must accept total liability for the injury, or if it is known that the ox has been accustomed to gore in the past, and its owner has not kept it in, he shall pay ox for ox, and the dead beast shall be his.'

These provisions do not consider the possibility that the animals involved might be of very different values. It is an entirely arbitrary procedure which is outlined here in which the assumption is made that one ox is as valuable as another. No doubt the fact that the law provided a quick settlement of the dispute was itself an important element in accepting its rough and ready nature. But there is no reason to assume that when there was a serious discrepancy in value between the two beasts, pecuniary adjustments could not have been made with the aid of assessors who are themselves mentioned in another case of injury in Exod. 21.22. The principle of the law is plain. The injured party was to be restored to the position he was in before the injury occurred.

The law, however, recognized that in the case of theft of animals simple compensation was not a sufficient deterrent. In this case punitive damages were awarded, five oxen for an ox and four sheep for a sheep (Exod. 21.37). While this penalty might deter the poor, it proved no deterrent to the rich as the famous story told by Nathan to David following the king's adultery with Bathsheba and murder of Uriah indicates (2 Sam. 12.1-6). For the rich man of that story only to have compensated the poor man for loss of his beloved ewe lamb by punitive damages under civil law was entirely inadequate. As David exclaims, he ought to be treated like a murderer and suffer the penalty of the criminal law—execution. The irony, of course, is that David has not committed the civil offence of theft of animals: he has committed the crimes of adultery and murder and does indeed deserve the death penalty.

As far the law was concerned animals were then part of a person's personal property and remedies for injury lay under the civil law. Thus Exodus sets out further provisions for the loss of an animal in another's charge (Exod. 22.9-12). While normally the shepherd would have been responsible to the owner for loss including theft, if he could show that the domestic animal had been killed by a wild beast by producing the indigestible left-overs, he was absolved from liability. With the probable exception of adultery, the earliest Hebrew sexual law concerns bestiality. Exodus 22.18 enacts: 'Whoever lies with a beast shall be put to death'. However the concern of the law was not with the dignity of the animal but more probably with the practice of seeking union with a deity through sexual intercourse with an animal subsequently sacrificed. No precise evidence for such a practice has been found in Canaan. However, the fact that Hittite law specifically forbids copulation with cattle, sheep and pigs and not horses or mules is held to be due to the former's status as sacred animals.

Exodus 23.12 enacts that the sabbath provisions apply not only to humans but domestic animals as well. Both are to have rest from routine daily labour. This does not mean that neither humans nor animals were to undertake any activity that day. As the incident in 2 Kgs 4.22-24 indicates, the reason for the husband's annoyance that one of his beasts and a servant must be released for his wife's sudden journey to the prophet is that she is to make it on a weekday and not the sabbath when such expeditions were normally undertaken. The purpose of the sabbath law was not to secure a day of total inactivity, but rather to act as a declaration of political sovereignty. The Hebrews were a free people who could order their working life without any restraint placed on them by other powers. This is in stark contrast to their admitted origins as Pharaoh's slaves in Egypt. Now they only owed allegiance to Yahweh who had released them from such slavery. Domestic animals, servants and aliens were all to enjoy their freedom.

I have already referred to the goring ox in connection with injury to another ox. But more central to this essay is the law on injury to persons by such a beast. Exodus 21.28 enacts: 'When an ox gores a man or woman to death, the ox shall be stoned, and its flesh shall not be eaten: but the owner of the ox shall be clear'. In my view this provision extends the law on murder to include animals. Exodus 21.12 has already ruled: 'Whoever strikes a man so that he dies shall be put to death'. Similarly an ox which gores a man is to be executed in the normal way by stoning which would have been carried out by the local community. Its flesh is regarded as taboo and must not be eaten for blood guilt rests upon it.

Before I go any further, I ought to pause to take note of the Hebrews' understanding of blood. For them life was the gift of God to whom it belonged (Jer. 38.16). The *nepeš*—that is, the life force or vitality of humans and animals—was held to have its seat in the blood. Consequently it could never be appropriated by a human. Yet this is what the murderer did (2 Sam. 4.11). He literally took possession of the victim's blood. This explains the ironic reply of Cain when God questions him about Abel's whereabouts (Gen. 4.9). To God's, 'Where is Abel your brother?', Cain replies, 'I do not know; am I my brother's keeper?' In fact of course he was: he had literally taken control of Abel's blood from Yahweh to whom it rightly belonged. Hence God's answer, 'What have you done? The voice of your brother's blood is crying to me from the ground' (Gen. 4.10). Abel's blood seeks release from Cain. Normally this could only be achieved by the execution of the murderer which explains why the ox who has killed a man must also be executed. While normally only the ox would have been executed, if it could be shown that the owner knew that it had a propensity to gore, then he too would be executed as a co-murderer (Exod. 21.29). Later this was modified by allowing the owner to pay compensation—though the ox was still treated as a murderer (Exod. 21.30). This applied too in the case of an ox goring a slave to death, though here the compensation was fixed, presumably at the average price for a slave (Exod. 21.32). Nonetheless, even though a slave was treated as his master's personal property, the ox was regarded as his murderer. In every case where the ox caused a man's death, it was executed.

It is time now to leave the law collections and turn instead to the opening chapters of Genesis. The source J, probably written at the time of the united monarchy of David and Solomon also by the wise at the royal court, is responsible for the Garden of Eden narrative. This describes how in the search for a companion for the man, the animals were made and brought to him for naming.

Two things are worth noting. First, the animals are formed by God in exactly the same way as the man himself—out of the ground. Like the man they are earthy and to the earth they shall return. J recognized that it was from the first God's intention that the man and the animals should share both a common origin and a common destiny. Neither were intended to be immortal. But second, the animals are not equal with the man. He alone is given responsibility for tilling the garden, ordering God's creation. So the man names the animals thereby indicating that he has power over them. Here we see reflected J's background among the wise in his description of a recognized order to the animal world. Indeed Solomon himself was said to have excelled in such matters being able to specify every variety of plant and beast (1 Kgs 4.33-34). So in spite of the man's natural affinity with the animals as fellow creatures of earth, no suitable partner is found. Thus J rules out any thought of sexual union between the human and animal worlds reflected as we have seen in the prohibition against bestiality in Exodus probably dating from the same period.

Dominion over the animals means for J that it is natural for humans that they should use them both for food and sacrifice to God. Indeed the two are linked because in order to eat meat the animal had to be taken to the local sanctuary for slaughter where its blood was drained from it by being poured out on the altar and so returned to God to whom it belonged. Later following the centralization of all worship at Jerusalem by Josiah and the consequent destruction of the local sanctuaries (2 Kgs 23) this duty became impracticable, and the killing of animals for food was secularized, but the blood had first to be poured out on the earth (Deut. 12.20-21). Both Abel (Gen. 4.4) and Noah (Gen. 8.20-22) offer animal sacrifices to God, who in the case of Noah's sacrifice is described in very human terms as unashamedly enjoying it to the full.

This is in striking contrast to the P narrative written in exile in Babylon which does not envisage any sacrifice being made until after the giving of the law to Moses at Sinai (Exod. 25-31). So while in P's version of the flood narrative Noah embarks with pairs of every animal, bird and reptile (Gen. 6.19), J lays down that the vessel shall be filled with seven pairs of clean animals and one pair of unclean (Gen. 7.2). For immediately on disembarkation, specimens of every clean animal and bird are sacrificed as a thank offering. In order to ensure the survival of the clean species, more than one pair is required in the ark, whereas unclean animals could be restricted to a pair. For P no distinction between clean and unclean animals was necessary. Similarly in the patriarchal narratives although in the J passages the patriarchs freely sacrifice at different Canaanite sanctuaries, in the P stories no sacrifices are offered.

But more important for the purposes of this essay is P's assertion that both humans and animals were created to be vegetarian. This is quite explicitly stated in P's seven-day creation account: 'And God said, behold I have given you every plant yielding seed which is upon the face of all the earth, and every tree with seed in its fruit, you shall have them for food. And to every beast of the earth, and to every bird of the air, and to everything that creeps on the earth, everything that has the breath of life, I have given every green plant for food. And it was so. And God saw everything that he had made, and behold it was very good' (Gen. 1.29-31). What P perceives is an awareness that the killing of living beings for food by other living beings is deeply offensive to the very nature of the God who created both with his own life force. Animals and humans share a common solidarity in that both owe their existence to God alone. One ought not to be at the disposal of the other. That cannot be what God had in mind when he commanded the man to exercise dominion over the animals.

But the J narrative upon which P was building his own account followed on P's idyllic picture of creation with a succession of stories which showed how that idyll had been destroyed as people's sin spread further and further throughout God's creation. For P writing in exile in Babylon the world had long ceased to be ordered and peaceful as God intended. The slaughter of animals for food was necessary, and following the flood narrative P describes God as permitting it: 'And God blessed Noah and his sons, and said to them, Be fruitful and multiply, and fill the earth. The fear of you and the dread of you shall be upon every beast of the earth, and upon every bird of the air, upon everything that creeps on the ground and all the fish of the sea: into your hand they are delivered. Every moving thing that lives shall be food for you: and as I gave you the green plants I give you everything. Only you shall not eat flesh with its life, that is its blood' (Gen. 9.1-4).

In recognizing the reality of this situation and allowing humans to eat meat, P was not abandoning his first principles. The end of vegetarianism was a necessary evil, though even here humans are not given an entirely free hand: the blood of the animal must first be drained from it and returned to God its true owner. In spite of his apparent compromise, P is not afraid to draw attention to that uncomfortable tension in which humans live—a tension which contradicts their true nature as conceived by God.

This discussion on blood leads P on to reiterate the ancient principles of the law of murder. Clearly he has J's account of Cain's murder of Abel in mind (Gen. 4). As has already been noted, when a person was killed, the murderer was thought to gain possession of the blood which cried to God for release from its captor (Gen. 4.9-10: Job 16.18). P pictures Yahweh as the Seeker of that blood which has been taken out of his control: 'For your lifeblood I will surely require a reckoning: of every beast I will require it and of man: of every man's brother I will require the life of man. Whoever sheds the blood of man, by man shall his blood he shed: for God made man in his own image' (Gen. 9.5-7). The reason that the discussion on murder follows on the concession of eating meat, but not the blood, is that deep in P's psyche is the recognition that killing animals is akin to murder: it can so easily be fuelled by blood lust. In emphasizing the sanctity of a person's life, P indirectly heightens the tension in the granting of permission to kill animals for food. It cannot be seen as natural but a mere necessity. Perhaps one day things might again be different.

So as the animals accompany Noah and his family from the ark, God reminds the whole of the animal creation that even if vegetarianism is now no longer possible, nonetheless God's intention in creating humans in his own image (Gen. 1.26) remains valid. By this God meant that humans were literally to reflect him in his world which the gift of torah enabled them to do. Humankind's rule over creation is not to be one of exploitation but of ensuring that God's will prevailed. Like J, P saw that there was a proper distance between God and humans symbolized by the two trees in Eden. For unlike God, humans were both mortal and could not know good and evil, that is the kind of knowledge which God alone had. But P saw that there was also a proper nearness of God and humans: alone of all creation they were made for communion with God: they alone were responsible to him—indeed they were indispensable to him, if God's purposes were to be fulfilled.

In Gen. 9.1-7 P seeks to confirm that in spite of the catastrophe of the flood, God's promise and blessing to humans at creation stands. They are still to have total dominion over the created order save that they must continue to recognize the ancient principle that all blood belongs to God, the creator of life. In other words in the awful conditions of exile, with the whole question of Israel's future in doubt, P asserts that she is still the elect people. Despite her failure, God will not let Israel go but continues to bless her. This explains why Gen. 9.1-7 frames its discussion of the eating of animals and murder with the repeated command to be fruitful and multiply. It was through Israel alone that God's purposes could be fulfilled.

And those purposes from the call of Abraham onwards were that paradise should be restored. But it was not the paradise of Eden but the paradise of Eden transformed by the creation account in which humans and animals lived together without fear and in *šālōm*—peace. This vision is contained in the Messianic prophecy of Isa. 11.1-9. Although often attributed to the eighth-century prophet himself; this oracle, both on grounds of content and its redactional position in the context of the book, belongs to the postexilic age. It assumes that the Davidic dynasty has been reduced to a mere stump (11.1). It is best understood as an oracle of hope indicating that the deposed Davidic king will be restored, thus fulfilling the promise of Isa. 9.1-6. However Isa. 11 goes a stage further than the kingdom of justice and righteousness prophesied in Isa. 9. It now carries a remote eschatological hope which extends the just rule of the king to include the re-establishing of that very order of nature as originally intended by God. Following the setting up of a just social order by the messianic ruler, nature herself is to resume her true order. No longer will there be any distinction between wild and domestic animals. Instead all will live together in a perfect harmony in which small children will be guaranteed their safety even from that ancient enemy the snake. Indeed in the summary of this oracle echoed in Isa. 65.25, dust is designated as the snake's food—again indicating an end to the hostility between the animal world and humans. Postexilic theology thus contains both a vision of an idyllic past and of its resumption in the future when humans and the animal world live in peaceful harmony. Is this an idle dream?

It is time to draw together conclusions from this study of animals in *Torah*. For there is no point to the study of scripture unless the ever living word of God is allowed to speak to our own times. We shall have little difficulty in supporting *Torah's* humanitarian attitude to animals: indeed we rather pride ourselves on this when comparing ourselves with other nations. Yet there are aspects of contemporary life from factory farming to hunting and shooting which should give us pause for thought. Are the Deuteronomic economic considerations relevant to our farming methods? While big game hunting has given way to concern for the preservation of the species, can we be quite certain that our traditional hunts and large shoots contain no element of blood lust? But it is the surprisingly little known and widely ignored injunction of the P writer that disturbs the most. Are we simply to accept that the eating of meat is a necessity—even a necessary evil? Is the Utopian picture of our intended origin and the prophetic vision of its return in the eschatological age mere pious dreaming? Certainly evolution with its observation of the survival of the fittest has taught us that there never was such an idyllic period in the past. Is it an illusion to contemplate, let alone work for, its realization in the future? Introduce any children to a farmyard and then let them know that you have killed and eaten the animals they have seen there, and there will be utter and automatic revulsion on their part. Is this an instance of what Jesus meant when he said: 'Truly, I say to you, unless you turn and become like children, you will never enter the kingdom of heaven' (Matt. 18.3)?

So far the only world humans have known is one in which they have had to fight for their survival. The killing of domestic animals for meat and of wild and domestic animals for clothing as well as wild animals for protection, has enabled them to develop to their present advanced state. Even now medical experimentation on animals ensures humans a longer life.

Yet do we not see that the prophetic vision may not be an idle dream? The killing of animals is no longer necessary for human survival: medical experimentation may itself become redundant: there are many cases of the domestication of wild animals. Of course it is a long view. Paradise is not around the corner whether in the realm of political and economic justice or a return to the primaeval golden age of natural harmony. But just as people of goodwill continue to work for that prophetic vision of peace and justice described elsewhere in Isaiah and Micah as turning swords into ploughshares (Isa. 2.4; Mic. 4.3), and continue to work despite the many setbacks which they encounter, should not they also do the same for a restoration of that paradisal world of nature in which God said, 'Behold I have given you every plant yielding seed which is upon the face of all the earth and every tree with seed in its fruit, you shall have them for food' (Gen. 1.29).

At the moment of Israel's defeat and total collapse resulting in exile in a heathen land, her theologians gave humankind an idyllic picture of the life which God intended politically, economically, and in the realm of nature. Both the political and economic vision raises awkward questions for many of us used to privilege and wealth: the vision of the common bond that exists between humans and the animal world should do the same for all of us.

Chapter 8

RESPECT FOR LIFE IN THE OLD TESTAMENT[*]

The sixth commandment reads: Thou shalt not kill. But this is not to be understood as giving unqualified support to those causes which advocate pacifism, the abolition of capital punishment or vegetarianism. The Hebrews were constantly at war, executed their criminals and ate meat. Yet it is fair to say that while all these activities carried a sacrificial connotation, they were also regarded as a necessary evil. God did not create humans for physical violence.

The Hebrews' attitudes to life derived from their creation theology. They understood all life to owe its origin to God to whom the life force (*nepeš*) belonged. This applied to both humans and animals (Jer. 38.16). Simple observation confirmed that loss of blood caused death. Consequently the blood was said to contain the *nepeš* (Gen. 9.4; Lev. 17.11, 14; Deut. 12.23), and ownership attributed to God. While blood was central to the ritual of the cultus, for through its use it secured the right relationship between God and his people, steps had to be taken to make sure that it was not appropriated by humans. This is clearly seen in the rules about eating meat.

From earliest times the Hebrews ate meat. The animal was taken to the local sanctuary for slaughter, its blood being poured out on the altar as a sacrificial act, and so returned to God. Later, following the centralization of all worship in Jerusalem in the wake of Josiah's reform, and the consequent destruction of all local sanctuaries (2 Kgs 23), this duty became impracticable, and the killing of animals for food was secularized. This could still be undertaken locally, but the blood had first to be poured out on the earth (Deut. 12.20-21) which swallowed it up (Gen. 4.11). Although the Holiness Code written just before the exile may have attempted to reverse this secularization (Lev. 17.1-14), in fact the totally

---

*   A talk given to a day conference at King's College, London, on 17 March 1983.

changed conditions of postexilic Israel prevented this. To this day orthodox Jews only eat meat from which the blood has been drained.

For the Priestly theologians of the exilic period the eating of meat is
seen as a concession given by God. For in their creation account (Gen. 1)
humans and animals were created as vegetarian. It is due to humankind's
rebellion symbolized by the generation of Noah that the world ceased to
be an idyllic place in which the animals were at peace with humans.
Instead they lived in fear of them for God has given humans authority to
kill them for food. Humans are, however, not given an entirely free hand:
before eating meat, the blood of the animal, its life force, must be drained
from it and returned to its creator, God (Gen. 9.4).

Nonetheless the ideal of a world in which there was no bloodshed
neither within the animal kingdom nor between humans and the animals is
preserved in the messianic prophecy of Isa. 11.6-9; 65.25. The messianic
kingdom can only reflect what was God's will in creation, that all in whom
he has placed his life force should live in *šālōm*, peace and harmony. Then
wild and domestic animals will lie down together in peace and children
play in safety by snakes' nests. Until then humans are given dominion
over the animals: they are to be instruments in his ordering of the world in
accordance with God's will. But as created by God, they are always to be
reverenced by humans.

So among the large number of humanitarian and charitable provisions of
Hebrew law, none of which could be enforced in the courts but were left to
natural moral sense to obey, there are a number of enactments concerning
animals. For instance engagement in a legal suit does not absolve a litigant
from his duty to rescue his opponent's animal in distress (Exod. 23.4-5).
Nor should a threshing ox be prevented from feeding itself while working
(Deut. 25.4), nor a mother bird be taken as well as her eggs or fledglings
(Deut. 22.6-7). And it is not merely the poor who are to benefit from the
rule that there should always be land left fallow, but wild beasts as well
(Exod. 23.10). While the Old Testament recognizes that this is not an ideal
world, and makes concessions until the messianic kingdom comes, it remains everyone's duty to do all in their power to reverence animal life.
While animals, like all God's creation, were made for humans, they must
still order that creation in accordance with God's will. What that will is is
left to them to discern from their own moral sense and in the light of the
nature of God as revealed in his Torah, understood as the complete
expression of his will.

The late Priestly provision of Gen. 9.1-7 dating from exilic times sums up this Hebrew attitude to life. Its aim is to differentiate between humans and animals. While animals may be slaughtered for food, God himself demands death for the killing of a human whether by his fellow human or a beast. This had always been the case in pre-exilic Israel as the law in Exod. 21 makes clear. So murder results in the execution of the murderer whether he is a human (Exod. 21.12) or an ox (Exod. 21.28). Indeed the word *rāṣâ* found in the sixth commandment and translated 'kill' is only used absolutely or with a person as object, never of an animal.

It is the Priestly justification for this difference in attitude to the slaughter of animals and humans which is new. Unlike the animals, humans are made in the image of God, that is for relationship with him (Gen. 1.26) They were created both to hear and be heard by God—to act as the representatives of the creator in his creation, to master and control it.

The creation narratives record the first murder (Gen. 4). As soon as Cain has killed his brother, God is on the spot to interrogate the offender: 'Where is Abel your brother?' To this Cain replies, 'I do not know; am I my brother's keeper?' God then answers Cain, 'What have you done? The voice of your brother's blood is crying to me from the ground.' In this exchange, part of the Yahwist's creation account probably dating from the time of Solomon, we have set out the Hebrews' ideas concerning murder.

When a man committed murder, he was understood to take possession of his victim's blood (2 Sam. 4.11). Literally this blood was on his hands—that is, in his control—and God as owner had to take action to recover it. So in such circumstances God is described as the seeker of the blood of the murdered man (Gen. 9.5; 42.22; Ps. 9.13; Ezek. 3.18, 20; 33.6, 8). And this seeking is what God is doing when he confronts Cain. For by his action, Cain had taken possession of his brother's blood which as God explains had been crying to him as its rightful owner to come and repossess it (Gen. 4.10; cf. Job 16.18). Cain's answer to God is singularly ironic. He denies knowledge of his brother's whereabouts by claiming in a pun that it is not part of brotherly duty for him to shepherd the shepherd (Gen. 4.9). By his action Cain has in fact taken possession of his brother's blood, become Abel's keeper.

The idea that where life was taken the ownership of the blood was transferred to the killer lies behind two Hebrew expressions about blood. The first refers to shedding innocent blood (Deut.19.10, 13; 21.8-9, 27.25)—that is the blood of someone who has not committed a crime and therefore does not deserve to suffer the pre-exilic criminal law penalty of execution. For instance where a killing took place by accident—as when a man goes into the forest with his neighbour to cut wood, and his hand swings the axe to cut down a tree, and the head slips from the handle and strikes his neighbour so that he dies (Deut. 19.15)—in such a case it is not murder and the accidental killer must be protected from an attempt to treat him as a murderer. If he were executed it would be innocent blood which was shed and an action intended to free the community of blood guilt would in fact bring blood guilt upon it for there was no blood to be released from the accidental killer's hands (Deut. 19.10). So cities of refuge were established to which the unintentional killer could flee for an impartial trial. Earlier legislation described such a killing as an act of God (Exod. 21.13). The refusal of the Deuteronomic legislators to attribute an accident to divine causation is an early example of coming to terms with the 'God of the gaps' theology.

The second phrase deriving from these ideas about the transference of blood following a killing describes a person's blood as remaining upon him or upon his head (Lev. 20.9, 11-13, 16; Josh. 2.19; 2 Sam. 1.16; 1 Kgs 2.37). This indicates that where a crime has been committed, and death is exacted according to the requirements of the criminal law, the victim's blood would not pass into the hands of his executioners, but remain on the victim himself. Indeed execution was seen as a sacrificial act by which the local community sought to propitiate God for the criminal's action and so avoid divine retaliation falling on them. But nowhere is there any indication that individuals could take the law into their own hands. All crimes were a matter for the local community which tried, and on conviction, executed the criminal.

Execution was by communal stoning which enabled all members of the community physically to take part in this corporate act of propitiation and would have made them collectively liable for any miscarriage of justice. It appears that where the land or people were already suffering what was interpreted as divine punishment, the corpse of the criminal might be exposed until that suffering stopped, thus signifying that God had been appeased (cf. Num. 25.4-5). This would explain the execution of the seven sons of Saul by the Gibeonites in the first days of the barley harvest which had failed for the third time, and Rizpah's watch over their bodies until the rains came (2 Sam. 21). The Deuteronomists in ordering a criminal's burial on the same day as his execution evidently considered this practice not only improper but positively harmful, preventing the very thing it was designed to achieve—the prosperity of the land (Deut. 21.22-23). Even the bodies of criminals were to be respected for they too were part of the created order and belonged to God. Of course, when the messianic kingdom came there would be no need for capital punishment for everywhere God's Torah would be kept. Until then those who put themselves outside the elect community by their actions towards God or their neighbour must be executed—sacrificed to the God whose law they had broken.

Both the necessity to propitiate God for a murder and the fact that it is the murderer who has possession of his victim's blood is confirmed from the ancient provision dealing with the case of murder by person or persons unknown (Deut. 21.1-9). No attempt is made to provide a substitute for the offender because only the actual murderer has possession of his victim's blood. Instead the elders take an unmated and unworked heifer to a valley where there is permanent running water and in which the soil has not been disturbed by ploughing or sowing, and there break its neck. The elders wash their hands over the animal and disclaim all responsibility for the murder. No blood is shed and the animal's corpse is simply abandoned. Nor is any attempt made to shift any guilt on to the heifer as in the case of the ritual scapegoat in the law of the Day of Atonement (Lev. 16.21). Rather the washing, confession and abandonment of the animal's corpse in the open countryside alone effects expiation for the murder and ensures that God will take no further action against the community or its land.

While in pre-exilic Israel criminals were always executed, in postexilic law with the exception of murder excommunication from the cult community replaced execution. This reflects the new situation of post-exilic Judaism which constituted a worshipping community centred on the temple rather than a political entity. Yet for murder execution is still required. The reason remains the necessity to free the blood of the victim to God to whom it belonged. He must be compensated for the loss which he has suffered. It is this principle which underlies the *lex talionis*.

This occurs three times in the Old Testament, once in each of the major legal collections. In all three places (Exod. 21.23-25; Lev. 24.17-22; Deut. 19.21) it is a late addition having no direct connection with the material into which it is inserted. Its origin is most probably to be sought in Babylon. For postexilic Israel it acts as a shorthand expression to indicate that in every case of loss due compensation is to be made to the injured party whether an individual or in the case of murder God himself. So Lev. 24.17-18 attaches the first talionic provision 'life for life' both to the tort of killing an animal and also to the crime of murder. There is certainly no indication that at any time Israel practised literal retaliation as a form of punishment. Indeed there is only one case where any kind of mutilation was prescribed by the law, indecent assault by a woman on a man's private parts (Deut. 25.11-12) which resulted in the loss of the offending hand. The mutilation is not ordered simply because of the woman's immodesty, but rather because by her action she might have damaged the man's testicles, and thereby affected his ability to have children. He could consequently be left in the position of being unable to father a son, and therefore having his name blotted out (cf. Deut. 25.6). This accounts for the position of this law after the provision on levirate marriage, also concerned with the continuance of a man's name.

Like the slaughter of animals for food, and the execution of the criminal, killing in war was also regarded as sacrificial—the foe being pictured as the enemy of God whose holy war it was. So war began with sacrifice (1 Sam. 7.9; 13.8-12) and required the participants to keep themselves clean by abstaining from sexual intercourse throughout the campaign (1 Sam. 21.5-6; 2 Sam. 11.11-13; cf. Deut. 23.10). Sometimes the enemy were formally dedicated to God by the infliction of the ban. This could be of varying severity; (1) total destruction of all persons and property (Deut. 20.16-18; 1 Sam. 15.3); (2) total destruction of all persons but not property (Deut. 2.34-35, 3.6-7); (3) destruction of all males only (Deut. 20.10-15). Failure to carry out the ban as at Jericho could lead to direct divine punishment (Josh. 7). In Deuteronomic eyes the ban is what ought to have been inflicted on the Canaanites which would have ensured that the Israelites would never have been led into apostasy by them. How often the ban was in fact inflicted in ancient times remains uncertain, but evidence for it is found on the ninth-century BCE Moabite stone. This records that Mesha, king of Moab, exterminated the inhabitants of the Israelite city of Nebo whom he had dedicated to his God, Ashtar-Chemosh.

Nonetheless war is to be avoided if possible so preventing unnecessary loss of life. Before attacking a city overtures of peace are to be made, and only after these are rejected is battle to start. In this case males are to be executed, but if the city surrenders without fighting then no one is to be harmed (Deut. 20.10-18). Only the Canaanites are to be utterly exterminated, but that is a late theological rubric which was never entertained in reality. Further, there was a limit to the ferocity with which war might be prosecuted. While trees which did not yield fruit might be cut down and used for siege works, this was not so of trees which supplied food. It was important that after the war there should be a regular supply of food (Deut. 20.19-20). Further a woman prisoner whom an Israelite might marry was to be treated humanely. She acquired full rights as a wife and so if her husband subsequently tired of her she could not be sold off as a slave (as prisoners usually were) but had to be divorced in the normal manner and sent off a free woman (Deut. 21.10-14). Characteristically Deuteronomic humanitarian law ensured that certain people were exempt from military service. These included anyone who had built a new house which he had not yet dedicated, planted a vineyard and not yet used it, betrothed himself to a woman, but had not yet taken her, and even those who were afraid (Deut. 20.5-8). Further Deut. 24.5 allows a newly married man a year's exemption from military service to enable him to found a family. The laws of warfare indicate that for the Hebrews victory was not to be won at any price. Even in war one had a duty to act humanely as the clear horror of the war crimes listed in Amos 1–2 indicates.

But war, like eating meat and capital punishment, would cease when the messianic age dawned. This could not be until the nations accepted God's Torah. But the prophetic vision points to a time when Israel will act as a light to the nations (Isa. 49.6) mediating to them that Torah which is his will for all his creation. So the nations will come to Jerusalem to receive it and return to their own lands to practise it, so enabling the beating of swords into ploughshares as peace encompasses the whole world (Isa. 2.2-4; Mic. 4.1-4).

Finally we must consider those without legal status and so without the protection of the courts. Only free adult males were both responsible under the law and could appeal to the courts to enforce it. All other persons were denied legal status. These included women, children and slaves, who could be disposed of by men as they liked under family law, part of the general body of customary law, mostly unwritten. It was of no concern to the courts but instead was administered in the home by the head of the household acting unilaterally. Change of a dependent's status was achieved either by a declaration being uttered by the head of the household and/or by his performance of a prescribed ritual. This applied to betrothal, marriage, divorce, adoption and the making of slavery permanent.

But in spite of the absolute authority of the head of the household in cases of family law, he nonetheless never had power of life or death over those under his protection. So for instance there was no question of a father being able to kill his daughter for consenting to her seduction before marriage or his wife for her adultery after marriage as in other ancient Near Eastern law. Nor was any child ever punished instead of his father for a crime which the father had committed, nor except for apostasy, when it appears that the whole male line was exterminated in order to blot out the father's name (Exod. 22.19), was any child executed along with his father for one of his father's crimes. Yet in other ancient Near Eastern law injury to another's son or daughter could result in corresponding injury being inflicted on one's own child. And although Naboth and his sons were executed (2 Kgs 9.26) almost certainly for apostasy (repudiating God and the king), later Deuteronomic law even put an end to that practice (Deut. 24.16).

Even slaves were to be protected from vicious masters. So if a slave died as a result of a disciplinary beating, the master would be prosecuted, though to be murder the death had to occur during or immediately after the beating which caused death. The law presumed that no master would want to deprive himself of his property (Exod. 21.20-21). Similarly a slave was able to bring an action for assault against a master in the case of permanent injury (Exod. 21.26-27).

But respect for life in Hebrew law also had its positive side. This is found in the so-called laws of humaneness and righteousness to some of which we have already referred. These were designed to protect those without legal status, the widow, orphan and foreigner and those whose status is threatened, the poor. Such people were not to be left to the mercies of a free economy. Those with sufficient means are placed under a moral duty to ensure that those without are protected. So loans are to be made free of interest, and a limit is placed on the legal rights of a creditor (Exod. 22.24-26). Later Deuteronomic law provided that all debts were to be written off at the end of every seventh year and enjoined that even when this year of general release was imminent, loans were still to be made though there could be no hope of recovery (Deut. 15).

As we have seen, these provisions though commonly termed laws, in a technical sense are not laws at all. They envisage no legal action for their breach and specify no penalties. Rather they are a sermon to society at large which bases its appeal on a sense of moral responsibility and justice. They recognize that there was a limit on the courts' power to secure order in society, but that true order went much deeper than what could juridically be enforced. How far practice matched ideals we cannot of course know but it was for breach of such unenforceable provisions that the eighth-century prophets condemned a self-righteous and prosperous northern kingdom, a charge later repeated against southern Judah.

Respect for life in Hebrew Torah was not then confined to the negative 'Thou shall not kill'. It included the positive injunctions to charity which was no optional extra but part of God's will alongside his criminal, civil and cultic law. It is a principle which has sustained the Jewish people to modern times and one which needs reasserting both nationally and internationally. Respect for life involves ensuring that economic pressures do not result in those made in the image of God going under, but in securing for them a satisfactory quality of life which will enable them to enjoy their relationship with their God which is his will for all—for all owe their creation to him who provided their *nepeš*.

Chapter 9

THE ATTITUDE OF TORAH TO WEALTH

At the end of the seventh century BCE, the Deuteronomists encapsulated the story of Israel's origins in the liturgy of the offering of the first fruits (Deut. 26.5-11). Once held by von Rad[1] and others as an ancient creed, this passage summarizes the theological self-understanding of the immediate pre-exilic generation.[2] In contrast to the stateless existence of the patriarch Jacob and the period of slavery in Egypt, the Hebrews can now rejoice in the possession of the rich land of Canaan.[3] Yet their occupation is not due to their own endeavour, but results solely from God's action. It is his gift.

Earlier in their Work, the Deuteronomists described in some detail the richness of the land which God had destined for Israel:

> For the Lord your God is bringing you into a good land, a land of brooks and water, of fountains and springs, flowing forth in valleys and hills, a land of wheat and barley, of vines and fig trees and pomegranates, a land of olive trees and honey, a land in which you will eat bread without scarcity, in which you will lack nothing, a land whose stones are iron, and out of whose hills you can dig copper. And you shall eat and be full (Deut. 8.7-10a).

By this lavish description, the authors were witnessing to the Hebrew conviction that riches were a sign of divine blessing. Israel was not called to renounce the world, but to leave the desert and enjoy what God of his grace had so richly provided, the land flowing with milk and honey. Wealth then is Israel's appointed destiny. Indeed when God gives, he can only give in abundance as Isaac found:

---

1. G. von Rad, 'The Form-Critical Problem of the Hexateuch', in *idem, The Problem Hexateuch and Other Essays* (Edinburgh: Oliver & Boyd, 1966), pp. 1-78.
2. Nicholson, *Exodus and Sinai*, pp. 20-23.
3. Phillips, *Deuteronomy*, pp. 173-74.

And Isaac sowed in that land, and reaped in the same year a hundredfold. The Lord blessed him, and the man became rich, and gained more and more until he became very wealthy. He had possession of flocks and herds, and a great household (Gen. 26.12-14a).

Yet the land is not given to Israel unconditionally. Although he wills his people to luxuriate in the abundance which he provides for them, the land ultimately remains God's to dispose of as he deems fit. Like Adam in Eden, Israel has been placed in Canaan to order it according to divine will.

The Hebrews acknowledged God's sovereignty by offering him the first fruits of the harvest. Indeed all property was recognized as remaining in God's possession, though to be used by man during his brief life on earth. So when David dedicated the material for the building of the temple, the Chronicler described him as saying:

> But who am I, and what is my people, that we should be able thus to offer willingly? For all things come from thee, and of thy own have we given thee. For we are strangers before thee, and sojourners, as all our fathers were; our days on the earth are like a shadow, and there is no abiding. O Lord our God, all this abundance that we have provided for building thee a house for thy holy name comes from thy hand and is all thy own (1 Chron. 29.14-16).

The terms for Israel's possession of the land are contained in Torah. While originally *tōrâ* meant a ruling or instruction on a particular issue, for the Deuteronomists it came to mean the complete expression of the will of God.[4] This explains why the Hebrew law collections place alongside criminal and civil provisions to be pursued through the courts, moral injunctions which no court could enforce. For what obedience to Torah demands is that society which God intended when he gave Israel the land. Briefly we must establish the Hebrews understanding of that society, before setting out how Torah could ensure it. For failure to do so would inevitably result in Israel suffering the same fate as the nations whom God had driven out from Canaan in order that his people might possess the land (Deut. 8.20). This was the situation facing the immediate post-exilic generation.

Like the story of origins, the Hebrew concept of the ideal society willed by God was formed prior to the introduction of the monarchy. It reflected a pastoral and agricultural community in which each family exercised its own autonomy, possessing house and land which provided economic livelihood

4. Lindars, 'Torah in Deuteronomy', pp. 117-36.

and ensured personal independence. Local administration would have been in the hands of the heads of each household, the elders, ensuring that all had a say in the community's affairs including the administration of justice.[5] The introduction of the monarchy with its centralized economic power threatened this individual freedom.[6] With the growth of a capitalist society in which money rather than payment in kind was accepted as the normal medium of exchange, considerable disparity in wealth arose. The solidarity of the existing social order in which through their ownership of realty all were protected by their participation in the local legal machinery broke down. The result was that realty became increasingly concentrated in the hands of fewer and fewer who lived in the cities among a swiftly expanding urban population without personal economic interest in the land and lacking legal protection. Former land-owners were reduced to the status of day labourers and an enormous increase in slave labour occurred, together with urban unemployment (cf. 1 Sam. 22.2). Although abuse of justice was an unfortunate fact of life in pre-monarchic days, under the monarchy it became the norm. This is clearly indicated by those early anti-monarchic texts, probably from the time of Solomon, which show that initial opposition to the monarchy was not theological, but economic and social (1 Sam. 8.1-3, 11-17; 12.3-5).[7]

It was this breakdown of the pre-monarchic ideal of individual worth which led both Isaiah and Micah to condemn the widespread seizure of realty and consequent growth of a large landless population without any personal stake in the community's fortunes (Isa. 5.8; Mic. 2.2). So what was still for the Deuteronomistic historians the recognized ideal economic and social pattern for Israel—'every man under his vine and under his fig tree' (1 Kgs 5.5)—became for postexilic Israel an eschatalogical hope (Mic. 4.4;[8] Zech. 3.10).

Before studying the individual measures by which the legislators hoped to protect disadvantaged Israelites, and their development under the monarchy, the fragmentary nature of the biblical law collections must be recalled. Neither the Book of the Covenant (Exod. 21.1-23.19),[9] the

---

5.   Phillips, *AICL*, pp. 17-20; Davies, *Prophecy and Ethics*, pp. 100-102.
6.   For a full discussion see E. Neufeld, 'The Emergence of a Royal-Urban Society in Ancient Israel', *HUCA* 31 (1960), pp. 31-53.
7.   Mayes, *The Story of Israel*, p. 94.
8.   Mic. 4.1-4 is best understood as an exilic text. Cf. J.L. Mays, *Micah* (OTL; London: SCM Press, 1976), pp. 95-96.
9.   On the composition of the Sinai narrative Exod. 19–24, see Phillips, 'A Fresh

Deuteronomic laws (Deut. 12–26), nor the Holiness Code (Lev. 17–26) are all-embracing codes, nor can any entirely comprehensive legal system be developed from them. For instance, much of the regular commercial dealings of ordinary life are absent, which does not necessarily mean that such practices were unknown, but does make overall interpretation of Israelite society more difficult. The concern of the compilers of the collections was theological rather than legal: the designation of God's will in certain religious, social and moral situations which confronted his people.

Only the legal precedents of Exod. 21.12–22.16 known as the *mišpāṭîm* designating prescribed remedies for specific actions have any claim to be considered as addressed to judges: the remaining collections are in effect sermons to the nation. How far the nation took notice of such injunctions, or how far they remained the ideal aspirations of those who devised them, cannot be ascertained. But the fact that the collections nowhere attempt to narrow their scope to what can be enforced in the law courts, indicates that in the eyes of their compilers there was no limit to the concerns of Torah, which explains the miscellaneous subject-matter of their contents. Further, whenever a man found himself with the opportunity for ensuring righteousness, then even if the collections contained no ruling on the situation confronting him, he still had a duty to do 'what is right and good' (Deut. 6.18).

We are now in a position to examine the individual measures by which the legislators sought to combat the new economic situation following the establishment of the monarchy and the resulting sudden growth of wide class differences in Israelite society. These are contained in the Book of the Covenant (Exod. 21.1–23.19) whose promulgation both on grounds of content and form is best seen as occurring during the united monarchy of David and Solomon.[10] Following the breakdown of clan solidarity, the protection of those dependents without legal status (widows, orphans and resident aliens), as well as the disadvantaged poor, became the general responsibility of the king (Ps. 72; Isa. 11). Indeed this support for the underprivileged was widely regarded as the role of monarchy throughout the ancient Near East, being in no sense peculiar to Israel.[11] The Book of the Covenant is the Israelite attempt not only to standardize criminal and civil law throughout the kingdom, but also to ensure that wider order in

Look', pp. 39-52, 282-94 (reprinted above as Chapter 2).

10. Phillips, *AICL*, pp. 158-61, and *idem*, in a review of *The If-You Form*, by Gilman, pp. 425-26.

11. Fensham, 'Widow, Orphan', pp. 129-39.

society which was always the aim of Torah, and which depended on the individual moral response of those addressed.

The contents of the Book of the Covenant fall into two categories: (1) a series of general rulings and detailed precedents on criminal and civil matters which carry specified penalties to be enforced by the courts (Exod. 21.12–22.19); and (2) a mixture of humanitarian and cultic injunctions which envisage no legal action for their breach and specify no penalties but rely on the moral and religious response of the community (Exod. 22.20–23.19), to which must be added the laws of slavery which now head the collection (Exod. 21.1-11).

The criminal and civil laws need hardly concern us except to note that they were enforced regardless of the rank and wealth of the parties, for in Israel all were equal under the law. Yet, morally speaking, wealth could still thwart the ideal of justice. This is well illustrated by the case set out in Nathan's parable (2 Sam. 12.1-6).[12] In response to the prophet's account of the rich man's seizure of the poor man's one ewe lamb, David asserts that the perpetrator of this appalling act deserves to die. Morally it is as if he had committed the crime of murder. Yet the king ruefully notes that under the law he must be treated as a civil offender and pay the prescribed damages of four sheep. Although the civil law required payment of punitive damages for theft of animals (Exod. 21.37; 22.2b), these had clearly been devised as a deterrent to the poor. As far as the rich were concerned, the law could be treated with contempt for they would always have the resources with which to compensate the injured. Ensuring that all were equal under the law did not then necessarily result in upholding true justice. In civil law, wealth remained and remains a determining factor.

It is, however, with the humanitarian provisions of the Book of the Covenant that we are principally concerned. Exodus 22.20–23.19 contains provisions on those who in the new economic conditions of the united monarchy found themselves at the mercy of others: the resident alien (Exod. 22.20; 23.9), the widow and orphan (Exod. 22.21-23), the poor (Exod. 22.24-26; 23.3, 6, 10-11), and even animals (Exod. 23.4-5, 10-11).

The resident alien was a person of foreign origin permanently living in Israel. Hitherto, like the widow and orphan, he would have relied for protection on the head of the clan to which he had attached himself by becoming a dependent member. Now with the breakdown of clan society all those dependents without legal status were forced to rely solely on charity.

---

12. For a full discussion see Phillips, 'The Interpretation', pp. 242-44 (reprinted below as Chapter 14).

The change from an agricultural society in which all derived their main-tenance directly from the land to one in which commerce (concentrated in the growing cities) played an ever-increasing role also resulted in a new definable class of 'poor'. These were the landless urban population depen-dent on others for employment. In addition, the plight of the small peasant farmer became increasingly acute. Should his crop fail, he had to obtain help either by direct loan or through a pledge in the hope that the follow-ing harvest would restore his fortunes.

Although other ancient Near Eastern legislation attempted to limit interest rates,[13] Hebrew law was unique in enacting that no interest was to be exacted on loans to impoverished fellow Israelites (Exod. 22.24).[14] No advantage was to be taken of a fellow-citizen's ill-fortune. Exorbitant interest rates were the chief cause of debt slavery in neighbouring coun-tries. As with all the humanitarian regulations, there was no means of enforcing the prohibition, and we cannot be certain that it was kept. The silence of the Old Testament on any provisions for interest or the period over which repayment was to be made cannot be taken as conclusive evidence of obedience, for many commercial undertakings go unmen-tioned. Yet the fact that of the prophets only Ezekiel alludes to its possible breach (Ezek. 18.8) is evidence of possible early observance which may not have continued (cf. Ps. 15.5; Prov. 28.8).[15]

Despite good intentions, the prohibition on usury may have been less effective than the legislators intended. For without any return the wealthy had little incentive to lend to those already in financial difficulty. This would explain why Deuteronomic legislation had to remind Israelites of their duty to lend to their fellow citizens in need (Deut. 15.9). No doubt a pledge often provided a means round this difficulty, which in the case of land could have been cultivated by the creditor to his financial advantage (Neh. 5).[16]

In any event it should be noted that what is in mind is borrowing to alleviate pressing financial need rather than the provision of loans for the purpose of production. Of these no mention is made in the Old Testament.

13. R.P. Maloney, 'Usury and Restrictions on Interest-Taking in the Ancient Near East', *CBQ* 36 (1974), pp. 1-20.

14. H. Gamoran, 'The Biblical Law against Loans on Interest', *JNES* 30, 1971, pp. 127-34.

15. Gamoran, 'The Biblical Law', pp. 133-34. For a discussion of the dating of Ps. 15, see Phillips, *AICL*, pp. 186-87.

16. Davies, *Prophecy and Ethics*, pp. 68-69.

This should not, however, be interpreted as meaning that limits were set on the nature of Israelite commerce. Venture capital may well have been supplied. But along with legal provisions for tariffs on services and merchandise, and laws regarding rentals, tenancy of land, and sale of land for purely commercial and profit motives, such loans were of no interest to Israel's legislators whose ideals remained those of the pastoral and agricultural society of her origins.

A limit was, however, placed on what could be pledged by those faced with total poverty. In no circumstances was a man's outer garment in which he would have slept to be kept by a creditor overnight (Exod. 22.25-26). Such a pledge was of course symbolic, enabling the creditor to prove his loan. That such a provision should have been required in the Book of the Covenant illustrates the extreme poverty of some in early monarchic Israel who despite the prosperity of the Solomonic era possessed nothing to pledge save what they stood up in.

For this reason, provision was made for the landless urban poor to take part in the harvest through a continuous method of crop rotation which left orchards and land uncultivated every seventh year (Exod. 23.10-11).[17] This provision has nothing to do with the later sabbatical year (Lev. 25.1-7) which was a theological rather than a humanitarian ideal and in contrast operated in a fixed seventh year. Further, in recognizing that wild animals also needed man's help to survive, Exod. 23.10-11 saw that it was in man's interest to preserve the ecological balance. The order must extend to all God's creatures, which explains the provision on rescuing an 'enemy's' ox or ass, the enemy being someone with whom one was engaged in a legal dispute (Exod. 23.4-5). This is why the provision appears in a series of injunctions concerned with the proper administration of law (Exod. 21.1-3, 6-9). These reassert the principle that justice is to be meted out without consideration for the personal circumstances of the parties. As in the case of Nathan's parable, it was not up to the courts to engage in a process of reverse justice in favour of the poor (Exod. 23.3), but to ensure that all men had access to what the law provided and upheld (Exod. 23.9).

Although apparently humanitarian in nature, the laws on slavery come at the beginning of the Book of the Covenant (Exod. 21.1-11). The chief source of slaves in the ancient Near East was foreign prisoners of war who were enslaved for life (cf. Deut. 20.10-14; 21.10-14). But economic conditions also ensured a regular supply of native-born slaves. These would include minors sold by poor and indebted parents, or adults either selling

17. Ginzberg, 'Studies', pp. 351-52.

themselves into slavery or being declared insolvent (2 Kgs 4.1; Neh. 5.1-5; Amos 2.6; Exod. 22.2b). It is these debt slaves who are the subject of Exod. 21.1-11.

Three issues are dealt with in the slave legislation: (1) the right of a male *'ebed 'ibrî*, usually rendered in English as 'Hebrew slave' to freedom after six years' service (Exod. 21.1-4); (2) a procedure for renouncing that right and making slavery permanent (Exod. 21.5-6) and (3) protection for the female slave taken into concubinage (Exod. 21.7-11).

Much discussion has centred on the interpretation of the phrase *'ebed 'ibrî*. Many scholars influenced in particular by the fifteenth-century slave legislation from Nuzi have interpreted the term *'ibrî* as referring to a slave of a particular legal or social class. However, there are a number of reasons for believing that the authors of the Book of the Covenant intended *'ibrî* to be understood as a gentilic referring to Israelite slaves, which explains the positioning of the laws of slavery at the beginning of the Book of the Covenant.[18] While such slavery had become an unpleasant fact of life since the settlement in Canaan, and many Hebrew slaves would have been forced to ensure their security by taking advantage of the provision for making slavery permanent, nonetheless such a situation was to be deplored.

The Hebrews had not left slavery in Egypt in order to enslave each other. For the compilers of the Book of the Covenant, the release of the male Hebrew slave was not in the end a merely humanitarian provision like those concerning widows, orphans, resident aliens, animals and the poor from which they separated it. Rather it was restoring to a member of Israel his rightful place in the community which by his enslavement he had lost. For this reason the right to restoration of legal status is placed before the rest of the enactments of the Book of the Covenant, which the slave when freed is bound both to obey and enforce. Economic conditions may have made the original concept of Hebrew society as a community in which each adult male had a stake in its affairs an ideal, but in the face of growing disparity in wealth, and an ever-increasing Israelite slave population, the need to reaffirm that ideal was urgent. Torah was about what ought to be, not necessarily about what was.[19]

---

18. For a full discussion see Phillips, 'The Laws of Slavery: Exodus 21.2-11', *JSOT* 30 (1984), pp. 51-66 (reprinted above as Chapter 5).

19. The tenth commandment may also originally have formed another example of this concern for a slaveless society (Phillips, 'The Decalogue', [reprinted above as Chapter 1]).

As we have already observed, the humanitarian provisions of the Book of the Covenant were unenforceable, relying on the moral good sense of those addressed. That they needed persuading is indicated by the motive clauses used to support the provisions on the resident alien (Exod. 22.20b; 23.9) and the widow and orphan (Exod. 22.21-23). In contrast to the injunctions themselves, these clauses are in the plural form, indicating that they are later additions. They are probably part of that revision of the Sinai narrative undertaken after the fall of Samaria during Hezekiah's reign.[20] They seek further to encourage those addressed to do what they already ought but cannot be forced to do by directly appealing to the emotions. Two motives are adduced. The first relates to the story of origins and is designed to evince sympathy:

> You shall not wrong a stranger or oppress him, for you were strangers in the land of Egypt (Exod. 22.20).

The second threatens the exercise of divine justice and is intended to instil fear:

> You shall not afflict any widow or orphan. If you do afflict them, and they cry out to me, I will surely hear their cry; and my wrath will burn, and I will kill you with the sword, and your wives shall become widows, and your children fatherless' (Exod. 22.21-23).

Later the Deuteronomists were to advocate a more fundamental reason for obeying such injunctions—sound economics.

Before turning to subsequent legislation to see how it reinforced the humanitarian concerns of the Book of the Covenant, I must note how the eighth-century prophetic protest confirmed torah. While Hosea largely concentrated on apostasy, Amos, Micah and Isaiah sought to condemn their contemporaries for their failure to exercise justice and protect those who could not protect themselves, those without legal status and the poor. In this they echoed the injunctions of the Book of the Covenant, presupposing its tradition of social justice.[21]

Although their oracles are chiefly directed at the rich, nowhere do the prophets indict them simply for possession of wealth: rather they are condemned for its enjoyment while exploiting or ignoring the needs of others (Isa. 1.23; 3.14-15; Amos 4.1; 5.11-12; 8.4-6; Mic. 6.11). While

20. See Phillips, 'A Fresh Look at the Sinai Pericope', pp. 47-52, 292 (reprinted above as chapter 2).

21. For a full discussion see Phillips, 'Prophecy and Law', pp. 217-32 (reprinted below as Chapter 10).

specific abuses such as shady business deals are referred to, much of the condemnation is in the same general terms as the injunctions in the Book of the Covenant.

The people clearly resented the prophetic protest. At the beginning of Amos' ministry, the northern kingdom of Israel was enjoying great prosperity, naturally interpreted as a sign of divine blessing. And the general absence of prophetic reference to breach of criminal and civil law provisions must indicate an outwardly law-abiding society. Certainly the picture which Amos presents is of a prosperous people confident that their own prosperity resulted from faithfulness to their God seen in their excessive religious zeal (Amos 4.4-5; 5.21-24), and, we must assume, outward maintenance of law and order (Amos 8.4-6).

Further, despite the vivid prophetic language, it must be recognized that it was not always readily apparent what 'doing justice' (Mic. 6.8) meant in the particular situation facing Israel. We have already noted the general nature of the humanitarian provisions of the Book of the Covenant, with their lack of specific directions as to what constituted appropriate action in any given situation. What guidelines had Israel for determining when 'oppression' was being inflicted? If we transfer the problem to our contemporary situation, and ask whether in the face of so much world poverty we are guilty of 'oppression' both in our own personal lifestyle and our nation's use of resources, then Israel's dilemma becomes clearer.

The prophetic answer was to appeal to natural law.[22] So Amos cites a succession of heinous war-crimes committed by foreign powers which everyone would condemn not because God had specifically prohibited them, but because they contravened all known standards of decency (Amos 1.1–2.3). He concludes his sermon with a stinging condemnation of Israel, citing by way of example a series of inhuman acts committed against those unable to protect themselves (Amos 2.6-8). These are not to be identified with specific practices prohibited by recognized legal sanctions. Rather they are particular actions which like the war-crimes should automatically have been seen to be abhorrent in Israel. It was for this reason that Amos summoned foreigners to view life in Samaria (Amos 3.9-10). Although unacquainted with Israel's law, they are expected to condemn her. Israel does not then need a detailed list of every act which God would condemn: she is quite capable of determining for herself her own moral responsibility. The laws of humaneness and righteousness had

22. Barton, 'Natural Law', pp. 1-14; *idem, Amos's Oracles against the Nations* (SOTSMS, 6; Cambridge: Cambridge University Press, 1980); 'Ethics', pp. 1-18.

made it clear what was generally required. If animals could act according to natural law (Amos 6.12; Isa. 1.2), then God's people should also be able to do his will.

The prophets therefore confirm that Torah can never absolve the community from exercising moral responsibility. Hebrew law is not just a series of detailed prescriptions, obedience to which secures God's blessing. From earliest times it appeals to conscience and requires moral judgments to be made. It was this lack of moral response which the eighth-century prophets found wanting, and for which they condemned their people. Prophecy and law are therefore seen as interdependent, and the prophetic response itself influenced later legislation. The law and the prophets cannot then be divorced either historically or theologically, for they belong together as witness to the nature of the God with whom Israel had to deal, and whose character was enshrined both in the story of her origins and the clan society based on individual worth and protection established after her liberation.

Later legislation at the end of the monarchic period (c. 600 BCE) re-iterated and reinforced the concern for humaneness and righteousness already found in earlier law and the prophets. So the Deuteronomists re-enacted the absolute ban on usury in respect of fellow Israelites,[23] food and anything else which might form the subject of a loan being added to money (Deut. 23.20-21). They also extended the humanitarian legislation designed to protect animals (Deut. 22.1-4, 6-7, 10, 25.4) and alleviate poverty. While they repeated the necessity for the proper exercise of justice towards the resident alien and the orphan (Deut. 24.17), and the ban on holding a man's cloak in pledge overnight (Deut. 24.12-13), they extended the law on pledges in three ways. An absolute ban was placed on taking in pledge millstones (Deut. 24.6) or a widow's garment (Deut. 24.17), and on entering another's house to take possession of a pledge

---

23. E. Neufeld, 'The Prohibitions against Loans at Interest in Ancient Hebrew Laws' *HUCA* 26 (1955), pp. 355-412 (399ff.) interprets the Deuteronomic prohibition of exacting interest on loans 'to your brother' as widening the original scope of the original injunction in Exod. 22.24. The ban now applies to loans for any purpose and not just to alleviate poverty. In my view the legislators remain concerned with the poor rather than the supply of venture capital, whatever was the position concerning loans for production. It is perhaps worth adding that although biblical Hebrew has terms for trade and commerce, there is no word for business. This probably indicates the small-scale nature of commercial life in ancient Israel reflected in the scarcity of direct material on business in the Old Testament.

(Deut. 24.10-11). Like a man's cloak in which he slept at night, millstones were one of the necessities of life, being used in the daily process of grinding and baking. No one was to be deprived of the means of survival. Later Job was to condemn both the taking of an orphan's ass and a widow's ox in pledge (24.3). Customary law probably forbade uninvited entry into another's house: legal entitlement to possession of property was not to override this custom. In addition Deut. 24.14-15 enacted that those who worked on a day-to-day basis for their keep were to be paid at the end of each day's work in order that they might not go hungry.

This concern for the proper feeding of the poor and needy (Deut. 10.18-19), who now included the country Levites deprived of support through the Deuteronomic policy of centralizing all worship at the one sanctuary in Jerusalem, resulted in two new measures: (1) Deut. 24.19-21 ordered that what was forgotten or missed from the harvest of crops or fruit at the first gleaning should not subsequently be recovered, but left for the resident alien, orphan and widow; and (2) regular provision for those without land was now connected with the annual tithe: every third year each Israelite was to devote his tithe to helping the resident alien, orphan, widow and Levite (Deut. 14.28-29; 26.12-15). Like the fallowing law of Exod. 23.10-11, which probably fell out of use because it could no longer achieve its purpose in the face of the ever-increasing number of landless poor, this provision was not intended to be observed simultaneously throughout Israel, since it sought to provide an annual harvest for those in need.

The seven-year cycle now became associated by the Deuteronomists with a new enactment requiring the cancellation of debts, which unlike the fallowing and tithe provisions was to operate simultaneously throughout Israel in one fixed year, the year of release (Deut. 15.1-6). This necessitated an injunction encouraging the rich to lend generously even when that seventh year was imminent, so making the chance of repayment slight (Deut. 15.7-11). The type of loan envisaged here involved the pledge of a person as security, who on non-payment of the debt was taken by the creditor who used his services as compensation. As a result of the Deuteronomic law not only would the enforcement of repayment have been prohibited, but anyone seized as pledge would also have been released. While borrowers were under a moral duty to repay loans (Ps. 37.21), the law found it preferable that those who could afford to lend should lose their money, rather than that anyone should lose his freedom (cf. Neh. 10.30).

The Deuteronomic legislators intention was then to minimize those occasions where Israelites found themselves forced into debt slavery. Where this unfortunately occurred, these legislators, in contrast to the authors of the Book of the Covenant (Exod. 21.1-4), required positive economic encouragement to be given to the Hebrew slave to exercise the right of release after six years' service:

> And when you let him go free from you, you shall not let him go empty-handed; you shall furnish him liberally out of your flock, out of your threshing floor, and out of your wine press' (Deut. 15.13-14).

Further, in accordance with their radical innovation of extending legal responsibility to adult Israelite women (Deut. 5.21; 7.3; 13.7; 15.12-17; 17.2-5; 22.22), this right to release now applied to female slaves as well.

The Deuteronomists also introduced a new motive clause encouraging obedience to those apparently uneconomic and unenforceable laws: divine blessing would follow, which, as always, was understood in material terms (Deut. 14.29; 15.4-6, 10, 18; 23.21). Adding to the earlier motives of sympathy or fear expressed in the Book of the Covenant, the Deuteronomists directly appeal to self-interest. So following the law on release of debts, Deut. 15.4-5 comments:

> But there will be no poor among you (for the Lord will bless you in the land which the Lord Your God gives you for an inheritance to possess) if only you will obey the voice of the Lord your God, being careful to do all this commandment which I command you this day.

I shall return to this economic motive later. We should, however, note that these laws only applied within the Israelite community of faith. Interest could he charged on loans to foreigners (Deut. 23.21), who could be pressed for repayment (Deut. 15.3). However, Israel was not to borrow from foreigners: economic vassaldom meant trusting in other nations and their gods, rather than in Israel's God who ensured their welfare (Deut. 15.6) through their obedience to even those apparently unprofitable provisions of Torah.

The Priestly legislation of the Holiness Code coming from the immediate pre-exilic period reaffirms the basic principles which I have already established. So Lev. 19.9-10, 23.22 asserts the necessity of leaving some of the harvest for the poor and resident aliens, Lev. 19.13 of paying the day worker his wages after work, Lev. 19.15 of ensuring the impartiality of justice regardless of the personal circumstances of the parties, and Lev. 19.33-34 of treating the resident alien as if he were native born.

But the Priestly legislators, conscious of Israel's continual failure to ensure individual economic freedom (Jer. 34.8-22; Ezek. 22.12) idealized the principles of earlier law by creating the sabbath and jubilee years. First they took over the idea of fallowing (Exod. 23.10-11), severed it from the concept of crop rotation by applying it to a fixed seventh year, and spiritualized it by connecting it with sabbath rest (Lev. 25.1-7). Their purpose was to assert God's ownership of the land by returning it once every seven years to its original state undisturbed by humans. While the owner, his household and cattle were to live off what the land naturally produced in the seventh year, there is now no thought of feeding the poor as in the original fallowing provision of Exod. 23.10-11.

Second, the Priestly legislators created the jubilee year, a fixed fiftieth year celebrated as a sabbath year of sabbath years (Lev. 25.8-12) in which realty, other than houses in walled cities, was restored to its former owners (Lev. 25.25-34) and slaves freed (Lev. 25.39-55). Legal ownership of both slaves and property was held to be vested in God, so that while a man might through necessity be forced to part with his freedom or his inheritance, neither was lost permanently. As far as land was concerned, he simply sold so many years' crops (Lev. 25.13-17). Usury was again forbidden, together with certain methods designed to circumvent it (Lev. 25.35-38). But the jubilee release is not to be confused with the ancient duty of a relative to re-purchase property in order to retain it within the family (Jer. 32.6-15; Ruth 4.1-4), which the jubilee year provisions somewhat illogically reiterate (Lev. 25.25). For in contrast to the jubilee release, the redeemed land did not return to the impoverished relative but was retained by the purchaser.

While Neh. 10.30 may indicate that an attempt was made to keep the provisions of the sabbatical year which is again reflected in 1 Macc. 6.49, 53,[24] the provisions of the jubilee year appear to have been no more than theological idealism. Indeed many slaves would have been dead long before the 50 years for jubilee release would have been reached. And the eventual return of the land to its original owner would have meant that no relative would have sought to redeem it by purchase, from the family's point of view a much more efficient procedure than the return of the land to an owner who had already proved himself to be economically incompetent. Nonetheless these provisions indicate that in the eyes of Torah economic factors alone cannot govern commercial and business undertakings. Every individual has a right both to his personal freedom and the

---

24. Ginzberg, *Studies*, pp. 358ff. believes that this attempt was restricted to a small observant minority around Jerusalem.

possession of land from which he can maintain himself and his family. The fact that houses in walled cities were not to be handed back indicates that the jubilee law's concern was the provision of sustenance rather than participation in the administrative and judicial proceedings of the local community, which would long have passed out of the hands of the heads of houses into those of professional judges. Freedom and the ability to maintain oneself were what 'every man under his vine and under his fig tree' meant for the Priestly legislators.

Wealth then is God's intention for humankind, for without it one can have no control over one's destiny. The possession of Canaan with its agricultural and mineral wealth enabled the Hebrews under the united monarchy of Solomon to exercise power throughout the ancient Near East. Despite the dangers which wealth brought, the puritan practices of the Rechabites (Jer. 35), who sought to retain a desert lifestyle after the settlement in Canaan, were not God's will. Instead Torah proclaims that the freedom which wealth brings is the right of each individual within the community. So the Book of the Covenant, the law collection of the united monarchy, enacts that those who enjoy the power which wealth gives must use it for securing for others that basic freedom over one's own life which remained and remains the Hebrew ideal.

Torah, however, recognized that the free surrender of superfluous wealth was against the individual's basic instinct ever to amass more. The Book of the Covenant was therefore expanded in order to encourage such charity by playing on the emotions of sympathy (Exod. 22.20; 23.9) and fear (Exod. 22.21-23). But as ought to have been obvious if Torah really was God's will for his people, there was a much better economic motive for the wealthy seeking to eradicate poverty. Not only would such charity prevent violent action being taken by those who had nothing to lose, it also provided the means for stimulating economic activity from which the wealthy themselves ultimately benefit. The Deuteronomic recognition that obedience to the apparent unprofitable injunctions of Torah would lead to material blessing is not then mere pietistic hope but sound economic sense. So when under Marshall Aid post-war Americans gave up a fixed percentage of their total production of goods and services to friends and ex-enemies alike, they not only averted the collapse of the post-war world economic system: they brought, as Torah said such charity would, economic blessing to America herself.[25]

25. For further discussion on some of the issues raised here see A. Phillips, 'Should the Primate of All England Eat York Ham?', *Theology* 85 (1982), pp. 339-46.

The attitude of Torah to wealth thus confirms God's injunctions to Adam that God and humans are on the same side. It is human instinct to doubt this, and once one thinks oneself self-sufficient to go one's own way, relying on one's wealth for future preservation (Deut. 8.11-18). The result, as the prophets proclaimed, is economic and political chaos as humans exploit other humans for their own gratification. The eradication of poverty and the establishment of a world free of hunger and disease will only be secured as people co-operate with the God who wills this end. Torah recognizes that people are not called to make a choice between God and the world. Rather they are to affirm both, and in fellowship with the Creator enjoy his creation in which, from the moment of setting Adam in Eden, God destined us to luxuriate.

Chapter 10

PROPHECY AND LAW

As late as 1965, in his monograph *Prophecy and Covenant*, Clements held that central to the preaching of the canonical prophets was the concept of the Sinai covenant. Their unique contribution was to have reactivated the idea of the covenant, which had fallen into neglect. Indeed, Clements went so far as to assert that, without the prior fact of the covenant, the prophets would be unintelligible to us.[1] Clements, of course, recognized that the actual term for covenant (*bᵉrît*) was only found twice in the eighth-century prophets, in Hos. 6.7 and 8.1, but he argued that to elect someone must lead to some kind of special relationship between him who elects and him who is elected, in which the obligations of the latter are set out. The use of the term 'covenant' to describe such a relationship was 'only of secondary importance'.[2]

But a decade later, in the wake of Perlitt,[3] Clements, in his second monograph, *Prophecy and Tradition*,[4] accepted that the covenant theology only gradually emerged to reach its classical expression in the Deuteronomic literature. The attempt to see the prophet as fulfilling the office of covenant mediator based on Deut. 18.15-22 must be abandoned, for it was the Deuteronomists who interpreted the prophets as preachers of *tōrâ* and spokesmen of the covenant between Yahweh and Israel. Further, reliance on Mendenhall's thesis[5] relating the covenant to the Hittite suzerainty treaties, allegedly reflected in the prophetic curses and lawsuit oracles, must also be given up. Instead, the prophets are to be seen as drawing on

---

1. R.E. Clements, *Prophets and Covenant* (SBT, 43; London: SCM Press, 1965), p. 126.
2. Clements, *Prophets and Covenant*, p. 54.
3. Perlitt, *Die Bundestheologie*.
4. R.E. Clements, *Prophets and Tradition* (Oxford: Basil Blackwell, 1975).
5. G.E. Mendenhall, 'Ancient Oriental and Biblical Law', pp. 26-46; 'Covenant Forms', pp. 50-76.

the various ways in which disaster could occur in the ancient Near East and employing the legal metaphor of a court action. The attempt to explain so many concepts within the prophetic corpus as deriving from the political suzerainty treaties implied a strange lack of theological creativeness on Israel's part when confronted with radically changed circumstances, which one would expect to be reflected in new theological insights. Indeed, the use of the political treaty form probably entered Israel's theology precisely in this way, following the fall of the Northern Kingdom and the threat to Judah's own existence. This, of course, is not to deny the creativity of the prophets but merely to indicate that they did not use an already existing literary model which was only assimilated into Israel's theological thought when new circumstances made it useful.

But, while Clements admitted that 'we cannot reconstruct a consistent covenant theology as a distinctive and coherent tradition underlying the preaching of the prophets', he nonetheless went on to argue that 'we can see that the traditions which the prophets inherited and used had a place in the emergence of a distinctive covenant ideology in Israel'.[6] So if, in the light of Perlitt and Nicholson,[7] the redactional work of the Deuteronomists within the prophetic corpus must now be recognized, caution must be expressed against a too-ready rejection of the development of that covenant theology over a considerable period of time, in which the prophets themselves played a part. So Barr[8] not only questions whether the covenant of Yahweh with Israel became significant so late but, in his reply to Kutsch,[9] indicates that syntactical and linguistic, rather than ideological and theological, restrictions might explain its use in one kind of linguistic context and not in another.[10] As Clements notes in his *Old Testament Theology* (1978), while *berît* clearly acquired a new emphasis in the Deuteronomic vocabulary, it is unlikely that it was an entirely 'novel introduction' in the seventh century to describe Israel's relationship with Yahweh.[11]

6.   Clements, *Prophets and Tradition*, p. 23.

7.   Perlitt, *Die Bundestheologie*; Nicholson, *Exodus and Sinai*.

8.   J. Barr, 'Some Semantic Notes on the Covenant', in H. Donner, R. Hanhart and R. Smend (eds.), *Beitrage zur Alttestamentlichen Theologie* (Festschrift W. Zimmerli; Gottingen: Vandenhoeck & Ruprecht, 1977), pp. 23-28.

9.   E. Kutsch, *Verheissung und Gesetz: Untersuchungen zum sogenannten 'Bund' im Alten Testament* (BZAW, 131; Berlin: W. de Gruyter, 1973).

10.   Cf. R. Martin-Achard, 'Trois ouvrages sur l'alliance dans l'Ancien Testament', *RTP* 110 (1978), pp. 299-306.

11.   R.E. Clements, *Old Testament Theology* (London: Marshall, Morgan & Scott, 1978), p. 101.

Deuteronomic covenant theology is, then, not in itself to be understood as an innovation, but as the end of a process, which is finally assimilated into a system, as set out in the Deuteronomic History work,[12] and applied to the prophetic material (e.g. Amos 2.4; Hos. 8.1). The law and the prophets are thus seen in conjunction very early, which explains the almost total absence of the canonical prophets from the Deuteronomic History. But without a clear point of contact, this redactional activity would have been inexplicable.

A different approach was adopted by Bergren,[13] who concentrated on the offences actually cited by the prophets in their indictment. His argument rested not only on Mendenhall's thesis about the covenant origins of Israel but also on Alt's distinction, formulated in 1934, between apodictic and casuistic law.[14] He contended that, whenever the prophets used law as a basis for their condemnation of Israel, their accusation was grounded solely on the breach of apodictic law. Nowhere is there any appeal to casuistic law, though the prophets clearly knew such law (Jer. 2.34; 3.1), thus showing that the old dualism between genuine Israelite law and other law continued in the prophetic preaching. The reason for this, in Bergren's view, was that the prophets understood that God had made a covenant with Israel, conceived of as a treaty, by which it was committed to a certain standard of behaviour as set out in the apodictic law, and which God himself would enforce. Indeed for Bergren, relying on Westermann's analysis of the forms of prophetic speech,[15] it is in the prophetic judgment speech that the law and the prophets come together. Thus he maintained that comparison of Alt's apodictic laws and the content of the accusation portion of the prophetic judgment speech indicates that the latter was entirely dependent on the former. But in spite of tabulating the prophetic accusations and relating them to the Pentateuchal legislation, Bergren made no real attempt to ask why appeal was made to certain laws and not to others. While he admitted that apodictic and covenant law are not coextensive, for the prophets are unconcerned with cultic requirements, even though these can be prescribed in apodictic form, he nonetheless relied on form to the exclusion of content.

---

12. Mayes, *Deuteronomy*, pp. 60-71.

13. R.V. Bergren, *The Prophets and the Law* (Monographs of the Hebrew Union College, 4; Cincinnati: Jewish Institute of Religion, 1974).

14. Alt, 'The Origin'.

15. C. Westermann, *Basic Forms of Prophetic Speech* (London: Lutterworth Press, 1967).

But Alt's thesis must now be very severely modified (see the full discussion by Schottroff).[16] In the first place, studies by Mendenhall, Gevirtz and Kilian have shown that the apodictic form in the second person singular is by no means unique to Israelite law but is found over a wide area of the ancient Near East.[17] And second, while scholars such as Gerstenberger and Gilmer have refined Alt's rigid division between apodictic and casuistic law, others like Wagner have abandoned it.[18] Indeed I argued that while the form may be able to tell us something of the legal *Sitz im Leben* in which the law evolved, it can tell us nothing about the geographical one.[19] Apodictic law simply denotes a situation in which those in authority—the head of the family or clan, elders, king, God—can determine public policy, enforcing this by sanctions if possible, while casuistic law has to define whether, in a particular case, that policy has been infringed.[20] The prophetic appeal is not to a particular form of law but rather to its breach by certain actions interpreted by the prophets as forbidden by Yahweh. When these are examined, two distinct traditions emerge.

Amos specifically sets out his charge against Israel. After a series of oracles denouncing the foreign nations for various war crimes (1.3–2.3), he condemns Israel for the exploitation of those who were not in a position to protect themselves (2.6-8). While scholars have disputed what precise actions were envisaged in the examples of exploitation listed by Amos, it is clear that the prophet was not introducing new ideas but formally indicting Israel for particular actions that fall under the rulings on humaneness and righteousness found in the Book of the Covenant (Exod. 22.20-26;

16. W. Schottroff, 'Zum alttestamentlichen Recht', in W.H. Schmidt (ed.), *Verkundigung und Forschung: Altes Testament* (BevT, 22; Munich: Chr. Kaiser Verlag, 1977), pp. 3-29.

17. Mendenhall, 'Ancient Oriental and Biblical Law', pp. 29-30; S. Gevirtz, 'West Semitic Curses and the Problem of the Origins of Hebrew Law', *VT* 11 (1961), pp. 137-58; R. Kilian, 'Apodiktisches und Kasuistisches Recht im Licht agyptischer Analogien', *BZ* 7 (1963), pp. 185-202.

18. Gerstenberger, *Wesen und Herkunft*; Gilmer, *The If-You Form*; V. Wagner, *Rechtssatze in gebundener Sprache und Rechtssatzreihen im israelitischen Recht: Ein Beitrag zur Gattungsforschung* (BZAW, 127; Berlin: W. de Gruyter, 1972).

19. Phillips, *AICL*, p. 13.

20. G. Liedke, *Gestalt und Bezeichnung alttestamentlicher Rechtssatze: Eine formgeschichtlich-terminologische Studie* (WMANT, 39; Neukirchen-Vluyn; Neukirchener Verlag, 1971); M. Weinfeld, 'The Origin of Apodictic Law: An Overlooked Source', *VT* 23 (1973), pp. 63-75.

23.1-3, 6-9). His further citations of oppression by the rich and perversion of justice are only similar examples of this original indictment. Thus the women of Samaria are condemned not for their indolent and selfish lives, nor for their possession of wealth, but because they are only enabled to live as they do through the exploitation of the needy (4.1). It is this that makes their conduct so unacceptable.

For Amos, *mišpāt* is being turned into a source of bitterness, and *ṣᵉdāqâ* entirely discarded (5.7; 6.12). Indeed, those who try to uphold justice are rejected (5.10) and, as a result, there is no check on the economic and social exploitation that now characterizes Israelite society and for which no legal redress can be obtained (5.11-12). Indeed, in a wistful aside, Amos indicates that the only possible hope for Israel lies in the proper administration of justice (5.15). For Amos is under no illusion that the cult can, of itself, secure Israel's future. No matter how extravagant Israel's religious practice is, it becomes worthless if that religion lacks content (4.4-5; 5.21-24). And although Israel's business community scrupulously keeps the Sabbath law, its observance is bitterly resented as an interruption to the sharp practices whereby fortunes are being made (8.4-6).

Amos does not, then, spring surprises but simply argues that Israelite society ought to reflect that *mišpāt* and *ṣᵉdāqâ* of which the precise content should have been obvious. To indicate this, he summons foreign powers as independent witnesses to observe the state of Samaria. Instead of justice and righteousness, they are confronted with oppression and exploitation (3.9-10). Even as foreigners unacquainted with Israel's law, they are expected to condemn such action.

What is striking in Amos' indictment of Israel is the total lack of reference to those wrongs against person or property for which the law provided sanctions. While Wolff interprets 3.10 as referring to murder and robbery,[21] comparison with Ezek. 45.9 indicates rather that general exploitation which characterizes Amos' charges. Had Amos been able to cite a more obvious breakdown of law and order beyond the laws of humaneness and righteousness, he would presumably have done so. Of course, it is not to be supposed that on occasion such capital crimes as murder and adultery were not committed. Rather, we must assume that where such actions occurred, they were dealt with under the law. Certainly, the picture that Amos presents is not of an outwardly lawless society but rather of a prosperous people, confident that their prosperity

21. H.W. Wolff, *Joel and Amos* (Hermeneia; Philadelphia: Fortress Press, 1977), pp. 193-94.

arose through faithfulness to Yahweh seen not only in excessive religious zeal but also, we must assume, in the maintenance of law and order. Hence we find the business community constrained by the sabbath requirement. Amos' indictment is that beneath this outwardly prosperous and law-abiding society (4.1; 6.1, 3-6) there lies rank disorder. But the recognition of that disorder was by no meant obvious to those in control of Israelite society, who could take a justifiable pride in their prosperity.[22] That the nation's very election should be renounced must have seemed even more unlikely (3.2).

Micah exhibits the same concern with social justice as Amos. So he condemns the deprivation of the small country farmers of their real estate by the wealthy and powerful Jerusalem citizens (2.1-5). As a result, their victims lose their status as free Israelites and become part of the landless poor, dependent on others for their maintenance and without a place in the running of society. There is, however, no indication that illegal means were used to evict them. The same concern for the oppressed occurs in 2.8-9.

In Mic. 3.1-4, 9-11, the prophet turns to the other main theme of Amos' condemnation, the perversion of justice. His language could hardly be more graphic. What precise actions were envisaged by the bloodshed of 3.10 are not specified: it may be a merely metaphorical reference to the oppression of the helpless, but it might also involve legal processes where-by innocent people were condemned to death (cf. Isa. 1.15). Yet, in spite of their conduct, it is clear that the authorities still envisaged Yahweh's support, which again indicates that, though their condemnation was obvi-ous enough to the prophet, it was not at all obvious to his contemporaries whom he condemns (3.11). Certainly excessive religious practice will not protect them (6.8). The oracle on, the exploitation of the poor, particularly through crooked business transactions (6.9-16), and the description of a society in which no one could be trusted (7.1-6), add nothing new and may only in part be from Micah's hand. Like Amos, although Micah may give examples of particular actions he condemns, he does not cite specific laws but appeals to the general concept of humaneness and righteousness. With such ideas his hearers were expected to be familiar, which makes their apparent non-recognition of the situation all the more surprising and again raises questions as to just how lawless was contemporary society.

The same concern for humaneness and righteousness is found in Isaiah.

22. McKeating, *Amos, Hosea and Micah*, p. 23.

So the prophet affirms that Israel's relationship with Yahweh rests not on the appropriate performance of cultic rites but on the proper administration of justice and the protection of the defenceless in society (1.16-17). This theme of maladministration of justice and oppression of the poor and defenceless continues in 1.21-3; 3.14-15 and the woe oracles of 5.8-25; 10.1-4. And in a masterful play on words, a general condemnation of Israel for its lack of *mišpāt* and *ṣᵉdāqâ* concludes the song of the vineyard (5.7).

Once more then we find an eighth-century prophet charging Israel with two interrelated groups of offences—the oppression of those who cannot defend themselves and the perversion of justice. What has now become quite apparent is that here lies the hub of these three prophets' indictment. It was neither cultic wrongs nor serious capital offences that dominated their preaching, for the references to idolatry in both Micah (1.7; 5.11-13) and Isaiah (2.8, 18, 20) must be regarded as redactional, as also the comment on murderers (1.21).[23] Nor is there any appeal to the Decalogue or to the covenant. Their indictment rests solely on those rulings on humaneness and righteousness already made part of the Book of the Covenant, to which I must now turn.

In contrast to the formal legal corpus of Exod. 21.12–22.16, with its specifications of precise legal offences and appropriate sanctions to be enforced through the courts, the laws of humaneness and righteousness are not, in a technical sense, laws at all, for they envisage no legal action for their breach and specify no penalties. Rather, they are addressed directly to the recipient and envisage unquestioning obedience. Their basis is an appeal to his sense of moral responsibility for those who are not in a position to protect themselves and to his sense of justice. These humanitarian and juridical provisions reflect the break-up of a clan-dominated society, in which the orphan and widow would readily have found protection, and which would have centred upon the family tent encampment. Instead, they indicate a settled agricultural community, owning its own property, readily engaging in commerce and exhibiting considerable disparity of wealth among its members. Such a thriving capitalist society marks an advanced state of development from the early days of the settlement in Canaan and would most naturally reflect the period of the united monarchy.

This is confirmed from Gilmer's analysis[24] of the If-You form in which

23. Kaiser, *Isaiah 1–12*, p. 39 (1983).
24. Gilmer, *The If-You Form.*

these humanitarian provisions appear, both in the Book of the Covenant and in Deuteronomy. Following Gerstenberger and Weinfeld,[25] he argues that this form, with its stress on persuasion, indicates a wisdom background 'which finally comes to focus in the royal court where it was employed in the instruction of officials and in the broader context of law'.[26] It is in such a royal court milieu that Deuteronomy was produced. But the same *Sitz im Leben* can be argued for the laws of humaneness and righteousness in the Book of the Covenant. Indeed, as I had already argued on different grounds,[27] the Book of the Covenant is best seen as a handbook of justice for the new Davidic state, whose king, as elsewhere in the ancient Near East, was to maintain law and order (Ps. 72; Isa. 11). Thus, from its inception the royal court, through its civil servants (a more neutral term than wisdom circles), would have initiated the codification of Israelite law which, because of Israel's peculiar constitution as the people of Yahweh, would always have been done on a theologised basis.

It is this tradition that Amos, Micah and Isaiah have taken over. They discern that within an apparently orderly society there are inhuman and unjust practices, which render that society subject to the judgement of God. This explains what Wolff, Schmid and Barton have identified as their appeal to 'natural' law,[28] though there would seem to be no need to polarize this with 'revealed' law when thinking of the sources for prophetic morality.[29] Hosea 8.12 shows that there was already a clear complex of written law accredited to Yahweh, to which appeal could be made. The innovation of Amos, Micah and Isaiah was to hold that the nation's very election depended, not merely on conformity to cultic practice and the observance of the laws for which specific sanctions were provided, but also on those principles of natural law already enshrined—but of necessity very generally—in the rulings on humaneness and righteousness in the Book of the Covenant, a breach of which any rational man ought to have been able to discern for himself. No exploitation could be justified on the grounds of national prosperity or expediency. The elect community was to

25. Gerstenberger, *Wesen und Herkunft*; Weinfeld, *Deuteronomy*.

26. Gilmer, *The If-You Form*, p. 110.

27. *AICL*, pp.158-61.

28. Wolff, *Joel and Amos*; H.H. Schmid, *Gerechtigkeit als Weltordnung: Hintergrund und Geschichte des alttestamentlichen Gerechtigkeitsbegriffes* (BHT, 40; Tübingen: J.C.B. Mohr, 1968); Barton, 'Natural Law'. pp. 1-14.

29. W. Zimmerli, *The Law and the Prophets: A Study of the Meaning of the Old Testament* (Oxford: Basil Blackwell, 1965), p. 67.

exhibit that same sense of responsibility for all within its ranks as characterized it from its inception. This prophetic reliance on the rulings on humaneness and righteousness indicates the unprofitability of so much recent discussion on wisdom and prophecy, whether in the attempt to identify a particular prophet with the wise, or to differentiate the prophets from a ruling class of wise.[30] Rather, these prophets offer a different assessment of Israel's situation from that of those who guided and administered the nation. Their analysis was confirmed by the subsequent widespread Deuteronomic emphasis on humanitarianism, which even included the desacralization of the holy-war legislation.[31] But this was not the only, nor in the end the dominant, tradition inherited from the prophets.

Bergren does not mention Hosea, presumably because he recognized the totally different standpoint of that prophet. For nowhere does Hosea make any direct reference to the exploitation of the poor and needy, except perhaps in a sarcastic comment on crooked trading practices (12.8). Instead, his emphasis falls on Israel's apostasy, summed up in the word 'harlotry'. It openly embraces other gods, and indulges in idolatry (4.17; 8.4-6; 11.2; 13.2; 14.9). As a result, Yahweh will no longer make himself known to it as I AM (1.9)—a direct reference to the disclosure of the divine name in Exod. 3.14. But since there is no mention of apostasy or idolatry in Amos, Israel is not to be thought of as suddenly embracing Baalism. Rather, Hosea is to be understood as attempting to purge Yahwism of those aspects of fertility religion to which it had, from the first, been attached. In Hosea's view, Yahweh was being treated as if He were a mere nature deity. Indeed, popular religion may have continued to address Yahweh as Baal.[32] But it is Yahweh and not Baal who is the giver of fertility to the land (2.10), which is to be induced neither through ritual associated with cult prostitution (4.11-14) nor through sacrifice but which follows automatically from knowledge of him (6.6). It is this failure of knowledge that leads to Israel's condemnation, from which there will be no escape in political alliances (5.13-14; 7.11-13; 8.9-10).

Hosea's formal indictment of Israel is set out in 4.1-3. *ᵉmet* and *ḥesed*

---

30. N. Whybray, 'Prophecy and Wisdom', in R. Coggins, A. Phillips and M. Knibb (eds.), *Israel's Prophetic Tradition* (Cambridge: Cambridge University Press, 1982), pp. 181-99.

31. Gilmer, *The If-You Form*, p. 109.

32. R.E. Clements, 'Understanding the Book of Hosea', *RE* 72 (1975), pp. 405-423 (pp. 412ff.).

indicate that intense loyalty that Yahweh has a right to expect from his people. *da'at ʳelōhîm*, lack of which is the theme of Hosea (4.6; 6.6; cf. 2.22; 5.4; 6.3; 8.2 and 13.4), describes that personal, intimate relationship that Israel can have with Yahweh as a result of its election. There can be no doubt that the five absolute infinitives of 4.2 refer to those crimes covered by the third, ninth, sixth, eighth and seventh commandments, all of which affected the person of the individual Israelite and demanded the death penalty.[33] Although neither vocabulary nor order correspond with the Decalogue, it is difficult not to recognize an explicit reference to it, particularly as the order of crimes can be accounted for by association: two kinds of spoken crime, two kinds of murder (the man-thief, to which Alt showed the eighth commandment referred, is called 'the stealer of life' in Deut. 24.7) and adultery.[34] The vocabulary results from the need to use single words. Such anarchy could only lead to the end of all life (4.3).

But since there seems little indication either in Amos or Hosea of the widespread chaos envisaged by 4.2, it would appear that the Decalogue is being used theologically, as a blanket expression indicating total renunciation of Yahweh in the most complete way possible. Hosea's interest is not in the crimes of the Decalogue but rather in Israel's lack of loyalty to God, consequent upon its syncretistic cult. Murders are mentioned in 6.8-9, but these probably relate to irregularities concerning the cities of refuge.[35] Nor should we understand 4.13-14 to refer to sexual promiscuity in society at large. Rather, reference is being made to the adoption of Canaanite sexual cultic practices involving brides, of which there is evidence elsewhere in the ancient world.[36] Only in the reference to theft and robbery in 7.1 is there any indication of general lawlessness, though these were not crimes covered by the Decalogue but civil wrongs.[37] This lack of general anarchy, together with the fact that the prophetic judgment speech presents the indictment twice, first negatively and then positively, raises the strong presupposition that the theological use of the Decalogue is due to Deuteronomic redaction designed to define 'knowledge of God' as the Decalogue, for it was part of Deuteronomic theology that the Decalogue alone was given to Israel at Horeb (Deut. 4.13; 5.22). Wolff[38] has noted

33. *AICL*, pp. 145-58; Wolff, *Hosea*, pp. 67-68.
34. Alt, 'Das Verbot'.
35. Dinur, 'The Religious Character', p. 142.
36. Wolff, *Hosea*, pp. 85-88.
37. *AICL*, pp. 132-41.
38. Wolff, *Hosea*, p. 31.

how many ideas characteristic of Deuteronomic thought occur first in Hosea. Another such idea was the interpretation of *tōrâ* as summarizing the complete expression of the will of Yahweh revealed to Israel at Horeb, obedience to which determined its future.[39] It is this use of 'my *tōrâ*' in 8.1, paralleled by 'my *bᵉrît*', which Perlitt has shown to be Deuteronomic (cf. Amos 2.4).[40] Uniquely, then, among the eighth-century prophets we have in Hosea appeal both to the Decalogue and *bᵉrît*. Clearly, the redactor intends Hosea's preaching to be understood against the background of an utterly rejected Decalogue, *the covenant law* of Sinai.

While the humanitarian concerns of the other eighth-century prophets were to be emphasized by the Deuteronomists, Hosea's anti-Canaanite stance was to have even greater consequences in the reforms of Hezekiah and Josiah and the legislation that accompanied them. I have already argued that Exod. 32–34 reflects Hezekiah's reform and, together with Exod. 19–24, forms the literary precedent for Deuteronomy.[41] Thus Exod. 34.10-16 warns against fraternizing with the Canaanites, orders the destruction of their sanctuaries and cult objects, and counsels against inter-marriage—a warning that may be compared with the later absolute pro-hibition in Deut. 7.3. Then comes the command against making a molten god (Exod. 34.17), in the context, clearly referring back to the golden calf of Exod. 32, itself to be identified with the bulls of Jeroboam I, of so much concern to Hosea. This explains why Hezekiah was not afraid to destroy the bronze serpent Nehushtan, even though its creation was attributed to no less a person than Moses. Finally there follows the revision of the festal calendar of Exod. 23.14-17, which now requires the centralization of the celebration of the three main festivals in Jerusalem (Exod. 34.23-24).

That Deuteronomy is to be seen as a new version of the Sinai narrative, deliberately intended to supersede this earlier account, can be seen by comparing Exod. 32–34 with Deut. 9–10. Whereas in Exod. 32–34 Moses himself is instructed to write a different set of laws (Exod. 34.11-26) on the new tablets, in Deut. 10.4 it is specifically asserted that the Decalogue was rewritten on the second set of tablets by God himself. Nicholson correctly recognized the importance of the Deuteronomic assertion that the Decalogue alone was given at Horeb (Deut. 4.13; 5.22) but missed the point of that assertion.[42] It does not indicate that the Deuteronomists did

---

39. Lindars, 'Torah in Deuteronomy', pp. 117-36.
40. Perlitt, *Die Bundestheologie*, pp. 146ff.
41. *AICL*, pp. 167-79; and see Chapter 2 above.
42. Nicholson 'The Decalogue'.

not know the Sinai pericope in its present form in Exodus, but that they wished to suppress it.

Exodus 34.10, 27-28 does, of course, envisage the second set of tablets as $b^e r\hat{\imath}t$, as indeed in its present context Exod. 19.5; 24.7-8 understands the first. While Nicholson,[43] following McCarthy,[44] has properly stressed the centrality of theophany in the original Sinai narrative, the latter has pointed both to the similarity and to the dissimilarity of these covenant references with Deuteronomic usage.[45] But as Patrick has indicated in reply to Perlitt and Nicholson,[46] this covenant framework is much more at home in what have come to be known as proto-Deuteronomic circles (see literature cited by Childs[47]), which I would identify as those responsible for Exod. 32–34, and whose activity is also to be found within Exod. 19–24, not only in $b^e r\hat{\imath}t$ passages but also in such parenetic material as the anti-Canaanite epilogue to the Book of the Covenant (Exod. 23.20-33). Indeed, the present arrangement of Exod. 19–24; 32–34 is to be understood as their response to the fall of Samaria, reflected in the destruction of the tablets, which they introduce into the narrative. Here lies the beginning of the understanding of Yahweh's relationship with Israel in terms of the political treaty-form, later to find full expression in Deuteronomy. The court-authors concerned to record Hezekiah's reform would have been well aware of such treaties.

The influence of Hosea's prophecy accounts, then, for Exod. 19–24; 32–34, which leads on to Deuteronomy and itself explains the reason for the Deuteronomic redaction of the prophecy. But the influence of the other eighth-century prophets can also be detected in Exod. 22–23 in the strengthening of the legally unenforceable laws of humaneness by the addition of clauses encouraging obedience (Exod. 22.20b, 22b–23; 23.9). These motive clauses indicate that, like the prophetic speeches, the law collections were addressed to the people at large and not simply to legal officials. They were not so much codes to be administered as a way of life to be followed.[48] That these clauses are not part of the original injunctions can be seen by their plural form of address. So while Exod. 22.20 now

43. Nicholson, *Exodus and Sinai*.

44. D.J. McCarthy, *Treaty and Covenant* (1963).

45. McCarthy, '*berit* in Old Testament History', p. 114.

46. Patrick, 'The Covenant Code Source', pp. 422-33; Perlitt, *Die Bundestheologie*; Nicholson, *Exodus and Sinai*.

47. Childs, *Introduction*, p. 166.

48. Gemser, *The Importance of Motive Clauses*, pp. 50-66.

seeks to obtain justice for aliens by reminding Israelites that they were once aliens in Egypt, Exod. 22.22-23 utters a direct threat against those who afflict the widow and the orphan. Yahweh will kill the offenders, thus ensuring that their wives and children have the same insecure status as those whom they had oppressed—another example of the principle of poetic justice to which Barton has pointed in the eighth-century prophets.[49] The Deuteronomists were later to introduce the further inducement that obedience to apparently uneconomic laws would bring material blessing from Yahweh (Deut. 15.10, 18; 23.21). This idea also characterizes the Deuteronomic addition to the fifth commandment, which now promises not only possession of the land (Exod. 20.12), but prosperity too (Deut. 5.16).

The two traditions that I have isolated in the eighth-century prophets come together in Jeremiah, itself heavily redacted by the Deuteronomists, not only in the prose sermons but also in the narrative material.[50] Like Hosea, Jeremiah condemns Israel for its apostasy. Though some of the references to this come from what appear to be Deuteronomistic material (Jer. 3.6-11; 11.1-14; 16.10-13), there is clear evidence elsewhere to confirm that this was a dominant theme in Jeremiah's prophecy. Thus his opening indictment, now intended by the Deuteronomists as an introduction to the book, summarizes his charge against Israel as apostasy (1.16), which is then fully set out (2.1–3.5). Israel is pictured as a harlot (2.20; 3.1-5) or adulteress (5.7-9; 9.1; 13.27; 23.9-12), peculiarly apt descriptions in view of its preoccupation with fertility rites involving sexual acts.

Something of the great variety of popular religion in the time of Jeremiah can be seen from the references to particular apostate cultic practices. Jeremiah 7.16-20 and 44.17-19, 25 describe the making of cakes for the queen of heaven, clearly some fertility rite. Another specific practice was the cult of Molech, centred in the valley of Ben-Hinnom outside Jerusalem. While it is not certain precisely what was involved, the fact that Jer. 7.31; 19.5 and 32.35 repeat that this rite was no command of Yahweh probably indicates that the participants saw him as the object of their devotions. It is true that Baal has been inserted in Jer. 19.5 and 32.35, and this conforms with Deut. 12.31, but to say that Yahweh never commanded child sacrifice to Baal seems hardly necessary, even to the most obtuse of Israelites. References to astral cults occur in Jer. 8.2; 19.13. These are particularly associated with the last years of the Davidic monarchy (2 Kgs

---

49. Barton, 'Natural Law'.
50. Nicholson, *Preaching*.

21.3-5; 23.4-5; Zeph. 1.5), and the commandment against images was extended to cover them (Deut. 4.15-24). Though much of this material derives from Deuteronomistic editing, there can be no doubt that the religious practices of Judah in Jeremiah's time were seen by the prophet as a betrayal of Yahweh—a going after other gods. Yet it is clear from the Temple sermon (Jer. 7; cf. Jer. 26) that the people themselves saw their religion as a guarantee of their security, hence their reliance on sacrifice (Jer. 6.20-21; 7.21-23; 11.15-16)—a reliance as misplaced as that on the presence of Yahweh in his temple.

The temple sermon introduces the other tradition of eighth-century prophecy, the laws of humaneness and righteousness. Although Jer. 7 in its present form is a Deuteronomistic composition, that it is based on an actual incident in Jeremiah's life is confirmed from Jer. 26. Echoes of Jeremiah's original sermon may be found in the people's threefold chant about the Temple. Verses 5-7 announce that if the people amend their ways and their doings, then Yahweh will let them continue to dwell in the land that He had given them. What amending their ways and their doings consists of is defined in vv. 5b–6—the proper exercise of justice and the refusal to oppress the alien, orphan and widow, to shed blood or to go after other gods.

I have identified the exercise of justice and the protection of those who could not defend themselves as the basis of the prophetic indictment of Amos, Micah and Isaiah. This tradition is also found in Jeremiah in his general condemnation of Judah (5.26-28; 6.13-14 = 8.10-11) and his summons to the king to administer justice (21.11-12), with his specific condemnation of Jehoiakim for failing to do so (22.13-19; cf. 23.5-6).

But in describing the actual breach of law for which Jeremiah indicts his people, Jer. 7.9 makes specific reference to the Decalogue, the eighth, sixth, seventh and ninth commandments being mentioned alongside the burning of incense to Baal and going after other gods. Nicholson sees this reference to the Decalogue as a possible echo of the prophet's original oracle,[51] but it seems to me more likely that, as in Hos. 4.2, this specific citing of the Decalogue is due to the Deuteronomists themselves again using the Decalogue theologically as a blanket statement to indicate the total renunciation of Yahweh. Once more man-theft is associated with murder. The fact that the Deuteronomists felt it necessary to set out this crime in their law shows that the commandment retained its importance (Deut. 24.7). But outside Jer. 7.9, no reliance is placed on the Decalogue

---

51. Nicholson, *Preaching*, p. 69.

for Judah's condemnation. While Jer. 9.1-8 paints a general picture of dishonesty, this is a very different matter from the general breakdown of society that would follow the total abrogation of the Decalogue. Indeed, all the evidence indicates that, once again, those in authority thought that the nation was secure (6.14; 8.11). It would therefore seem much more likely that Jeremiah's original charge concerned oppression of the defenceless and maladministration of justice, together with apostasy, thus showing that the prophet had inherited from his eighth-century predecessors the two prophetic traditions that we have isolated.

But the fact that references to the Decalogue only found their way into Hos. 4.2 and Jer. 7.9 due to Deuteronomistic redaction does not necessarily mean that the Decalogue itself originated with the Deuteronomists, any more than that the covenant idea did. A final paragraph is no place to argue the date of the Decalogue, but two points may be made. First, examination of the Book of the Covenant indicates that the compiler is consciously trying to distinguish crimes prohibited by the Decalogue, and carrying the death penalty, from civil offences, for which compensation was required. So murder (Exod. 21.12) is contrasted with assault (Exod. 21.18-19), and man-theft (Exod. 21.16) with theft of property (Exod. 21.37, 22.2b-3). But, exceptionally assault of parents (Exod. 21.15) as well as their repudiation (Exod. 21.17) carries the death penalty; seduction of a virgin (in contrast to adultery) results in damages (Exod. 22.15-16). In my view, the compiler aims to assimilate local indigenous legal practice, long administered by the elders in the gate, to the over-riding principles of Yahwism contained in the Decalogue.[52] And secondly, the Decalogue has been inserted before the Deuteronomic legal corpus (12–26), not as a summary of the more important Deuteronomic laws, but rather to give those laws a proper pedigree by presenting them as deduced from the Decalogue itself, the only law written on the tablets given at Horeb. As I have indicated earlier, prophetic silence about the Decalogue and its provisions can be due to other reasons than ignorance of its existence.

---

52. Phillips, 'Another Look at Murder'.

Chapter 11

TORAH AND MISHPAT: A LIGHT TO THE PEOPLES

There can be little doubt that Israel regarded the Babylonian conquest and her subsequent exile in a heathen land as the most cataclysmic event in her history. The destruction of the temple, the captivity of the king and leading citizens and the absorption of her land into the Babylonian empire seem to mark her end as a distinct people, the people of Yahweh. Could there be any future?

But one element in Israel's life was not destroyed, her law, though paradoxically Israel's theologians considered that its breach had led to her apparent hopeless situation. For it was not Babylonian military prowess which had brought this about, but Yahweh himself who could no longer tolerate Israel's disobedience. But ironically if there was to be any future, that future depended on Israel continuing to express faith in Yahweh, and the only sure vehicle for that faith was his law.

In the aftermath of the disaster of 586 the Deuteronomists produced what was on the face of it one of the most remarkable testimonies to faith ever written. By modelling the book of Deuteronomy on the political suzerainty treaty form they clearly indicated that they understood the continuation of the covenant relationship with Yahweh to be determined by Israel's obedience to the stipulations he had laid upon her. Whether earlier generations had interpreted Israel's relationship with Yahweh in the same way need not concern us.[1] But for the Deuteronomists Israel's election contained within it the threat of rejection if she failed to keep the covenant law laid upon her by her suzerain, Yahweh. Yet though they understood that threat to have been implemented by the events of 586, the Deuteronomists nonetheless produced their great theological work, Deuteronomy–2 Kings. Their hope, apparently illogical, was that despite all that had occurred, Yahweh might yet once more exercise his grace, that

1. Nicholson, *Exodus and Sinai*.

there might be another entry into the promised land.

The event which apparently prompted the Deuteronomists to articulate their hope was the release of King Jehoiachin from prison in 561. Undoubtedly this caused enormous excitement throughout Judaism both in Palestine and Babylon. Could this be the prelude to yet another mighty act of Yahweh? For those who had eyes to see, was he even now preparing to deliver his people? So in spite of their own theological position, the Deuteronomists were prepared to recognize that Yahweh could not let his people go. This was their testimony of faith.

But if there was to be a future, that future could only be built on Yahweh's Torah. Hence the Deuteronomists reiterate the importance of absolute obedience to the covenant law, which they set out in every detail. If ever again Israel is given the chance to cross the Jordan she will know what she has to do in order to ensure that she should not once more be cursed for her failure. It is thus no accident that it is the Deuteronomists who reinterpret the word *tōrâ* from its earlier use as a specific direction following a particular question to designate the whole corpus of the law. It therefore comes to stand for the complete expression of the will of Yahweh. So, as Barnabas Lindars has indicated, the usual translation 'the book of the law' would be better rendered 'the book of divine instruction'.[2] This development was probably the work of the scribal school now widely thought to have been behind Deuteronomy[3] for it is in the wisdom literature that Torah is used quite generally of the teaching of the wise rather than in the priestly sense as an answer to a query. In any event, for the Deuteronomists the individual laws are intended as a comprehensive list to deal with every situation which Israel may face in the promised land, and thus enable her at all times to fulfill Yahweh's will. Consequently the Torah must on no account be varied either by addition or subtraction (Deut. 4.2; 12.32). This is not an uncommon element in ancient Near Eastern law codes as the conclusion of the Babylonian codes of Lipit Ishtar[4] and Hammurabi[5] indicate. But it may at first seem surprising that the Deuteronomists considered their code complete when it makes no reference to the civil law provisions which are so important in the Book of the Covenant. But as I have pointed out in my commentary on Deuter-

---

2.   Lindars, 'Torah in Deuteronomy', pp. 117-36.
3.   Weinfeld, *Deuteronomy*; Gilmer. *The If-You Form*.
4.   *ANET*, p. 161a.
5.   *ANET*, p. 178b.

onomy,[6] the reason for this was that such provisions were not understood as part of the covenant law on which Israel's continued election depended, but rather as domestic issues to be settled between the parties through the payment of damages. The Deuteronomic law is not concerned with the protection of property but with establishing that society which reflects Yahweh's will. Hence its stress on sole allegiance to him and the exercise of charity to those in need. For it was by an act of charity, the exercise of his grace, that Yahweh had chosen Israel and brought her to the promised land, and might yet do so again.

It is then on the strength of the history of Yahweh's dealings with his people that the Deuteronomists appeal to their contemporaries to remain faithful. For if Yahweh is to continue to exercise his grace towards Israel, there must still be a people whom he can deliver. For the Deuteronomists, then, despite judgment having been carried out under the law, that law must not be considered obsolete. For it is with those who still acknowledge its validity that Yahweh can do, if he so wills, his further mighty work. In other words, though Israel's future depends on the initiative of Yahweh, Yahweh is himself dependent on there being a faithful people on whom he can lavish his illogical generosity (cf. Hos. 11.8-9), and who will then once more be able to practise his Torah in their own land and so entirely fulfill his will. Then they will enjoy unparalleled prosperity as they luxuriate in the rich ordering of life which obedience to Torah always brings. This was the vision which the Deuteronomists offered their generation.

The Deuteronomists produced their work sometime between the release of Jehoiachin from prison in 561 and 540, for they show no awareness of the threat to Babylon from the rise of Cyrus, nor make any mention of the return from exile in 538. Whether they wrote in Babylon or Palestine remains uncertain. Their work was shortly followed by the prophecies of Deutero-Isaiah.

This unknown prophet of the exile, like the Deuteronomists, proclaimed a message of hope against a background of total failure. No attempt is made to gloss over Israel's sin which had brought her to her present position. But the emphasis of Deutero-Isaiah's prophecy and the basis for his hope is that Yahweh who is both lord of creation and lord of history (e.g. Isa. 51.9-11) is still in control, though the responsibility for Israel's future rests entirely on the exiles.

---

6. Phillips, *Deuteronomy*, p. 32.

Deutero-Isaiah was not the first prophet to proclaim a return from exile. Ezekiel had done so many years before. But the generation to whom Ezekiel had preached was already dead, and there still seemed to be no end to Israel's sojourn in Babylon. The only sensible conclusion must be to accept that Yahweh's judgment had been final, as the Deuteronomic covenant theology implied (though the Deuteronomists hoped that this was not so), and identify with foreign and apparently victorious gods. Against such a background Deutero-Isaiah announces that even now Yahweh is breaking in to perform his new mighty act. Israel's redemption was not merely imminent but accomplished (Isa. 48.20). His message is then one of realized eschatology. It is no accident that this all-conquering Persian prince has appeared in the east, but part of the divine plan. Israel's punishment is over and the whole world will witness her triumphant procession across a transformed environment back to her own land (Isa. 40.1-11). And this new exodus in which water will be abundantly available to the chosen people (Isa. 43.19-21) will be no secret flight (Isa. 52.12), but will take place in full sight of the nations. It may have looked as if Yahweh had abandoned his people, but there had in fact been no bill of divorce (Isa. 50.1). But unlike the Deuteronomists who make no attempt to reassess Yahweh's relationship with his people, but still see Israel as subject to the threat of total rejection, Deutero-Isaiah assures the exiles that this relationship will be for all time. In the future nothing will be able to sever Yahweh's covenant with his people for in the new exodus from Babylon, unlike its predecessor from Egypt, no obligations will be laid on them. Deutero-Isaiah arrives at this 'new covenant' theology of sheer grace (cf. Jer. 31)—a theology also to be found in Ezekiel and the Priestly Work— by omitting any reference to the Sinai covenant (Exod. 19–24, 32–34).[7] Instead he concentrates on Israel's three ancient covenant traditions—all covenants of promise without obligation: the covenants with Noah (Gen. 8.21-22), Abraham (Gen. 17), and David (2 Sam. 7). Thus the covenant with Abraham is proclaimed as still in force (Isa. 51.2-3), the covenant with Noah reiterated (Isa. 54.9-10), and the covenant with David reapplied to the nation (Isa. 55.3). The only element of hesitation in the prophet's triumphant message is whether the exiles will have sufficient faith to recognize in the events now engulfing them the hand of Yahweh who wills that they should continue to be his people and he their God. Their future is assured for ever, if only they will appropriate what is at present at hand.

7.   Cf. Zimmerli, *The Law and the Prophets*, pp. 86-90; Phillips, *God B.C.*, pp. 43-47.

But is it only in the abandonment of the Deuteronomic threat theology that Deutero-Isaiah differs from the Deuteronomists? Could it also be said that his attitude to the foreign nations marks a complete reversal of Deuteronomic concern? Certainly this view was once generally accepted. Deutero-Isaiah was seen as charging the chosen people, now specifically designated as 'a light to the nations' (Isa. 42.6; 49.6), with an active mission to the world. Having been individually elected to receive Yahweh's revelation, they are now to set about sharing it with all nations. But studies of Deutero-Isaiah by de Boer,[8] Snaith[9] and Martin-Achard[10] have challenged such an interpretation. Far from Deutero-Isaiah being the apostle of missionary zeal, his prophecies have been understood as narrowly nationalistic and particularist. So de Boer argues that Deutero-Isaiah's 'only purpose is to proclaim deliverance for the Judean people'.[11] an assessment which both Snaith and, more judiciously, Martin-Achard support. So the latter writes: 'The chief concern of the prophet of the Exile is not the salvation of the Gentiles but the liberation of his own people and its triumphant return to Jerusalem; the heathen are scarcely more than an instrument in the hands of Israel's God'.[12] The result of such an interpretation is that Deutero-Isaiah is held responsible for the allegedly narrow and exclusive attitude of postexilic Judaism, and any tension between his prophecy and the work of Nehemiah and Ezra is removed. But in my view this interpretation of Deutero-Isaiah's work does as much violence to his prophecy as the interpretation it rightly overthrows.[13] While Deutero-Isaiah nowhere bids Israel actually to go out in mission to the foreign nations, he is nonetheless positively concerned about their relationship with Yahweh. While he rejoices over Yahweh's unexpected deliverance of Israel, he by no means sees this in narrow nationalistic terms, but as having definite repercussions on the nations who are thereby brought to acknowledge Yahweh as the one sovereign God. As a result, Yahweh's

8. P.A.H. de Boer, 'Second Isaiah's Message', *OTS* 9 (1956), pp. 80-101.

9. N.H. Snaith, 'The Servant of the Lord in Deutero-Isaiah', in H.H. Rowley (ed.), *Studies in Old Testament Prophecy* (Edinburgh: T. & T. Clark, 1950), pp. 187-200, and *idem*, 'Isaiah 40-66: A Study of the Teaching of Second Isaiah and its Consequences', in *Studies on the Second Part of the Book of Isaiah* (VTSup, 14; Leiden: E.J. Brill, 1967), pp. 154-65.

10. R. Martin-Achard, *A Light to the Nations* (Edinburgh: Oliver & Boyd, 1962).

11. Martin-Achard, *A Light*, p. 90.

12. Martin-Achard, *A Light*, p. 13.

13. J. Lindblom, *Prophecy in Ancient Israel* (Oxford: Basil Blackwell, 1963), pp. 427-28.

Torah and *mišpāṭ* now become of universal significance and the means whereby world order can be achieved.

The Deuteronomic attitude to foreign nations is clear enough. In the Deuteronomists' opinion Israel's failure to destroy the Canaanites on first entry into the land had led to her subsequent apostasy, and so to Yahweh's judgment for her unfaithfulness. Consequently the Deuteronomists urge that were the Jordan ever to be crossed for a second time, then this time the indigenous population must be utterly exterminated. Of course one has only to compare the prophecy of Hosea with Deuteronomic theology to recognize that this Deuteronomic assessment is decidedly one-sided. In fact in every department of her life and not least in her understanding of her God, Israel's debt to Canaan was immense. But for the Deuteronomists writing in the aftermath of the Babylonian conquest and exile, it was Canaanite religious practice which had polluted the pure Yahwistic faith and led to Israel's renunciation by her God. Hence the Deuteronomists concentrate on ensuring the isolation of Israelite religion from all Canaanite customs and practices (Deut. 14; 18.9-14; 21.22-23; 22.5; 23.18-19). Thus while under earlier regulations marriages with Canaanite women had been frowned upon (Exod. 34.16), now they are totally banned with both men and women (Deut. 7.3; Josh. 23.12; Judg. 3.6). The Deuteronomists see Israel as a religious ghetto in faithful obedience to Yahweh revelling in the richness of the land which he wills to give her. They know that they are better off than any of the other nations both in their God's concern for them and the nature of his will, his Torah (Deut. 4.7-8), and are content to leave the other nations to their inferior gods. Their conversion is thus never contemplated. But within Israel—that is the whole territory of the promised land—Yahweh is to enjoy his people's exclusive worship. What happened outside is no concern of theirs. In this respect, as in my view in their covenant threat theology, the Deuteronomists were merely reiterating the recognized pre-exilic position. While Yahweh is seen as having power to do with the nations as he likes, both in using them as his agent and also inflicting judgment upon them, it is only with Israel that he has entered into a specific relationship and only from her that he expects unwavering allegiance (Amos 3.2).

The basis for the view that Deutero-Isaiah specifically charged Israel with a mission to the world lies in the fact that he is the first Old Testament theologian explicitly to articulate the doctrine of monotheism, that is, that there is only one God (Isa. 41.4; 43.10-13; 44.6-8; 45.5-6, 14, 18, 22; 46.9; 48.12). Earlier Israel had, of course, worshipped only one God, but had freely acknowledged the existence of other gods with whom she was forbidden to have any dealings. This milestone in the development of Israel's religious understanding was no doubt prompted by finding that in Babylon the same things were being claimed for Marduk as for Yahweh. The exponents of the missionary view of Deutero-Isaiah's ministry then argue that the immediate effect of the declaration of monotheism was to bring the other nations which could hitherto be comfortably ignored into a definite relationship with Yahweh, for as the only God he must have been responsible for their creation. This accounts for the new world view of Deutero-Isaiah. Logically this must be the case. If there is only one God, the creator of all, then all must be of intimate concern to him. The Deuteronomic ghetto theology cannot be maintained. But it does not necessarily follow from this that the only way in which Yahweh can express his concern is by charging Israel with an active mission to the nations. They can equally well get to know Yahweh and his will by coming themselves to Israel to be taught by her.

The missionary view of Deutero-Isaiah's prophecy is based on four key texts: Isa. 42.1-4; 49.1-6; 51.4-5; and 55.3-5. In Isa. 42.1-4, the first of the so-called servant songs (Isa. 42.1-4[9]; 49.1-6[13]; 50.4-9[11]; 52.13–53.12), Yahweh designates his chosen servant through whom he wills that his *mišpāṭ* shall be brought forth to the nations. A final note adds that even those most distant places, the coastlands or isles (v. 4) await Yahweh's *tōrâ*. In this task the servant strengthened by Yahweh's spirit is assured of success, even when others might have been discouraged. The hint that this discouragement will consist of severe personal suffering is confirmed in the later songs.

But before we go any further we must ask who is this servant? Despite the multitude of words which have been written on this subject[14] there can to my mind be no doubt who has formed Deutero-Isaiah's model. For as we would expect in a work depicting a second exodus, it can only be Moses for he alone of all Israel's heroes was specifically said to have suffered vicariously at Yahweh's behest.[15] The first intimation of this

---

14. For the history of the study of the servant songs, cf. C.R. North, *The Suffering Servant in Deutero-Isaiah: An Historical and Critical Study* (Oxford: Oxford University Press, 2nd edn, 1956); H.H. Rowley, 'The Servant of the Lord in the Light of Three Decades of Criticism', in *idem*, *The Servant of the Lord and Other Essays on the Old Testament* (Oxford: Basil Blackwell, 2nd edn, 1965), pp. 3-60; W. Zimmerli and J. Jeremias, *The Servant of God* (SBT, 20; London: SCM Press, 1957).

15. A. Bentzen, *King and Messiah* (London: Lutterworth Press, 1953); G. von Rad,

occurs in the account in Exodus of the incident of the golden calf (Exod. 32.32), in my view the work of the proto-Deuteronomists,[16] where Moses is described as offering to atone for Isarel's sin. It is on this incident that the Deuteronomists have built. For them Yahweh takes the initiative and specifically refuses to allow Moses to enter the promised land (Deut. 1.37; 3.26-28; 4.21). Instead he is instructed to look across the Jordan at the full extent of that land, and so to take possession of it on Israel's behalf, for this was the recognized legal way by which the conveyance of land was effected (cf. Gen. 13.14-17).[17] But although himself innocent of any offence, Moses must die in Transjordan for Israel's rebellion in the desert. This theological assessment was too much for the Priestly theologians who reinterpreted Yahweh's refusal to allow Moses entry into the promised land as due to actual sin on his part (Num. 20.12; Deut. 32.51).[18] But it is this explicit example of vicarious suffering, the work of the Deuteronomists, who incidentally continually describe Moses as 'the servant of God', which has directly influenced Deutero-Isaiah.

But establishing the model for the suffering servant does not mean that we have discovered that servant's identity. Who is to be the new Moses of the new exodus? From Isa. 49.3 the answer would seem to be Israel,[19] but Isa. 49.6 makes it plain that this cannot be all Israel. Rather the servant must be that righteous remnant of Israel who remain faithful to Yahweh and by accepting Deutero-Isaiah's message secure the future of all Israel. It is those individuals who in the face of the apparent inactivity of Yahweh are still prepared to acknowledge and trust him. It seems then to me that we are to see in the dying generation of the faithful exiles a direct parallel to Moses who like them had to die in a heathen land beyond the Jordan in order that his people might enter the promised land. Their faithfulness in suffering would ultimately have worldwide significance. The servant will not have laboured in vain: he need not be discouraged.

Old Testament Theology, 2 (Edinburgh: Oliver & Boyd, 1965), pp. 250-62.

16. Phillips, 'A Fresh Look', pp. 39-52, 282-94 (reprinted above as Chapter 2).

17. Phillips, 'A Fresh Look', p. 30. Cf. Mt. 4.8-9; Lk. 14.18. This method of conveying land is also found in Roman law.

18. In Ps. 106.32-33 an attempt is made to reconcile the two traditions.

19. Many commentators have sought to excise 'Israel' from Isa. 49.3 as a late interpolation (e.g. S. Mowinckel, *He That Cometh* [Oxford: Basil Blackwell, 1956], pp. 462-64; C. Westermann, *Isaiah 40–66* [OTL; London: SCM Press, 1969], pp. 208-210). But manuscript evidence would argue for its retention (cf. C.R. North, *The Second Isaiah* (Oxford: Clarendon Press, 1964), pp. 187-88.

According to Isa. 42.1-4 the servant's task is to bring forth, that is manifest, *mišpāṭ* among the nations. This word is usually rendered in English
by judgment or justice. But neither term adequately expresses its meaning.
In Exod. 21.1 the plural *mišpāṭîm* is used collectively of the various
injunctions of the Book of the Covenant (Exod. 20.20–23.33). Originally
mišpāṭîm here referred only to the specific decisions on criminal and civil
cases, for the laws on humaneness and righteousness (Exod. 22.20-26;
23.1-9) are a later addition.[20] Thus the *mišpāṭîm* represented actual court
rulings which also acted as precedents for the future. But these precedents
did, of course, directly reflect the will of Yahweh who was regarded as the
author of all such decisions. Consequently further injunctions which could
not be enforced in the courts, the laws of humaneness and righteousness,
could be subsumed under the title *mišpāṭîm* as they too were seen to reflect
the divine will. Collectively then *mišpāṭ* could be understood as indicating
the kind of conduct which Yahweh wanted his people to put into effect in
their lives. Thus Jeremiah understands *mišpāṭ* as a synonym for the way
(*derek*) in which Yahweh wishes Israel to walk (5.4-5). It is then in this
sense of applied law, that is applying Yahweh's will to the whole stratum
of life, that *mišpāṭ* is to be understood in Isa. 42.1-4. It is this that the
servant is to establish among the nations so that the whole world lives
the kind of life that Yahweh wills. It comes then as no surprise to find both
in Isa. 42.4 and the very similar passage Isa. 51.4 *mišpāṭ* used in parallel
with *tôrâ* in its novel Deuteronomic sense of divine instruction, that is
the collective expression of the will of Yahweh. Further investigation
indicates that it is only in this Deuteronomic sense that *tôrâ* is used by
Deutero-Isaiah (Isa. 42.21, 24; 51.7). As in the case of the suffering
servant, we here find another instance of direct Deuteronomic influence on
Deutero-Isaiah.

The servant's task then is to bring forth *mišpāṭ* to the nations. But
in effecting this, he is not left unaided. At his call, Yahweh endows him
with his spirit. The same gift of the spirit occurs in Isa. 11.2 where the
Messianic king is similarly equipped in order that he might perform his
task of establishing justice. Indeed it is possible that as in Isa. 53.3
promises concerning the Davidic monarch have again been reapplied to

20. I. Lewy, 'Dating of Covenant Code Sections on Humaneness and Righteousness', *VT* 7 (1957), pp. 322-26. These provisions could have been the work of wisdom
circles and may well be associated with the period of the establishment of the Davidic
monarchy. Cf. Phillips, *AICL*, pp. 158-61, and my review of Gilmer, *The If-You Form*,
p. 425.

faithful Israel. For there can be no doubt that for Deutero-Isaiah the prophecy of Isa. 11 will be fulfilled not by a restoration of the Davidic line and the reign of an ideal king, but rather by the work of the servant in establishing *mišpāṭ* among the nations. It was this universalistic aspect of the servant's mission that a later editor of Isaiah felt obliged to add to the original, and in my view Isaianic Messianic prophecy (Isa. 11.10).

But curiously the servant is to achieve his task without crying or lifting up his voice. This would seem to rule out a mission to the nations to proclaim Yahweh's will such as Amos' mission to the northern kingdom. But perhaps in view of Isa. 11 we should see here a reference to the royal proclamation of the law following the king's coronation. In v. 3 we learn that the exercise of *mišpāṭ* can only bring life even in apparently hopeless situations (cf. Isa. 40.6-8). Finally the song hints that the servant will fulfil his commission solely by his persistent endurance in the face of personal adversity. Until then the far-off places must wait for Yahweh's *tōrâ*.

In what is usually regarded as an addition to the first song, Isa. 42.6 designates the servant as *berit 'ām* ('covenant of the people') and *'ōr gōyim'* ('a light to the nations'). Both phrases occur again in Isa. 49.

The precise meaning of *bᵉrît 'ām* is very uncertain. Indeed the phrase 'give as a *bᵉrît'* occurs nowhere else in the Old Testament. For this reason the New English Bible here rejects the normal translation of *bᵉrît* as 'covenant' and follows the suggestion originally made by Torczyner that *bᵉrît* should here be derived from a root *brr* meaning 'give light', 'shine'.[21] Luke 2.32 ('a light for revelation to the Gentiles, and for glory to thy people Israel) lends some support to this suggestion. But it is perhaps better to understand *bᵉrît* in its usual sense as derived from *brh* 'bind together', than look for a new word found nowhere else in the Old Testament. The servant then can be understood as the one who binds up. *'ām* (people) is in the singular and should as is normal in Deutero-Isaiah be interpreted as such and here understood as referring to Israel[22] It is true that in two instances; the preceding verse Isa. 42.5 and Isa. 40.7 *'ām* singular is to be taken in a plural sense, and understood as referring to the nations at large. But in view of the parallel passage in Isa. 49, it is clear that the servant's task is first to bind up scattered Israel (Isa. 49.8) and thereby to act as a light to the nations (Isa. 49.6). This means that the action which Isa. 42.7 goes on to describe, giving sight to the blind and

21. H. Torczyner, 'Presidential Address', *JPOS* 16 (1936), pp. 1-8 (7).
22. J. Skinner, *The Book of the Prophet Isaiah Chapters XL-LXVI* (Cambridge: Cambridge University Press, 1917), p. 32.

releasing the prisoners, does not, as a number of commentators have argued, refer to the nations. For the use of the blind elsewhere in Isa. 42 and the parallel passage in Isa. 49.9 indicate that in Isa. 42.7 too reference is being made to the exiles. Thus the servant's role as a light to the nations is intimately connected with Israel's forthcoming deliverance from Babylon. It is through this miraculous event that the servant will be able to bring the nations into relationship with Yahweh. But while the initiative for the deliverance lies with Yahweh, whether or not he can do so is entirely dependent on the servant's faithfulness.

It is this faithfulness that is in doubt in the second servant song, Isa. 49.1-6, significantly addressed to the most distant nations. In the face of the futility of his endeavours, the servant is tempted to give up. This results in Yahweh not only confirming the servant's tasks to restore Israel, but also extending the scope of his commission to involve the salvation of the whole world (Isa. 49.6). The following verse indicates how that salvation is to be effected. It will occur as the direct consequence of Yahweh's deliverance of his people (Isa. 49.7). In the face of such a miraculous turn of events the nations leaders will come and prostrate themselves before Israel in Zion. It is through Yahweh's glorification of the once despised people that Israel will assume a commanding role among the nations and become the hub of the whole world (Isa. 55.5). Just as once David through his military prowess became a leader among nations (Ps. 18.43-45) so now Israel through Yahweh's grace will inherit the role of David (Isa. 55.4-5). For following the totally unexpected vindication of Israel, the survivors of the nations will have no alternative but to acknowledge that Yahweh alone is God (Isa. 45.20-25) and therefore to submit to his authority. The servant will then through divine grace be able to fulfil his commission of being a light to the nations without himself undertaking a mission to the world, but through the world coming to the servant. He will then be able to bring the nations into a relationship with Yahweh and illuminate to them his divine will. For it must not be forgotten that the purpose of his commission was that Yahweh's salvation should no longer be limited to Israel but stretch to the end of the earth. It is for this that the most distant places wait (Isa. 42.4). And the way whereby the servant is to achieve this task is through revealing to the nations Yahweh's *tōrâ* and *mišpāṭ* which they will now accept and practise. That this is Yahweh's end purpose is confirmed from Isa 51.4-5 where *tōrâ* and *mišpāṭ* are themselves seen as *'ōr 'ammîm*, a light to the peoples, here specifically in the plural, who expectantly wait for Yahweh's rule. But again it is stressed that the ultimate initiative for bringing Yahweh's salvation to the farthest places does not lie with Israel, but with Yahweh himself. So he assures his people that the covenant with Abraham (cf. Isa. 41.8) is still in force, and despite all appearances to the contrary Israel's land will be restored to the pre-fall paradisal state (Isa. 51.1-3). Here we appear to have another echo of Isa. 11 which also pictures a return to paradise as wild and domestic animals lie down together in peace and children play in safety by snakes' nests. But more—Isa. 51 goes on to describe how the ancient hope that Abraham will be the father of all peoples (Gen. 12.3) is now to be fulfilled through the dissemination of Yahweh's *tōrâ* and *mišpāṭ* even to the farthest places. As a result they too must enjoy the paradisal state for Gen. 12.3 is the Yahwist's answer to the curse of Babel when all the nations of the world became scattered from Yahweh's presence (Gen. 11). It is the servant's task to secure the reversal of that curse and a return to the original paradisal state where people dwelt together in unity and peace. For Yahweh who began the history of salvation in the call of Abraham is still in control of that history, and when history ends, symbolized in the apocalyptic language of the destruction of the heavens and the earth, his salvation will still endure (Isa. 51.6).

What then can we say of the motive behind Deutero-Isaiah's prophecy? Martin-Achard observes 'that actually about two-thirds of Deutero-Isaiah's utterances are devoted to persuading his contemporaries that the hour of Israel's liberation and its return to the Holy Land had come... The monotheistic and universalistic elements that we find in Isaiah xl–lv are not the essence of the prophet's message; their function is to corroborate his proclamation that the People of Yahweh will be comforted'[23] (Isa. 42.10-13; 43.7; 45.23; 49.26). But he fails to appreciate that the motive behind the whole work is Deutero-Isaiah's appreciation that it is not merely Israel's fate that is at issue but Yahweh's too. Without a community who in the face of all the evidence to the contrary will remain faithful, Yahwism is doomed. Israel's eventual restoration may be due to another divine act of grace, but that restoration is dependent on there being a faithful remnant to restore. Hence for all the assurances which Deutero-Isaiah lavishes on his hearers, he himself remains anxious about the outcome. It is by no means assured, and Yahweh himself is powerless to assure it. If the exiles as a whole apostatize, there will be no future. And Deutero-Isaiah knows that the cards are stacked against Yahweh. Ezekiel's

23.   Martin-Achard, *A Light*, p. 14.

prophecy had not been fulfilled; many of those to whom he preached were dead. Deliverance may be at hand; Cyrus may even now be coming from the east. But until that deliverance is recognized as a fact, then the faithful remnant must continue to fulfil their role through dogged endurance. There is no other way. A destiny far beyond the exiles' wildest dreams awaits them—far more than a mere Deuteronomic re-entry into the promised land—but that destiny can only be achieved through the passive acceptance of their present suffering which makes them utterly repugnant to the nations. This is the servant's task and Deutero-Isaiah drives it home in the third and fourth servant songs (Isa. 50.4-9; 52.13–53.12). But if the faithful persevere they will be vindicated and through their vindication bring salvation to the world. Their suffering will therefore be seen to have been on behalf of even those nations who had hitherto despised them.

But what will be the status of the foreign nations following Israel's vindication? Deutero-Isaiah does, of course, exult over the forthcoming destruction of Israel's enemies and the nations' humiliation before her (Isa. 49.26). But Israel's vindication can only be publicly manifested through the defeat of her enemies, and Yahweh's salvation only reach the farthest places in so far as those places accept his authority. This will inevitably mean humiliation as the nations discover that their whole future blessing depends on Israel and her God (Isa. 45.14). Further, in his appeal to the suffering faithful, it was inevitable that Deutero-Isaiah should emphasise the reversal of fortunes which Yahweh's act of deliverance would bring. Those who had enslaved Israel would themselves act as slaves in helping in her own restoration (Isa. 49.22-23). But this does not mean that the nations were to be kept in a permanent state of slavery. While they were to continue to be dependent on Israel, for from the call of Abraham she had been Yahweh's chosen means of enlightenment in the world, they too are to enjoy his blessing. Nor is there any hint in Deutero-Isaiah of their political absorption into Israel. They remain independent but united to Israel through their acknowledgment of the one and only God. While Deutero-Isaiah's prophecy is naturally much more concerned with the immediate issue—the preservation of a faithful remnant through whom Yahweh can redeem the world—that world's redemption remains his ultimate aim (Isa. 45.20-25). For without it there could be no return to Eden. And that will only come about through the universal acknowledgment of Yahweh's *tōrâ* and *mišpāṭ*. It is as mediator of the law that Israel acquires her title 'a light to the nations', but it is the law itself that constitutes that light.

The high hopes of Deutero-Isaiah did not materialize following the return from exile, but in the work called Trito-Isaiah those hopes are kept alive. Whether the author wrote before or after the rebuilding of the temple remains uncertain. Central to his message lies Yahweh's *tōrâ* and *mišpāṭ*. Thus at its very opening Trito-Isaiah dramatically extends Deutero-Isaiah's renunciation of Deuteronomic theology in respect of the nations. While Isa. 56.1 still looks forward to that miracle through which Yahweh's salvation will come and a new age dawn, Isa. 56.3-8, in complete contradiction to Deut. 23.2-9, ordains that both a foreigner and a eunuch are to be admitted to the worshipping community of Israel provided they keep the law. As in other postexilic material, sabbath observance is emphasized, being one of the clear outward distinguishing marks of membership of Judaism. The other, circumcision, may well be alluded to in the reference to 'my covenant' since the Priestly theologians re-interpreted circumcision as the specific sign of the covenant and trans-ferred it to the eighth day after birth (Gen. 17).[24] But the importance of Isa. 56 is that Judaism is open to any who wish to enter: previous race is to be no bar. All that is required is that those who seek membership of the elect community should obey the *tōrâ*. Nor are these converts to Judaism to be treated in any way as second class citizens. They have absolute right of entry to the temple and their sacrifices are entirely acceptable to Yahweh. They act as a sign of the coming new age.

Isaiah 60–61 pictures that new age, though this is now realized not in some specific historical event, but rather as a miraculous change in Israel's fortunes. Since the return from exile had taken place, there was now no 'historical' deliverance to look forward to. Nonetheless this miraculous change of fortune continued to be seen in terms of a return of the exiles, for in fact following Cyrus's edict very few Jews had gone back to Palestine. In addition the foreigners who had destroyed the Judaean cities would rebuild them and their kings who had enslaved Israel minister to her. The climax comes in Isa. 61 which is directly modelled on Isa. 42. So the prophet speaks as the Messianic prince of Isa. 11 to whom Yahweh had given his spirit. Part of his commission is to bind up the broken-hearted, a reference to the restoration of life in Isa. 42.3. As in Isa. 42.7 the captive exiles are to be released and Israel restored to her former glory. The prophecy then dramatically describes Israel as priest nation to the world. Just as in pre-exilic Israel the laity did all the manual work and

---

24. Köhler, *Hebrew Man*, pp. 37-39.

supplied the non-property owning clergy with their livelihood, so the foreign nations will serve Israel who will eat their wealth and glory in their riches—riches brought about by the nations now being in communion with Yahweh. But Isa. 61.5 must not be interpreted in narrow nationalistic terms as if all Israel was to do was to enjoy herself at the expense of the now servile nations. She has a particular responsibility to be their priest, the chief of whose duties was, of course, to teach *tōrâ* (Deut. 33.10). Isaiah 61.5-7 thus pictures the fulfilment of the servant's commission in Isa. 42.1-4 with Israel establishing throughout the world the practice of the complete will of Yahweh, his *mišpāṭ*. That the servile role of the nations is not to be taken literally in Isa. 61.5-7 is confirmed by Isa. 62.8-9 and 65.21-22 where restored Israel is shown as now being able to enjoy the fruits of her own agricultural and building work. The importance of the vision of Isa. 61.5-7 is that it confirms that in the new age Israel is not destined for political superiority to be maintained by force of arms, but rather is to be the servant of the servants of Yahweh maintaining world peace through the dissemination of his *tōrâ* and *mišpāṭ*. Israel, now no longer a nation but a worshipping community, is thus at last able to fulfil her pre-conquest designated role as a kingdom of priests (Exod. 19.6)—a role which her long period of nationhood had paradoxically prevented her from realizing.

Zechariah 8.20-23 also takes up the theme of Israel as the priest nation, though there it is applied individually to each Jew who himself is to be a priest to the world. But as in Deutero-Isaiah it is because of what God has done for Israel that the foreign nations will come to her and not through any achievement on her part. Both in restoring Israel and willing to dwell in her midst in the rebuilt temple, Yahweh declares his nature to the nations of the world who now, through Israel, have the means of enjoying his grace. So a new age of salvation dawns, and that salvation is for the whole world. For it is God's world, and all people part of his creation and so eligible for membership of his elect community which is humankind itself.

The final chapter of Trito-Isaiah confirms that it will not be through Israel's missionary endeavour that the farthest lands will hear of Yahweh's *tōrâ* and *mišpāṭ*. Building on Isa. 45.20-25 where the survivors of the nations are brought to acknowledge Yahweh as the only God, Trito-Isaiah now pictures those survivors themselves going out to the most distant countries to proclaim Yahweh's glory (Isa. 66.19). As in Isa. 56, Trito-Isaiah again recognizes that through acceptance of Yahweh's *tōrâ* and *mišpāṭ* these foreigners become full members of the cult community. Consequently they are even eligible for the priesthood (Isa. 66.21). Nationhood is now of no concern to Yahweh: obedience to *tōrâ* alone determines a man's acceptability. Further, as in Isa. 51.6, Trito-Isaiah argues that even when the existing creation has passed away, and a new one is made, the promise to Israel, the priest nation to the world, will endure with 'all flesh' coming to worship in Jerusalem (cf. Zech. 14.16-19).

The vision of the foreign nations coming to Jerusalem to learn Yahweh's *tōrâ* and the resultant paradisal peace is again pictured in Isa. 2.2–4 also found in Mic. 4.1–4 with an additional verse. The history of the composition of this oracle remains a matter of dispute. Its striking inconsistency with the rest of Micah usually leads commentators to deny its authenticity to that prophet: but there are still many who would regard it as genuinely Isaianic as the additional note Isa. 2.1 asserts. But its close relationship to the new universalistic thought of Deutero- and Trito-Isaiah makes such an identification highly implausible.[25]

The oracle is modelled on a picture of the nations streaming to Jerusalem to celebrate the annual pilgrimage feast of Tabernacles at the centre of which lay the proclamation of Yahweh's *tōrâ*. But a number of commentators here interpret *tōrâ* not in the Deuteronomic sense, followed in Deutero-Isaiah, of a comprehensive term expressing the complete will of Yahweh, but rather its earlier though continued use (Hag. 2.11-13) as a specific instruction for a particular case?[26] The foreign nations are then seen as individual plaintiffs coming to Zion to have their individual cases heard by Yahweh, and after his judgment, return home. But in my view this is too narrow an interpretation for in Isa. 2.3 (Mic. 4.2) the nations specifically indicate that they seek general instruction in Yahweh's ways—that is how in any given situation which may confront them they are to act. Only with such knowledge can they be said to walk in his paths. Isaiah 2.4 (Mic. 4.3) is not to be interpreted as in a temporal sequence with the preceding verse, but rather as a statement of consequence. In Isa. 2.3 (Mic. 4.2) the nations come to Zion for general instruction in Yahweh's *tōrâ*, just as long before Israel had gone to the mountain of the Lord, Sinai, for a similar comprehensive body of teaching (Exod. 19–24, 32–34). Isaiah 2.4 (Mic. 4.3) then points out that the nations' acceptance of the validity of Yahweh's law immediately results in an enormous increase in

---

25. Cf. Kaiser, *Isaiah 1–12*, pp. 48-56; Mays, *Micah*, pp. 95-96 and the literature cited by both authors.

26. E.g. Lindars, 'Torah in Deuteronomy', p. 121; Mays, *Micah*, p. 97.

the area of his jurisdiction. Further, since the nations now become part of the one people of God subject to his *tōrâ*, war now becomes irrelevant. Law thus achieves its avowed aim of ensuring absolute *šālōm*, that is order, harmony and peace over all humankind. Instead of agricultural implements being forged into weapons of war, each man can now cultivate his own land in the knowledge that eternal peace reigns, a prophecy reversed in Joel 4.10. Yahweh himself and not a Davidic king performs the role of the ideal Messianic prince (Isa. 11) ensuring world peace and justice, and so, as the additional verse in Mic. 4.4 points out, freeing the farmers from fear of military call-up (1 Kgs 4.25). Jerusalem thus becomes the centre of a transformed world no longer concerned for power and domination, but only that Yahweh's will might prevail. Here we see her in effect fulfilling her role as priest to the world.

But the promise of this oracle depends solely on the grace of Yahweh. It is not for humankind to achieve but results from the prior action of Yahweh in establishing the primacy of Mount Zion. The oracle is strictly eschatological: it will be realized in the latter days, not just in the distant future (Gen. 49.1; Num. 24.14), but in Yahweh's one last act of grace whereby his kingdom will be inaugurated and history brought to its goal. The coming of the kingdom depends then entirely on divine initiative. Israel of herself cannot inaugurate it. But the possibility of such an inauguration will depend on their being a faithful mediator, a new Moses, who will be available on the eschatological day to act as Yahweh's servant. Hence the importance of Isa. 2.5 (Mic. 4.5). Israel's part is to provide that continuity of faith without which Yahweh cannot bring about the eschatological reign of peace, but the gift of that reign and the time of its dawning depends entirely on Yahweh, and on Yahweh alone.

It was this concern to ensure the survival of a distinct people of Yahweh which dominated the reforms of Ezra and Nehemiah in connection with mixed marriages (Ezra 9–10; Neh. 13). Whether we have a description of two separate historical occasions or whether the same traditions have been related to both Ezra and Nehemiah need not detain us.[27] In order to justify their action, both make direct appeal to Deuteronomic law (Deut. 7.1-6; 23.4-6). Indeed the Chronicler specifically adopts the Deuteronomic idea that the return from exile marked a second entry into the promised land. Those returning were to separate themselves entirely from the peoples of the lands—interpreted as if they included all foreigners (Ezra. 9.1). It is

27. Cf. R.J. Coggins, *The Books of Ezra and Nehemiah* (CBC; Cambridge: Cambridge University Press, 1976).

those who have been through the exilic experience who constitute the true Israel and in whom hope for the future lies. So it is the returning exiles who dedicate the rebuilt temple though they are joined by those who forsake the pollutions of the people of the land (Ezra. 6.21). Seeing the threat to the survival of Israel as a distinct people, accentuated by the fact that she was no longer a political entity but only a worshipping community, and illustrated for example in the loss of knowledge of that community's language (Neh. 13.23-24), Ezra and Nehemiah took drastic action against all foreign elements. Marriages were in future to be an internal Jewish matter (cf. Mal. 2.10-12), foreign wives were to be divorced (Ezra 9–10; Neh. 12.23-29), and those of mixed blood removed from the community (Ezra 10.44; Neh. 13.1-3). *Tōrâ*, most probably now to be understood as the Pentateuch, and again interpreted as the full expression of Yahweh's will, was alone to define membership of Israel.

Yet it must not be thought that these reforms entirely put the clock back by a return to the Deuteronomic ghetto theology. For particularism and universalism are not terms which cannot co-exist. On the contrary, the basic postexilic ideal was of a particular nation, Israel, acting as priest to all other nations. It was through Israel faithfully maintaining her identity in obedience to *tōrâ* that Yahweh in his own time would be able to bring all peoples into that communion which he willed for them. While the universaliatic eschatological hope of Israel found in Deutero-Isaiah, Trito-Isaiah and Proto-Zechariah was of no immediate concern to Ezra and Nehemiah, their action did nothing to invalidate it. Indeed their particularist stance based on strict adherence to *tōrâ* enabled Israel to survive the Seleucid period and kept that eschatological hope alive.

Nor despite Nehemiah's appeal to Deut. 23.4-6 (Neh. 13.1-2) must it be thought that individual proselytes could not be incorporated into Israel as envisaged by Trito-Isaiah (Isa. 56). While marriages were to be made within the worshipping community of Israel, those who were prepared to separate themselves from the pollution of the peoples of the land by accepting Yahweh's *tōrâ* would find themselves members of that community (Ezra 6.21). While one cannot imagine that in the time of Ezra and Nehemiah there would have been many converts to Judaism, by continuing to insist on obedience to *tōrâ* as the sole criterion for membership of the chosen people, the reformers paradoxically left the way open for foreign converts from future generations.

It has, however, often been alleged that in the books of Ruth and Jonah we have a direct challenge to the particularist theology of Ezra and

Nehemiah. The former tells the story of a Moabite woman who adopts Judaism and becomes the great-grandmother of the greatest hero in Israel's history, King David. The latter depicts the repentence of the most wicked city in the world, Nineveh, in response to the preaching of Yahweh's prophet. Those who regard these books as missionary tracts then argue that their authors sought to imply that Israel ought to be making greater efforts to bring knowledge of Yahweh to those outside Judaism, for who could tell what the consequences of such evangelism might be.

Examination of the book of Ruth does not substantiate this view. In the first place the genealogy of 4.18-22 has been incorporated into the book either from 1 Chron. 2.4-15 or derived from the same source. Nor is 4.17b a genuine part of the narrative. For at this point the story requires that the name of the child should be specifically related to Naomi. It is therefore clear that the original tale had no connection at all with David.[28]

Second, the total lack of any reflection on the significance of marriage with a foreigner—for or against—(cf. 1.4; 4.6) rules out the conclusion that the book was a polemical attack on the mixed marriage policy of Ezra and Nehemiah. At the time the book was written, such marriages were entirely acceptable and unremarkable. Indeed the point of the tale lies not in Ruth's foreignness, but her faithfulness which the former only serves to heighten. The story comes from the same sort of popular wisdom background as the legend of Job which forms the framework to the biblical book. Adversity faithfully endured will be richly rewarded.

In my view, the book of Ruth is clearly postexilic. But since the narrative shows no bias over mixed marriages one way or the other, it could hardly have been compiled in the period following the reforms of Ezra and Nehemiah. Further the fact that the heroine is of all races a Moabitess (cf. Neh. 13.1) suggests to me that it most probably comes from the time following the deliberate rejection of Deut. 23.2-9 by Trito-Isaiah (Isa. 56). It, would therefore reflect the period before the reforms of Ezra and Nehemiah when foreign marriages were widely entered into (Mal. 2.10-12) and, despite the Deuteronomic law, a foreigner was encouraged to take his place in the Jewish worshipping community (Isa. 56).

The result of Jonah's announcement of Nineveh's imminent punishment is the repentence of its king and people, and their pardon by Yahweh. But nowhere is it said that they were called to repent of their idolatry nor that they embraced Yahwism. Nor is the sacrifice of the sailors and their vows

28. O. Kaiser, *Introduction to the Old Testament* (Oxford: Basil Blackwell, 1975), pp. 191-92.

to be interpreted as a sign of conversion. In the heat of the moment they try to propitiate a dangerous god. But there is no indication that they rejected their former gods for the sole worship of Yahweh. They merely acted prudently. And, despite the clearly didactic nature of the book, it contains no evidence at all that it was written in opposition to the measures taken by Ezra and Nehemiah.[29] Indeed the situation envisaged by the book seems akin to that in Jer. 18.7-8 where Yahweh declares his intention to pardon a nation if that nation turns from its evil. Without saying anything about monotheism, Jeremiah's concern is to emphasize the worldwide authority of Yahweh. He is a free agent and can condemn and pardon whom he wills. The same idea of overall authority is present in Amos 9.7-8. In my view, in the book of Jonah we are very much closer to this earlier thought about Yahweh's authority over the nations—seen again, of course, in his use of Cyrus—than to the universalistic passages of Deutero-Isaiah, Trito-Isaiah and Proto-Zechariah which all interpret Yahweh's relationship to the foreign nations in terms of Israel herself acting as the go-between. It is thus Yahweh's sovereignty rather than his magnanimity which is the prime stress of Jonah which the incident of the gourd further emphasizes. What occasioned the need to assert this?

Now the ironical aspect of the book of Jonah is that the Assyrian capital was, of course, destroyed by the Babylonians in accordance with Yahweh's plans (Isa. 10.12-15, 24-27; 14.24-27). But the author of Jonah is clearly countering the claim that another Nineveh threatened by Yahweh with destruction has not been destroyed but surprisingly pardoned. In other words the book indicates Israel's sense of insecurity and doubt in the power of her God when faced with the continued presence of a certain heathen nation which confronts her. The author of Jonah meets this despair with the assertion that the world situation, however unexpected, is all part of Yahweh's plan: he has everything in his control.[30] Can we be more specific still? I believe we can.

---

29. Two studies of Jonah have both rejected this interpretation: R.E. Clements, 'The Purpose of the Book of Jonah' (VTSup, 28; Leiden: E.J. Brill, 1975), pp. 16-28; G.I. Emmerson, 'Another Look at the Book of Jonah', *ET* 88 (1976), pp. 86-88. See further S.D.F. Goitein, 'Some Observations on Jonah', *JPOS* 17 (1937), pp. 63-77.

30. At a different level this is also the point of the beginning of the story in which Jonah seeks to avoid an unpleasant and dangerous task. P.R. Ackroyd, *Exile and Restoration* (OTL; London: SCM Press, 1968), pp. 244-45, has revived the suggestion that the incident of the great fish should be interpreted allegorically. Jonah represents Israel swallowed up by the fish, Babylon.

Deutero-Isaiah's prophecy had asserted that Yahweh was master of world events. Even now Israel's deliverance was being put into effect and Babylon would be destroyed (Isa. 47. Cf. Isa. 41.11-13; 51.23). But in fact this destruction had not occurred. Instead the Persian prince, Cyrus, had been welcomed as a liberator by those conservative Babylonians who had disapproved of the policies of Nabonidus. There can be little doubt that the insignificant nature of the return from exile, the failure to rebuild the temple, and the 'escape' of Babylon from punishment led to considerable uncertainty among loyal Yahwists. In my view the aim of the author of Jonah was to counter such uncertainty. Thus he asserts that the God of grace who had not forgotten Israel in Babylon, but who had delivered her from exile, was still in control of world events. Babylon had not escaped Yahweh's punishment through her own strength or the strength of her gods: Yahweh had pardoned her. It might be argued that there is no evidence of any Babylonian repentence. But the fact that the older influential groups ousted by Nabonidus, including the priests of Marduk, welcomed Cyrus, Yahweh's anointed, would amply justify a picture of repentence and account for Yahweh's pardon of the city which Cyrus could then enter in peace. After all Deutero-Isaiah makes very strong claims for Cyrus though he never became a Yahwist. The purpose of the author of Jonah is then clear. Like the author of Ruth he seeks to encourage faithfulness in Yahweh whose providence can be trusted and whose grace knows no bounds. Further, again like Ruth, the book may also derive from scribal wisdom circles. If my reasoning is correct it ought then to be attributed to the period following Deutero-Isaiah whose theology of the sovereignty of Yahweh over history it upholds. In this period the lot of Israel remained desperate and hostility to Babylon, by no means as violent in Deutero-Isaiah as elsewhere (Jer. 50–51; Isa. 13–14; 21) continued (cf. Zechariah). Thus the didactic nature of Jonah can be explained without any recourse to a Jewish opposition party to the reforms of Ezra and Nehemiah of which there is no biblical evidence.

Finally, we should note that this interpretation finds support from the one Old Testament reference to the prophet Jonah outside the book called after him. For in 2 Kgs 14.25 it is recorded that Jeroboam II restored the borders of Israel in accordance with the prophecy of Jonah the son of Amittai. In other words this unique biblical reference to Jonah's ministry concerns the proclamation of Yahweh's sovereignty over the nations and his control of the extent of their territories. And just as the historic Jonah had sought to reassure his insecure contemporaries about their future (2

Kgs 14.26), so the book of Jonah does the same for their successors. Yahweh is lord of history and despite any appearances to the contrary remains totally master of events. The book of Jonah is then quite properly included among the prophets even though it contains no specific oracles.

In conclusion then my investigation confirms de Boer's, Snaith's and Martin-Achard's assertion that Israel was neither summoned to nor contemplated an active missionary role to the foreign nations, and Ruth and Jonah are not to be understood as protests against this lack of evangelization. But this does not mean that postexilic prophecy is to be interpreted as narrowly nationalistic concerned only with Israel's vindication and exaltation over the nations. On the contrary, this prophecy repeatedly looks forward to Yahweh's redemption of the whole world. But in order that Yahweh can realize this universalistic hope—and it is clearly recognized that it is entirely his affair—sufficient of his people must remain faithful to him to enable Israel to fulfil her role as priest nation to the world. Thus the concern of all postexilic theology is to ensure the survival of that faithful community in the face of so much discouragement and unfulfilled hopes. The only way of achieving this was through demanding strict adherence to Yahweh's *tōrâ* and *mišpāṭ*. And in acceptance of its authority by the faithful remnant ultimately lay the key to the unity of all humankind and the realization of the goal of Israelite history in the return to the paradisal state of Eden which as a result of postexilic prophecy would embrace all people (Isa. 11.10). Yahweh's *tōrâ* and *mišpāṭ* are not then as in pre-exilic times concerned only with maintaining Israel's election: rather they are of universal significance, and are aptly termed 'a light to the peoples'.

Chapter 12

THE BOOK OF RUTH: DECEPTION AND SHAME

The book of Ruth tells the story of a Bethlehem couple Elimelech and Naomi and their two sons, Mahlon and Chilion, who because of famine sought refuge in Moab. There Elimelech died, and the sons married Moabite girls, Orpah and Ruth. The sons too died and although married for ten years left no children. As the introduction to Ruth puts it: 'the woman was bereft of her two sons and her husband' (1.5).

Hearing that agricultural prosperity had returned to Judah, Naomi set out to go back to Bethlehem, and her two daughters-in-law accompanied her. Naomi, however, urged them to return to their own people and marry again. While with much weeping Orpah turned back, Ruth clung to her mother-in-law declaring: 'for where you go I will go, and where you lodge I will lodge; your people shall be my people, and your God my God' (1.16).

Back in Bethlehem Ruth according to the custom of widows (Deut. 24.19) followed behind the harvesters gathering grain. She found herself in the field of Boaz, a wealthy relative of Elimelech. Boaz was clearly attracted to her, treated her with favour, and ordered the young men not to molest her. Naomi hearing all this, and seeing the quantity of grain which Ruth brought back, correctly sized up the situation. Yet although Ruth continued to work in Boaz's field throughout the harvest, the latter made no definite move towards her.

As the harvest ends, Naomi realizes that if she is to secure the union of Ruth and Boaz she has to act fast. So she conceives her plan. One night when Boaz has finished winnowing and has eaten and drunk, Ruth suitably anointed and dressed is told by her mother-in-law to go to Boaz's threshing floor and note where he lies down. Once he is asleep, she is to uncover his feet and lie down beside him. Everything falls out as Naomi plans. The well-fed and merry Boaz falls asleep and Ruth obeys her mother-in-law's injunction. At midnight Boaz awakes and finds Ruth beside him. She reveals her identity and asks him to spread his skirt over her, that is to marry her (cf. Ezek. 16.8). Boaz blesses her for going after him and not young men, but tells her that he is not her husband's closest relative, but that there is one nearer. Legally he must be given first option of marrying Ruth. If he declines, then Boaz will. Whatever happens, all will be settled in the morning. Ruth remains with Boaz until just before dawn, and then secretly returns to Naomi laden with grain. Naomi realizes her plan has worked.

Next morning Boaz goes to the gate of the town and, as the nearest relative passes by, asks him to stop. There in front of a court of ten elders he sets out the issue. But instead of raising the question of marriage to Ruth, he announces that Naomi who has recently returned from Moab is selling a plot of land which belonged to Elimelech. He calls on the nearest relative to exercise his duty and redeem it for the family. When the nameless nearest relative agrees to fulfil his family obligation, he is then told by Boaz that he must also marry Ruth. This he declines to do. So Ruth and Boaz are free to marry. They produce a son Obed, the grandfather of King David.

In spite of the brevity of the book, there remains no scholarly consensus on such basic questions as when it was composed or for what purpose. Efforts to connect the book with a fertility cult drama win little contemporary support.[1] The same is true of the theory that it constituted a missionary tract counteracting the ruthless nationalistic marriage policy of Ezra and Nehemiah (Ezra 9–10; Neh. 13.1-3, 23-27) by depicting the great King David as descended from a mixed marriage. In spite of the emphasis placed on Ruth's nationality—six times she is called a Moabitess (1.22; 2.2, 6, 21; 4.5, 10) and once a foreigner (2.10)—the total lack of any reflection on the significance of *marriage* with a foreigner rules out such a polemical purpose. The author sees nothing unusual in the marriage of Mahlon and Chilion (1.4); nor does the nearest relative use Ruth's foreignness as an excuse not to marry her (4.6). Clearly when the book was written mixed marriages were both acceptable and unremarkable.

Nor is the connection with David to be thought original, which rules out the suggestion that the author's purpose was to legitimatize David's Moabite ancestry by making Ruth fully Jewish. The genealogy in 4.18-22

---

1.   W.E. Staples, 'The Book of Ruth', *AJSL* 53 (1936–37), pp. 145-57; *idem*, 'Cultic Motifs in Hebrew Thought', *AJSL* 55 (1938), pp. 44-55; H.G. May, 'Ruth's Visit to the High Place at Bethleham', *JRAS* 75 (1939), pp. 75-79; S.L. Shearman and J.B. Curtis, 'Divine–Human Conflicts in the Old Testament', *JNES* 28 (1969), pp. 235-40.

is copied from 1 Chron. 2.4-15, and is intended to amplify 4.17b. The people's wish that Boaz's house should be like that of Perez (4.12) cannot be harmonized with the genealogy in which Perez is seen as an ancestor of Boaz. Nor are Elimelech or Boaz ever mentioned as ancestors of David in the narrative itself. But further 4.17b is itself not a genuine part of the narrative. The fact that the son of Ruth and Boaz is described as born to Naomi (4.17a) requires that the child should have a name connected with Naomi (cf. 1 Sam. 4.21). The original name has been removed in order to make the child David's grandfather, who according to tradition was called Obed (4.17b).[2] The story has then been transferred into a narrative concerning David after it acquired a fixed literary form. The purpose was to provide David with a genealogy missing in Samuel. The fact that the author has set his account in the period of the judges and that David was recorded as having contact with Moab (1 Sam. 22.3-4) no doubt facilitated this, and explains the book's position in the Septuagint after the book of Judges, whereas in the Old Testament it is part of the Writings.

Although recently there have been a number of advocates for an early date to Ruth,[3] on balance a postexilic date still appears more probable. The author sees himself far removed from the events described (1.1) and seems familiar with the Deuteronomistic historian's presentation of the judges as rulers of Israel.[4] He is also obliged to explain an ancient custom of transference of legal rights (4.7) presumably because by his time such transference was achieved by deed (cf. Jer. 32.6, 15). Further, the symbolic names given to the characters in the book[5] show that the narrative has a theological rather than a historical purpose. The author's adoption of a classical style appears a conscious imitation which the Aramaisms and some late Hebrew words seem to confirm.[6] Finally, the book's position in the third part of the Hebrew canon would support a late date for its composition.

2. For a different view see A.A. Anderson, 'The Marriage of Ruth', *JSS* 23 (1978), pp. 171-83.

3. R.M. Hals, *The Theology of the Book of Ruth* (Philadelphia: Fortress Press, 1969), pp. 54ff.; Leggett, *The Levirate*, pp. 143-46; E.F. Campbell, *Ruth* (AnBib; Garden City, NY: Doubleday, 1975), pp. 23ff.

4. J. Gray, *Joshua, Judges and Ruth* (NCBC; London: Oliphants, 1967), p. 399.

5. D. Daube, *Ancient Jewish Law: Three Inaugural Lectures* (Leiden: E.J. Brill, 1981), p. 33.

6. M. David, 'The Date of the Book of Ruth', *OTS* 1 (1942), pp. 55-63. David believes that Deut. 24.19 was a new law giving widows a right which they did not previously have. Cf. Exod. 22.21.

If the book is postexilic, it clearly could not have been compiled in the aftermath of the activities of Ezra and Nehemiah (cf. Neh. 13.1). Probably it is best dated prior to their period when foreign marriages were widely entered into (Mal. 2.10-12) and despite Deuteronomic law (Deut. 7) with its specific reference to Moabites (Deut. 23.4-8) a foreigner was encouraged to take his place in the Jewish worshipping community (Isa. 56).

The legal background to the story of Ruth is fraught with many difficulties that have as yet received no entirely satisfactory solution. Indeed it is often argued that the author did not understand the institutions about which he was writing. While this is possible, it should not necessarily be assumed for we do not know for certain when he wrote and our knowledge of Old Testament legal practice for all periods remains very limited, especially when as here we are dealing with customary law.

Traditionally the plot of Ruth has been held to hang on two legal practices which the author has cleverly entwined: levirate marriage and the *gō'ēl*'s duty to redeem realty.

The law on levirate marriage is contained in Deut. 25.5-10. This required that when a man died childless, his unmarried brother living with him should marry the widow and the first son of the union would be regarded as the son of the deceased brother and so bear his name and inherit his property. The marriage served the double purpose of preserving the name and inheritance of the dead brother as well as protecting his widow who would otherwise have no male to look after her.[7] But levirate marriage was part of customary law, that is, it could not be enforced by the courts. Thus the Deuteronomic provision makes no attempt to force an unwilling brother to fulfil his duty or to punish him for failure, but provides the widow with the opportunity of publicly humiliating him. This is an example of the shame motif prominent in Deuteronomy.[8] The unwilling brother is summoned before the local court and if he still refuses to undertake his levirate duty, the widow pulls a sandal off his foot and spits in his face. A sandal was used symbolically to indicate transfer of rights over persons or property (cf. Amos 2.6). The widow's action indicates that the brother-in-law has surrendered his right to marry her and honour his dead brother by giving him a son. Her action is deliberately ironic, for by his failure the brother-in-law inherits his brother's property. Instead of acquiring property by having a sandal handed to him to mark the con-

---

7. E.W. Davies, 'Inheritance Rights and the Hebrew Levirate Marriage: Part 1 and 2', *VT* 31 (1981), pp. 138-44, pp. 257-68.

8. D. Daube, 'The Culture of Deuteronomy', *Orita* 3 (1969), pp. 27-52.

veyance as was the general custom (Ruth 4.7), he acquires it through having a sandal taken from him. Consequently his family is always to be known as the household which acquired its property through 'him that had his sandal pulled off' (Deut. 25.10). Had the legislators intended to punish a defaulting brother they could have prevented him inheriting the property.

Commentators often point out that the law in Deut. 25.5-10 only covers brothers living together, and have therefore questioned whether the duty of levirate marriage extended to any further male relatives. But Deuteronomy is dealing with a custom which had already grown unpopular and was widely ignored. If anyone could be shamed into performing the duty of raising an heir for a deceased relative then it could only be his unmarried brother still living with him. This explains the Deuteronomic concentration on brothers, but does not rule out the possibility that other male relatives could perform the duty. Indeed, as T. Thompson and D. Thompson have shown, the Hebrew words for brother-in-law and sister-in-law derive from the custom of levirate marriage because these were the parties usually involved, but they originally designated progenitor/progenitress, thereby indicating that the custom envisaged a much wider range of possible relationships able to fulfil it.[9]

Indeed the unpopularity of the custom explains why the Priestly legislators extended the law to permit daughters to inherit property, and so continue the name of their deceased and sonless father (Num. 27.1-11). But it is doubtful if the customary law of levirate marriage was ever formally abolished. While Lev. 20.21 seems to prohibit marriage with a brother's wife and Lev. 18.16 all sexual relations between them, these regulations probably only applied during the lifetime of the brother, whereas levirate marriage operated after his death (cf. HL 195).[10]

Apart from Ruth, the only other instance of levirate marriage in the Old Testament is that of Tamar (Gen. 38) to which the author or Ruth refers (4.12). On the death of Tamar's first husband, her father-in-law Judah ordered his second son Onan to fulfil the duty of levirate marriage. Onan, however, interrupted intercourse to spill his seed and was struck dead by God. Although recognizing that Tamar ought to marry his third and last son Shelah, Judah delayed the marriage fearing that through contact with this dangerous woman his last boy might die too. He would therefore be left without an heir. In retaliation Tamar disguised herself as a prostitute

9. T. Thompson and D. Thompson, 'Some Legal Problems in the Book of Ruth', *VT* 18 (1968), pp. 77-99.
10. Davies, 'Inheritance Rights', p. 267.

and tricked Judah into having sexual intercourse with her resulting in the birth of the twins Perez and Zerah. I shall need to return to this story later.

Despite recent criticism to the contrary,[11] in my view Naomi's exultation when she hears of Ruth's meeting with Boaz (2.20) and Boaz's reaction to Ruth's request for marriage (3.10-13) confirm that levirate marriage forms the basis of the plot of Ruth. Indeed Naomi has often been understood to have earlier recognized the futility of this custom in her case in acknowledging that she has no more sons who could do a brother's duty (1.11). But if this is so, her further comments on the possibility of future marriage cause difficulty. While Naomi admits that she is too old to marry again, she adds that even if the impossible happened and she did in fact marry and have sons, her daughters-in-law, already married for ten years, would be far too old by the time these further sons would be ready to marry and raise children (1.12-13). Yet there is nothing in the Old Testament to indicate that such sons born to Naomi from another husband would have been regarded as heirs of Elimelech and therefore under a duty to perform levirate marriage. A number of solutions to the problem have been proposed. First ~~it has been suggested that this is an example of the~~ author's ignorance of ancient legal customs. But I have already indicated that this should not be assumed: it could only be accepted as an answer once all other possibilities had been dismissed. T. Thompson and D. Thompson investigate the possibility that levirate marriage extended further than has commonly been thought. A son of Naomi by another husband would inherit Naomi's property which could then be understood as returning to the direct family line.[12] But the fact that the duty of levirate marriage makes its appeal to blood relationship, and then has great difficulty in getting even a brother to carry it out, makes such a wide coverage unlikely.

Many have seen Naomi's outburst as the author's way of indicating the sheer hopelessness of her situation in being unable to provide by any means husbands for her daughters-in-law. Indeed Rowley argued that the possibility of levirate marriage never entered her head until Ruth reported

11. D. R. G. Beattie, 'Ruth III', *JSOT* 5 (1978), pp. 39-48; J.M. Sasson, 'The Issue of *ge'ullah* in Ruth', *JSOT* 5, (1978), pp. 52-64; *idem*, *Ruth: A New Translation with a Philological Commentary and a Formalist-Folklorist Interpretation* (The Biblical Seminar, 10; Sheffield: *JSOT* Press, 2nd edn, 1989); B. Green, 'The Plot of the Biblical Story of Ruth', *JSOT* 23 (1982), pp. 55-68.

12. Thompson and Thompson, 'Some Legal Problems', pp. 96-99.

her meeting with Boaz (2.20).[13] This seems the best explanation, for Naomi must have known of the existence of other male relatives of Elimelech at Bethlehem. The custom had however virtually ceased to be fulfilled.[14] Thus since levirate marriage was not a practical proposition, Naomi counselled her daughters-in-law to remain with their own people, for in Israel they could only expect to suffer at the hands of the young men who would satisfy themselves free from any criminal charge of adultery (Lev. 20.10; Deut. 22.22) or civil suit for seduction (Exod. 22.15-16; Deut. 22.28-29). There is then nothing inconsistent between Deuteronomic law with its concentration on brothers living together and the more complex situation presented by the author of Ruth.

The legal suit before the elders does not, however, initially concern Ruth but a plot of land belonging to Elimelech. Boaz announces that Naomi is selling this and calls on her husband's nearest relative as *gō 'ēl* to fulfil his duty to redeem it (Lev. 25.25), and so keep it within the family: the exercise of this right of redemption was normal legal practice designed to preserve family solidarity as the example in Jer. 32.7-8 confirms, though again it is doubtful if the courts could force the *gō 'ēl* to act. At this point Boaz introduces Ruth.

Though the use of *qānâ* in 4.5 is not to be interpreted as indicating that either the nearest relative nor Boaz was literally to purchase Ruth,[15] the way in which the author phrases Boaz's remarks at first sight appears to indicate that a legal obligation to marry Ruth accompanied the redemption of the property. Yet Hebrew law knows nothing of any duty of the *gō 'ēl* to marry the widow. Certainly Ruth 3.10 appears to indicate that she was free to marry whom she liked.

Beattie attempts to solve the problem by reading Kethibh *qānîtî* instead of Qere *qānîtā* in Ruth 4.5.[16] He translates: 'On the day you acquire the field from Naomi's hand, I am acquiring Ruth the Moabite, the wife of the deceased, to raise up the name of the deceased over his inheritance'. According to Beattie, Boaz thereby indicates that his and Ruth's son as

---

13. H.H. Rowley, 'The Marriage of Ruth', *HTR* 40 (1947), pp. 77-99 (95ff.), repr. in *idem, The Servants of the Lord*, pp. 164-90.

14. David, 'The Date', pp. 58-59.

15. D.H. Weiss, 'The Use of קנה in Connection with Marriage', *HTR* 57 (1964), pp. 244-48.

16. D.R.G. Beattie, 'Kethibh and Qere in Ruth IV 5', *VT* 21 (1971), pp. 490-94, *idem*, 'The Book of Ruth as Evidence for Israelite Legal Practice', *VT* 24 (1974), 251-67 (263-64).

heir to Mahlon would eventually claim the land as his own. For Davies this interpretation makes the possibility of redemption not less but more attractive, for the nearest relative would have the use of the land (albeit for a limited period) free from the necessity of supporting the widow. It would therefore not lead to a change of mind.[17] This is not necessarily the case. The real objection is that it neither explains Boaz's sudden introduction of the redemption of land into a narrative hitherto entirely concerned with the question of levirate marriage, nor why Boaz felt any necessity to come to court if all along he was free to marry Ruth without reference to the nearest relative. In my view it is because he must get the nearest relative's waiver of his prior right to levirate marriage that any court action is needed, even if Boaz masks his intention by raising a hitherto unmentioned subject, redemption of land.

Beattie counters this objection both by rejecting the idea that the book of Ruth concerns *levirate* marriage and by arguing that in his nocturnal conversation with Ruth, Boaz introduces the question of redemption of the land.[18] Similarly Sasson, while recognizing that the weakness of Beattie's argument was that the existence of the field had not yet been disclosed,[19] nonetheless held that Ruth sought two different things: (1) marriage with Boaz; and (2) that Boaz might become her mother-in-law's redeemer.[20] Yet the story does not indicate that Naomi was looking for a redeemer. Had she been in financial difficulty she could quite easily have approached the nearest relative and asked him to redeem the land. As his immediate response in court indicates, he would only too readily have come to her aid. There was no problem over redemption of land, certainly no need to go to the elaborate lengths to which Naomi puts Ruth. But redemption of land was not Naomi's concern, nor in my view does it enter into the plot until Boaz surprisingly and unprompted mentions it in court. Naomi's sole desire is to perpetuate her husband's name, and she knows that only through levirate marriage, and in no other way, can she achieve that. But, with the possible exception of brothers, the custom had long since fallen out of use. It is only when against all the odds a relative of Elimelech

17. E.W. Davies, 'Ruth IV 5 and the Duties of the *gō'ēl*', *VT* 33 (1983), pp. 231-34 (232).

18. Beattie, 'Ruth III' pp. 39-48.

19. J.M. Sasson, 'Ruth III: A Response', *JSOT* 5 (1978), pp. 49-51.

20. Sasson, 'The Issue', pp. 52-64; *idem*, *Ruth*. See also D.R.G. Beattie, 'Redemption in Ruth and Related Matters: A Response to Jack M. Sasson', *JSOT* 5 (1978), pp. 65-68.

shows unexpected interest in her daughter-in-law (2.20) that Naomi realizes that all is not lost, and conceives her plan to force Boaz's hand. How she does this we shall consider later, as also why Boaz should bring up redemption of land at all.

Davies argues that since the primary purpose of levirate marriage was to give an heir to the deceased husband who would inherit his property, the two legal elements in the Ruth narrative are not to be divorced.[21] Without land to inherit, the name of the deceased could not be revived. By insisting that the nearest relative should both redeem the land and marry Ruth, Boaz was making explicit what had always been implicit in levirate duty. The reason Davies thinks that the nearest relative changed his mind was that he had supposed he would have to marry Naomi who was past child-bearing and so was in no danger of subsequently losing the property, whereas Boaz indicates that he must marry Ruth to whom Naomi must have renounced her rights. Ruth was certainly young enough to have a child who could inherit the property.

This is a more plausible explanation than Daube's suggestion that the nearest relative refused to redeem the property precisely because he was tricked by Boaz into thinking that he would have to marry Naomi, and since, so Daube argues, he could not take another wife until he had provided her with a child—a virtual impossibility—feared the extinction of his line.[22] Of such a monogamous restriction there is no evidence. Yet on Davies's argument it is difficult to believe that *if* the purpose of levitate marriage was to perpetuate the deceased's name through the land, it was not apparent to the nearest relative from the start, as it must have been to everyone else, that if he redeemed the land he would have to marry Ruth, the widow of one of Elimelech's sons Mahlon, who for ten years after his father's death with his brother Chilion was legal owner of that land (4.9).

But redemption of land and levirate marriage are two quite distinct practices of customary law, and should not be confused. It is the particular circumstances of Ruth's position that in her case results in the nearest relative having two separate responsibilities towards her. Boaz first gets the nearest relative to consider redemption which was a not unattractive proposition, before suddenly springing on him the other customary duty of levirate marriage which ruled out redemption on financial grounds.

At this point we perhaps ought to ask how in any event Naomi was in a position to put the land up for sale. While realty passed from father to son

---

21. Davies, 'Ruth', pp. 231-34.
22. Daube, *Ancient Jewish Law*, pp. 40-42.

and later daughters followed by other male relatives (Num. 27.1-11), there is no record of widows inheriting. Indeed we might well ask why had the property not already passed to the nearest kinsman on the death of Elimelech's two sons? The problem is not solved by arguing that the land was being retained until the issue of levirate marriage was resolved, for the author clearly believed that legal title would pass to the purchaser following the sale. The *gō'ēl* is apparently faced with redeeming property which it seems should already under Hebrew law have passed to him. Is this an example of the inexactness of the author over legal procedures which he did not properly understand? Yet it seems unlikely that if widows did not inherit realty, the author should have based the climax of his narrative on a legal situation which everyone would have known to be impossible. Beattie, who argues for an early date for the book, holds that inheritance by widows must have been the custom in early times before the law was written.[23] But this cannot be accepted. The fact that such a right of inheritance by a widow does not appear in the law collections does not necessarily mean, as Beattie infers, that it must have existed prior to their composition: it could equally well have arisen after they were compiled. The fact that it is with Deuteronomic law that women first start acquiring rights and obligations under the law which made them equal with men (Deut. 5.21; 7.3; 13.7; 15.12-17; 17.2-5; 22.22) would seem to point in this direction.[24] Further, contracts at Elephantine allow a childless widow to inherit from her husband (and cf. Jdt. 8.7; 16.24).

We must therefore assume that when levirate marriage virtually ceased to be practised, first the Priestly legislation extended inheritance to daughters, and then at some subsequent unknown date the law provided that if a man died childless—that is without either son or daughter to inherit—the widow was entitled to ownership of his property. In this way one of the original purposes of levitate law would be preserved—the protection of the widow, even if the name of her husband was lost.

If then we accept that Naomi had the right to put up the land for sale (presumably on Ruth's behalf), what does Boaz mean by apparently indicating that if the *gō'ēl* exercised his right to redeem, he must also marry Ruth? In my view what we have in Ruth is an example of that same shame technique which characterized the law of levitate marriage in Deut. 25.5-10. Boaz first reminds the nearest relative of his customary duty to redeem the property which he is happy to do. As Jer. 32.6-15 confirms, it will

---

23. Beattie, 'The Book of Ruth', pp. 251-67.
24. Phillips, *AICL*, pp. 15-16; *idem, Deuteronomy*, p. 50.

become his and pass with his estate. He may even have congratulated himself that he was acting honourably towards the two widows. It never enters his head that he might be expected to perform another duty under customary law, namely levitate marriage, since with the possible exception of brothers that custom had long since fallen out of use. Boaz then indicates that if the nearest relative is willing to perform one legal custom to his advantage, he should in logic be willing to perform the other which was not. As Rowley recognized, either the nearest relative must play the part of kinsman or he must not.[25] He could not decently choose one and reject the other. The peculiarity of this case skilfully created by the author was that one custom (levitate marriage) made the other (redemption of land) financially ridiculous.[26]

Undoubtedly the nearest relative is taken off guard. He had not anticipated the request that he should perform levitate marriage and had no intention of doing so for there could then be no possible profit for him since the land would pass to Ruth's son as heir to her deceased husband (4.5). Wrong-footed by Boaz, the nearest relative renounces his right of redemption pleading financial reasons as his excuse, and leaves the court. Boaz then makes considerable show of exercising both customary laws even though such action is to his financial disadvantage. He had other reasons for acting so generously.

Since Ruth is not present in court, she cannot enact the shame ritual prescribed by Deuteronomic law for brothers-in-law who refuse levitate marriage. Indeed her absence was probably intentional on Boaz's part since her presence would have given the game away as to what his real objective was, and, as we shall see, that was not in his interest. Hence his reference to Naomi selling the land. The last thing he wanted was that anyone should think about Ruth.

Yet it is clear that the author still intended the story to be understood in terms of a shame motif by the fact that he never names the nearest relative. Because he has failed to fulfil the customary law, and so would deny Elimelech's name in Israel, the author ironically denies him a name. Thus Campbell's contention that the nearest relative acted like a 'normal solid responsible citizen' is not the author's view.[27]

Why was it then that Boaz raised the issue of redemption of property in

25. Rowley, 'The Marriage of Ruth', pp. 89ff.
26. There is no need to speculate whether or not Boaz and/or the nearest relative were already married.
27. Campbell, *Ruth*, p. 159.

the first place? Could he not simply have asked the nearest relative whether or not he was intent on marrying Ruth? The answer in fact lies in ch. 3 which we must examine in a moment. For having delayed all summer to take any action over Ruth, Boaz then found himself in a compromising situation. Yet using his wits, he managed to cast himself in the role of a righteous and generous benefactor—the man who unlike the nearest relative was prepared to act without self-interest. Facing as we shall see shame himself, he managed to reverse the situation and ended up being honoured by all.

But before we examine ch. 3, one problem remains. If Naomi knew that there was land belonging to her husband's family in Bethlehem, why did she not encourage Ruth to return with her, for even though levirate marriage was unlikely to take place, an attractive widow with property would surely find a husband easily enough and protect Naomi herself.

The answer is that Naomi's sole concern is the preservation of the line of Elimelech. Despite its biblical title, that is what the book is about (4.14-16), namely how a sonless widow in the most hopeless situation yet managed to secure her husband's name. Faced with her disastrous position in Moab and knowing that the chances of levirate marriage are nil, Naomi has no motive for encouraging what in any event would have been an extraordinary act, the young widow's abandonment of her family, country and religion. It is Ruth's astonishing loyalty to her mother-in-law which opens up possibilities for Naomi of which she never dared to dream, though she did not at first realize this. While Naomi could have kept both herself and her daughter-in-law on Elimelech's land and even married off Ruth, that would not have secured an heir for her late husband. Only the ancient but virtually defunct custom of levirate marriage could do that. So she resigns herself to her bitter state (1.20-21).

But given that Naomi and Ruth had land of their own, why did Ruth need to go and glean elsewhere? Could she not have supported herself and her mother-in-law from the property? Bettan suggests that as the widows arrived in Bethlehem at the beginning of the harvest, their land would have been uncultivated. Ruth had therefore to seek sustenance elsewhere.[28] It is, however, extremely unlikely that land which could be cultivated would have been left untilled for ten years. 2 Kings 8.1-6 describes a similar situation in which the land was cultivated during the owner's absence and

---

28. I. Bettan, 'The Book of Ruth', in *idem*, *The Five Scrolls: A Commentary on the Song of Songs, Ruth, Lamentations, Ecclesiastes, Esther* (Cincinnati: Union of American Hebrew Congregations, 1940), p. 60.

recovery obtained by a widow. More likely Ruth, whom the author indicates took the initiative, had another purpose in mind. Having committed herself to live in Israel, she needed to establish herself within the community in the best possible way. Naomi is content to let Ruth go. Unable to secure levirate marriage for her, she could hardly do other in view of her daughter-in-law's loyalty. But when Ruth returns and reports her meeting with Boaz, a meeting in which he clearly takes delight, Naomi recognizes that the possibility of levirate marriage is by no means over, as her reference to the living and the dead in 2.20 shows.

Indeed it seems probable that it was design not chance which brought Ruth to Boaz's field. Although Hals sees the hidden hand of God in this accidental meeting,[29] elsewhere in the narrative it is the different participants in the story who determine what occurs. Had the author wanted to indicate that God directed Ruth to Boaz's field he could quite easily have said so as the numerous references to his activity elsewhere in the story indicates. Ruth knew her mother-in-law's concern for an heir to Elimelech, and she knew too that under the customary law of Israel to which she had committed herself that was possible. Conversation among the women would have established Boaz's relationship to her: his wealth would have been readily apparent. Indeed Ruth may well have ascertained that the nearest relative was by no means so rich.[30] But in any event, when it dawned on Naomi that Boaz was faltering in bringing about what she so earnestly desired, she took drastic action.

Whatever the legal situation, there can be no doubt that the whole story turns on one's interpretation of Ruth's nocturnal visit to the threshing-floor. Discussing this visit, Carmichael writes: 'the nature of this scene, far from being a matter of pure idyll and innocence, is heavy with underlying sexual allusion'.[31] Only the very naive could disagree. But the trouble with spotting sexual allusion is that once one starts, it is very difficult to stop. Carmichael's interpretation of Ruth is in fact already determined by his understanding of the shame ritual in Deut. 25.5-10.[32] This he believes re-

29. Hals, *The Theology*, pp. 11ff. Sasson, *Ruth*, pp. 38ff., rules out all suggestion of chance and translates 2.2: 'Should I go to the fields and glean among the ears of grain, in the hope of pleasing him?' See further W.F. Stinespring, 'Note on Ruth 2:19', *JNES* 3 (1944), p. 101.

30. This is the opinion of Neufeld, *Ancient Hebrew*, p. 37 n. 4.

31. Carmichael, *Women, Law*, p. 74.

32. Carmichael, *Women, Law*, pp. 65-70. See also his article, 'A Ceremonial Crux: Removing a Man's Sandal as a Gesture of Female Contempt', *JBL* 96 (1977), pp. 321-36.

enacts Onan's withdrawal from sexual intercourse with Tamar and the spilling of his seed. For Carmichael the sandal represents the female genitals and the foot the male sexual organ, while the spitting by the woman symbolizes the spilling of Onan's semen. The woman is in effect saying that the defaulting brother-in-law is an Onan. To call the name of his house the house of the drawn-off sandal means the house of conception denied.

Carmichael finds support for his contention in the arrangement of the laws in Deut. 25. The levirate law (Deut. 25.5-10) is preceded by the law which declares that an ox should not be muzzled when treading out the grain (Deut. 25.4). It is entitled to the first-fruits of the crop. Similarly the levirate law guarantees that an Israelite should not be denied the first-fruits of his inheritance in the land by his treading, that is sexual intercourse. But in Carmichael's view there is a limit to the length which a woman could go in shaming a man. This accounts for the next Deuteronomic enactment (Deut. 25.11-12) which deals with a woman immodestly seizing a man by his private parts when he is in a fight with her husband. Carmichael argues that while in the shame procedure of the levirate marriage provision, the woman figuratively exposes a man's genitals, on no account is she to be allowed to do so in fact.

Turning to Ruth, Carmichael finds innumerable sexual allusions. Much of these centre around the idea of treading.[33] It is to the threshing-floor that Naomi sends Ruth, the place of treading. She is instructed to lie at his feet to be trodden. In inviting him to spread his skirt over her, it is symbolically implied that he will expose his private parts. Carmichael believes that by uncovering his feet, that is by taking off his sandals, Ruth offers herself as his new sandals. By treading Ruth, Boaz will produce the first-fruits of Elimelech's line. This is confirmed for Naomi when Ruth returns home laden with the first-fruits of the harvest which Boaz has placed in the folds of her garment. She carries the grain in front of her as if pregnant with child. Even the place names have sexual connotations—Bethlehem the place of fertility, Moab the place of infertility. The deaths of Mahlon and Chilion indicate a dearth of child-producing males in Moab and echo the story of Lot's daughters forced to have intercourse with their father resulting in the birth of Moab and Benammi (Gen. 19.30-38). Removing the sandal for legal purposes, the nearest relative unwittingly alludes to Onan's denial of conception. The reason he refuses to do his duty, in Carmichael's view, is that he fears like Onan he may be tempted to spill his seed in

---

33. C.M. Carmichael, '"Treading" in the Book of Ruth', *ZAW* 92 (1980) pp. 248-66.

order to inherit Elimelech's land for himself, and so would meet a similar fate to Onan. In this way his inheritance would be destroyed.

Let us consider Carmichael's thesis starting with Deut. 25. The inner connection of the laws in Deuteronomy is a complicated business to which Carmichael has given important consideration.[34] The compiler must have devised the arrangement of the material. Certainly the laws on levirate marriage and the immodest woman are related, though not in the way Carmichael supposed. The woman's aim is not simply to expose the man's genitals, but by seizing them to procure her husband's victory in the brawl. As a similar Assyrian provision confirms,[35] by her action in crushing the assailant's testicles she has threatened his ability to have children. It is this possibility of childlessness rather than any idea of immodesty that provides the link with the law of levirate marriage and explains this unique example of mutilation in Israel's criminal law.[36] There is no need then to interpret the shame procedure of Deut. 25.5-10 as figuratively exposing the brother-in-law's genitals.

While 'feet' often refer to the private parts of both men and women (Exod. 4.25; Deut. 28.57; Judg. 3.24; 1 Sam. 24.3; 2 Kgs 18.27 = Isa. 36.12; Isa. 7.20; Ezek. 16.25), nowhere in the Old Testament must sandals be understood as a euphemism for female genitals.[37] On the other hand sandals were clearly used in a legal context not only in the passages under discussion (Deut. 25.9-10; Ruth 4.7-8), but also in Amos. 2.6; 8.6. Further, as Carmichael admits,[38] while spitting elsewhere stands for contempt (Num. 12.14; Isa. 50.6; Job 30.10), there is no Old Testament reference to an allusion to semen, but only in post-biblical material. The attempt to explain the shame ritual of Deut. 25.5-10 as figuratively a re-enactment of the Onan incident is unconvincing. Rather as I indicated earlier, the woman's action is calculated to bring shame on the defaulting brother-in-law as to the way in which he acquires ownership of his brother's property. By removing the sandal, the widow indicates that her brother-in-

---

34. Carmichael, *The Laws*. See further in support of Carmichael: J.T. Noonan, 'The Muzzled Ox', *JQR* 70 (1980), pp. 172-75; L. Eslinger, 'More Drafting Techniques in Deuteronomic Laws', *VT* 34 (1984), pp. 221-26.

35. MAL A 8.

36. Phillips, *AICL*, pp. 94-95; *idem*, *Deuteronomy*, p. 170.

37. Carmichael's attempt ('"Treading"', p. 258) to bring in Song 7.2 is unacceptable. It is the girl's own feet in her sandals to which reference is made, the lover being engaged in describing her beauty from toe to head.

38. Carmichael, *Women, Law*, pp. 68-69.

law has no legal rights over her, but spits with contempt on him because by his refusal to marry her he legally takes possession of the property of her husband whose name is in consequence for ever lost in Israel.

Returning to the story of Ruth, the narrative itself indicates awareness of the story of Tamar (4.12). Carmichael also points to the story of Lot's daughters,[39] but because he is conditioned by his interpretation of the levirate law in Deut. 25.5-10 to identify feet with the male sexual organ and sandals with the female genitals, he fails to draw out the author's daring use of this material, which explains his emphasis on Ruth as a Moabitess. In fact sandals are never mentioned in Ruth 3,[40] in contrast to Ruth 4 where a single sandal is used for its normal biblical legal purpose. Nor, we may add, does Naomi believe that if Ruth returned to Moab, she could not have children: indeed that was the sensible thing to do instead of entrusting herself to a foreign society in which she would have no secure place.

Genesis 19 narrates that after the destruction of Sodom and Gomorrah, Lot's two daughters find themselves without male kinsmen through whom they can continue their father's line. As a result they make Lot drink wine, and then on successive nights each girl lies with him. Lot is quite unaware of what has happened. The plan works and each girl bears a son, the older Moab and the younger Benammi.

Naomi's plan also depends on Boaz being merry with wine and consequently having no clear memory of what happened. Ruth, suitably anointed and dressed, waits for the well-satiated Boaz to lie down to sleep. Then stealthily she comes and uncovers his feet and lies down beside him. What Ruth does is to expose Boaz's genitals by removing his skirt.[41] When he awakes he finds himself half naked and someone beside him. Ruth identifies herself and asks Boaz quite literally to spread his discarded skirt over her. Boaz imagines that Ruth has done what her ancestress, Lot's daughter, did before her. Because of his hesitation over her all summer, she has had to take extreme measures. There can now be no delaying, for Boaz undoubtedly believes that like Lot's daughter, the

39. Carmichael *Women, Law*, pp. 80, 83.
40. Carmichael admits this but argues that the reader must recognize the hidden significance of the event ('A Ceremonial Crux', p. 333; 'Book of Ruth', p. 258).
41. I have already argued for the literal interpretation of uncovering the skirt in Deut. 23.1 where the same word *knp* is used (A. Phillips, 'Uncovering the Father's Skirt', *VT* 30 [1980], pp. 38-43, reprinted as Chapter 17 below). Carmichael is forced to interpret *knp* symbolically because of his concern to introduce the idea of sandals (not mentioned in the text) into the narrative.

mother of Moab, Ruth may be pregnant with his child. And since he has
warned off the young men and openly shown that he was attracted to Ruth
in his generous treatment of her, there would be no doubt in the neigh-
bourhood whom the father was believed to be. This would not matter were
Ruth an ordinary widow at the mercy of men: but she was the widow of
Boaz's kinsman to whom he owed a duty under customary law. If he the
rich Boaz were not to be shamed, he must freely fulfil that duty. But if he
acted quickly no one need know that he had in fact been deceived into it
(3.14). It is therefore wrong to interpret his sending away of Ruth secretly
before dawn as an attempt to save her reputation: as a widow she had no
right to one.[42] Rather Boaz seeks to save his own reputation and keep
Naomi quiet at the same time by signalling by the gift of grain that he will
now do what he ought all along to have put in motion. There is, though, a
nice irony to the story which despite 4.13 Beattie misses, believing that
Boaz and Ruth had sexual intercourse. By her action Ruth has frightened
Boaz, who because he was drunk has no means of knowing that she has
not in fact had sexual intercourse with him, while Lot who was also drunk
had no idea that his daughters had. Deception characterizes both stories. It
is this deviousness, so characteristic of Old Testament stories, which
commentators have missed. The Moabite precedent spurs Boaz to action:
happily for him the nearest relative, who ever since Naomi and Ruth
returned from Moab has shown no interest in fulfilling his duty, renounces
it and Boaz can save face.

The stories of Lot's daughters, Tamar and Ruth, all concern women
unable to secure sons who as a result have to take unorthodox action to
achieve their ends. In each case, the male is from an older generation, a
father, father-in-law, and in Ruth's case not one of the young men (3.10).[43]
None of the women acquires any moral blame for their action for necessity
has determined it. Even the Deuteronomist does not bar an Ammonite or a
Moabite from the assembly because of their unusual ancestry but because
of their treatment of Israel (Deut. 23.4-5). And Judah is forced to admit
that Tamar is more righteous than he as her apparent act of adultery was

42. Nor did she run any risk of a charge of adultery for, unlike Tamar, she was not
understood to be betrothed to anyone, and therefore free to go after whom she liked
(3.10).

43. For the common pattern of these stories see H. Fisch, 'Ruth and the Structure of
Covenant History', *VT* 32 (1982), pp. 425-37. For the consequences of Boaz's old age
for the interpretation of 4.11, see C.J. Labuschagne, 'The Crux in Ruth 4:11', *ZAW* 79
(1967), pp. 364-67.

caused by Judah's failure to allow her betrothed Shelah to perform his customary duty. Similarly no blame can attach to Ruth for her immodest act: by it she enabled Boaz to do his moral duty.[44]

But in order to minimize suspicion, and to present himself in the best possible light, Boaz does not immediately raise the issue of levirate marriage with the nearest relative. He could have done that; indeed, were he truly honourable, he ought to have done that when Ruth first came to his attention. He had after all known of her arrival in Bethlehem before he ever met her. Instead, Boaz opens the court proceedings by announcing the sale of land by Naomi. This is not because he first needed to secure the land for Naomi's heir. Had the wealthy Boaz agreed to enter into levirate marriage with Ruth at the beginning of the barley harvest he would have achieved that. Rather his aim is to divert attention from what has now become the dire necessity of immediately entering into marriage with Ruth. For the sudden marriage of the rich Boaz with the foreign widow could only result in widespread comment and provoke malicious gossip.[45] By making the redemption of land appear to be the legal issue before the court, Boaz found a way of securing his reputation. Indeed, since there appears to have been no communication between Naomi and Boaz concerning the land, Boaz's introduction of its sale must have been a deliberate ruse on his part. By this means he succeeds in contrasting himself favourably with the nameless nearest relative prepared to look after his own financial interests, but not to do what customary law required for his childless deceased relative whose foreign widow had entrusted herself to Israel. Not only would Boaz redeem the land, he would also marry Ruth even though that meant financial loss on his part. Thus the nearest relative is shamed and Boaz appears as a generous and disinterested benefactor who gains universal praise. His crafty action justifies the meaning of his name as 'sharp-witted',[46] and answers Beattie's question: 'How, in the orthodox exegesis of Ruth, can such a name be seen as appropriate for Boaz?[47]

---

44. On the connection of Ruth and the story of Lot's daughters in later Jewish exegesis, see A. Baumgarten, 'A Note on the Book of Ruth', *JANESCU* 5 (1973), pp. 11-15.

45. Though his interpretation is different from mine, E. Robertson, 'The Plot of the Book of Ruth', *BJRL* 32 (1950), pp. 207-228 (220), recognized Boaz's problem. Gray, *Joshua*, p. 421, notes that Boaz first raised the redemption of land to allay gossip.

46. M. Noth, *Die israelitischen Personennamen in Rahmen der gemeinsmitischen Namengedung* (BWANT, 3.10; Stuttgart: W. Kohlhammer, 1966), p. 228.

47. Beattie, 'Ruth III', p. 46.

The book of Ruth is then about levirate marriage, a custom long since defunct as far as relatives outside brothers were concerned. It describes a hopeless situation which against all the odds suddenly becomes hopeful, but which is only realized by deception, though to avoid shame the deceived himself deceives and shames. It is to achieve the latter that Boaz introduces redemption of land, and for no other purpose.

Finally, we must ask why this book was included in the third part of the canon, the Writings. Many scholars have seen the story coming from the same sort of popular wisdom background as the legend of Job which forms the framework to the biblical book. Adversity faithfully endured will be richly rewarded. Yet the book nowhere stresses the faith of either Naomi or Ruth: indeed, both have to take matters into their own hands in order to achieve their purpose, confirming that God only helps those who help themselves. This would also rule out the idea that the author's aim was to point to God's hidden control of history.[48] Rather it is the shame motif which forms the clue to the purpose of the book. While Ruth abandons herself entirely to her mother-in-law, so making her destiny with Israel, her dramatic act meets with no response within Israel. Although there were ancient customary laws which should have ensured her a proper place in Israelite society, these were ignored and she remained at the mercy of any male who would take advantage of her. Neither the nearest relative, nor the wealthy Boaz, even though both in heart in mind he knew what he ought to do, made any move to fulfil the customary law, even though such failure meant the loss of an Israelite's name for ever.

The story is thus an indictment on Israelite society for failing as so often in the past to give effect to the principles of Hebrew law which went far further than those actions which the courts could enforce. For Torah sought to ensure that ordered society which was the will of God himself and reflected his very character. The author, drawing on two traditions in Genesis of women whose place in society was in total jeopardy, has constructed his own story of a woman similarly situated who like them used deception to secure her future. She should never have been put in such an invidious position which involved for her a shameful act, the necessity of which in turn shamed the man who should have prevented it. Well might Boaz have recited the words of his fellow procrastinator Judah: 'she is more righteous than I' (Gen. 38.26). It is with ensuring righteousness—right relations within the community of faith—that the

---

48. This is the interpretation of Hals, *The Theology*.

author is concerned, and makes the book of Ruth another example of the overriding importance of justice in the theology of Israel. If a political *Sitz im Leben* is to be sought, then the book may well reflect the difficulties of the returning exiles, many of whom would have married foreign wives, in being assimilated back into the life of Israel (Neh. 5).

We can then conclude that the author's purpose was not to set out Ruth as a model of Hebrew piety, but rather to chastise his contemporary society for failing in its ancient calling to reflect the very will of God himself. It is a story of deception and shame only made necessary by the failure of Israel to respond as she should to the foreign widow who had declared to her mother-in-law: 'Where you go I will go, and where you lodge I will lodge; your people shall be my people, and your God my God' (1.16). She had a right to believe that Israel's law would be her law.

CHAPTER 13

THE PLACE OF LAW IN CONTEMPORARY SOCIETY

The following paper was given to the first Jewish-Anglican Consultation held under the joint Chairmanship of the Archbishop of York and the Chief Rabbi at Amport House, Andover, Hampshire, from 26 to 28 November 1980, on the theme 'Law and Religion in Contemporary Society'. It sought to answer three questions:

1. What is the legitimacy or need of an objective law of God beyond situational ethics?
2. Is the religious objection to 'permissiveness' (at least to the extent acceptable by society) more than a mere return to religious triumphalism?
3. Have Jews and Christians any insights to the line to be drawn between individual personal freedom and the authority of the State?

The New Testament does not contain a comprehensive system of ethics which we can call 'the ethics of the New Testament' and to which we can appeal as the authoritative law of God, nor does it appear that Jesus ever contemplated the creation of such a system. The books which now make up the collection which the Church has canonized came into being as the works of individual writers who, as Houlden points out, 'wrote for their own reasons in their own circumstances, unaware of the future role of their work. In so far as any of them were aware of any of the rest, their purpose seems to have been to correct and supersede them rather than to complement them.'[1] Much of the earlier material is so dominated by the belief in the imminent end of the present world order that it has little practical ethical value, for instance Paul's attitude to slavery. But with the loss of the idea of an immediate parousia the writers were increasingly forced to

---

1. J.L. Houlden, *Ethics and the New Testament* (London: Mowbrays, 1975), p. 3.

recognize that Christians needed guidance as to how they were to live in the world, a world radically transformed through the Christ event. As Robin Nixon wrote, 'Law in the sense of legalism is rejected, but the whole concept of law does not disappear'.[2] Nonetheless the ethical guidance given is limited to those issues of immediate concern to the authors and those addressed. The overall New Testament picture is then of necessity sparse, fragmented and subject to the particular theological insights of the author who may deal with the original teaching of Jesus in varied ways, as in the case of divorce.

At first sight the Old Testament seems to present a very different picture. For while initially *tōrâ* meant an individual instruction or ruling on a particular issue, the Deuteronomists reinterpreted it to designate the whole corpus of law seen as the complete expression of the will of Yahweh. As Barnabas Lindars has indicated, the usual translation 'the book of the law' would be better rendered 'the book of divine instruction'.[3] But historical criticism has also shown that despite this comprehensive understanding of Torah, it too came into being by a process of correction and supplementation, and that its overall content was also fragmentary and unsystematic, and in certain areas such as family law, sparse. But because it was interpreted as embracing the totality of God's will, it played a determining part in Israel's life for which there is no New Testament equivalent. While at no time did Israel understand Torah to have created her relationship with her God which was and remained entirely dependent on his gracious election, obedience to Torah nonetheless determined who was within that relationship, that is who constituted Israel. Those who broke Torah must be removed from the community. In my view, in spite of the reservations of many contemporary scholars, this idea goes back to earliest times in the formation of Israel in terms of obedience to the Decalogue.[4] So in the prescriptions of the Book of the Covenant (Exod. 20.23–23.19) we see indigenous Canaanite practice being brought into line with this fundamental law, thereby enabling Israel to preserve her identity. Both Deuteronomy and the Priestly legislation continue this process of setting out what it is that makes Israel Israel in the face of contemporary threats to that identity. Of

2.   Robin Nixon, 'Fulfilling the Law: The Gospels and Acts', in B.N. Kaye and G.J. Wenham (eds.), *Law, Morality and the Bible* (Leicester: Inter-Varsity Press, 1978), pp. 53-71 (71).

3.   Lindars, 'Torah in Deuteronomy', pp. 117-36.

4.   See Phillips, *AICL*.

necessity those issues which make up Torah reflect the author's immediate concerns and theological understanding, which were not necessarily those of their predecessors. So within the Pentateuch itself correction, expansion and addition to Torah is found, but for the postexilic community this compilation was God's law, the entire revelation of his will for his people, obedience to which defined that community. The revelation of God's law was then seen as an act of blessing, for it enabled the elect to respond to God and to remain within their election enjoying the blessings which God gave to his obedient people. Indeed without such a revelation of his will, God's nature, his righteousness (Deut. 4.7-8), could not have been known and response to him made. It was that nature as seen in his law which engendered that full-blooded love (Deut. 6.5) which so characterizes the Old Testament attitude to law seen most fully expressed in the Psalter. Indeed as the prophet we call Second Isaiah indicates, it is Israel's mission to bring Yahweh's Torah to the nations (Isa. 42.1-4). Only then can there be a return to the paradisal state of Eden (Isa. 2.2-4; 11.1-10).

Yet despite this apparent unambiguous position as to what God's law was, Judaism was by no means content to fossilize Torah in its Pentateuchal straitjacket. As Torah itself had developed by a dialectic process of received tradition interacting with contemporary conditions, for instance the sexual legislation in Lev. 18, so Torah continued to be subject to the same tension of continuity and change in the development of *halakah*. *Torah* as part of the word of God does not return to him empty (Isa. 55.11), but is made real for every generation in the situation which confronts it. This includes, to use Gordis's words, both 'new social, economic, political and cultural conditions' that pose 'a challenge or even a threat to accepted religious and ethical values' as well as 'new ethical insights and attitudes' even when the conditions remain the same.[5] Situationism is not then the enemy of Torah but its interpreter. By such a dynamic process continuity is preserved and through the decision of contemporary Jewish leaders the will of God is made real to each generation. The principle upon which they worked both in the Midrashic and Mishnaic methods was that Torah should have the sole purpose of securing that righteousness which was God's will for his world.

The rabbis achieved this in various ways. Where particular laws were still recognized as sound, all the rabbis had to do was apply them to new situations; where a particular area was devoid of legislation, the rabbis

---

5.   R. Gordis, 'A Dynamic Halakhah: Principles and Procedures of Jewish Law', *Judaism* 28 (1979), pp. 263-82.

applied principles and practices of related fields of Jewish law. But where the laws were seen by later generations as no longer morally supportable, then the rabbis, in order to maintain their claim to divine authority, first tried to preserve continuity with Torah by using a variety of legal techniques to get round the enactment: imposing so many restrictions that it could not be applied; deliberately misinterpreting it; inventing legal fictions. But where such a course proved impossible, in the last resort the rabbis were prepared to amend the law. Clearly this brought into question the divine authority of Torah, but the rabbis continued to uphold this by arguing that on the one hand all common law traditions in the oral law were revealed to Moses, but that on the other hand God revealed his will in each generation. As Dorff points out: 'Since the bulk of tradition was maintained in each generation this organic growth was tolerated'.[6] Indeed without this willingness to recognize new situations, whether external or internal, Torah would have become obsolete and the whole system fallen into disuse. By the process of preserving continuity but allowing change, Torah retains a creative role in everyday Jewish living, a role which puts God at the centre and in which the believer can know that he is doing his will.

What was important was that the principles enshrined in Torah should continue to be applied even when changed conditions stood the original enactment on its head. So by what at first sight looks like an abrogation of the law of the release of debts set out in Deut. 15.1-6, Hillel by permitting the creditor to transfer the debt to the courts, and allowing the latter to collect it on his behalf after the year of release, enabled economic help to go on being offered even in the years immediately before the year of release. By this ruling the restless word of God continued to effect the purpose for which it was spoken, the establishment of righteousness. This could even be the case when the ruling of the rabbis changed the purpose of the original enactment. So while Deut. 21.15-21 clearly intended the eldest son to inherit two-thirds of his father's estate, the rabbis ruled that he should receive only twice the share of any brother. If he had five brothers, he would receive two-sixths of the estate instead of the two-thirds intended by the original Deuteronomic enactment. While this had sought to keep family property intact, a vital concern in the predominantly agricultural society of sixth-century Palestine, with the changes in the economic structure of the Jewish community now scattered throughout the

---

6. Elliot N. Dorff, 'The Interaction of Jewish Law with Morality', *Judaism* 26 (1977), pp. 455-66.

Diaspora, righteousness became directed at ensuring that proper financial provision was made for all sons.

It is clear then that from the time of the Decalogue to our modern period law consists of the application of inherited principles to the situation confronting the contemporary legislators. Law is then a living tradition which marks the grateful response of believers to their gracious election by God. By obedience to law believers maintain their position within that community, and so are free from all claims upon them other than the claims of God which in any event they meet through their obedience. This is to appropriate that salvation already secured by God's election—salvation from both the tyrannies of other gods and humankind and also from one's self. Law then secures for humankind a freedom which without it they could not have. But the balance between freedom and enslavement is very fine: it is the difference between law and legalism into which, as the prophetic protest makes plain, law was always threatening to degenerate and become itself the very tyranny from which it should liberate.

The New Testament proclaims the same message—the possibility of freedom from tyranny. But this is no longer achieved through obedience to law, but by acceptance of Christ who fulfils law (Mt. 5.17-20). Salvation is thus 'in Christ'. Consequently Jesus had no need to establish a rival Torah to determine who made up the new Israel. Christianity rests entirely on the authority of Jesus alone, what he was and did. The Christian is called to identify with Christ by taking up his cross and following (Mt. 16.24). It is in this self-denying cross that his ethics are located. This explains why the Christian is unwilling 'to give overriding importance to the prevention or relief of pain'.[7]

But this does not mean that Jesus or his followers can be indifferent to Torah. Jesus' quarrel with contemporary Judaism was with legalism rather than the law itself, for Torah was being used to mask the gracious nature of the God who had revealed it. So by his attitude to the tax collectors and sinners—an attitude which cost him his life—Jesus threatened the whole exclusive structure of Judaism. As his disputes over sabbath observance indicate, central to his ministry was his desire to secure the appropriation of God's grace which no 'situation' could limit. Indeed by his radical reinterpretation of Torah (Mt. 5.21-48) he showed that no man could consider himself justified by his own merit for in the end all fall short of the will of God. Acceptance of even the most righteous is due to God's

---

7.   Basil Mitchell, *Law, Morality and Religion in a Secular Society* (Oxford: Oxford University Press, 1967), pp. 110-11.

grace alone. In the end Pharisee and tax collector stand together in the same position before God (Lk. 18.9-14). Torah, which was always in danger of being interpreted legalistically as a minimum moral standard securing acceptability by God, becomes with Jesus an impossible ideal which he alone could fulfil.

But if the New Testament indicates that acceptance of salvation lies in Jesus rather than the law, the fact that Jesus understood his ministry in terms of the fulfilment of Torah meant that initially his followers remained under the umbrella of Judaism worshipping within the Jewish ecclesiastical structure and interpreting Torah. But the recognition of the universalistic nature of Christ's revelation led to a radical reassessment of the position of Torah. On the one hand this resulted in the abrogation of much ritual and ceremonial law which differentiated Jews from Gentiles, such as circumcision. But on the other it subjected lax Gentile morality to the ethical insights of the Torah of Jesus the Jew. The effect of canonization was to confirm this position by ensuring that Christian ethics remained rooted in their Jewish heritage, a position maintained by Article 7 of the Anglican Articles of Religion.

While then membership of the Israel of the new covenant was not determined by obedience to any Christian law, Mosaic Torah was not rejected. But it was now subjected to the new 'situation' created by the Christ event. Christian ethics thus continued and continue the Rabbinic dialectic between inherited tradition and situational insight. They must therefore take into account 'new moral, economic, political and cultural conditions', as well as 'new ethical insights and attitudes', and it is only when they fail to do so that the Church becomes guilty of triumphalism, as for instance in the Roman Catholic attitude to birth control. The physical and human sciences are not extraneous to Christian ethics but are an integral element in them. Neither Judaism nor Christianity can then support a moral 'fundamentalism': like the law of Moses, the words of Jesus are also subject to this dialectic tension. The Bible then knows neither in Old Testament nor New Testament of an unalterable law of God despite the Deuteronomic injunction (Deut. 4.2; 13.1), but only of his restless word which must be made real to each generation. So for Christians, the Spirit, under whose direction all ethical rulings must be made, continues to guide into all truth (Jn 16.13).

But for the Church to abrogate moral leadership by reducing Christian ethics to the exercise of 'situational' love is to subject individuals to the tyranny of both others and their own selves, and discounts both ignorance and sin. It is from such tyranny that law liberates. Law and love are not then antithetic. As we have seen, Old Testament law was regarded not only as an expression of God's will but also of his love for his people, enabling them to respond to that love with love. It is this idea which John takes up in Jesus' urging his disciples to keep his commandments (Jn 14.15, 21; 15.10), and is to be the basis of Christian ethics (1 Jn 5.3). The situationists are thus right in pointing out that ethical decisions must be made in the light of the reality of the actual situation concerned including the insights of the physical and human sciences, and that love must characterize that decision: but to leave such a decision to each individual without any guidance inevitably results in chaos as everyone does what (they think) is right in their own eyes (Judg. 21.25). Significantly the New Testament does not envisage the guidance of the Spirit being given to the individual in the particular situation confronting him or her, but rather in Moule's words to the 'Christian worshipping congregation listening critically' (1 Cor. 14).[8] Christian ethics are not an individual's personal property determined according to one's own insight, but the possession of the whole people of God seeking to establish that righteousness which is his will for his world. Indeed it is the overriding weakness of situation ethics that the good thing can become reduced to 'the most loving thing' which in the particular instance confronting me, I do. But even if it were in fact true that a particular action was the most loving thing, indeed in the special circumstances the 'right' thing as opposed to all other actions, it does not necessarily make it 'good'. Indeed such a position denies the tragic reality that many of the decisions which we make involve a choice of the lesser of two evils. When I use arms to defend my wife and children, it may be a 'loving thing' that I do, it may even be the 'right' thing, but it is not a 'good' thing, and by pretending it is the situationists dehumanize and despiritualize me by denying me my conscience and the opportunity of repentance. They also make nonsense of the uncompromising nature of Christ's teaching which remains God's will, even if it is an ideal impossible of attainment. Evil remains evil and no amount of rationalization will make it other. Ironically this kind of situationism, like legalism, denies that we are accepted by the gracious God in spite of what we do and are. As James Packer has written of such situationism: 'It is only in its denial that any particular action is intrinsically immoral, evil

8.   C.F.D. Moule, 'Important Moral Issues. Prolegomena: The New Testament and Moral Decisions', *ET* 74 (1962–63), pp. 370-73.

and forbidden that situationism goes astray. Unfortunately, this one mistake is ruinous.'[9]

Torah is only condemned in the New Testament when it prevents someone enjoying God's grace which obedience to Torah was intended to facilitate. But the casuistry necessary in any legal system in order that principles may go on being effective in the varied practical situations which confront one is not necessarily to be condemned, even if such rulings are relative to the time and place of formation as the history of the growth of *halakah* makes plain. The Christian Church does humankind no service by renouncing its Jewish legal heritage: rather like the rabbis its task is to make real God's will in the ever new situations facing humankind, even if its conclusions can only be provisional and constantly subject to the dialectic tension of tradition and situationism under the guidance of the Spirit speaking to the congregation. As Harold Berman writes: 'Love needs law. Indeed, from both a Judaic and a Christian standpoint, and from a humanist standpoint as well, this is law's chief justification and also its chief purpose, namely, to help create conditions in which love may flourish.'[10] This is the point that Paul makes in Rom. 13.8-10. One cannot hold that apart from love 'there are no unbreakable rules'[11]—unless one is God. And the effect of acting as if this were true is in the end to behave as if one were God, but being human leaves one the agent of 'caprice, arbitrariness, and oppression—not love'.[12]

If then for Judaism and Christianity law is both an expression of God's love and gives content to the love that they are to show for others, should Jews and Christians seek to impose their law through the authority of the State on those who do not share their beliefs? Clearly if Jews and Christians hold their law to be God's will, it is proper for them to seek to influence those who legislate. Indeed not to do so is to reduce Jewish and Christian ethics to the realm of 'club' rules. Since God made all humankind in his image, that is for relationship with him, his law must be

9. James Packer, 'Situations and Principles', in B.N. Kaye and G.J. Wenham (eds.), *Law, Morality and the Bible* (Leicester: Inter-Varsity Press, 1978), pp. 151-67 (161).

10. Harold J. Berman, *The Interaction of Law and Religion* (London: SCM Press, 1974), pp. 88-89.

11. J.A.T. Robinson, *Christian Morals To-day* (London: SCM Press, 1964), p. 16, and *idem*, *Christian Freedom in a Permissive Society* (London: SCM Press, 1970), p. 16.

12. Berman, The *Interaction*, p. 88.

applicable to all whether or not they acknowledge it. But the doctrine of creation itself limits the authority of the State over the individual. For while God created humankind to work with him, he also gave them freedom to reject his sovereignty. Consequently Jews and Christians have no right to expect the State to assume an authority which even God chooses to surrender by seeking to impose his law on those who do not accept it. What God wills is that all should be free to enter into relationship with him—not that they should be coerced into obeying his will.

What is at stake then is whether by what I am (e.g. a member of the IRA), do (e.g. incite to racial hatred), or have (e.g. great wealth) others' freedom is threatened or curtailed. If so, then the State must legislate even if it infringes my personal freedom. Principally this will result in the State concerning itself with the poor and oppressed (who are not necessarily minority groups). So in Jewish and Christian eyes the State has the duty to restrict anyone's freedom over their property by imposing taxes in order to ensure the deprived the opportunity to be free to be themselves. No State can, then, be other than a welfare State. Indeed it is characteristic of Torah that persons matter more than property—that those who have not, have a right to support from those who have. Charity is part of law because it helps to restore to humankind that essential freedom which is God's will for them. While it is proper for Jew and Christian to support the maintenance of freedom of choice (e.g. how I spend my money), this can never be justified at the expense of others (e.g. deciding to whom to sell my house on racial grounds). Calls to uphold freedom, on examination, all too often turn out to be freedom for some at the expense of others. Of course the State cannot create that love which Jews and Christians seek to express through their law: but law can direct us towards the expression of that love which without it would never have been realized.

But has the State the right to infringe my own personal freedom when my actions in no way curtail the freedom of others? Since, as we have seen, individuals have the right to reject God's will, can the State limit that right (e.g. by prohibiting the termination of my life at my request). While the Wolfenden Report rejected the intervention of the criminal law in the private lives of sane adults, the Devlin-Hart debate which resulted has shown that some limitation of personal freedom is acceptable both to protect the individuals from themselves (e.g. drug abuse) and the essential institutions of that society of which they are members (e.g. marriage). The problem is to know where to draw the line. In the end Jews and Christians will have to determine whether to legislate or not to legislate is the lesser of two evils both for the individual and society at large, for even private acts influence public morality. But since God shows himself unwilling to terminate our essential freedom to choose to behave as we like, even when we thereby injure ourselves, the onus lies on those who would infringe personal freedom to show that this leads to lesser disorder. They must, however, bear in mind that above all they ought not to bring the law into contempt—for it is a short step from dishonouring and disregarding one enactment which restricts freedom to dishonouring and disregarding law in general. Then anarchy results.[13]

13. Mitchell, *Law*, p. 135, indicates the issues which should be considered before legislating: (a) So far as possible, privacy should be respected; (b) It is, as a rule, bad to pass laws which are difficult to enforce and whose enforcement tends therefore to be patchy and inequitable; (c) It is bad to pass laws which do not command the respect of the most reasonable people who are subject to them; (d) One should not pass laws which are likely to fail in their object, or produce a great deal of suffering, or other evils such as blackmail; (e) Legislation should be avoided which involves punishing people for what they very largely cannot help.

Part II

SHORTER ESSAYS

Chapter 14

The Interpretation of 2 Samuel 12.5-6

As a result of investigation into ancient Israel's criminal law, it has become possible, I believe, to distinguish civil law actions in tort from criminal prosecutions, and I suggest that an appreciation of this distinction may lead to a new interpretation of 2 Sam. 12.5-6.

The offence which the rich man in Nathan's parable had committed was theft, which in Israel was a tort resulting in an action for damages.[1] The general principle of the civil law was that an injured party should be restored as far as possible to the position he was in before the tort was suffered. Thus where an ox gored another ox to death, the living ox was sold, and the proceeds of sale, together with the dead animal's carcass, were divided between the parties (Exod. 21.35). But if the owner of the living ox knew that his beast had a propensity to gore, then he must give to the owner of the dead animal another ox of the same monetary value as the dead animal, and would himself take the carcass (Exod. 21.36). The goring ox would, of course, lose its value being a dangerous animal, and was therefore not to be given to the plaintiff as compensation for his loss.

But in the case of theft of animals, a prospective thief would not be deterred by the knowledge that if he were caught, he would only have to return to the plaintiff an animal of the same value as the stolen beast. Consequently the law enacted that in the case of an ox the thief must restore fivefold, and for a sheep fourfold (Exod. 21.37).[2] These punitive damages are not to be regarded as a fine, for they are paid to the plaintiff and not to

---

1. In ancient Israel there was a crime of manstealing (Exod. 21.16; Deut. 24.7), to which the commandment against theft originally referred (Exod. 20.15; Deut. 5.19). A. Alt, 'Das Verbot', pp. 333-40.

2. The major difficulty in legislating against theft is to determine at what moment the offence is completed. Initially it appears that the tort was not committed until the animal was killed or sold, but that later it was extended to include being in wrongful possession of another's animal. In this later case, the punitive damages were fixed at twofold (Exod. 22.3). Daube, *Studies*, pp. 90-93.

the state. A thief who could not pay the requisite damages was to be sold (Exod. 22.2b). The poorer the potential thief, the greater was the deterrent value of these measures.

Consequently the poor man in Nathan's parable, whose lamb had been stolen, was entitled to sue in tort for fourfold restitution (2 Sam. 12.6). The LXX here reads sevenfold. While it is possible that the punitive damages were later increased[3] it is more likely that sevenfold is a later proverbial expression indicating that perfect restitution must be made.[4] A later scribe might have altered the MT to fourfold to conform to the law[5] but it would seem more probable that the LXX rendering is due to a recollection of the proverbial saying preserved in Prov. 6.31, which also reads sevenfold. As the amount of compensation was fixed by law, it is unlikely that David would need to resort to a proverbial saying.

What then is the meaning of 2 Sam. 12.5? It has already been noted that the damages prescribed for theft would be little deterrent to the rich. It would therefore seem reasonable to suppose that David's angry outburst, in which he describes the rich man as a *ben-māwet*, reflects the inadequacy of the civil law in this particular case.

The expression *ben-māwet* occurs elsewhere only in 1 Sam. 20.31 and 26.16 (in the plural). In 1 Sam. 20.31, Saul indicates that David has acted so badly that he deserves to die, but when Jonathan challenges him to specify the offence, Saul cannot. David has done nothing to which Saul can legally take exception.[6] In 1 Sam. 26.16 David accuses Abner and Saul's men of such negligent behaviour that they deserve to be executed as criminals for their failure to guard the Lord's anointed. But there is no suggestion that they have committed any crime for which the death penalty could be exacted. Similarly, David, when he uses the term *ben-māwet* indicates that the rich man in Nathan's parable had committed such a heinous offence that he deserves to be indicted on a criminal charge and suffer the penalty of the criminal law, capital punishment (2 Sam. 12.5), but that because he has in fact committed no *crime*, the state cannot intervene, and so the injured party is left to sue for full compensation under the civil law (2 Sam. 12.6). David thus contrasts the criminal and civil law, state prosecution and the action by the plaintiff, capital punish-

---

3   Cook, *The Laws of Moses*, pp. 215-16.

4.   De Vaux, *Ancient Israel*, p. 160.

5.   Driver, *Notes on the Hebrew Text*, p. 291.

6.   Saul had already attempted to murder David, both directly (1 Sam. 18.10-11) and indirectly (1 Sam. 18.25).

ment and damages. The rich man deserved death for his callous act, but was protected by the law itself.

With the expression *ben-māwet* should be compared the phrase *'īš māwet* found in 2 Sam. 19.26 (in the plural) and 1 Kgs 2.26, which also indicates those who should certainly die. 2 Samuel 19.26 refers to Saul's family. The speaker is Mephibosheth who seeks to flatter David into again showing him mercy by recalling that, although in David's eyes all Saul's family deserved death, Mephibosheth himself had been previously spared.[7] In 1 Kgs 2.26 Abiathar, who had supported Solomon's rival Adonijah in the succession struggle, though worthy of death is given a free pardon.[8]

Both *ben-māwet* and *'īš māwet* are therefore emphatic expressions, indicating those who in the eyes of the speaker should without doubt be executed. Can this be yet another case where *māwet* is used superlatively?[9] If this is so, then, as in other cases where *māwet* has been treated as a superlative,[10] its primary meaning is still apparent. The expressions are first understood as referring to those who ought to be executed being 'death's men' or 'sons', that is, they already belong to that realm of weakened life which the Hebrew understands as the state of *māwet*.[11] Because of their emphatic use, these expressions can then come to be understood in a superlative sense and thus mean 'the deadly man', 'the arch villain'.

Therefore in the case under discussion, David describes the rich man as an arch villain who is morally guilty, but regretfully notes that the criminal law cannot touch him. The climax of the narrative is now reached with Nathan's dramatic disclosure to David that he is the rich man of the parable. But he is not simply a *ben-māwet*, a man who deserves to die, but who can only be sued in tort: he is, by his murder of Uriah, an actual murderer who should suffer execution under Israel's criminal law. It is only due to Yahweh's direct pardon that David is to be spared (2 Sam. 12.13).

---

7.   As 2 Sam. 21 appears to be presupposed by 2 Sam. 9, it is probable that Mephibosheth is making a specific reference to the seven sons of Saul whom David handed over to the Gibeonites to execute. Similarly Shimei also appears to refer to this event (2 Sam. 16.5-8). Hertzberg, *I and II Samuel*, pp. 299-301, 345-46, 381-85.

8.   Similarly Joab is not executed for his support of Adonijah, but on a criminal charge of murder (1 Kgs 2.32).

9.   D.W. Thomas, 'A Consideration of Some Unusual Ways of Expressing the Superlative in Hebrew', *VT* 3 (1953), pp. 209-24 (219-24); S. Rin, 'The מות of Grandeur', *VT* 9 (1959), pp. 324-25.

10.   E.g. Judg. 16.16; 2 Kgs 20.1; Isa. 53.12.

11.   A.R. Johnson, *The Vitality of the Individual in the Thought of Ancient Israel* (Cardiff: University of Wales Press, 2nd edn, 1964), pp. 88-90.

Chapter 15

THE CASE OF THE WOODGATHERER RECONSIDERED

In a short note in *Vetus Testamentum*,[1] Professor Weingreen has argued that the principle of *sîg lattôrâ* ('a fence around the Torah'), well known in rabbinic thinking and practice, can in fact be found within the Old Testament. By this principle the rabbinic law sought to forbid acts which although not harmful in themselves, nevertheless might lead to a breach of religious prohibitions. In support of his view, Weingreen cited the case of the sabbatarian woodgatherer (Num. 15.32-36), the law on the giving of false evidence (Deut. 19.19), and the prohibition of the making of idols and of their worship (Exod. 20.4-5). It is the purpose of this reconsideration to argue that Weingreen has allowed himself to read back later practices into earlier material where it was unknown. Let us examine his examples in reverse order.

Weingreen asserts that the basic prohibition in Exod. 20.4-5 is against the worship of idols, and not their manufacture. If one orders an image, there is a clear intention that one is going to worship it: therefore, argues Weingreen, the manufacture shows intention to break the law, and is itself treated as a culpable act.[2]

But it has been generally held that as elsewhere in the Decalogue the original commandment merely consisted of a short apodictic injunction, namely *lō' ta*ᵃ*śê-l*ᵉ*kā pesel* ('you shall not make for yourself a graven image'), and that Exod. 20.4b-6 formed a later addition.[3] Clearly the intention of this original second commandment was to prohibit any images of Yahweh, for by the first commandment all relations with any other deity

---

1.   J. Weingreen, 'The Case of the Woodgatherer (Numbers XV 32-36)', *VT* 16 (1966), pp. 361-64.
2.   Weingreen, 'The Case of the Woodgatherer', p. 364.
3.   Cf. J.J. Stamm and M.E. Andrew, *The Ten Commandments in Recent Research* (SBT, 2; London: SCM Press, 2nd edn, 1967), pp. 18-22, 81-89.

had already been forbidden. In other words the commandment ensured that the Yahweh cult was to be imageless.[4]

That Exod. 20.4b-6 was a later addition is confirmed by the plural suffixes in the injunction *lō' tištaḥᵃwâ lāhem wᵉlō' tā'ābdēm* ('you shall not bow down to them and serve them') for these suffixes cannot refer to the singular *pesel* of Exod. 20.4a.[5] Further, the phrase 'bow down and serve' is used neither of Yahweh nor of idols. It is therefore evident that direct reference is being made to the phrase *'ᵉlōhîm 'ᵃḥērîm* ('other gods') mentioned in the first commandment.[6] This is supported by the use of the term *'ēl qannā'* ('jealous god'), an expression which is only applied to Yahweh when his claims over Israel are being threatened by other deities (Exod. 24.14; Deut. 4.24; 5.9; 6.15. Cf. Josh. 24.19).[7] Thus the first two commandments are now understood as one.[8] Whereas under the original apodictic injunction *pesel* had referred to an image of Yahweh, now through the addition of Exod. 20.4b-6 it was understood to indicate an image of a heathen deity.

There can, therefore, be no question of accepting the worship of idols as the primary prohibition, and accordingly Exod. 20.4-5 does not provide an example of the operation of the principle of *sîg lattôrâ*.

Weingreen sees in the Deuteronomic law on false evidence (19.19) an example of intention to commit an act being treated as equal to the performance of that act itself.[9] Since the Deuteronomic 'purging' formula is only used where capital punishment is to be inflicted (12.6; 17.7, 12; 21.21; 22.21, 22, 24; 24.7; cf. 19.13; 21.9), it is clear that the false witness in Deut. 19.19 must have attempted to have secured the execution of 'his

---

4.   Whether or not the Old Testament provides evidence that there were images of Yahweh, the fact that the commandment may subsequently have been broken is no argument against its existence (H.H. Rowley, 'Moses and the Decalogue', *BJRL* 34 [1951–52], pp. 81-118 (105-106). In any event there can be no doubt that the official cult remained imageless for neither at Kadesh, Shechem, Shiloh nor in the temple was any image of Yahweh erected.

5.   H.G. Reventlow, *Gebot und Predigt im Dekalog* (Gütersloh: Gerd Mohn, 1962), p. 31, argued that the plural suffixes referred directly to the expanded v. 4. But this cannot be maintained (Knierim, 'Das erste Gebot', pp. 26ff.).

6.   W. Zimmerli, 'Das zweite Gebot', in W. Baumgartner *et al.* (eds.), *Bertholet Festschrift* (Tübingen: J.C.B. Mohr, 1950), pp. 550-63.

7.   Obbink, 'Jahwebilder', pp. 264-74.

8.   On the different methods of counting the commandments, cf. S. Goldman, *The Ten Commandments* (Chicago: University of Chicago Press, 1956), pp. 28ff.

9.   Goldman, *The Ten Commandments*, pp. 363-64.

brother' through conviction to a criminal charge.[10] For this he himself is to be executed. But in my view this is not to be understood as an example of intention to commit murder (albeit through the due processes of law) being regarded as the same thing as murder itself. The giving of false evidence is understood as a crime in its own right. Indeed Deut. 19.16-21 is in fact only an expansion of the ninth commandment (Exod. 20.16), and therefore this crime ranks alongside the other crimes prohibited by the Decalogue such as murder, adultery and manstealing.[11] Where evidence was not given under oath,[12] it was essential that the accused criminal who faced the prospect of execution should be protected from an unscrupulous witness (cf. 1 Kgs 21), particularly as it is probable that under Israelite law the accused was assumed guilty until proved innocent.[13] Thus we must again reject Weingreen's hypothesis.

Finally, we come to Professor Weingreen's starting point, the case of the woodgatherer (Num. 15.32-36)[14] In the first place the form of the story is due to the Priestly legislator who has adopted the practice of putting new legislation into the framework of a particular narrative case, perhaps due to a recollection of Exod. 18.13-27. Another instance of the use of this practice is provided by Lev. 24.10-23. Secondly, there are two other sabbath provisions of the Priestly legislator which also concern fire, namely Exod. 35.3 which forbids domestic fires, and Exod. 16.23 which implies that cooking is not to be undertaken on the sabbath. In my view these three sabbath provisions of the Priestly legislator are to be taken together, and understood as a deliberate act on his part to extend the scope of the sabbath law enactment to include even domestic activity. Since all earlier references to the sabbath enactment relate to actual occupational work (Exod. 23.12; 34.21; cf. 2 Kgs 4.22-23, Amos 8.5) this interpretation would seem to be justified, and is in accordance with the acknowledged emphasis placed on sabbath observance in the exilic and postexilic period.

---

10. As elsewhere (Exod. 21.23-25; Lev. 24.17-20) the talionic provisions in Deut. 19.21 are a later addition. In the first place the only possible punishment under Deut. 19.19 is death, and therefore only the first phrase is applicable. Secondly, as there need be no actual death for a man to be convicted of giving false evidence in a criminal action, even this first talionic provision has no inherent connection with the subject matter of Deut. 19.16-21 (Morgenstern, 'The Book', pp. 76-77).

11. Cf. Alt, 'Das Verbot', pp. 333-40.

12. M. Greenberg, 'Witness', in *IDB* IV (1962), p. 864.

13. Von Rad, *Deuteronomy*, p. 59.

14. Von Rad, *Deuteronomy*, pp. 361-64.

The collection of firewood simply provides an example of the sort of domestic act which was now prohibited as 'work', the performance of which would constitute the crime of sabbath breaking as set out in the fourth commandment. There is thus in my view no need to resort to the principle of *sîg lattôrâ* to explain the case of the woodgatherer. It is just part and parcel of the new Priestly legislation extending the sphere of sabbath observance.

Chapter 16

NEBALAH: A TERM FOR SERIOUS DISORDERLY AND UNRULY CONDUCT

It is clear that $n^e b\bar{a}l\hat{a}$ indicates action which is to be utterly deplored. Thus while with one exception KB treats the word as 'a euphemism for heavy sin',[1] and BDB holds that it always amounts to something disgraceful,[2] the *Interpreter's Dictionary of the Bible* describes it as 'an understatement for outright sinfulness'.[3] Its connection with outrageous sexual offences has often been noted,[4] but its use is considerably wider. Thus while it is applied to Shechem's rape of Dinah (Gen. 34.7), to Amnon's rape of Tamar (2 Sam. 13.12), to attempted sodomy and communal rape (Judg. 19.23-24; 20.6, 10), to adultery (Jer. 29.23) and to a woman's loss of virginity before marriage (Deut. 22.21), it is also used of Achan's breach of the ban on Jericho (Josh. 7.15), of Nabal's normal behaviour (1 Sam. 25.25), of the defence of God by Job's friends (Job 42.8), and of deceptive words (Isa. 9.16; 32.6) including false prophecy (Jer. 29.23).

The noun $n^e b\bar{a}l\hat{a}$ is, of course, related to the verb *nābal* usually rendered 'to be foolish, senseless', the opposite of *ḥākam* 'to be wise'. Behind the Hebrew concept of wisdom lies the idea that life is ordered by basic rules which one can discern from one's experience.[5] The wise were those skilled in seeing the order in things, how one thing related to another, how society functioned, how the natural world and science worked. They looked at relationships, objects and ideas, and tried to discern their pattern, structure, rule and order. Their concern was that people should be able to live the best and fullest lives, and not come to any mishap. And as part of

---

1. KB, p. 590a.
2. BDB, p. 615a.
3. *IDB*, II (1962), p. 303.
4. G. von Rad, *Genesis* (OTL; London: SCM Press, 3rd edn, 1972), p. 332, and *idem*, *Deuteronomy*, p. 142.
5. Cf. the discussion in G. von Rad, *Wisdom in Israel* (London: SCM Press, 1972).

their exercise of wisdom, the wise were expected to be able so to manipulate words that order might either be maintained or restored. They were those who knew what to say in an awkward situation, and by saying it brought about peace and harmony. The judgment of Solomon in the case of the two prostitutes and the one surviving child nicely illustrates this (1 Kgs 3.16-28).

Folly, therefore, consists in failing to observe life's essential rules. The fool is unable to see the order in things, says the wrong thing at the wrong moment, and takes action which results in unruliness and disorder.[6] Thus anyone or anything acting in an unruly or disorderly manner can be described as 'unwise' or 'foolish'. Such is an embryo which cannot find its way out of the womb for birth at the appropriate time (Hos. 13.13):[7] so too was Job's wife when she counselled her husband to curse God and die, that is to commit suicide (Job 2.9-10). Since God gave, he could also take away (Job 1.21).[8] It was simply illogical to renounce him in adversity having acknowledged him in prosperity. Job's wife had looked at her husband's pitiful condition and failed to see its proper place in the order of things. Instead she spoke as one of the foolish women. Consequently to treat someone as a fool, meant for the Hebrew to act towards him in an unruly or disorderly manner (Nah. 3.6). This might amount to actual rebellion whether by a son against his father (Mic. 7.6) or Israel against Yahweh (Deut. 32.15).[9]

It is this idea of lack of order, unruliness, which lies behind the use of $n^eb\bar{a}l\hat{a}$. As the examination of the particular texts will confirm, $n^eb\bar{a}l\hat{a}$ is reserved for extreme acts of disorder or unruliness which themselves result in a dangerous breakdown in order, and the end of an existing relationship. It is this which explains the very serious nature of the term. $n^eb\bar{a}l\hat{a}$ can then best be rendered as 'an act of crass disorder or unruliness' or 'acting in an utterly disorderly or unruly fashion'. Does this cover all the instances of its use?

---

6.   Von Rad, *Wisdom*, pp. 64-65.

7.   Von Rad, *Wisdom*, pp. 20, 142.

8.   The Hebrews believed that if one blasphemed, then God would automatically strike one dead. Cf. Brichto, *The Problem of 'Curse'*, pp. 147, 164-65.

9.   The same idea of violent action is present in Jer. 14.21 where Yahweh is urged not merely not to dishonour his glorious throne, but ironically not to rebel against it, so leading to the withdrawal of his presence and the end of the covenant relationship.

1. *nᵉbālâ Applied to Sexual Acts*

a. *Genesis 34.7*

Israelite law provided that where a virgin was seduced, her lover had to make good the father's loss by paying him damages equivalent to the amount of the bride price which he could have expected to have received on his daughter's marriage (Exod. 22.15). But in this primitive story much more is involved than the mere seduction of a girl within the local community: Dinah and Shechem belong to different clans with different laws and customs. This explains Jacob's hesitation in consenting to the marriage and the insistence on circumcision, for normally it was the custom only to marry among one's kin (Gen. 24.4; 28.2; 29.19).[10] By his rape of Dinah, Shechem had done something which 'ought not to be done', that is he had broken customary law (Gen. 20.9; 29.26; 2 Sam. 13.12)[11] which separated one clan from another. Inevitably his utterly disorderly and unruly conduct (*nᵉbālâ*) could only lead to conflict between the clans which could no longer co-exist alongside each other.

b. *2 Samuel 13.12*

Similarly Amnon's rape of his half-sister Tamar is another instance of action which 'is not done in Israel', that is a breach of customary law. The custom here is the ancient prohibition on casual sexual relations outside marriage with women whom one could expect to find living under the same family roof.[12] Although the situation of the royal household in Jerusalem with separate houses for the royal princes is very different from that of the primitive patriarchal family of three or four generations living together in one tent, the ancient taboo still applies. While Amnon could certainly have married Tamar with his father's consent (cf. Gen. 20.12), to force her was indeed an act of crass disorder, extreme unruliness (*nᵉbālâ*), which inevitably led to bloodshed within the royal family.

c. *Judges 19.23-24; 20.6, 10*

The attempted sodomy on the Levite, and the ravishing to death of the concubine are another appalling instance of breach of the customary law,

10. Köhler, *Hebrew Man*, p. 90; de Vaux, *Ancient Israel*, pp. 30-31.

11. Falk *Hebrew Law*, pp. 29-30.

12. This customary law lies behind the list of relatives in Lev. 18.6-18, now considerably expanded. Cf. Elliger, 'Das Gesetz Leviticus 18', pp. 1-25; Porter, *The Extended Family*; Phillips, *AICL*, pp. 123-29.

this time of the law of hospitality.[13] Having been welcomed as a guest at Gibeah, the Levite was entitled to protection. This explains the old man's offer of his daughter to the Benjaminites in order that the law of hospitality should not be broken (cp. Gen. 19.1-11). The Benjaminites utterly disorderly and unruly conduct ($n^e b\bar{a}l\hat{a}$) inevitably led to war with Israel.

d. *Deuteronomy 22.21*

A woman found guilty of pretending to be a virgin on marriage was to be executed as if she were an adulteress (Deut. 22.20-21), even though the sexual intercourse complained of might have taken place before marriage or betrothal. It is probable that the original purpose of the law of adultery was not simply to protect the husband's property, which his wife certainly was, but rather to ensure that the husband might be certain that his wife's children were his own. This was vital in a society which did not believe in life after death but rather that a man's personality went on in his children. This would explain the extension of adultery to include a wife's sexual intercourse before marriage.[14] Her action can be described as utterly unruly and disorderly ($n^e b\bar{a}l\hat{a}$) for it resulted in the inevitable breakdown of the marriage.

e. *Jeremiah 29.23*

Similarly the exiled prophets Ahab and Zedekiah are charged with disorderly and unruly conduct ($n^e b\bar{a}l\hat{a}$) not only for their false prophecy, but also for their adultery.[15]

2. *$n^e b\bar{a}l\hat{a}$ Applied to Non-Sexual Acts*

a. *Joshua 7.15*

Achan's action in appropriating property subject to the ban at Jericho inevitably brought divine punishment on Israel inflicted through her unexpected defeat by the men of Ai (Josh. 7.1-6). His looting of what had already been dedicated to God was both utterly disorderly and unruly in

---

13. De Vaux, *Ancient Israel*, p. 30.

14. The ancient rite in Num. 5.11-31 may, in fact, be a method of assessing paternity. Cf. Phillips, *AICL*, pp. 118-20.

15. Further, in Hos. 2.12 the unique word *nablūt* is applied to the stripping of adulterous Israel, serving as a euphemism for her private parts, the place of her disorderly and unruly conduct. She was to be shown up as the common prostitute she was. Cf. Phillips, 'Family Law', pp. 352-53 (reprinted above as Chapter 6).

itself ($n^e b\bar{a}l\hat{a}$) and brought further disorder. By transgressing the ancient sacral taboo of the ban, he had broken the customary law of the holy war with disastrous results to his people. If order is to be restored, Israel must root out the offender and destroy him.

b. *1 Samuel 25.25*

Abigail describes her husband's normal way of life as $n^e b\bar{a}l\hat{a}$ of which his action in refusing David and his men sustenance is another instance. By custom David was entitled to the payment of tribute for protecting Nabal as the latter's herdsmen readily recognize. Clearly Nabal ought to have seen that the inevitable outcome of his refusal would be a punitive raid by David and his men since the arrangement between them had now been summarily brought to an end. 'Disorder', 'Unruliness' (*nābal*) is his name and utterly disorderly and unruly ($n^e b\bar{a}l\hat{a}$) his conduct.[16]

3. $n^e b\bar{a}l\hat{a}$ *Applied to the Spoken Word*

a. *Job 42.8*

Job's friends are accused of $n^e b\bar{a}l\hat{a}$ for the way in which they sought to defend God from Job's charges. They had failed to enter into the reality of Job's experience and instead were content to repeat the orthodox theological position that suffering was God's punishment for sin. But while innocent suffering cannot be explained, to deny its existence is to fly in the face of reality and create yet even more difficulty for those trying to come to terms with the problem of evil. As Job finds out, the friends' unruly and disorderly views ($n^e b\bar{a}l\hat{a}$) prevent any constructive theological discussion. The friends had failed to recognize that the order of life contained within it an irrational and inexplicable disorder. As a result their relationship with God is broken and it is only as a result of Job's prayer that it can be restored.[17]

b. *Isaiah 9.16*

The poem Isa. 9.8-21, 25-30 indicates that the people do not learn from the punishment already inflicted by God, but instead of turning back to him,

16. For the compiler, the story contains the additional implication that Nabal was guilty of even greater foolishness in failing to recognize David's true identity. He is no runaway slave, but Yahweh's chosen king.

17. Even if the epilogue was originally written to conclude a lost prose story, it now presupposes the present poem and acts as a conclusion to it and a judgment on the arguments there advanced.

continue in their rebellion. Consequently they can only expect further acts of divine judgment. They had misunderstood his nature and for their disorderly and unruly speaking ($n^e b\bar{a}l\hat{a}$) must expect yet more disorder to fall upon their community.

c. *Isaiah 32.6*

Here again $n^e b\bar{a}l\hat{a}$ is used of the rebel against God. It is a particular mark of his disorderly and unruly action that he should misinterpret the nature of God by uttering false statements about him. As a result the people are led astray, and this inevitably leads to disorder within society. So the hungry hunger, and the thirsty thirst.

d. *Jeremiah 29.23*

The disorderly and unruly conduct ($n^e b\bar{a}l\hat{a}$) of the prophets Ahab and Zedekiah not only covers their adultery, but also their false prophecy. As prophets they were meant to mediate the will of God to men: anything else could only lead to disorder. False prophecy was very much a live issue in Jeremiah's time both for the prophet himself personally (Jer. 26–29),[18] and also in the unsuccessful Deuteronomic attempt to root it out (Deut. 13.2-6; 18.22).[19]

This brief examination of the texts where $n^e b\bar{a}l\hat{a}$ appears shows that it is certainly not a term reserved for sexual offences of a particularly abhorrent kind. Rather $n^e b\bar{a}l\hat{a}$ is a general expression for serious disorderly and unruly action resulting in the break up of an existing relationship whether between tribes, within the family, in a business arrangement, in marriage or with God. This shows its extreme gravity and perhaps explains why the word is so rarely used. It indicates the end of an existing order consequent upon breach of rules which maintained that order. Its earliest use particularly connects it with breach of the customary law where there was, of course, no means of obtaining satisfaction through the courts, but only through taking direct actin. Later it came to be applied more generally to other instances of total collapse in existing relationships, but it remains surprising that it was so little used of Israel's rebellion against Yahweh.

18. T.W. Overholt, *The Threat of Falsehood* (SBT, 16; London: SCM Press, 1970).

19. Von Rad, *Deuteronomy*, pp. 96-97, 122-25; Phillips, *Deuteronomy*, pp. 94-95, 126.

Chapter 17

UNCOVERING THE FATHER'S SKIRT

Deuteronomy 23.1 reads: 'A man shall not take the wife of his father'. The first half of the verse prohibits marriage with a stepmother, thus depriving the heir of his ancient right of inheriting his father's wives and concubines, and having sexual relations with them (Gen. 35.22; 49.4; 2 Sam. 3.7; 16.22; 1 Kgs 2.22; 1 Chron. 2.24).[1] Since a son by a first marriage would often be the same age as a later wife of his father, marriage with one's stepmother could clearly be an attractive proposition. For the Deuteronomist such a union was considered totally improper and absolutely forbidden. It is difficult to say how widespread such a practice was at that time. A man would have had to be of some means to support more than one wife (cf. Deut. 21.15-17). Certainly the majority of the cases cited in the Old Testament concern the royal family where possession of the King's harem was essential to the man who would succeed to the throne.[2] But the fact that Deut. 23.1 specifically prohibits marriage in contrast to promiscuous sexual relations mentioned twice in the Holiness Code (Lev. 18.8; 20.11) and again in the cursing liturgy against secret offenders (Deut. 27.20) would appear to indicate that the Deuteronomist was depriving men of a right which was still being practised. No penalty is prescribed in Deut. 23.1, but it is probable that death was intended, the offence being treated as an extension of the crime of adultery (cf. Lev. 20.11).

The second half of Deut. 23.1 is usually interpreted as a restatement of the first, the father's skirt being understood in a transferred sense as referring to his wife.[3] Support for this interpretation comes from (1) Ruth

1.   W. Robertson Smith, *Kinship and Marriage in Early Arabia* (London: A. & C. Black, new edn, 1903), pp. 104ff.
2.   M. Tsevat, 'Marriage and Monarchical Legitimacy in Ugarit and Israel', *JSS* 3 (1958), pp. 237-43.
3.   Driver, *Deuteronomy*, p. 259; Carmichael, *The Laws*, pp. 169-71, and *idem*, 'A Ceremonial Crux, p. 333.

3.9 and Ezek. 16.8 where the expression to spread the skirt over a woman indicates taking her as one's wife, and (2) Deut. 27.20 which reads: 'Cursed be he who lies with the wife of his father for he has uncovered the skirt of his father'. But two things should make us cautious about interpreting Deut. 23.1 in the light of Deut. 27.20. In the first place Deut. 27.20 substitutes *kî'* ('for') for the *w^{e}lō'* ('and...not') of Deut. 23.1, and second it is not the normal practice for legislation to say the same thing twice. Interpreted in the light of Deut. 27.20, Deut. 23.1b becomes tautologous. This raises the question whether it should be taken either literally and understood as referring to uncovering and looking upon the private parts of the father, or euphemistically and understood as prohibiting actual sexual relations between son and father. Is there any evidence to support this?

Homosexual practices are prohibited neither in the Book of the Covenant nor in Deuteronomy, but are first made criminal in the Holiness Code (Lev. 18.22; 20.13). These provisions are intended to govern all sexual relations between males rather than the specific case of a son seducing his father. But in Lev. 18.7 we find specific reference to such relations: 'The nakedness of your father and the nakedness of your mother, you shall not uncover: she is your mother, you shall not uncover her nakedness'. Most commentators understand 'the nakedness of your father' as a later addition into what was originally a list of female relations whom one would have expected to find in one's tent encampment and with whom customary law forbad any casual sexual relations, and they accept translations which refer it to the mother, the father's wife.[4] But it is much more natural to understand Lev. 18.7a in its present form as prohibiting sexual relations with either of one's parents.[5] For sexual intercourse with the mother is prohibited not, as in the case of a stepmother (Lev. 18.8), because she has married the father, but simply because she is the mother. The conjunction in Lev. 18.7a should be given its ordinary meaning, and 'the nakedness of the father' understood literally. And here at any rate it is clear that it is not merely the immodest act of looking upon the sexual parts of the father which is prohibited, but actual physical relations.

Another possible though unlikely contemporary reference to such sexual relations occurs in Ezek. 22.10-11, where in his condemnation of the utter

---

4. Noth, *Leviticus*, pp. 135-36; J.R. Porter, *Leviticus* (CBC; Cambridge: Cambridge University Press, 1976), pp. 143, 145. On Lev. 18.6-23, see further Elliger, 'Das Gesetz Leviticus 18', pp. 1-25; Porter, *The Extended Family*.

5. Daube, *Studies*, p. 81, interprets Lev. 18.7a as prohibiting sexual intercourse with both father and mother.

sexual depravity of Jerusalem, Ezekiel lists in turn those who uncover their fathers' nakedness, those who have sexual intercourse with women during their menstrual period, men who commit adultery, have sexual relations with their daughters-in-law or stepsisters. Driver argues that the prophet draws on the language of Lev. 18.8 to condemn those who have sexual relations with their stepmothers.[6] The prophet could in fact have been quoting from either Lev. 18 or 20, for both list all the sexual depravities which he condemns. But the fact that the language of the second half of the verse condemning intercourse with a woman during her menstrual period seems to be drawn from Lev. 18.9 rather than Lev. 20.18 suggests that Ezekiel was in fact using Lev. 18. Further, since all the other offences which he lists concern sexual intercourse with a female, there is the strong presupposition that he was, as Driver argues, referring to Lev. 18.8 and not to Lev. 18.7a, however that is interpreted. Indeed, this addition may not yet have been made.

If we are correct in arguing that Deut. 23.1b prohibits some kind of sexual immodesty or act with one's father, can we find an explanation for the inclusion of such a provision in the Deuteronomic legislation?

Carmichael has argued that the Deuteronomist has been influenced by the patriarchal narratives in the drafting of his legislation. Behind Deut. 23.1 lies the story of Reuben's intercourse with Bilhah, his father Jacob's concubine (Gen. 35.22; 49.4).[7] Through his legislation the Deuteronomist is attempting to ensure that his fellow-Israelites will not follow the example of their forebear.[8] The weakness of Carmichael's argument is that within the Genesis story itself it is clear that Reuben's act was regarded with abhorrence. This was no marriage with a stepmother: it was the seduction of his father's concubine during his life. What the Deuteronomist is doing is ruling out a practice which had hitherto been considered not only legal, but entirely proper. In this respect Deut. 27.20 differs from Deut. 23.1 which further explains why the latter should not be interpreted in the light of the former. For the cursing liturgy is concerned with a secret sexual encounter between a stepson and stepmother, precisely the situation covered by Reuben's sexual intercourse with Bilhah. Deuteronomy 23.1a, however, prohibits a permanent union after the father's death.

Mention of uncovering a father's skirt would immediately bring to mind the offence of Ham who 'saw the nakedness' of his father Noah (Gen.

6. Driver, *Deuteronomy*, p. 259.
7. Carmichael, *The Laws*, pp. 169-71.
8. Carmichael, *A Ceremonial Crux*, p. 326.

9.20-27). It is difficult to tell from the text of Gen. 9 whether Ham simply looked upon his father's private parts or whether he engaged in sexual relations with him. Since, however, Gen. 9.24 specifically refers to Noah knowing what his son had done to him, we should perhaps understand this incident as more than an immodest looking at his drunken and naked father but rather as his actual seduction while unconscious—an act so abhorrent that the author is unwilling to spell it out.[9] But whatever were the particular circumstances of this particular abomination, Ham's son, Canaan, is cursed to be the slave of Ham's brothers and the Canaanites seen as the offspring of a perverted ancestor. Now it is well known that much of the Deuteronomic legislation is specifically anti-Canaanite seeking to ensure Israel's isolation from all Canaanite customs and practices (Deut. 14; 18.9-14; 21.22-23; 22.5; 23.18-19) and both in Deuteronomy and the Deuteronomic History there is much anti-Canaanite parenetic material. It is therefore no surprise that in addition to ruling out marriage with a stepmother, which is of course a law designed to engender further filial piety towards the father rather than to protect his wife, the Deuteronomist should also have added a prohibition against that abhorrent sexual practice involving a father and associated with the eponymous ancestor of the Canaanites. Its insertion into Lev. 18.7, now clearly identified as involving physical sexual relations, no doubt reflected the same anti-Canaanite feeling which led the Priestly legislators to reinterpret the crime of adultery to include all those unnatural sexual unions (Lev. 18.6-18; 20.10-21) which the Canaanites, the former inhabitants of the land, were held to have practised (Lev. 18.24-30; 20.22-26).[10]

At first sight it might look as if Hebrew law is not unique in providing such a regulation as Deut. 23.1b. For while Hittite Law, like the Book of the Covenant, Deuteronomy and the Code of Hammurabi, makes no mention of homosexuality in general,[11] HL 189 specifically forbids sexual relations between father and son for which it seems probable that the death penalty was exacted.[12] But here it is the father who takes the initiative, the offences being paederasty with one's own son, rather than the seduction of

9. B. Vawter, *On Genesis* (London: Geoffrey Chapman, 1977), p. 139. For another possible case of seduction during drunkenness, cf. Ruth 3.7.

10. Phillips, *AICL*, pp. 122-29.

11. In contrast MAL A 20 (*ANET*, p. 181) forbids sodomy though the suggestion has been made that this might only be in cases where the victim was in a specially close relationship to the offender. See Driver and Miles, *The Assyrian Laws*, p. 71.

12. *ANET*, p. 196; Neufeld, *The Hittite Laws*, p. 189.

the father. But in my view it is the case of Ham and his father Noah which has led to the Deuteronomic provision.

Finally, we must consider why Deut. 27.20 in contrast to Deut. 23.1 specifically identifies sexual relations with a stepmother as uncovering the father's skirt. For like the usual interpretation of Deut. 23.1 from which I have dissented, such an explanation appears to be tautologous unless it can be shown that by it a further idea is being added to the curse of the first part of the verse. The other curses concerning prohibited sexual relations in Deut. 27.22, 23 clearly show that the liturgy of Deut. 27 is dependent on the list of sexual offences in Lev. 18 for they deal with two relationships which were late additions to that list, those with the half-sister through a mother (Lev. 18.9) and the mother-in-law (Lev. 18.17 and cf. 20.14).[13] As I have noted, Lev. 18 would originally have consisted of a series of short apodictic injunctions not necessarily in written form directed at the full adult male in the prime of life forbidding him sexual relations with females whom he might find living in his tent encampment. As the introduction in Lev. 18.6 indicates, this old family law has now been extended to include any female relative whether found in the tent encampment or not (including the half-sister through a mother and the mother-in-law), and explanations given for the various prohibitions based on blood relationship rather than mere physical proximity. Thus sexual intercourse with the wife of a near male relative—a woman whom one might expect to find in the tent encampment—is now forbidden on the grounds that this uncovers her husband's nakedness (Lev. 18.8, 14, 16)—an idea also found in Lev. 20.11, 20, 21. In other words marriage with a near male relative effectively makes the woman herself into a blood relative and therefore as in the case of female near relatives, sexual relations with her are treated as an unnatural offence. It is then the necessity to make all women in the list in Lev. 18.6-18 into blood relatives that has led to the insertion of the apparently obvious explanation that sexually a wife belongs to her husband. The author of the curse in Deut. 27.20—though using the language of Deut. 23.1—accepted this explanation spelt out in Lev. 18.8 and Lev. 20.11 in drafting his curse against those who had secret sexual relations with a stepmother. Indeed it is possible that his use of the language of Deut. 23.1 may have been deliberate—an attempt to suppress the offensive suggestion that any Israelite could like Ham the father of Canaan commit in secret such an unspeakable offence on his father. Its mention in

13. For a discussion of the date and purpose of this cursing liturgy, cf. Phillips, *Deuteronomy*, pp. 180-83.

Deut. 23.1 and Lev. 20.7 is due to the theologized nature of the Deuter-onomic legislation and the Holiness Code which uses the tradition of Ham's abhorrent action for polemical purposes. The author of the cursing liturgy of Deut. 27 was not concerned with polemics but practical possibilities.

In conclusion, then, Deut. 23.lb should not be interpreted in the light of Deut. 23.la. It is drafted not as an explanation of the prohibition of marriage with a stepmother, but as a separate command, and laws do not repeat themselves. Deuteronomy 23.lb is a deliberate enactment of the Deuteronomist and is part of his anti-Canaanite material. It was added at the head of the list of prohibited sexual relations in Lev. 18.7-23 which the Canaanites, the former inhabitants of the land, were held to have com-mitted (Lev. 18.24-30) because no relationship was more abhorrent to the Israelites than that associated with Ham, the father of Canaan.

Chapter 18

DOUBLE FOR ALL HER SINS

Isaiah 40.2 describes Jerusalem as having 'received from the Lord's hand double for all her sins'. Commentators are quick to defend Yahweh from any charge of injustice. Accordingly the phrase is interpreted as 'characteristic of Oriental exaggeration',[1] being 'rhetorical exaggeration'[2] or 'rhetorical hyperbole'.[3] Reference is then made to the fulfilment of the prophecy of Jer. 16.18[4] (cf. Jer. 17.8; Rev. 18.6), though there *mišnê* is used rather than the rare noun *kepel*, found only here and in Job. 11.6, 41.5, and the cognate verb *kāpel* appears in Exod. 26.9, 28.16, 39.9 and doubtfully Ezek. 21.19. So von Rad,[5] following Tsevat's[6] assertion that *mišnê* in Deut. 15.18 and Jer. 16.18 means 'equivalent', 'double' or '*quid pro quo*', argues that *kiplayim* in Isa. 40.2 is to be interpreted in the same way. The nouns are in effect synonyms. Consequently von Rad sees the prophet as announcing that Jerusalem has now paid 'the equivalent', that is the appropriate penalty.

The fact that *kepel* everywhere else refers to something which is doubled should at least raise the question whether it is in fact to be understood literally. This was the contention of Tom[7] who noting the use of *kepel* in Exod. 26.9, 28.16, 39.9 and Job. 41.5 as indicating something placed exactly on top of its counterpart, argued that 'the double' of Isa.

1.   J. Muilenberg, 'Isaiah 40–66', *IB*, V (1956), pp. 381-773 (425).
2.   R. Levy, *Deutero-Isaiah: A Commentary* (London: Oxford University Press, 1925), p. 114; C.C. Torrey, *The Second Isaiah: A New Interpretation* (Edinburgh: T. & T. Clark, 1928), p. 305.
3.   G.W. Wade, *The Book of the Prophet Isaiah* (London: Methuen, 2nd edn, 1929), p. 249.
4.   It is possible that Jer. 16.18 reflects Isa. 40.2.
5.   G. von Rad, 'כפלים in Jes 40:2 = "Äquivalent"?', *ZAW* 79 (1967), pp. 80-82.
6.   Tsevat, 'Alalkhiana', pp. 125-26.
7.   W. Tom, 'Welke is de Zin van het "dubbel ontvangen" uit Jesaja 40:2', *GThT* 59 (1959), pp. 122-23.

40.2 meant that Jerusalem's sins were wholly covered. Her forgiveness is therefore absolute, and far from raising questions about God's justice, makes the consolation of the prophet's words of comfort even greater.

It is also possible that the prophet was referring to a punishment which had in fact been doubled. A number of commentators point out that 'double', damages are known in Hebrew law.[8] Thus in the Book of the Covenant, for the tort of theft of animals still in the thief's possession, the civil law provides that double damages are to be paid to the injured party (Exod. 22.3). Similar damages are also required for theft of property committed to another's care (Exod. 22.6). But these deterrent measures of the civil law, which in other instances demands even larger punitive damages (Exod. 21.37; 2 Sam. 12.6), have no bearing on Jerusalem's situation following Yahweh's judgment on her for her apostasy. The only way in which her punishment could be thought of as doubled is not in its amount, but in its duration. It has been twice as long as it should have been. It is my contention that this is what the prophet means by 'double for all her sins'—namely that whereas one generation properly experienced the destruction of Jerusalem and consequent exile, its duration has extended to another 'innocent' generation as well. Confirmation that *kepel* can be used of the doubling of a period of time is provided by Sir. 26.1.

That Yahweh could punish more than one generation was of course recognized in the well-known phrase 'to the third and fourth generation' (Exod. 20.5; 34.7; Num. 14.18; Deut. 5.9). This is a short-hand expression for total annihilation, for while a fourth generation was a rarity, a fifth was considered an impossibility. Exilic literature indicates that the extent of liability over more than one generation was one of the most important current theological issues (cf. Lam. 5.7). It was at this time that, as far as the courts were concerned, Deuteronomic legislation finally ruled out the possibility of anyone other than the criminal himself being held liable for his crime (Deut. 24.16).[9] Since this resulted in a higher morality being attributed to human justice than divine (cf. Deut. 5.9), ideas about the latter also had to alter. This should cause no surprise for theology is always shaped by human experience. So both Jer. 31.29-30 and Ezek. 18 reject the validity of the current popular proverb that one generation suffers for the sins of its predecessor. Instead both assert that each gene-

---

8.   Levy, *Deutero-Isaiah*, p. 114; J.L. McKenzie, *Second Isaiah* (AnBib; New York: Doubleday, 1968), p. 17.

9.   P.J. Verdam, ' "On ne fera point mourir les enfants pour les pères" en droit biblique', *RIDA* 3 (1949), pp. 393-416; Greenberg, 'Postulates', pp. 20-27.

ration's fate is in its own hands. In Jeremiah this new understanding of man's responsibility is placed in the future[10] while for Ezekiel it is a present reality to be grasped. His concern is to get the exilic generation in Babylon to stand on their own two feet and acknowledge Yahweh. While Israel had been rightly punished for her sins, those who now found themselves suffering punishment could yet experience God's grace. As Joyce[11] has pointed out, Ezekiel's aim is to assert the moral independence of generations. Not only can one generation no longer be condemned for the activities of its predecessor, but if it repents it is not even to be condemned for its own past behaviour. Ezekiel thus indicates that those addressed cannot blame the ancestors for their fate: their destiny rests entirely on their own response to Yahweh (18.30). The proverb to which they refer as an excuse for taking no action is false and must not be used. Instead of blaming the earlier generation, it is they themselves who must repent and turn to God.

For Deutero–Isaiah, a generation after Ezekiel, a different situation obtained. Those who had heeded Ezekiel's message had not experienced the promised restoration and had perished in a heathen land. A second generation, entirely innocent of the offences which had led to the exile, had now grown up both in Palestine and Babylon. Deutero–Isaiah's appeal is to this innocent generation. In fact, though they do not realize this, the exile is even now ending and Jerusalem's glorious future already dawning. The prophet's concern is that at the eleventh hour the faithful may renounce Yahweh and so lose what is already within their grasp. His hope is of a restored Jerusalem to which the exiles will return from every corner of the world to which they have been banished (Isa. 43.5-7), and from which God's law (*tōrâ*) and justice (*mišpāṭ*) would go out to the ends of the earth (Isa. 42.1-4; 51.4-5). Whether the prophet was writing in Jerusalem, or as is more usually supposed Babylon, the event which is to trigger off this process of restoration is the return of the exiles. Israel's immediate destiny lies with them. As I have argued elsewhere[12] the suffering servant is therefore to be interpreted as those innocent Israelites who in the exilic situation continue to remain faithful to Yahweh, even suffering death in

10. It is possible that Jer. 31.29-30 reflects Ezek. 18 rather than anticipates it.

11. P.M. Joyce, 'Individual Responsibility in Ezekiel 18?', in E.A. Livingstone (ed.), *Studia Biblica 1978* (*JSOTS*, 11; Sheffield: JSOT Press, 1979), pp. 185-96; cf. B. Lindars, 'Ezekiel and Individual Responsibility', *VT* 15 (1965), pp. 452-67.

12. Phillips, '*Torah* and *Mishpat*', pp. 112-32 (reprinted above as Chapter 11), and *idem*, 'The Servant', pp. 370-74.

Babylon, in order that Israel herself may experience the return to her own land. These innocents constitute the second Moses who like the Moses of the first exodus vicariously suffer in order that their people might cross the Jordan and possess the land (cf. Exod. 32.32; Deut. 1.37; 3.26-28; 4.21). For Deutero–Isaiah not only the guilty generation, but a subsequent innocent generation has suffered for sins for which it was not responsible, and is called to continue in that suffering even unto death (Isa. 53). But that generation has the consolation that its faith alone will secure a future for all Israel. While the exiles in Babylon are the means whereby Israel's future is to be assured, the faithful in Jerusalem, from where Yahweh's *tōrâ* and *mišpāṭ* is to go out to the ends of the earth, share in the unjust suffering of the innocent generation. Together they provide that continuity of faith without which God's plans for the future could not be realized.

In my view then Deutero–Isaiah accepts that while Israel was rightly punished, the length of that punishment has not been just. Jerusalem *has* suffered 'double for all her sins'. But in rejecting Ezekiel's hard individualism (Ezek. 14.12-20) by recognizing vicarious suffering as a vocation (Isa. 53), the prophet makes an appeal to justice irrelevant.

Chapter 19

THE UNDETECTABLE OFFENDER AND THE PRIESTLY LEGISLATORS

Milgrom has pointed to the apparent paradox in the different treatment prescribed in Lev. 5.20-26 from that in Num. 15.30-31.[1] While Num. 15.30-31. orders that the man who acted deliberately ('with a high hand') must be 'cut off', Lev. 5.20-26 allows him to expiate his sin by sacrifice. Although both pieces of legislation recognize that unintentional sin is to be atoned for by the requisite sacrifice (Lev. 5.14-19; Num. 15.27-29),[2] the offences in Lev. 5.20-26 were quite clearly committed intentionally. Why then were offenders not 'cut off'?[3]

Against Jackson,[4] Milgrom convincingly shows that the two clauses in Lev. 5.20-26 which speak of a false oath (Lev. 5.22, 24) apply to all the offences listed there. The trespass against God is that in various cases concerning the possession of disputed property, the offender has desecrated the holy name by swearing falsely (cf. Lev. 19.12). What are the characteristics of these property offences?

Milgrom rejected the often repeated assertion that in Lev. 5.21 *gzl* (robbery) covered *gnb* (theft).[5] Rather he confirms that throughout the Old Testament *gzl* stands for a non-furtive forcible act whereas *gnb* is characterized by furtiveness and stealth. *gzl* is done openly through naked aggression, while the man who commits *gnb* remains unknown until sub-

---

1. J. Milgrom, 'The Priestly Doctrine of Repentance', *RB* 82 (1975), pp. 186-205 (repr. in *idem, Cult and Conscience* [SJLA, 23; Leiden: E.J. Brill, 1976], pp. 84-89, 104-123).

2. Daube, 'Error', (1949), pp. 189-213, notes that the introduction of the concept of error into the law is a priestly innovation, though Num. 35 and Josh. 20 do not refer to homicide caused by error but accidental killing.

3. For the purpose of this note, it is not necessary to decide whether 'cut off' meant execution or excommunication. In either case it resulted in irrevocable severance from the community (*AICL*, pp. 28-32).

4. Jackson, *Theft*, pp. 24-27.

5. Milgrom, 'The Missing Thief', pp. 71-85.

sequently detected. This explains why *gnb* is absent from Lev. 5.20-26. All the offences concern property being claimed from their known possessor who is alleged to have improperly seized or withheld it from its rightful owner, the claimant. In the absence of evidence substantiating the claim, all the possessor has to do to retain possession of the property, or avoid paying compensation if he has disposed of it, is to swear an oath that it is his.[6] That determines the issue. Consequently *gnb* should not be described as 'omitted' or 'missing' from Lev. 5.20-26. In contrast to Lev. 19.11, 13, the legislators never sought to include it because their concern was with property dispute cases between *identifiable* parties.[7]

The practice of taking an oath when the court had no other means of settling a dispute over the ownership of property is already well attested in the Book of the Covenant (Exod. 22.6-11). While Exod. 22.6-8 seems to indicate the incorporation into Israel's law of a pre-Israelite method of trial by ordeal before the sanctuary *'elōhîm*, which, at any rate as far as Exod. 22.8 is concerned, resulted in both judgment and payment of damages, Exod. 22.9-11 simply requires an oath to be taken before Yahweh which must be accepted by the claimant.[8] No judgment is given nor any further action contemplated, the assumption being that if the oath is false divine punishment will inevitably follow (cf. Num. 5.11-31). The courts can do no more than leave the matter in God's hands.

It is this procedure which is referred to in Lev. 5.20-26. Therefore the situation envisaged is that the claimant has alleged that the possessor wrongfully holds his property, and in the absence of any determining evidence, the possessor has countered the claim by the oath procedure, but has sworn falsely. The claimant has now no means of recovering his property: the possessor has 'got away with it', at least until God takes action against him. One can hardly imagine an act of greater contempt for Yahweh.

---

6. For a discussion as to whether Lev. 5.20-26 required payment in kind or in money, cf. Daube, *Studies*, pp. 133-44; J. Milgrom, 'The legal terms *ŠLM* and *BR'ŠW* in the Bible', *JNES* 35 (1976), pp. 271-73 (repr. in *idem, Cult and Conscience*, pp. 137-40).

7. Milgrom acknowledges that a thief may have been tracked down or come under suspicion but believes that the final clause of 5.22b is intended to cover such contingencies. This is confirmed by Lev. 5.24a.

8. For a full discussion of the two different procedures reflected in Exod. 22.6-11, see *AICL*, pp. 135-37. It is possible that with the incorporation of Exod. 22.6-8 into the Book of the Covenant, the oath procedure was reinterpreted to correspond with Exod. 22.9-11. Evidence in court was not given under oath.

Clearly for the Priestly legislators this unhappy state of affairs should be terminated as soon as possible for it meant that there was within the community a man who quite deliberately had flouted the sanctity of God's name, and yet could take full part in cultic activities. But no one other than the undetected offender could remedy the situation. Nonetheless the law could encourage him to do so: this is the purpose of Lev. 5.20-26.

While Milgrom admits that a penalty for false swearing is nowhere stipulated in biblical law, he yet believes it to have been a capital offence in contrast to defrauding man which is a civil offence settled by the payment of damages.[9] But how could false swearing ever have been the subject of a prosecution? The cases Milgrom cites in support of his contention (Jer. 5.2-3; Zech. 5.4; Mal. 3.5) only indicate that God himself will act against those who swear falsely. Indeed, he was the only one who could because there was no means of detecting the offender. The whole point of the oath procedure was that it only came into force when the courts had to admit their own inability to administer justice and through the oath left it to God to do so. This explains why there is no biblical provision making false swearing a crime.[10]

The problem facing the Priestly legislators was what to do with the man who through their encouragement and weighed down by guilt feelings[11] admitted that he had sworn falsely. Should he be 'cut off', or could he make expiation? Numbers 15.30-31 would prima facie indicate that he ought to be 'cut off' for the Priestly legislators clearly regarded his act with total abhorrence (Lev. 19.12). The fact that they decided otherwise is not a mark of compassion, but of practical good sense.

Milgrom goes on to compare Lev. 5.20-26 with the later version of the same law in Num. 5.6-8. This provides that before making restitution to the defrauded man, the offender was required to make confession to God. He notes that in P such confession is only explicitly required for deliberate sin (Lev. 5.1-4; 16.21; 26.40; Num. 5.6-7). For involuntary sin, guilt or remorse suffices. Deliberate sin must both be articulated and responsibility assumed. For Milgrom this explains why the sinner who acts 'with a high

9. Milgrom, 'The Priestly Doctrine', p. 191.

10. In any event to have summoned the support of the law to make false oaths illegal would in effect have amounted to a repudiation of the efficacy of the oath itself. See further Brichto, *The Problem of 'Curse'*.

11. In *Cult and Conscience*, Milgrom contends that in cultic texts the noun *'šm* should be rendered 'reparation', 'reparation offering', while the verb without an object indicates the psychological state of the offender, his inner experience of feeling guilt.

hand' is denied atonement: 'sacrificial atonement is barred to the *unrepentant* sinner, to the one who "acts defiantly...", but not to the deliberate sinner who has mitigated his offense by his repentance'. Milgrom notes that only three deliberate sins are expiated by sacrifice: sin of false oath (Lev. 5.20-26; Num. 5.6-8); sin of withholding evidence (Lev. 5.1); sins of the community carried off by the scapegoat (Lev. 16.21-22). In these cases alone is there an explicit demand for confession. Milgrom therefore concludes that confession is the legal device fashioned by P to convert deliberate sins into inadvertent ones, and so qualify them for sacrificial expiation.

The flaw in Milgrom's reasoning is his introduction of the notion of deliberate *unrepentance* into Num. 15.30-31. Though the sinner who acted 'with a high hand' may have behaved 'brazenly', there is nothing in the text to indicate that he necessarily remains unrepentant: in contrast to Lev. 5.20-26, he is simply not given the chance to repent. Numbers 15.27-31 merely contrasts those who act unwittingly with those who act deliberately. Milgrom rightly assesses the issue: why is confession and expiation allowed in Lev. 5.1 and Lev. 5.20-26[12] and *not* in Num. 15.30-31? Leviticus 5.20-26 certainly seems to satisfy all the criteria of Num. 15.30-31. including the most brazen treatment of Yahweh. But the question cannot be answered by introducing into the text of Num. 15.30-31 a concept which is not there.

Leviticus 5.1 can be interpreted in two ways. Milgrom understands it to deal with the case of a man put on oath to give evidence but who deliberately withholds that evidence.[13] As in Lev. 5.20-26 there would be no means of detecting anyone guilty of this offence. Consequently it is here left to God to inflict direct divine punishment which is what is meant by 'he shall bear his iniquity'. If this interpretation is correct, then the offence results in a very similar situation to Lev. 5.20-26—namely, the presence in the community of someone who has deliberately abused God's sacred name, but who cannot be detected.

But Lev. 5.1 can also be understood to refer to a man who has heard another swear publicly, but does not report it.[14] There is good evidence to

12. Although Lev. 5.20-26 does not actually specify confession (cf. Num. 5.6-8), since the offender could not be detected, the expiatory rite could only be performed after confession.

13. Mt. 26.23 would provide an example of this interpretation (cf. Josh. 7.19; Jn 9.24).

14. Noth, *Leviticus*, p. 44.

suggest that the subsequent verses Lev. 5.2-4 should also be understood as failure to divulge known offences to the authorities.[15] Leviticus 5.1-4 would then be concerned not with the original perpetrator of the various offences, but the person who for whatever reason covered them up. Although the offender's action would not, as in Lev. 5.20-26, involve direct profanation of the divine name, his offence would remain undetected as well as the offence which he covered up.

Whichever is the correct interpretation of Lev. 5.1, it is clear that the Priestly legislators were both in Lev. 5.1 and 5.20-26 confronted with the problem of deliberate but undetectable offences which contaminated the cult. Certainly in the case of Lev. 5.20-26 such persons ought to be 'cut off' for their deliberate profanation of God's name, but to prescribe such a penalty would be self-defeating for then there would be no incentive for the offender to admit his guilt and so enable his sin to be removed from the community. Consequently the Priestly legislators realizing that there would be those troubled by guilt positively sought to encourage confession by ensuring that anyone who committed the undetectable offences of Lev. 5.1 and 5.20-26 would remain within the elect community and be treated with extreme leniency.

In the case of Lev. 5.20-26, the offender had to compensate his injured victim (Lev. 5.24), but the punitive damages payable were far less than those prescribed under the Book of the Covenant (Exod. 22.6-8).[16] And in contrast to Num. 15.30-31 there was now no question of the offender being 'cut off'. Instead even though he had acted deliberately, he could atone for his sin through the prescribed reparation offering.[17] The same leniency appears in Lev. 5.1 where the Priestly legislation bent over backwards to ensure that even the poorest of men would be able to make expiation (Lev. 5.7-13), clearly indicating their anxiety to obtain a confession perhaps supporting the interpretation that their main aim was to trace the man whose offence had been covered up.

Throughout their law, the Priestly legislators' one overriding interest

15. A. Spiro, 'A Law on the Sharing of Information', *Proceedings of the American Academy for Jewish Research* 28 (1959), pp. 95-101.

16. In his expanded version of 'The Priestly Doctrine', in *Cult and Conscience*, pp. 114-15, Milgrom notes that the priestly legislators appear to encourage the voluntary surrender of illegally acquired property, but he fails to understand that their primary concern is not with compensating the owner, but eradicating undetected deliberate sin within the community.

17. See above n. 11.

was the preservation of that holiness which God required and which maintained the life of the community. Perhaps drawing on the confession ritual of the Day of Atonement (Lev. 16.21), they provided that for the deliberate, but *undetectable*, offences of Lev. 5.1 and 5.20-26 the defaulter should confess and expiate his sin, so remaining within the elect community. That was preferable to his (and perhaps others) continued contaminating presence within the cult—a presence which in detectable cases Num. 15.30-31 made impossible.

Chapter 20

THE ORIGIN OF 'I AM' IN EXODUS 3.14[*]

Scholars have long recognized the overcrowding of Exod. 3.13-15. To Moses' question asking God how he should answer the people when they ask for his name, God supplies three answers (vv. 14a, 14b and 15). Various proposals have been made how best to interpret what must be additions to the original text.[1] These must, however, be judged against its overall purpose.

Clearly the original author's concern was to identify the God of the fathers with the God who had appeared to Moses at the burning bush. They are one and the same. The traditions of the Patriarchs and the exodus belong to one people. If this is the case, then it seems clear that v. 15 is the answer to Moses' question and that the use of the first person singular of the verb 'to be' in v. 14 is a later interpolation commonly interpreted as an attempt to explain the meaning of the divine name, Yahweh. This is confirmed by v. 14a being directly addressed to Moses alone, while v. 15 recognizes that God's answer is for the benefit of the people. This means that v. 14b should be seen as a redactional transition to v. 15. So the answer to Moses' question was (1) Yahweh and (2) who is to be identified with the God of the fathers. In the original composition of this passage there was, then, no attempt to explain the meaning of the name Yahweh. But in any event, is that the purpose of v. 14a?

There is only one other place in the Old Testament where *'ehyê* appears as a reference to God, though in no mainstream English version of the Bible we know is it rendered 'I am'. God commands Hosea to call his third child *lō'-'ammî*, 'for you are not my people and I a no *'ehyê* to you'. Commentators are quick to point out that this name refers back to

*   This note results from questions raised in an A level lesson at the King's School, Canterbury, being taught by Anthony Phillips. Among the pupils was his daughter, Lucy Phillips, who is the joint author of this note.
1.   E.g. Noth, *Exodus*, pp. 41-45; Childs, *Exodus*, pp. 60-70.

Exod. 3.14 and indicates that the covenant relationship with Israel established at Sinai is now terminated.[2]

But if as seems more probable covenant theology resulted from the
work of the eighth-century prophets,[3] the naming of Hosea's son should
perhaps be interpreted in its own right independently of Exod. 3.14. It
then becomes possible to see this passage as the source of the later interpolation of Exod. 3.14a. Further, the fact that there it is put in a positive
form appears to indicate that the author's concern was not etymological
but a desire to reaffirm Yahweh's relationship with his people. If this is so,
then Hosea should be credited with creating what is in effect a pun on the
divine name by using *lō'-'ehyê* to signify the termination of Israel's
election as Yahweh's people. Indeed in the language he uses, we appear to
have another example of his embryonic covenant theology found elsewhere in Hos. 6.7 and 8.1.[4] If this is so, then it is in the break-up of Hosea's
marriage and subsequent divorce that the ideas of Yahweh's covenant with
Israel took shape. Who though would be responsible for taking up Hosea's
pun and using it so positively in the interpolation of Exod. 3.14a?

My study of the Sinai narrative Exod. 19–24, 32–34 has set out the
arguments for a Proto-Deuteronomic authorship of the text in its present
form.[5] I argued that in the light of the fall of the Northern Kingdom,
Yahweh's relationship with southern Judah was redefined in terms of
the political suzerainty treaty form as a covenant. The tablets of stone on
which the terms of Yahweh's covenant with Israel were inscribed (Exod.
24.12) were introduced into the text to be broken indicating the end of
Yahweh's covenant relationship with the Northern Kingdom due to their
apostasy symbolized by the account of the golden calf (Exod. 32). Moses,
however, receives a new set of tablets (Exod. 34) whose provisions I
argued reflected Hezekiah's reform (2 Kgs 18). Provided Judah kept these
provisions, Yahweh's covenant relationship with her was assured.

No prophetic book more influenced Deuteronomic thought than Hosea.
The *raison d'être* for the Proto-Deuteronomic revision of the Sinai narrative lay in the fulfilment of Hos. 1.9 and the subsequent necessity both to
remind Judah that a similar threat hung over it, but that despite what had

2.　　Mays, *Hosea*, pp. 29-30; Wolff, *Hosea*, pp. 21-23.

3　　Perlitt, *Die Bundestheologie*; E.W. Nicholson, *God and his People* (Oxford:
Clarendon Press, 1986).

4.　　Nicholson, *God and his People*, pp. 187-88; J. Day, 'Pre-Deuteronomic Allusions to the Covenant in Hosea and Psalm LXXVIII', *VT* 36 (1986), pp. 1-12.

5.　　Phillips, 'A Fresh Look', pp. 39-52, 282-94 (reprinted above as Chapter 2).

happened to its northern neighbour, it was still Yahweh's elect people bound to him by covenant. Since it was normal literary practice for Hebrew authors to give away the conclusion to their works at their beginning (e.g. Exod. 19.3-8), it seems entirely probable that it was the Proto-Deuteronomists who inserted Exod. 3.14a into the narrative of the burning bush. With the fulfilment of the awful prophetic sign of the naming of Hosea's third child fresh in their minds, they used Hosea's pun to indicate at the beginning of their revised Sinai narrative that despite all that had happened, Yahweh was still *'ehyê* to what remained of his people. In the very uncertain political circumstances facing southern Judah, Exod. 3.14a constitutes a passionate commitment by Yahweh not just for the present but the future too. If Judah kept the covenant now summarized in the laws of the second set of tablets, Yahweh would remain *'ehyê* to them. The insertion of Exod. 3.14 was not therefore for etymological reasons but theological. It indicates yet again the important creative part Hosea's prophecy played in the development of Hebrew theology. Though he drew on his own intimate situation to lead him to enunciate his embryonic covenant theology, whose model the Proto-Deuteronomists recast in the light of the Assyrian suzerainty treaty imposed on Judah, it seems clear that it was in Hosea's time that covenant theology emerged, to which his prophecy gave a major impetus.

Chapter 21

OLD TESTAMENT AND MORAL TRADITION

While originally *tōrâ* (law) meant an individual instruction or ruling on a particular issue, it came also in the time of the Deuteronomists to be understood collectively as the complete expression of the will of God for his people. This explains why criminal and civil law provisions which could be pursued through the courts are found in conjunction with unenforceable moral enactments requiring the exercise of humaneness and righteousness. The Torah is thus the theological expression of how a man should act towards God and his neighbours in the world in which God has created both him, and it.

Although biblical Hebrew has terms for trade and commerce, there is no word for business. This probably indicates the small-scale nature of commercial life in ancient Israel reflected in the scarcity of direct material on business in the Old Testament. While the law prohibits false weights and measures (Lev. 19.35-36; Deut. 25.13-16), there are no legal provisions for tariffs on services and merchandise, no laws regarding rentals or tenancy of land, no mention of the sale of land for purely commercial and profit motives, and no provision of loans for the purpose of production, though this does not necessarily mean that such practices were not undertaken. For in interpreting biblical ethics a distinction must be made between the theological ideals and principles of the community of faith which produced the Hebrew scriptures, and the actual practice of Israelite society. Indeed theologically Israel's ideal community remained the pastoral and agricultural society of her origins (1 Kgs 4.25; Mic. 4.4; Zech. 3.10), in which the monarchy with the possibility of its centralized economic power was seen as an intrusion (1 Sam. 8.10-18).

Two principles can, however, be discerned: the first as old as patriarchal times, the second brought about by economic growth under the monarchy: (1) wealth was interpreted as a sign of God's blessing (Gen. 26.12-14; Job 42.12-13); (2) everything should be done to secure the individual's personal economic freedom. It was the prophets' achievement to recognize the interdependence of these principles (Amos 8.4-6; Mic. 2.8-9; Isa. 10.2).

With the development of a capitalist society under the monarchy in which money rather than payment in kind was accepted as the proper medium of exchange, considerable disparity of wealth arose. The solidarity of the existing social order in which individual families enjoyed independence broke down resulting in a gradually expanding population without personal economic interest in the land and lacking family protection. The ideal of each family living off its own property in perpetuity (1 Kgs 21.3) gave way to large estates (Isa. 5.8; Mic. 2.2) which became a capital asset for the rich who worked them with easily exploited contract labour (Lev. 19.13; Deut. 24.14-15) and slaves. These now included not only foreigners captured in war, but Hebrews, the victims of debt and dispossession (Exod. 22.2b; 2 Kgs 4.1; Isa. 50.1).

Early monarchic legislation (c. 1000–900 BCE) sought to protect both the threatened peasant farmer from his creditors and those denied legal status, the widow, orphan, slave and foreign resident. Slavery of a Hebrew was to be limited to six years' service, though economic reality in fact meant that most would have taken advantage of a procedure for making their slavery permanent (Exod. 21.2-6). Unique in the ancient Near East usury, understood as the exaction of any interest on loans of money, was prohibited (Exod. 22.24), for no one had the right to make a profit out of the needs of others. Indeed even legal rights were limited in the face of abject poverty (Exod. 22.25-26). The subsistence claims of the needy were to be ensured by a method of continuous crop rotation which left land and orchards uncultivated every seventh year to provide a harvest for those without land (Exod. 23.10-11).

But both the lack of penalties and the additional clauses encouraging obedience (Exod. 22.20b, 22-23; 23.9) indicate that such provisions could not be enforced through the courts but depended on a proper sense of moral responsibility towards those who were not in a position to defend themselves. Further, unlike criminal, civil and cultic law, the situations in which charity should be exercised could only be defined in very general terms. Yet, as the prophets indicated, this was no excuse for Israel's failure towards the poor and needy, for reasonable men ought to be able to discern for themselves when humanitarian action is required (Amos 1.1–2.8). But the prophets never indicted the rich merely for the possession of wealth: they were condemned for its enjoyment while exploiting or ignoring the needy (Isa. 1.23; 3.14-15: Amos 4.1; 5.11-12; 8.4-6; Mic. 6.11).

In the wake of the prophetic protest, the late monarchic legislation (c. 650–600 BCE) sought to strengthen earlier law. The absolute prohibition of usury was reiterated, food and anything else which might form the subject of the loan being added to money (Deut. 23.20-21). Economic encouragement was given to the slave to seek his freedom (Deut. 15.12-18), and the charitable legislation designed to alleviate poverty extended (Deut. 24.6, 10-15, 17-22). The regular provision of produce for those without land secured by the fallowing requirement of Exod. 23.10-11 was connected with the annual tithe: every third year this was to be devoted to those without property (Deut. 14.28-29). The seven-year cycle was now associated with the cancellation of debts which unlike the fallowing and tithe provisions was to operate simultaneously throughout Israel in one fixed year (Deut. 15.1-6). This necessitated an injunction encouraging the rich to lend generously even when that year was imminent, so making the chance of repayment slight (Deut. 15.7-11). Obedience to these apparently uneconomic and unenforceable laws, which did not protect non-resident foreign businessmen (Deut. 15.3; 23.20), was now openly encouraged on grounds of self-interest: divine blessing would follow, which, as always, was understood in material terms (Deut. 14.29; 15.4-6, 10, 18; 23.21).

The absolute prohibition of usury, together with methods intended to circumvent it (Lev. 25.35-38), and the provision of food for the needy (Lev. 19.9-10; 23.22) were again enjoined by the Priestly legislation of the exilic period (c. 600–540 BCE). But the Priestly legislators, conscious of Israel's continual failure to ensure individual economic freedom (Jer. 34.8-22; Ezek. 22.12), extended further the principles of earlier law. First they took over the idea of fallowing (Exod. 23.10-11), applied it to a fixed seventh year, and spiritualized it by connecting it with sabbath rest (Lev. 25.1-7). Then they created the jubilee year, a fixed fiftieth year celebrated as a sabbath year of sabbath years (Lev. 25.8-12), in which slaves were to be freed (Lev. 25.39-55) and realty other than houses in walled towns restored to former owners (Lev. 25.25-34). Legal ownership of both slaves and property was held to be vested in God so that while a man might through necessity be forced to part with his freedom or his inheritance, neither was lost permanently. As far as land was concerned, he simply sold so many years' crops (Lev. 25.13-17). But this jubilee provision is not to be confused with the ancient duty of a near relative to purchase property to keep it in the family (Lev. 25.25; Jer. 32.6-15; Ruth 4.1-4).

While the sabbatical year may have been celebrated (Neh. 10.30), the provisions of the jubilee year were no more than theological idealism. Indeed many slaves would have been dead long before the jubilee year was reached, and the eventual return of land to its original owner would have meant that no relative would seek to redeem it by purchase, from the family's standpoint a much more efficient procedure than the return of land to an owner who had already proved himself economically incompetent. Nonetheless the provisions indicate that for the community of faith economic factors alone cannot govern commercial and business undertakings. Every individual has a right both to personal freedom and the possession of land from which he can sustain himself and his family. But in postexilic Israel economic reality continued to fall short of theological ideals. While psalmists and sages equated charity with righteousness and justice, and encouraged it on the grounds that it brought divine blessing (Pss. 37.21-26; 112.5-6; Prov. 19.17), the only exception being acting as a surety (Prov. 6.1-5), Israelites still fell victim to economic pressures (Neh. 5.1-13; Job 24.2-3, 9).

Through canonization, the Jewish moral tradition was inherited by the Christian church. But as in rabbinic Judaism, it remained and remains subject to the tension between inherited tradition and the ever new situation in which God's will must be secured. There is then no moral fundamentalism within the Old Testament but a continual revision and development of ethical rulings in the face of contemporary moral problems. This means that a particular requirement of Old Testament law cannot be applied to contemporary ethical situations without first ascertaining how that requirement sought to express God's will in its original setting, and whether the principle behind such a requirement can still be ensured through its present application. It is, however, the Hebrew conviction that the needs of individuals override the maintenance of property rights which forms the basis of the Christian social tradition and which provides the continued justification for the use of the Old Testament in contemporary moral reasoning.

While government policy has rightly encouraged individual self-sufficiency in a property-owning democracy—each man under his vine and under his fig tree (Mic. 4.4)—it also recognizes that the economic needs of those who fail whether through misfortune or incompetence cannot be ignored. Charity—now subsumed into the welfare state and so part of national law—continues to provide as of right for those unable to support themselves. But it is in attitudes to taxation to fund investment in health, education, welfare and job creation that Hebrew moral tradition challenges contemporary political aspirations. Reduction of taxation may in the short term increase individual wealth: in the long it could impoverish the nation. As the Deuteronomists recognized, obedience to apparently uneconomic injunctions stimulates economic activity from which the wealthy themselves ultimately benefit.

BIBLIOGRAPHY

Ackroyd, P.R., *Exile and Restoration* (OTL; London: SCM Press, 1968).
Albright, W.F., *From the Stone Age to Christianity* (Baltimore: The Johns Hopkins University Press, 2nd edn, 1946).
—'The Judicial Reform of Jehoshaphat', in S. Lieberman (ed.), *Alexander Marx Jubilee Volume* (New York: Jewish Theological Seminary of America, 1950), pp. 61-82.
Alt, A., 'Das Verbot des Diebstahls im Dekalog', in *idem, Kleine Schriften zur Geschichte des Volkes Israel*, I (Munich: C.H. Beck, 1953), pp. 333-40.
—'The Origins of Israelite Law', in *idem, Essays on Old Testament History and Religion* (Oxford: Basil Blackwell, 1966), pp. 81-132 (repr. in Sheffield; JSOT Press, 1989).
Anderson, A.A., 'The Marriage of Ruth', *JSS* 23 (1978), pp. 171-83.
Baltzer, K., *Das Bundesformular* (Neukirchen–Vluyn: Neukirchener Verlag, 1960).
Barr, J., 'Some Semantic Notes on the Covenant', in H. Donner, R. Hanhart and R. Smend (eds.), *Beiträge zur Alttestamentlichen Theologie* (Festschrift W. Zimmerli; Göttingen: Vandenhoeck & Ruprecht, 1977), pp. 23-28.
Barton, J., 'Natural Law and Poetic Justice in the Old Testament', *JTS* 30 (1979), pp. 1-14.
—*Amos's Oracles against the Nations* (SOTSMS, 6; Cambridge: Cambridge University Press, 1980).
—'Ethics in Isaiah of Jerusalem', *JTS* 32 (1981), pp. 1-18.
Baumgarten, A., 'A Note on the Book of Ruth', *JANESCU* 5 (1973), pp. 11-15.
Beattie, D.R.G., 'Kethibh and Qere in Ruth IV 5', *VT* 21 (1971), pp. 490-94.
—'The Book of Ruth as Evidence for Israelite Legal Practice', *VT* 24 (1974), pp. 251-67.
—'Ruth III', *JSOT* 5 (1978), pp. 39-48.
—'Redemption in Ruth and Related Matters: A Response to Jack M. Sasson', *JSOT* 5 (1978), pp. 65-68.
Bentzen, A., *King and Messiah* (London: Lutterworth Press, 1953).
Bergren, R.V., *The Prophets and the Law* (Monographs of the Hebrew Union College, 4; Cincinnati: Jewish Institute of Religion, 1974).
Berman, H.J. *The Interaction of Law and Religion* (London: SCM Press, 1974).
Bettan, I., *The Five Scrolls: A Commentary on the Song of Songs, Ruth, Lamentations, Ecclesiastes, Esther* (Cincinnati: Union of American Hebrew Congregations, 1940).
Blenkinsopp, J., *Gibeon and Israel* (SOTSMS, 2; Cambridge: Cambridge University Press, 1972).
Boecker, H.J., *Law and the Administration of Justice in the Old Testament and Ancient East* (Minneapolis: Augsburg, 1980).
Brichto, H.C., *The Problem of 'Curse' in the Hebrew Bible* (JBLMS, 13; Philadelphia: Society of Biblical Literature and Exegesis, 1963).
—'The Case of the *SOTA* and a Reconsideration of Biblical "Law"', *HUCA* 46 (1975), pp. 55-70.

Buss, M.J., 'The Distinction between Civil and Criminal Law in Ancient Israel', in *Proceedings of the Sixth World Congress of Jewish Studies 1973* (Jerusalem: World Union of Jewish Studies, 1977), pp. 51-62.

Campbell, E.F., *Ruth* (AnBib; Garden City, NY: Doubleday, 1975).

Carley, K.W., *The Book of the Prophet Ezekiel* (CBC; Cambridge: Cambridge University Press, 1974).

Carmichael, C.M., *The Laws of Deuteronomy* (Ithaca, NY: Cornell University Press, 1974).

—'A Ceremonial Crux: Removing a Man's Sandal as a Gesture of Female Contempt', *JBL* 96 (1977), pp. 321-36.

—*Women, Law and the Genesis Traditions* (Edinburgh: Edinburgh University Press, 1979).

—'"Treading" in the Book of Ruth', *ZAW* 92 (1980), pp. 248-66.

Carroll, R.P., *From Chaos to Covenant* (London: SCM Press, 1981).

Cassuto, U., *A Commentary on the Book of Exodus* (Jerusalem: Magnes Press, 1967).

Cazelles, H., 'David's Monarchy and the Gibeonites Claim', *PEQ* 87 (1955), pp. 165-75.

Childs, B.S., *Exodus* (OTL; London: SCM Press, 1974).

—*Introduction to the Old Testament as Scripture* (London: SCM Press, 1979).

Clements, R.E., *Prophecy and Covenant* (SBT, 43; London: SCM Press, 1965).

—*God's Chosen People* (London: SCM Press, 1968).

—*Prophecy and Tradition* (Oxford: Basil Blackwell, 1975).

—'Understanding the Book of Hosea', *RE* 72 (1975), pp. 405-423.

—'The Purpose of the Book of Jonah' (VTSup, 28; Leiden: E.J. Brill, 1975), pp. 16-28.

—*Old Testament Theology* (London: Marshall, Morgan & Scott, 1978).

Coggins, R.J., *The Books of Ezra and Nehemiah* (CBC; Cambridge: Cambridge University Press, 1976).

Cook, S.A., *The Laws of Moses and the Code of Hammurabi* (London: A. & C. Black, 1903).

Dahood, M.J., 'Zacharia 9,1 'ên 'Ādām' *CBQ* 25 (1963), pp. 123-24.

Daube, D., *Studies in Biblical Law* (Cambridge: Cambridge University Press, 1947).

—'Concerning Methods of Bible-Criticism', *ArOr* 17 (1949), pp. 89-99.

—'Error and Accident in the Bible', *RIDA* 2 (1949), pp. 189-213.

—'The Culture of Deuteronomy', *Orita* 3 (1969), pp. 27-52.

—*Ancient Jewish Law: Three Inaugural Lectures* (Leiden: E.J. Brill, 1981).

David, M., 'The Date of the Book of Ruth', *OTS* 1 (1942), pp. 55-63.

—'The Manumission of Slaves under Zedekiah (A Contribution to the Laws about Hebrew Slaves)', *OTS* 5 (1948), pp. 63-78.

—'The Codex Hammurabi and its Relation to the Provisions of the Law in Exodus', *OTS* 7 (1950), pp. 149-78.

Davies, E.W., *Prophecy and Ethics: Isaiah and the Ethical Tradition of Israel* (JSOTSup, 16; Sheffield: JSOT Press, 1981).

—'Inheritance Rights and the Hebrew Levirate Marriage: Parts 1 and 2', *VT* 31 (1981), pp. 138-44, 257-68.

—'Ruth IV 5 and the Duties of the *gō'ēl*', *VT* 33 (1983), pp. 231-34.

Day, J., 'Pre-Deuteronomic Allusions to the Covenant in Hosea and Psalm LXXVIII', *VT* 36 (1986), pp. 1-12.

de Boer, P.A.H., 'Second Isaiah's Message', OTS 9 (1956), pp. 80-101.

de Vaux, *Ancient Israel: Its Life and Institutions* (London: Darton, Longman & Todd 1961; 2nd edn., 1965).

—*The Early History of Israel: From the Beginnings to the Exodus and Covenant of Sinai* (London: Darton, Longman & Todd, 1978).

Dinur, B., 'The Religious Character of the Cities of Refuge and the Ceremony of Admission into Them', *EI* 3 (1954), pp. 135-46.

Dorff, E.N., 'The Interaction of Jewish Law with Morality', *Judaism* 26 (1977), pp. 455-66.

Draffkorn, A.E., 'Ilani/Elohim', *JBL* 76 (1957), pp. 216-24.

Driver, G.R., 'Three Notes', *VT* 2 (1952), pp. 356-57.

—'Two Problems in the Old Testament Examined in the Light of Assyriology', *Syria* 33 (1956), pp. 70-78.

Driver, G.R. and J.C. Miles, *The Assyrian Laws*, I (Oxford: Clarendon Press, 1952).

—*The Babylonian Laws*, I (Oxford: Clarendon Press, 1952).

Driver, S.R., *Deuteronomy* (ICC; Edinburgh: T. & T. Clark, 3rd edn, 1902).

—*The Book of Exodus* (Cambridge: Cambridge University Press, 1911).

—*Notes on the Hebrew Text and the Topography of the Books of Samuel* (Oxford: Clarendon Press, 2nd edn, 1913).

Eichrodt, W., *Theology of the Old Testament*, I (OTL; London: SCM Press, 1961).

—*Ezekiel* (OTL; London: SCM Press, 1970).

Elliger, K., 'Das Gesetz Levitcus 18', *ZAW* 26 (1955), pp. 1-25.

Emmerson, G.I., 'Another Look at the Book of Jonah', *ET* 88 (1976), pp. 86-88.

Eslinger, L., 'More Drafting Techniques in Deuteronomic Laws', *VT* 34 (1984), pp. 221-26.

Falk, Z.W., *Hebrew Law in Biblical Times* (Jerusalem: Wahrmann Books, 1964).

—'Hebrew Legal Terms: II', *JSS* 12 (1967), pp. 241-43.

Fensham, F.C., 'Widow, Orphan, and the Poor in Ancient Near Eastern Legal and Wisdom Literature', *JNES* 21 (1962), pp. 129-39.

—'The Treaty between Israel and the Gibeonites', *BA* 27 (1964), pp. 96-100.

—'Aspects of Family Law in the Covenant Code in the Light of Ancient Near Eastern Parallels', *Dine Israel* 1 (1969), pp. 5-19.

Finkelstein, J., 'The Goring Ox: Some Historical Perspectives on Deodands, Forfeitures, Wrongful Death and the Western Notion of Sovereignty', *Temple Law Quarterly* 46 (1973), pp. 69-290.

Fisch, H., 'Ruth and the Structure of Covenant History', *VT* 32 (1982), pp. 425-37.

Fishbane, M., 'Accusations of Adultery: A Study of Law and Scribal Practice in Numbers 5:11–31', *HUCA* 45 (1974), pp. 25-46.

Gamoran, H., 'The Biblical Law against Loans on Interest', *JNES* 30 (1971), pp. 127-34.

Gemser, B., 'The Importance of the Motive Clauses in Old Testament Law' (VTSup, 1; Leiden: E.J. Brill, 1953), pp. 50-66.

Gerstenberger, E., *Wesen und Herkunft des 'apodiktischen Rechts'* (WMANT, 20; Neukirchen–Vluyn: Neukirchener Verlag, 1965).

—'Covenant and Commandment', *JBL* 84 (1965), pp. 38-51.

Gevirtz, S., 'West Semitic Curses and the Problem of the Origins of Hebrew Law', *VT* 11 (1961), pp. 137-58.

Gilmer, H.W., *The If-You Form in Israelite Law* (SBLDS, 15; Missoula, MT: Scholars Press, 1975).

Ginzberg, E., 'Studies in the Economics of the Bible', *JQR* 22 (1932), pp. 343-408.

Goiten, S.D.F., 'Some Observations on Jonah', *JPOS* 17 (1937), pp. 63-77.

Goldman, S., *The Ten Commandments* (Chicago: University of Chicago Press, 1956).

Good, E., 'Capital Punishment and its Alternatives in Ancient Near Eastern Law', *Stanford Law Review* 19 (1967), pp. 947-77.

Gordis, R., 'Hosea's Marriage and Message: A New Approach', *HUCA* 25 (1954), pp. 9-35.

—'A Dynamic Halakhah: Principles and Procedures of Jewish Law', *Judaism* 28 (1979), pp. 263-82.

Gordon, C.H., 'אלהים in its Reputed Meaning of Rulers, Judges', *JBL* 54 (1935), pp. 139-44.

—'Hos. 2:4–5 in the Light of New Semitic Inscriptions', *ZAW* 13 (1936), pp. 277-80.

—'Biblical Customs and the Nuzu Tablets', *BA* 3 (1940), pp. 1-12.

Gray, J., *Joshua, Judges and Ruth* (NCBC; London: Oliphants, 1967).

—*I and II Kings* (OTL; London: SCM Press, 2nd edn, 1970).

Gray, M.P., 'The Habiru-Hebrew Problem in the Light of the Source Material Available at Present', *HUCA* 29 (1958), pp. 135-202.

Green, B., 'The Plot of the Biblical Story of Ruth', *JSOT* 23 (1982), pp. 55-68.

Greenberg. M., 'Some Postulates of Biblical Criminal Law', in M. Haran (ed.), *Yehezkel Kaufman Jubilee Volume* (Jerusalem: Magnes Press, 1960), pp. 5-28 (repr. in Greenberg, *Studies in the Bible and Jewish Thought* [Philadelphia: Jewish Publication Society of America, 1995], pp. 25-41).

—' 'nsh in Exodus 20 20 and the Purpose of the Sinaitic Theophany', *JBL* 79 (1960), pp. 273-76.

—'Witness', in *IDB*, IV (1962), p. 864.

—Review of *AICL*, in *JBL* 91 (1972), pp. 535-38.

Gurney, O.R., *The Hittites* (Harmondsworth: Penguin Books, rev. edn, 1961).

Hals, R.M., *The Theology of the Book of Ruth* (Philadelphia: Fortress Press, 1969).

Hertzberg, H.W., *I and II Samuel* (OTL; London: SCM Press, 1964).

Hillers, D.R., *Treaty Curses and the Old Testament Prophets* (BibOr, 16; Rome: Pontifical Biblical Institute, 1964).

Hobbs, T.R., 'Jeremiah 3:1-5 and Deuteronomy 24: 1-4', *ZAW* 86 (1974), pp. 23-29.

Houlden, J.L., *Ethics and the New Testament* (London: Mowbrays, 1975).

Jackson, B.S., 'Some Comparative Legal History: Robbery and Brigandage', *Georgia Journal of International and Comparative Law* 1 (1970), pp. 45-103.

—'Liability for Mere Intention in Early Jewish Law', *HUCA* 42 (1971), pp. 197-207.

—*Theft in Early Jewish Law* (Oxford: Clarendon Press, 1972).

—'Reflections on Biblical Criminal Law, *JJS* 24 (1973), pp. 8-38 (repr. in *idem*, *Essays*, pp. 25-63).

—'The Problem of Exodus 21:22–5 (*IUS TALIONIS*), *VT* 23 (1973), pp. 273-304 (repr. in *idem*, *Essays*, pp. 75-107).

—'The Goring Ox', *Journal of Juristic Papyrology* 18 (1974), pp. 55-93 (repr. in *idem*, *Essays*, pp. 108-152).

—'From Dharma to Law', *American Journal of Comparative Law* 23 (1975), pp. 490-512.

—*Essays in Jewish and Comparative Legal History* (SJLA, 10; Leiden: E.J. Brill, 1975).

Jacobson, H., 'A Legal Note on Potiphar's Wife', *HTR* 69 (1976), p. 177.

Johnson, A.R., *The Vitality of the Individual in the Thought of Ancient Israel* (Cardiff: University of Wales Press, 2nd edn, 1964).

Joyce, P.M., 'Individual Responsibility in Ezekiel 18?', in E.A. Livingstone (ed.), *Studia Biblica 1978* (JSOTSup, 11; Sheffield: JSOT Press, 1979), pp. 185-96.

Kaiser, O., *Introduction to the Old Testament* (Oxford: Basil Blackwell, 1975).

—*Isaiah 1–12* (OTL; London: SCM Press, 2nd edn, 1983).

Kilian, R., 'Apodiktisches and kasuistisches Recht im Licht agyptischer Analogien', *BZ* 7 (1963), pp. 185-202.

Kline, M.G., *Treaty of the Great King: The Covenant Structure of Deuteronomy* (Grand Rapids: Eerdmans, 1963).

Knierim, R., 'Exodus 18 und die Neuordnung der Mosaischen Gerichtsbarkeit', *ZAW* 73 (1961), pp. 146-71.

—'Das Erste Gebot', *ZAW* 77 (1965), pp. 20-39.

Kohler, L., *Hebrew Man* (London: SCM Press, 1956).

Kornfeld, W., '*L'adultère* dans l'oriente antique', *RB* 57 (1950), pp. 92-109.

Kuhl, C., 'Neue Dokumente zum Verständnis von Hosea 2 4–15', *ZAW* 11 (1934), pp. 102-109.

Kutsch, E., *Verheissung und Gesetz: Untersuchungen zum sogenannten 'Bund' im Alten Testament* (BZAW, 131; Berlin: W. de Gruyter, 1973).

Labuschagne, C.J., 'The Crux in Ruth 4:11', *ZAW* 79 (1967), pp. 364-67.

Leggett, D.A., *The Levirate and Goel Institutions in the Old Testament with Special Attention to the Book of Ruth* (Cherry Hill, NJ: Mack Publishing, 1974).

Lemche, N.P., 'The "Hebrew Slave": Comments on the Slave Law Exodus XXI 2-11', *VT* 25 (1975), pp. 129-44.

—'The Manumission of Slaves—The Fallow Year—The Sabbatical Year—The Jobel Year', *VT* 26 (1976), pp. 38-59.

Levy, R., *Deutero-Isaiah: A Commentary* (London: Oxford University Press, 1925).

Lewy, I., 'Dating of Covenant Code Sections on Humaneness and Righteousness', *VT* 7 (1957), pp. 322-26.

Liedke, G., *Gestalt und Bezeichnung alttestamentlicher Rechtssätze: Eine form-geschictlich-terminologische Studie* (WMANT, 39; Neukirchen–Vluyn: Neukirchener Verlag, 1971).

Lindars, B., 'Ezekiel and Individual Responsibility', *VT* 15 (1965), pp. 452-67.

—'Torah in Deuteronomy', in P.R. Ackroyd and B. Lindars (eds.), *Words and Meanings* (Cambridge: Cambridge University Press, 1968) pp. 117-36.

Lindblom, J., *Prophecy in Ancient Israel* (Oxford: Basil Blackwell, 1963).

Lipiński, E., 'L' "Esclave Hébreu"' , *VT* 26 (1976), pp. 120-24.

Loewenstamm, S.E., 'The Laws of Adultery and Murder in Biblical and Mesopotamian Law', *Beth Miqra* 13 (1962), pp. 55-59 (Hebrew) (repr. in *Comparative Studies in Biblical and Ancient Oriental Literatures* [AOAT, 204; Neukirchen-Vluyn: Neukirchener Verlag, 1980], pp. 146-53 [English]).

—'The Laws of Adultery and Murder in the Bible', *Beth Miqra* 18–19 (1964), pp. 77-78 (Hebrew) (repr. in *idem, Comparative Studies*, pp. 171-72 [English]).

Lohfink, N., 'Zur Dekalogfassung von Dt 5', *BZ* 9 (1965), pp. 17-32.

Maier, J., *Das altisraelitische Ladeheiligutum* (BZAW, 93; Berlin: W. de Gruyter, 1965).

Maloney, R.P., 'Usury and Restrictions on Interest-Taking in the Ancient Near East', *CBQ* 36 (1974), pp. 1-20.

Martin-Achard, R., *A Light to the Nations* (Edinburgh: Oliver & Boyd, 1962).

—'Trois Ouvrages sur l'alliance dans l'Ancien Testament', *RTP* 110 (1978), pp. 299-306.

May, H.G., 'Ruth's Visit to the High Place at Bethlehem', *JRAS* 75 (1939), pp. 75-79.

Mayes, A.D.H., *Israel in the Period of the Judges* (SBT, 29; London: SCM Press, 2nd edn, 1974).

—*Deuteronomy* (NCBC; London: Oliphants, 1979).

—'Deuteronomy 4 and the Literary Criticism of Deuteronomy', *JBL* 100/101 (1981), pp. 23-51.

—*The Story of Israel between Settlement and Exile* (London: SCM Press, 1983).

Mays, J.L., *Hosea* (OTL; London: SCM Press, 1969).

—*Micah* (OTL; London: SCM Press, 1976).

McCarthy, D.J., *Old Testament Covenant: A Survey of Current Opinions* (Oxford: Basil Blackwell, 1972).

—'*bᵉrît* in Old Testament History and Theology', *Bib* 53 (1972), pp. 110-21.

—*Treaty and Covenant: A Study in Form in the Ancient Oriental Documents and in the Old Testament* (AnBib, 21A; Rome: Biblical Institute Press, new edn., 1978).

McKane, W., *Proverbs* (OTL; London: SCM Press, 1970).

McKeating, H., *Amos, Hosea, Micah* (CBC; Cambridge: Cambridge University Press, 1971).

—'The Development of the Law on Homicide in Ancient Israel', *VT* 25 (1975), pp. 46-68.

—'Sanctions against Adultery in Ancient Israelite Society with Some Reflections on Methodology in the Study of Old Testament Ethics', *JSOT* 11 (1979), pp. 57-72.

—'A Response to Dr. Phillips by Henry McKeating', *JSOT* 20 (1981), pp. 25-26.

McKenzie, J.L., *Second Isaiah* (AnBib; New York: Doubleday, 1968).

Mendelsohn, I., 'Slavery in the Ancient Near East', *BA* 9 (1946), pp. 74-88.

—'The Family in the Ancient Near East', *BA* 11 (1948), pp. 24-40.

—*Slavery in the Ancient Near East* (Oxford: Oxford University Press, 1949).

—*Religions of the Ancient Near East* (Oxford: Oxford University Press, 1955).

Mendenhall, G.E., 'Ancient Oriental and Biblical Law', *BA* 17 (1954), pp. 26-46.

—'Covenant Forms in Israelite Tradition' *BA* 17 (1954), pp. 50-76.

—'The Hebrew Conquest of Palestine', *BA* 25 (1962), pp. 66-87.

Milgrom, J., 'The Priestly Doctrine of Repentance', *RB* 82 (1975), pp. 186-205 (repr. in *Cult and Conscience* [SJLA, 23; Leiden: E.J. Brill, 1976], pp. 84-89, 104-123).

—'The Missing Thief in Leviticus 5:20ff.', *RIDA* 22 (1975), pp. 71-80 (repr. in *Cult and Conscience*, pp. 89-102).

—'The Legal Terms *ŠLM* and *BR'ŠW* in the Bible', *JNES* 35 (1976), pp. 271-73 (repr. in *Cult and Conscience*, pp. 137-40).

—'The Betrothed Slave Girl, Lev. 19:20-22', *ZAW* 89 (1977), pp. 43-50.

Mitchell, B., *Law, Morality and Religion in a Secular Society* (Oxford: Oxford University Press, 1967).

Morgenstern, J., 'The Book of the Covenant—Part 11', *HUCA* 7 (1930), pp. 19-258.

Moule, C.F.D., 'Important Moral Issues. Prolegomena: The New Testament and Moral Decisions', *ET* 74 (1962–63), pp. 370-73.

Mowinckel, S., *He That Cometh* (Oxford: Basil Blackwell, 1956).

Muilenberg, J., 'Isaiah 40–66', *IB* V (1956), pp. 381-773.

Neufeld, E., *Ancient Hebrew Marriage Laws* (London: Longmans, Green, 1944).

—*The Hittite Laws* (London: Luzac, 1951).

—'The Prohibitions against Loans at Interest in Ancient Hebrew Laws', *HUCA* 26 (1955), pp. 355-412.

—'The Emergence of a Royal-Urban Society in Ancient Israel', *HUCA* 31 (1960), pp. 31-53.

Nicholson, E.W., 'The Centralisation of the Cult in Deuteronomy', *VT* 13 (1963), pp. 380-89.

—*Preaching to the Exiles* (Oxford: Basil Blackwell, 1970).

—Review of *AICL*, by Anthony Phillips, in *Theology* 75 (1972), pp. 154-55.

—*Exodus and Sinai in History and Tradition* (Oxford: Basil Blackwell, 1973).

—'The Interpretation of Exodus xxiv 9–11', *VT* 24 (1974), pp. 77-97.

—'The Antiquity of the Tradition in Exodus xxiv 9–11', *VT* 25 (1975), pp. 69-79.

—'The Origin of the Tradition in Exodus xxiv 9–11', *VT* 26 (1976), pp. 148-60.

—'The Decalogue as the Direct Address of God', *VT* 27 (1977), pp. 422-33.

—Review of *Abraham in History and Tradition* (New Haven: Yale University Press, 1975), by J. van Seters, in *JTS* 30 (1979), pp. 220-34.

—'The Covenant Ritual in Exodus xxiv 3–8', *VT* 32 (1982), pp. 74-86.

—*God and his People* (Oxford: Clarendon Press, 1986).

Niditch, S., 'The Wrong Woman Righted: An Analysis of Genesis 38', *HTR* 72 (1979), pp. 143-49.

Nixon, R., 'Fulfilling the Law: The Gospels and Acts', in B.N. Kaye and G.J. Wenham (eds.), *Law, Morality and the Bible* (Leicester: Inter-Varsity Press, 1978), pp. 53-71.

Noonan, J.T., 'The Muzzled Ox', *JQR* 70 (1980), pp. 172-75.

North, C.R., *The Suffering Servant in Deutero-Isaiah: An Historical and Critical Study* (Oxford: Oxford University Press, 2nd edn, 1956).

—*The Second Isaiah* (Oxford: Clarendon Press, 1964).

Noth, M., *Das System der zwölf Stämme Israels* (BWANT, 4.1; Stuttgart: W. Kohlhammer, 1930).

—*Exodus* (OTL; London: SCM Press, 1962).

—*Die israelitischen Personennamen in Rahmen der gemeinsmitischen Namengedung* (BWANT, 3.10; Stuttgart: W. Kohlhammer, 1966).

—*Leviticus* (OTL; London: SCM Press, rev. edn, 1977).

Obbink, H.T., 'Jahwebilder', *ZAW* 47 (1929), pp. 264-74.

Overholt, T.W., *The Threat of Falsehood* (SBT, 16; London: SCM Press, 1970).

Packer, J., 'Situations and Principles', in B.N. Kaye and G.J. Wenham (eds.), *Law, Morality and the Bible* (Leicester: InterVarsity Press, 1978), pp. 151-67.

Patrick, D., 'The Covenant Code Source', *VT* 27 (1977), pp. 145-57.

Paul, S.M., *Studies in the Book of the Covenant in the Light of Cuneiform and Biblical Law* (VTSup, 18; Leiden: E.J. Brill, 1970).

Pedersen, J., *Israel: Its Life and Culture*, 1-2 (Oxford: Oxford University Press and Cophenhagen: Branner og Korch, 1926).

Perlitt, L., *Die Bundestheologie im Alten Testament* (WMANT, 36; Neukirchen–Vluyn: Neukirchener Verlag, 1969).

Phillips, A., 'The Interpretation of 2 Samuel XII 5–6', *VT* 16 (1966), pp. 242-44.

—'The Case of the Woodgatherer Reconsidered', *VT* 19 (1969), pp. 125-28.

—*Ancient Israel's Criminal Law: A New Approach to the Decalogue* (Oxford: Basil Blackwell, 1970).

—*Deuteronomy* (CBC; Cambridge: Cambridge University Press, 1973).

—'Some Aspects of Family Law in Pre-Exilic Israel', *VT* 23 (1973), pp. 349-61.

—'NEBALAH—A Term for Serious Disorderly and Unruly Conduct', *VT* 25 (1975), pp. 237-42.

—Review of *The If-You Form in Israelite Law* (SBLDS, 15; MT: Scholars Press, 1975), by H.H. Gilmer, in *JTS* 27, 1976, pp. 424-26.

—*God B.C.* (Oxford: Oxford University Press, 1977).

—'Another Look at Murder', *JJS* 28 (1977), pp. 105-126.

—'The Servant—Symbol of Divine Powerlessness', *ET* 90 (1978–79), pp. 370-74.

—'Torah and Mishpat—a Light to the Peoples', in W. Harrington (ed.), *Witness to the Spirit* (*Proceedings of the Irish Biblical Association*, 3; Manchester: Koinonia Press, 1979), pp. 112-32.

—'Another Example of Family Law', *VT* 30 (1980), pp. 240-45.

—'Uncovering the Father's Skirt', *VT* 30 (1980), pp. 38-43.

—Review of *Women, Law and the Genesis Traditions* (Edinburgh: Edinburgh University Press, 1979), by C.M. Carmichael, in *JJS* 31 (1980), pp. 237-38.

—'Another Look at Adultery', *JSOT* 20, 1981, pp. 3-25.

—'The Place of Law in Contemporary Society', *Christian Jewish Relations* 14 (1981), pp. 43-51; (*South African Outlook* 111 [1981], pp. 3-6; and *ExpTim* 93 [1982], pp. 108-112).

—'A Response to Dr. McKeating', *JSOT* 22 (1982), pp. 142-43.

—'Prophecy and Law', in R. Coggins, A. Phillips and M. Knibb (eds.), *Israel's Prophetic Tradition* (Festschrift P.R. Ackroyd; Cambridge: Cambridge University Press, 1982), pp. 217-32.

—'Should the Primate of All England Eat York Ham?', *Theology* 85 (1982), pp. 339-46.

—'Double for all her Sins', *ZAW* 94 (1982), pp. 130-32.

—'Respect for Life in the Old Testament', *King's Theological Review* 6 (1983), pp. 32-35.

—'The Decalogue—Ancient Israel's Criminal Law', *JJS* 34 (1983), pp. 1-20.

—'The Laws of Slavery: Exodus 21.2-11', *JSOT* 30 (1984), pp. 51-66.

—'A Fresh Look at the Sinai Pericope—Part 1', *VT* 34.1 (1984), pp. 39-52.

—'A Fresh Look at the Sinai Pericope—Part 2', *VT* 34.2 (1984), pp. 282-94.

—'The Undetectable Offender and the Priestly Legislators', *JTS* 36 (1985), pp. 146-50.

—'The Book of Ruth—Deception and Shame', *JJS* 37 (1986), pp. 1-17.

—'The Attitude of Torah to Wealth', in Andrew Linzey and Peter J. Wexler (eds.), *Heaven and Earth: Essays on Theology and Ethics* (Worthing: Churchman Publishing, 1986), pp. 69-86.

—'Animals and the Torah', *ExpTim* 106 (1995), pp. 260-65.

—'Old Testament and Moral Tradition', *ExpTim* 108 (1997), pp. 231-32.

Phillips, A. and Phillips, L., 'The Origin of "I AM" in Exodus 3.14', *JSOT* 78 (1998), pp. 81-84.

Ploeg, J. van der, 'Studies in Hebrew Law. II. The Style of the Laws', *CBQ* 12 (1950), pp. 248-59, 416-27.

—'Studies in Hebrew Law. III. Systematic Analysis of the Contents of the Collections of Laws in the Pentateuch', *CBQ* 13 (1951), pp. 28-43, 164-71, 296-307.

—'Slavery in the Old Testament' (VTSup, 22; Leiden: E.J. Brill, 1972), pp. 72-87.

Porter, J.R., *The Extended Family in the Old Testament* (Occasional Papers in Social and Economic Administration, 6; London: Edutext Publications, 1967).

—*Leviticus* (CBC; Cambridge: Cambridge University Press, 1976).

Rad, G. von, *Old Testament Theology* (2 vols.; Edinburgh: Oliver & Boyd, 1965).

—*Deuteronomy* (OTL; London: SCM Press, 1966).

—'The Form-Critical Problem of the Hexateuch', in *idem*, *The Problem of the Hexateuch and Other Essays* (Edinburgh: Oliver & Boyd, 1966), pp. 1-78.

—'כִּפְלַיִם in Jes 40:2 = "Äquivalent?"', *ZAW* 79 (1967), pp. 80-82.

—*Genesis* (OTL; London: SCM Press, 3rd edn, 1972).

—*Wisdom in Israel* (London: SCM Press, 1972).

Reventlow, H.G., *Gebot und Predigt im Dekalog* (Gütersloh: Gerd Mohn, 1962).

Rin, S., 'The מות of Grandeur', *VT* 9 (1959), pp. 324-25.

Ringgren, H., *Israelite Religion* (London: SPCK, 1966).

—'Israel's Place among the Religions of the Ancient Near East' (*VTS*, 23; Leiden: E.J. Brill, 1972), pp. 1-8.

Robertson, E., 'The Plot of the Book of Ruth', *BJRL* 32 (1950), pp. 207-228.

Robinson, J.A.T., *Christian Morals To-day* (London: SCM Press, 1964).

—*Christian Freedom in a Permissive Society* (London: SCM Press, 1970).

Rogerson, J., Review of *AICL*, by Phillips, in *PEQ* 104 (1972), p. 157.

Rossell, W.H., 'New Testament Adoption—Graeco-Roman or Semitic?, *JBL* 71 (1952), pp. 233-34.

Rowley, H.H., 'The Marriage of Ruth', *HTR* 40 (1947), pp. 77-99 (repr. in *idem, The Servant of the Lord and Other Essays on the Old Testament* [Oxford: Basil Blackwell, 2nd edn, 1965], pp. 169-94).

—'Moses and the Decalogue', *BJRL* 34 (1951–52), pp. 81-118.

—'The Servant of the Lord in the Light of Three Decades of Criticism', in *idem, The Servant of the Lord and Other Essays on the Old Testament* (Oxford: Basil Blackwell, 2nd edn, 1965), pp. 3-60.

Rudolph, W., *Hosea* (KAT, 13.1; Gütersloh: Gerd Mohn, 1966).

Sarna, N., 'Zedekiah's Emancipation of Slaves and the Sabbatical Year', in H.A. Hoffner (ed.), *Orient and Occident* (AOAT, 22; Neukirchen–Vluyn: Neukirchener Verlag, 1973), pp. 143-49.

Sasson, J.M., 'Ruth III: A Response', *JSOT* 5 (1978), pp. 49-51.

—'The Issue of *ge'ullah* in Ruth', *JSOT* 5 (1978), pp. 52-64.

—*Ruth: A New Translation with a Philological Commentary and a Formalist Folklorist Interpretation* (The Biblical Seminar; Sheffield: JSOT Press, 2nd edn, 1989).

Schmid, H.H., *Gerechtigkeit als Weltordnung: Hintergrund und Geschichte des alttestament-lichen Gerechtigkeitsbegriffes* (BHT, 40; Tübingen: J.C.B. Mohr, 1968).

Schottroff, W., 'Zum alttestamentlichen Recht', in W.H. Schmidt (ed.), *Verkündigung und Forschung: Altes Testament* (BEvT, 22; Munich: Chr. Kaiser Verlag, 1977), pp. 3-29.

Seebass, H., 'Der Fall Naboth in 1 Reg. XXI', *VT* 24 (1974), pp. 474-88.

Seters, J. van, *Abraham in History and Tradition* (New Haven: Yale University Press, 1975).

Shearman, S.L., and Curtis, J.B., 'Divine–Human Conflicts in the Old Testament', *JNES* 28 (1969), pp. 235-40.

Skinner, J., *The Book of the Prophet Isaiah Chapters XL–LXVI* (Cambridge: Cambridge University Press, 1917).

Smith, H.P., *The Books of Samuel* (ICC; Edinburgh: T. & T. Clark, 1912).

Smith, W. Robertson, *Kinship and Marriage in Early Arabia* (London: A. & C. Black, new edn, 1903).

Snaith, N.H., 'The Servant of the Lord in Deutero-Isaiah', in H.H. Rowley (ed.), *Studies in Old Testament Prophecy* (Edinburgh: T. & T. Clark, 1950), pp. 187-200.

—'Isaiah 40–66: A Study of the Teaching of Second Isaiah and is Consequences', in *Studies on the Second Part of the Book of Isaiah* (VTSup, 14; Leiden: E.J. Brill, 1967), pp. 154-65.

Sonsino, R., *Motive Clauses in Hebrew Law: Biblical Forms and Near Eastern Parallels* (SBLDS, 45; Chico, CA: Scholars Press, 1980).

Speiser, E.A., 'Leviticus and the Critics', in M. Haran (ed.), *Yehezkel Kaufmann Jubilee Volume* (Jerusalem: Magnes Press, 1960), pp. 29-45.

Spiro, A., 'A Law on the Sharing of Information', *Proceedings of the American Academy for Jewish Research*, 28 (1959), pp. 95-101.

Stamm, J.J., and M.E. Andrew, *The Ten Commandments in Recent Research* (SBT, 2; London: SCM Press, 2nd edn, 1967).

Staples, W.E., 'The Book of Ruth', *AJSL* 53 (1936–37), pp. 145-57.

—'Cultic Motifs in Hebrew Thought', *AJSL* 55 (1938), pp. 44-55.

Stinespring, W.F., 'Note on Ruth 2:19', *JNES* 3 (1944), p. 101.

Sulzberger, M., *The Ancient Hebrew Law of Homicide* (Philadelphia: J.H. Greenstone, 1915).

Talmon, S., 'The "Comparative Method" in Biblical Interpretation—Principles and Problems' (VTSup, 29; Leiden: E.J. Brill, 1978), pp. 320-56.

Thomas, D.W., 'The Root שׁנה = *Saniya* in Hebrew II', *ZAW* 55 (1937), pp. 174-75.

—'A Consideration of Some Unusual Ways of Expressing the Superlative in Hebrew', *VT* 3 (1953), pp. 209-224.

Thompson, T. and D. Thompson, 'Some Legal Problems in the Book of Ruth', *VT* 18 (1968), pp. 77-99.

Thompson, T.L., *The Historicity of the Patriarchal Narratives: The Quest for the Historical Abraham* (BZAW, 133; Berlin: W. de Gruyter, 1974).

Tom, W., 'Welke is de Zin van het "dubbel ontvangen" uit Jesaja 40:2?', *GThT* 59 (1959), pp. 122-23.

Torczyner, H., 'Presidential Address', *JPOS* 16 (1936), pp. 1-8.

Torrey, C.C., *The Second Isaiah: A New Interpretation* (Edinburgh: T. & T. Clark, 1928).

Tsevat, M., 'Alalkhiana', *HUCA* 29 (1958), pp. 109-134.

—'Marriage and Monarchical Legitimacy in Ugarit and Israel', *JSS* 3 (1958), pp. 237-43.

Vawter, B., *On Genesis* (London: Geoffrey Chapman, 1977).

Verdam, P.J., '"On ne fera point mourir les enfants pour les pères" en droit biblique' (*RIDA*, 3, 1949), pp. 393-416.

Wade, G.W., *The Book of the Prophet Isaiah* (London: Methuen, 2nd edn, 1929).

Wagner, V., *Rechtssätze in gebundener Sprache und Rechtssatzreihen im israelitischen Recht: Ein Beitrag zur Gattungsforschung* (BZAW, 127; Berlin: W. de Gruyter, 1972).

Weinfeld, M., 'The Concept of Law in Israel and among her Neighbours', *Beth Miqra* 17 (1964), pp. 58-63 (Hebrew).

—*Deuteronomy and the Deuteronomic School* (Oxford: Clarendon Press, 1972).

—'The Origin of Apodictic Law: An Overlooked Source', *VT* 23 (1973), pp. 63-75.

Weingreen, J., 'The Case of the Woodgatherer (Numbers XV 32-36)', *VT* 16 (1966), pp. 361-64.

—'The Concepts of Retaliation and Compensation in Biblical Law', *Proceedings of the Royal Irish Academy* 76 (1976), pp. 1-11.

Weiss, D.H., 'A Note on אשר לא ארשה', *JBL* 81 (1962), pp. 67-69.

—'The Use of קנה in Connection with Marriage', *HTR* 57 (1964), pp. 244-48.

Wenham, G.J., 'BETULAH: "A Girl of Marriageable Age"', *VT* 22 (1972), pp. 326-48.

—*The Book of Leviticus* (Grand Rapids: Eerdmans, 1979).

—'The Restoration of Marriage Reconsidered', *JJS* 30 (1979), pp. 36-40.

Wenham, G.J., and J.G. McConville, 'Drafting Techniques in Some Deuteronomic Laws', *VT* 30 (1980), pp. 248-52.

Westermann, C., *Basic Forms of Prophetic Speech* (London: Lutterworth Press, 1967).

—*Isaiah 40–66* (OTL; London: SCM Press, 1969).

Whybray, R.N., 'Prophecy and Wisdom', in R. Coggins, A. Phillips and M. Knibb (eds.), *Israel's Prophetic Tradition* (Cambridge: Cambridge University Press, 1982), pp. 181-99.

Wolff, H.W., *Hosea* (Hermeneia; Philadelphia: Fortress Press, 1974).

—*Anthropology of the Old Testament* (London: SCM Press, 1974).

—*Joel and Amos* (Hermeneia; Philadelphia: Fortress Press, 1977).

Yaron, R., 'On Divorce in Old Testament Times', *RIDA* 4 (1957), pp. 117-28.

—*Law of the Aramaic Papyri* (Oxford: Clarendon Press, 1961).

—'Matrimonial Mishaps at Eshnunna', *JJS* 8 (1966), pp. 1-16.

—'The Restoration of Marriage', *JSS* 17 (1967), pp. 1-11.

—'Ad secundas nuptias convolare', in *Symbolae Iuridicae et Historicae Martino David Dedicatae*, I (Leiden: E.J. Brill, 1968), pp. 263-79.

Zimmerli, W., 'Das zweite Gebot', in W. Baumgartner *et al.* (eds.), *Bertholet Festschrift*
(Tübingen: J.C.B. Mohr, 1950), pp. 550-63.
—*The Law and the Prophets: A Study of the Meaning of the Old Testament* (Oxford: Basil
Blackwell, 1965).
—*Ezekiel*, I (Hermeneia; Philadelphia: Fortress Press, 1979).
Zimmerli, W. and J. Jeremias, *The Servant of God* (SBT, 20; London: SCM Press, 1957).

INDEXES

INDEX OF REFERENCES

OLD TESTAMENT

INDEX OF MODERN AUTHORS